Business Communication

PROFESSIONALS & CONSULTANTS

A RHETORICAL APPROACH

Craig L. Engstrom
Elmhurst College

Kendall Hunt
publishing company

Kendall Hunt
publishing company

www.kendallhunt.com
Send all inquiries to:
4050 Westmark Drive
Dubuque, IA 52004-1840

Printed in the United States of America
10 9 8 7 6 5 4 3

Contents

Introduction: Preparing for Today's Job Market and Business Environment 1

Starting Point 1

The Interpretive Frame of Mind 2

Answering Anticipated Questions 5

    What's Needed to Succeed in Today's Workplace? 5

    What Is the Objective of This Text? 8

    How Does This Text Benefit Students? 8

    How Should Students Approach This Class? 9

    How Is This Text Different from Others? 14

Conclusion 16

References 17

Unit 1: Writing and Design Fundamentals 19

Chapter 1: Approaching Business and Professional Communications Rhetorically 21

Starting Point 21

Defining Rhetoric in Professional Communication 23

    A Definition of Interpretive Rhetoric 25

    A Definition of Narrative Rhetoric 26

    The Value of Interpretive-Narrative Theoretical Orientations 27

Using Rhetorical Criticism to Understand and Improve Business Communications 31

    Classes of Rhetoric 32

    The Five Canons of Rhetoric 33

    Classical Persuasive Appeals 38

    Rhetorical Situations and *Kairos* 40

Conclusion 43

Continuing Education: Recommended Texts and Resources 44

References 45

Chapter 2: Planning and Crafting Professional Communications **47**

Starting Point 47

The Basic Artifact Construction Process 49

    Step 1: Prepare and Research (Invention) 49

    Step 2: Organize and Outline (Arrangement) 63

    Step 3: Write (Style) 68

    Step 4: Complete (Memory and Delivery) 83

Conclusion 89

Continuing Education: Recommended Texts and Resources 90

References 90

**Chapter 3: Designing, Distributing, and Evaluating Professional
Communications** **93**

Starting Point 93

Design 94

    Document Formatting 95

    Embedded Objects 103

Distribution 104

    Factors Influencing Message Distribution 104

    Oral Delivery 108

    Designing and Using Presentation Aids 115

Evaluation 116

    Preparing Feedback 117

    Improving Reading and Listening 117

    Providing Constructive Feedback 118

    Receiving Feedback 121

Conclusion 121

Continuing Education: Recommended Texts and Resources 122

References 123

Unit 2: Crafting Business and Professional Communications **125**

Chapter 4: Crafting and Sharing a Résumé **127**

Starting Point 127

The Employment Search Process 129

    Understanding Occupations, Professions, and Institutional Environments 129

Searching for Opportunities 133

Continuing Education, Networking, and Counseling 136

Writing the Résumé 139

Rhetorical Situations 139

Applying the Five Canons 140

Writing the Application Letter 156

Salutation and Opening 156

Body 157

Closing 158

Speaking: Conversations and Interviews 160

Conversations 160

Interviews 160

Additional Employment Considerations 166

Dress and Appearance 167

Negotiating Salary and Benefits 167

Resignations 168

Conclusion 168

Continuing Education: Recommended Texts and Resources 168

References 169

Chapter 5: Crafting Concise and Extensive Communications 171

Starting Point 171

Applying the Five Canons 172

Invention 173

Arrangement 173

Style 175

Memory/Delivery 175

Concise Artifacts 177

Strategies for Crafting Concise Communications 177

Written Types of Concise Communications 178

Spoken Types of Concise Communications 190

Extensive Artifacts 195

Written Types of Extensive Communications 195

Verbal Types of Extensive Communications 202

Conclusion 205

Continuing Education: Recommended Texts and Resources 206

References 208

Chapter 6: Crafting Electronic Communications and Presentation Aids . . .209

Starting Point 209

Applying the Five Canons 211

Written Electronic Communications (Concise to Extensive) 213

    Text Messages 213

    Instant Messages 214

    Email 215

    Blogs 218

Spoken Electronic Communications (Concise to Extensive) 220

    Voice Messages 220

    Teleconferencing 222

    Podcasting 225

    Second Life 227

Social Networking and Collaborative Electronic Communications (Written and Spoken) 228

    Microblogs 228

    Social Networking Sites 229

    User-Generated Content (UGC) Sites 229

Presentation Aids 231

    Using Presentation Aids 232

    Infographics and Specific Visual Aids 239

Conclusion 243

Continuing Education: Recommended Texts and Resources 244

References 245

Unit 3: Developing Skills for the Workplace and Communication Consulting 249

Chapter 7: Facilitating Safe and Collaborative Work Environments 251

Starting Point 251

Setting a Productive Rhetorical Tone 254

Facilitating Safe and Caring Work Environments 256

    Physical Concerns 257

    Emotional Concerns 258

    Addressing Physical and Emotional Concerns 259

    A Special Note about Regulations 265

Facilitating Teams and Groups 266

    Facilitating Meetings 267

    Conflict and Collaboration 270

Conclusion 273

Continuing Education: Recommended Texts and Resources 273

References 274

Chapter 8: Gathering, Sharing, and Protecting Internal/External Communications 277

Starting Point 277

Setting the Right Rhetorical Tone 280

Gathering Information and Communication 280

    Effective Information Gathering 285

    Using Common Communication Research Methods 287

    Covert Data Gathering Methods 295

    Ethical Considerations of Data Collection 298

Sharing Information and Communications 300

    Saving "Hard" Files 301

    Saving Electronic Files 302

Protecting Information and Communications 307

Conclusion 308

Continuing Education: Recommended Texts and Resources 309

References 310

Chapter 9: Social Networking and Optimizing Online Presence 313

Starting Point 313

Applying the Five Canons 316

    Traditional Social Networking: Tips and Strategies 317

    Online Social Networking: Tips and Strategies 319

    An Important Note about Social Networking 322

Establishing Online Presence 323

    Websites 323

    Generating Content 327

    Social Networking and UGC Sites 331

Managing an Online Presence 336

    Monitoring Online Reputations 337

    Search Engine Optimization (SEO) 338

    Analyzing Results 345

Conclusion 345

Continuing Education: Recommended Texts and Resources 346

References 347

Appendices

Appendix A: Useful Tables and Figures **349**

Appendix B: Résumé Writing: A Look at the Consulting Process **365**

Overview 365

What Matters? Relevant and Contested Résumé Items 365

   Name and Contact Information 365

   Personal Statements and Objectives 366

   Education 366

   Experiences, Skills, and Other Interesting Substance 367

   Personal Data and References 368

   Example 1: Original Document 370

   Example 1: Round 1 Feedback 371

   Example 1: Round 3 Feedback 372

   Example 1: Final Version 374

   Example 2: Original Document 376

   Example 2: Final Document 378

Appendix C: A Mini Case of the HP Spy Scandal **379**

Overview 379

Outsourcing the Investigation, or "Plausible Deniability"? 380

Discussion Questions 381

References 381

Index **383**

Preparing for Today's Job Market and Business Environment

Image © maigi, 2012. Used under license from Shutterstock, Inc.

Starting Point

All communication courses prepare students for improved civic participation and professional success. However, students frequently describe courses dealing with business and professional communication as more practical. Perhaps this is a result of the applicability and immediate usefulness of knowledge gained in such classes. You've probably had a part-time job or currently work. You're likely involved in a social organization or club. During the semester, you will likely participate in a learning group as you complete class projects. This means you are likely to experience the pains of a meeting with a poorly planned agenda or the joys of working in a group with a transformational leader. You are likely to participate in or be the topic of gossip. You will contribute to and, perhaps at times, instigate conflict. In this way, you are already engaging in business and professional communication. This book helps you to better understand the reasons for work productivity or group dysfunction and prepares you to approach and manage situations with greater communicative competence.

Another reason students find this text more practical is that assignments—for example, writing a résumé, participating in a video interview simulation, and practicing sales pitches—seem more relevant than a five-page theory paper. Both the theory paper and the résumé are essential to your intellectual and personal growth, though for different reasons. While improving your writing skills, the theory paper builds your creative capacity to simultaneously think abstractly and analytically. The résumé, on the other hand, helps you practice technical writing and teaches you how to transform experience into narrative. Despite both assignments' pedagogical value, students usually prefer writing the résumé. Its utility is obvious—it can help you get a summer internship or launch your career. But relevance and importance are not the same things. While this class may be immediately relevant, it is no more necessary to your overall professional success than other communication courses or assignments.

This text builds upon knowledge you have obtained or will acquire across the communication curriculum. In additional to creative thinking and analytical skills, this course teaches technical communication skills that will be vital to your professional success—from launching your career to obtaining a promotion and pay raise; from obtaining money to start a business to staying competitive through online advertising. For those who are or would like to become consultants, you will learn how to turn unit concepts into profitable services. This course complements the skills and knowledge you will obtain during your academic tenure and throughout your career.

The remainder of this introduction builds upon this starting point. It aims to shift you into the proper frame of mind for reading and learning. It also addresses questions about the specific approaches taken in this book, including how this text differs from others with similar content.

The Interpretive Frame of Mind

> Michael, thank you for accepting my friend request. Tell me about what you do. I see you have written a book. What's it called? What's it about? I'm also working on a book and a project you might be interested in. I would like to discuss potential business opportunities with you. (Port, 2011, p. 180)

The preceding excerpt, by author and columnist Michael Port, highlights many of the changes and challenges of communicating in today's business environment, and also demonstrates that little has changed in our expectations of professional communication. It is relatively easy to network with today's social media technology, as the example shows. However, communicating through social networking services does not mean that we can be ignorant of proper communication etiquette. Just because we can send and receive messages at an accelerated pace does not mean that we should. The sender of the above message, as Port notes in the book, should have taken some time to do his or her due diligence.

Port complains that the sender of the Facebook email did not read his profile, which clearly outlines all four of his books. As Port notes, "to fast-forward the process and ask for business without first gaining some intelligence is more than ineffective, it's a turnoff" (p. 181). Consider Port's interpretation. The tone of the sender's email is seemingly impersonal, hurried, unrealistic, and selfish. The sender does not appear to ask his or her questions out of genuine interest, but with the aim of self-promotion—but it is not very good self-promotion because the sender offends the receiver. However, we miss an opportunity to learn from this example if we criticize only the sender. We do not know the intentions of the sender, so we should be cautious about our judgments as observers. To be considerate of Port's time, the writer may have been deliberately abrupt, but she or he was not successful in portraying this concern. This example highlights, therefore, one of the problems of receiving communication from others: A receiver can never fully know a sender's intentions. With communicators struggling to express and understand messages and motivations, there are many opportunities for miscommunication.

Little or poor training in verbal and written communication only enhances the potential for confusion. Thus, it is essential to spend time developing skills that will help you reduce possibilities for misunderstanding. For this reason, there are a large number of business and professional communication textbooks and courses. In the majority of books on this topic, however, emphasis is on written and spoken *expression*. While being able to speak and write well is important, communicating professionally also requires critical and conscientious *interpretation* of communication. In this book, therefore, we will spend time learning to be more observant, flexible and self-aware communicators.

Port is obviously entitled to his position, which, as a successful writer, is a credible one. Nevertheless, consultants and researchers of professional communication would question Port's decision to quickly accept an individual he does not know into his social network. He seems to criticize the sender of the message without much reflection on his own behaviors. It is unlikely he would so easily associate with others in offline situations, so why does he do so online? This example raises additional questions worthy of broader inquiry. How should professionals build and maintain online profiles? Should they accept a customer as a "friend" into their online social networks? What are the benefits and risks to including and excluding certain individuals? What type of communication is best suited for virtual and nonvirtual media? Since research in the area of virtual social networking is emergent, the answers to these questions are largely based upon anecdotal evidence. In other words, there is significant uncertainty regarding "best practices" in virtual communication.

The uncertainties of communicating virtually should make us conservative communicators. The rhetorical approach in this book, which focuses on the use of the traditional canons of rhetoric, adheres to a more conventional approach to business and professional communication. Globalization and technology have provided more means for us to communicate with each other, but the same methodical approach to effective persuasion used centuries ago still applies. Today's professional is likely to achieve greater success by using the rhetorical methods used by professionals in the ancient Greek *agora* (place of assembly). Utilizing persuasive and interpretive approaches, which include audience analysis, stock organizational patterns, stylistic and delivery adaptation, and which can be applied to each communicative situation—whether it is virtual or nonvirtual, written or spoken—is likely to reduce

Ancient agora in Athens. (Image © totophotos, 2012. Used under license from Shutterstock, Inc.)

misunderstandings and improve desired business and professional outcomes. As we craft résumés, interview for jobs, respond to emails, write wikis, comment upon others' work, pitch ideas, speak with upset customers, organize files, and so on, we will be more effective at our work by drawing upon and adapting the theories and practices of communication outlined by Socrates, Aristotle, Cicero, and many other notable historical rhetoricians. By learning contemporary business and communication principles through the rhetorical tradition, we not only adhere to the foundation of the communication studies discipline, we learn approaches that are amendable to any business or professional situation.

For example, through the canon of invention, you will learn to identify, in advance, audience desires and the possible interpretations they may have of your work. By doing so, you can then construct your message in a way that will be more appealing to the intended audience. By thinking about your audiences' needs, you will also become a better listener. An interpretive ethics entails being willing to open yourself to others' positions. In so doing, you allow yourself to empathize and learn. When you are more attentive to your audience and you adapt your messages and arguments, you create the possibility for a stronger fusion of understanding between you and other interlocutors. You invite them to learn from you, and you also learn from them. As emphasized in this book, business and professional communication is not solely about enhancing your position in a marketplace. It is about being an important contributor to creating the conditions for the possibility of better business and professional environments—to be a better professional *and* citizen. By being more attentive to rhetoric, you will (re)shape the symbolic environment in which you work and enhance your ability to achieve desired outcomes. In other words, if you want to work in a cordial work environment or be a member of an ethical profession, adopt a tone of friendliness and use ethical communication practices in conversations and documents. Contributing to professional and organizational development requires helping others understand your desires, intentions, needs, and so on.

Working through this book, you will acquire techniques to communicate well in business and professional contexts. You will learn how to persuade customers, colleagues, and other constituencies by crafting letters and other artifacts tailored to business and professional situations. You will enhance your communication by learning to do the following three things: Think rhetorically, interpret cautiously, and practice ethically. Practice these three things in conjunction with the practical advice provided in this book, and you will become a better professional, business owner, and consultant.

Answering Anticipated Questions

Now that you are somewhat familiar with the interpretive frame of mind, it is appropriate to address some of the questions that (communication) students, who are taking charge of their career through this course, are likely to ask.

What's Needed to Succeed in Today's Workplace?

Demographic trends nationally and internationally, from aging baby boomers to increasing diversity of populations in countries, promise to dramatically transform workforces and consumers. For example, the 2010 U.S. census data revealed a rapidly changing United States. In terms of population growth, Asians and Hispanics or Latinos comprised the largest growth, outpacing whites by an 8-to-1 ratio. Latinos now represent one of every six persons in the United States and will represent one of every five persons in the United States by 2020. For the United States, population growth over the decade 2000 to 2010 was highest in southern and mountain states, and this trend is likely to continue (**http://2010.census.gov/2010census/data**). Learning to work within these changes by adapting your business communication strategies will not only increase business sales, for example, but could lead to the enactment of new business and professional opportunities.

Internationally, the system of trade and governance is likely to continue to change. According to the National Intelligence Council (2008), Brazil, Russia, India, and China (commonly referred to as "BRIC countries"—pronounced "brick") will continue to grow in power and influence, which will bring new stakes and rules to the business and diplomacy game. There will be an unprecedented transfer of wealth from West to East. Coupled with unparalleled economic and population growth, there will be growing demand for energy, food, and water. Increasing economic disparity and global climate change will likely intensify political turbulence. These challenges, though they may create a feeling of uncertainty, present opportunities for people who learn to communicate across different cultural backgrounds and in second or third languages. Shifting centers of influence, increased competitiveness for jobs, shifting purchasing power, fluidity in organizational boundaries, and other challenges are opportunities for people with a cosmopolitan ethic.

Today's work environment is demographically rich, creating new opportunities. (Image © olly, 2012. Used under license from Shutterstock, Inc.)

Technologically, the biggest challenges for the global workforce are keeping pace with new developments in hardware and software and mitigating external security threats. Employees, even those not working specifically in IT departments, will need to be familiar with cloud computing, which refers to accessing computation resources on demand through a virtual network. Workers will need to understand how to access virtual software, save and protect documents, and collaborate with others in the production of virtual documents. For example, individuals who are uncomfortable or unfamiliar with "Google Docs" (**https://docs.google.com**) may face increased stress or sanctions in the workplace. If you have never experienced someone editing your work at the very moment you are typing, you cannot know how you will respond to this type of feedback. Mobile and smart devices will also continue to change at an accelerated pace. Learning how to work with, control, and protect data on these devices will be essential to workplace success.

Technology also comes with ethical implications and risks. For example, computers allow for increased surveillance of workers' practices. They also allow people to engage in their own intelligence gathering on potential employers and competitors. But such surveillance can lead to information overload and decreased employee morale (Smith & Tabak, 2009). What is more, corporate espionage can also create legal ramifications, as Patricia Dunn, a former chairperson of Hewlett-Packard, discovered when she hired private investigators to spy on the HP board members (Norander, 2008). The result was her dismissal and the imprisonment of several private detectives. The 2010 Deepwater Horizon oil spill, commonly referred to as the "BP oil spill" or "Gulf oil spill," and the Fukushima Daiichi nuclear power plant crisis following the 2011 earthquake and tsunami in Japan demonstrate the risks of technology. As technology becomes more complex, we have increased risk of what organizational theorist Karl Weick calls a "cosmology episode," or a total "collapse of sensemaking" (Weick, 1993). Complex technology, according to Weick and Roberts (1993), requires organizations to create a "collective mind" capable of thinking as a smart system, especially during a crisis. Knowing how to develop crisis-response protocol, effective communication systems for sharing information, and proper training processes is vital for managers in today's workplaces. Although this text cannot help you fully develop these skills, it provides you with an introduction to some critical tools and approaches to honing such competencies.

The following are some other skills that are important for success in business and professional situations.

- **Strong rhetorical and interpretive skills.** Employers will expect that professionals understand various rhetorical situations, understand how to respond to changing discourses, and anticipate others' potential interpretations.

- **Flexibility and stress management.** Workers are expected to work autonomously and be flexible enough to work in different environments and situations marked by too little or too much information. Employees will need to be more comfortable handling uncertainty and working through ambiguity.

- **Technical skills.** Employers often cannot afford to give managers office assistants. In some small companies, employees will be responsible for both internal and external communication. Workers must be able to write well, have some mechanical or artistic capacities, and work with multiple types of computer programs (e.g., document processing and scheduling systems).

- **Analytic and organizational skills.** Employers expect workers to know how to collect, analyze, and organize large amounts of data. When necessary, employees must be willing to make strategic decisions and understand how to evaluate outcomes.

- **Negotiation and collaboration skills.** Employees must be willing to work through conflict, have strong interpersonal skills, and understand collaborative techniques.

- **Intercultural and international sensitivity.** Employees should be able to work with people from different national and organizational cultures.

- **Ethics and professionalism.** Employees need to be able to create a credible image and be willing to participate in shaping their profession.

- **Listening skills and a willingness to follow directions.** Listening in the workplace has long been held to be an important skill by researchers and practitioners (Flynn, Valikoski, & Grau, 2008). Because both minor mistakes and large-scale catastrophes are often a result of an accumulation of errors (Weick, 1993), it is critical that employees learn to develop attentiveness and a faculty for interpreting (often vague) information in the workplace.

Employers expect their employees to engage in the art of impression management. Working autonomously, employees will need to control their actions to mitigate negative interpretations. With increased electronic surveillance, the slightest offhand remark, in the wrong place and time, can have political implications. For example, the CEO of British Petroleum, Tony Hayward, came under significant scrutiny for not appearing sensitive to the magnitude of the BP oil spill crisis by saying, "What the hell have we done to deserve this?" ("The bumbler from BP," 2010). What Hayward meant is unclear, but journalists seemed to think it was corporate self-pity, not a comment encompassing the reflection of the crisis. Had Hayward simply added a clarifying word—"What the hell have we [*humans*] done to deserve this?"—the interpretation would have been narrower. By adding "humans," the offhand comment would be a question seemingly directed at some higher power.

The cost of inattentiveness and distractions in the workplace come at a high price. A Microsoft study, for example, suggests that following a work disruption due to reading email, it takes workers approximately 15 minutes to refocus their attention to pre-disruption levels (Robinson, 2010). Thus, improving business and professional communication skills will require you to learn to listen, follow directions, organize your workflow, and control your impulse to attend constantly to business communication.

What Is the Objective of This Text?

The primary objective of this text is to prepare students for success in contemporary workplaces marked by intense competition due to globalization, fluctuating unemployment, and job and workplace instability. Thus, this book aims to help you learn the skills that are vital to obtaining and retaining jobs, managing employees, helping organizations gain a competitive advantage, and working through crisis situations. In order to accomplish these overarching objectives, you must not only work smarter, you must have technical expertise in using Web 2.0 and new media technology. Although you cannot learn all the technical skills necessary to become and remain competitive in a semester-long class, you can certainly acquire some of these skills, find out where to obtain others, and discover how to market those you do possess.

How Does This Text Benefit Students?

In an unpredictable business environment, it is imperative to be more flexible, comfortable with uncertainty, engage the world as a *bricoleur* (i.e., a Jack-or-Jane-of-all trades), and, among other things, learn to be better team member, negotiator, data collector, and electronics user. As you gain mastery in these areas, you gain credibility among other professionals. Furthermore, the more you expand your skills and knowledge, the more likely you are to be successful at operating or managing an organization. You may also earn more money. For example, a student using negotiation strategies learned in this course may be able to obtain an extra $1,000 in his or her yearly salary. While this may not seem significant, when calculating the employee-employer contribution to retirement and pay increases over time, the lifetime earnings differential becomes noteworthy.

For example, if a 22-year-old recent graduate who will retire at age 68 negotiates for a starting salary of $41,000 instead of $40,000, and assuming that she or he receives an average 3% annual pay increase, the difference in earnings will be an extra $85,000 for his or her 46 years of full-time employment. While this may not seem like a significant difference, we cannot forget that retirement contributions would also be more substantial. Without considering employer contribution to retirement, and holding all other things equal, if we simply assumed that the recent graduate invested the extra $1,000 in annual income into a fund that yields 7% annually, the gap widens to almost $290,000.

There are obviously many assumptions in the above scenario. However, the point is clear: better negotiators increase their financial opportunities. Of course, there is much more to life than money, and being a better negotiator has other relational benefits. For example, better negotiators are usually more amicable business associates, friends, and life partners.

How Should Students Approach This Class?

Students are likely to get more out of any course when they can translate content into practice. This requires you to have your own objectives for this class. Besides bringing an interpretive approach to this course, spend some time thinking about, in advance, what skills you already possess and what you personally hope to gain from each project. In short, take charge of your education and career; to make your degree(s) ultimately a reflection of the knowledge and skills that you actually possess, engage in the readings and activities seriously. If you have a bachelor's or master's degree in Communication Studies, but you do not know how to write well or understand the technology and etiquette for successfully engaging in a video conference, then you are adding to the devaluation of the communication degree. Answering the following questions will help you get more out of this course.

What do you want to do?   Base your career choices on your skills, interests, and values. By aligning skills to a job, you will make fewer mistakes and build communicative confidence. If you work in positions that require skills you do not possess, you will make costly mistakes and experience higher levels of stress. If you align your interests with a job, you will feel more motivated to go to work every day. If your personal values match the values of a profession, you will experience a better quality of life. To choose the career that fits you, answer some of the following questions.

- **What would you not get bored doing every day?** Every job has its dull moments. But sometimes the doldrums of everyday routines are displaced by other activities. For example, significant free time or a fun workplace may complement a routine job. An office assistant's duties, for example, are routine. He or she may answer phones, file paperwork, and facilitate communication. While this may be boring for some, the fact the she or he gets to meet different people, and often has plenty of "downtime" to converse with others, may align with his or her more social attitude. A manager's position may have fewer dull moments, but it often comes with making uncertain decisions that can have significant consequences. Although salary often reflects the degree of difficulty of a job, this alone may not be enough to overcome a person's belief in living a stress-free life. One way to take an inventory of career skills and beliefs, values, and interests is to create a list of them. Another way to approach creating an inventory is to generate a list of past work or leadership experiences that aligned with your personal values and lifestyle(s). Try keeping a journal for a few weeks and note all things that you enjoy doing. A formal inventory is also an option. Students can take these, often for a fee, at a university's career services office. The most popular are the Myers-Briggs Type Indicator (**www.myersbriggs.org**), Career Assessment Inventory (**www.pearsonassessments.com**), and the Common-Metric Questionnaire (see www.**pstc.com** and **http://commonmetric.com**).

- **Do you prefer autonomy?** Some individuals enjoy the freedom that comes with making decisions independently and determining their own work process. However, this is not the preferred choice of others. Spend time thinking about how much independence you want. Would you enjoy working from home and telecommuting? How much surveillance of your work practices are you willing to tolerate? Are you contented working with machines, or do you prefer human contact? Are you comfortable with the assumed risks of making your own decisions, or do you want someone to help you make decisions? The answers to these questions may help you find a better career, or they may help you find the right company to work for in a career.

- **What are your personal goals?** Some professions have better pay than others do, but high salary is often associated with more demanding careers. Some jobs are stressful and time intensive. Some careers demand workers to relocate or travel frequently. Some occupations are physically tiring, while others are mentally draining. These factors increase stresses in other areas of your life. If you have demanding family needs, then you may not be comfortable with a job that has high requirements for your time. If you must to make complex decisions at home, you may not want to be doing this all day at work. It is important that you think about your personal desires and align these with your professional ones. While a fair wage and benefits are important, your overall well-being is much more essential to a happy life.

- **What kind of environment do you prefer to work in?** Spend time thinking about the type of corporate or external organizational cultures that are right for you. Are you okay with bureaucracy? Do you want to work in a profession where the general institutional environment is dynamic and competitive? Alternatively, do you prefer flatter structures with unclear reporting relationships? Do you prefer a stable environment? Do you want to work in an organization that is diverse or homogeneous? The answers to these questions require you to reflect on some of your core values. While the above issues may not seem to be the most important factors of career success and overall happiness, they do play a role in the other day-to-day operations that will have more immediate impact on what you do in the workplace. For example, a more flexible structure may provide a surface-level sense of autonomy. However, if there are no clear reporting relationships, power plays may be frequent and people may be able to demand more of your time. Formal structures can buffer you from interaction with others.

- **Other questions to consider.** In addition to the above general categories, here are some other questions you should consider:
  - Are you more emotional or analytical?
  - Do you prefer working with numbers or languages, or with both?

- Do you want a career that requires a lot of reading or writing?
- Are you comfortable working in a cubicle or would you prefer to work outside?
- Are you okay acting as a spokesperson?
- Do you prefer a small or large company?
- Is location important to you? If so, then what kind of place or local community do you prefer?
- Do you want to work among young urban professions who hit the trailhead after work, soccer moms and dads who incessantly talk about last weekend's game, or people who love spectator sports?
- Would you prefer to have an eclectic mix of ethnicities in the workplace?
- Do you prefer a profession or workplace that actively promotes alternative lifestyles, or would you be comfortable in a more conservative environment?

Because you want to appear open-minded, you may be inclined to answer some of the questions untruthfully. However, it is in your best interest to be honest in your assessment.

Some of the above questions are specific, while others are broad. None of the above questions is mutually exclusive. By now, however, you should get the point. As an exercise, you need to ask questions to engage in introspective self-assessment. By doing a self-assessment, you will better understand what you want to do and what you bring to your profession.

What kind of work environment do you prefer? Would you feel comfortable in a "gossipy" environment? (Image © CREATISTA, 2012. Used under license from Shutterstock, Inc.)

What can you offer others? A work relationship is never one-sided. While it is important that you choose the right profession and find a company that aligns with your values, a company hires people for productivity and cultural fit. As part of your self-assessment, consider what kind of skills and knowledge you possess that others are willing to pay for. You may already have a good sense of these things; you may even already have a résumé that describes them. If you do not, a few minutes of brainstorming can help you identify what you can offer employers. Even if you already have a résumé, doing the following activity may help you remember forgotten achievements.

Start by listing your proudest achievements, activities you have participated in, and some of your personal characteristics. Then tease these out by thinking more deeply about them. For example, in working toward an achievement (e.g., class president), what sort of skills did you gain or enhance? Did you become a better speaker? Do you know a little about campaign management? You probably know a little about leadership and team building. Did you attend any conferences or leadership academies that gave you knowledge others might not possess? Is this knowledge useful to others? Can you lead a team or manage an organization? What about your personal characteristics? Do you feel you were a charismatic or an authoritative class president? How would others describe you? Be truthful when responding to these questions.

If you have an idea of a field of interest, list the skills you know the career demands. While you are at it, you may want to verify your assumptions by interviewing professionals in the field, by exploring information bulletins like the Bureau of Labor Statistic's *Occupational Outlook Handbook* (**www.bls.gov/oco**) for career overviews and employment projections, or by reading literature produced by professional associations (e.g., the National Communication Association's *Spectra* or the Public Relations Society of America's *Strategist*; see **www.natcom.org** and **www.prsa.org**).

As you work through your lists, see if you can identify patterns of skills. Which of them do you think would be valuable to employers? What might make you an effective consultant (i.e. which ones would be valuable to a small business owner on a short-term hire basis)?

How can you enhance your value and how do you show it to others? While answering these questions, you may have found that you lack certain skill sets for your chosen profession or specific job of interest. Your participation in this class will get you on the right path for developing specific communication skills. However, not all of your coursework, in this class or others, is likely to develop all the skills needed to succeed in your career search. Similarly, your evening or summer job at Subway as a sandwich artist, while demonstrating your work ethic, may not be building crucial skills and knowledge that are going to be valued by a future employer. Whether you apply for a sales position in a small green technology startup or as an insurance adjuster for a larger and more conservative company like Liberty Mutual, you need to demonstrate that you have "added value" beyond the technical job functions. If you do have the necessary skills, you still need to demonstrate that you have them in your cover letter, résumé, or preemployment interview. Pointing to projects you have completed will demonstrate your competencies and build your credibility.

So where can you obtain these skills? Clearly, projects completed in courses are one way to demonstrate your skills. However, course projects appear less legitimate than cocurricular activities. Participating in competitions or attending conventions that highlight your work adds credibility. By volunteering, you may be able to demonstrate other core competencies that may not be associated with a club or sport. For example, demonstrating your search engine optimization (SEO) skills can be achieved by volunteering for workplace web projects, engaging in freelance work, shadowing workers, offering free labor, or completing an internship or externship. Of course, doing any of the above requires personal initiative.

Should you be motivated enough, there are many creative ways to demonstrate and enhance your skills. Here are two specific ways.

- Post an announcement to freelancer websites that advertise your skills. Someone may need your skills and be willing to pay for them. If you do the job well, you get an example of a completed project and a reference. If you are nervous about your technical abilities, then simply be honest with the client and offer her or him a discount or money-back guarantee. The following are a few websites on which to consider posting your freelance services: **www.craigslist.org**, **www.ifreelance.com**, **www.freelance.com**, and **www.freelanceswitch.com**.

- Provide your talents to a *crowdsourcing* project. Crowdsourcing is a new and innovated way for outsourcing. Companies seek a solution to a problem by using (usually) unidentified groups of people (a "crowd"). The crowd works collaboratively to solve the "open call" problem (Surowiecki, 2004). Although your work proposal may not be accepted, it still produces outputs that demonstrate your creativity and expertise. (Note: You can use the proposal as a writing sample that demonstrates your technical writing abilities.) The following websites are educational or suitable for freelancers with expertise in communication, graphic design, SEO, corporate branding, and so on: **www.mturk.com**, **www.crowdsourcing.org**, **www.chaordix.com**, **www.blurgroup.com**, and **www.idealist.org**.

As you gain skills and experience, continue to develop your portfolio and publish it for others to see. We'll cover ways to create and distribute your résumé. However, if you're ready to get started today, begin by thinking about the way you plan to promote yourself. Always keep a running list of your activities, skills, and work. Even if these do not immediately show up in your résumé, you never know when they may be useful. As your life's work (or *curriculum vitae*) accumulates and you feel confident that it sufficiently promotes your work, put it into formats that can easily be shared. Here are some ways to share résumés online.

- Obtain a personal URL. The two most popular domains right now for personal sites are .me and .name. Your URL (short for Uniform Resource Locator, or colloquially "web address") could be, for example, *www.yourname.me*. Once you obtain a personal URL, publish your portfolio on the Internet. This requires some coding skills. However, many website hosts offer user-friendly software or templates, so the HTML (hypertext markup language) coding required is minimal.

- Start a blog. Use these sites to embed videos, pictures, and descriptions of your work. Two popular blog hosting sites are **www.blogger.com** and **www.wordpress.org**.
- Using a portable document format (PDF) file, upload your work to a portfolio-sharing site, such as **www.behance.com**, **www.visualcv.com**, and **www.issuu.com**.

Have you declared the right major?   As you become more serious about career exploration and professional requirements for a field of interest, you may discover that you are pursuing the wrong academic major. While communication degrees are an excellent asset, especially because the process of obtaining them teaches many critical skills for both life and professional success, the discipline cannot serve the needs of every professional niche. In these circumstances, consider a dual major or an alternative major. Good decisions regarding your career require serious exploration of the skills needed to succeed in your desired profession. Align your education with skills development.

When aligning your major with your career ambitions, consider what courses you're required to take and which "elective courses" you can take. Think about how these courses are taught. For example, if you are planning a career in marketing research, and your school's communications department requires a course in statistics and has a quality research methods course, then you may be well on your way to obtaining the needed knowledge to succeed. The business school at your university may offer a marketing degree, but the methods courses may not be as good. This could hinder your ability to collect data and develop marketing campaigns. If you want to be a consumer ethnographer, which has starting salaries of upward to $80,000 (**www.indeed.com/q-Ethnographic-jobs.html**), then seek out a communications program that offers courses in qualitative research too. Not all communications departments offer courses in ethnography; however, it is almost a certainty that your business school does not. If you want to work in distribution or supply chain management, you may consider augmenting your communications degree with other courses. Surprisingly, many experts in supply chain management would not recommend business classes; instead, they suggest analytic philosophy classes. A philosophy degree is one of the top-earning liberal arts degrees in the United States, and companies like FedEx and Amazon hire analytic philosophers to work on shipping logistics (see The best and worst jobs, 2011).

It may seem odd to receive advice to leave the communication discipline in a communication-oriented textbook that is written for a communication course. However, to honestly assess your career, you must consider the possibility that a communication degree, in certain circumstances, may not be the best for you. Although you are invited to critique the communication studies discipline, most students are likely to see that it is one of the best degrees available to students in the social sciences and humanities. A communication degree undoubtedly prepares students for better civic engagement and for success in the workplace.

How Is This Textbook Different from Others?

The majority of business and professional communication textbooks on the market are rather good. However, each book has certain features that make it unique. This book is no exception, and some of its distinguishing features are worth noting.

Fewer chapters and "add-ons."   This book has fewer chapters than the traditional 15-chapter textbook, which is designed to cover a different topic each week during a traditional semester. A shorter book invites instructors to supplement the course with their own materials, creates space for lengthier in-class discussions, and gives students more time to enhance outputs (e.g., stronger résumés). Each chapter should be covered over a two- to three-week period. This will improve conversations and give you more time to work on assignments. While many textbooks provide activities, this book provides very few. With so many do-it-yourself tutorials and examples online, there is no need to have a large number of add-ons. Because relevant webpages change frequently, students are encouraged to go to the book's companion site **(http://proCommunication.me)**, which offers a variety of links to tutorials and activities. This site also provides an online forum for collaborating and sharing with other students. For example, students can share do-it-yourself tutorials that both demonstrate their knowledge and teach others. In addition, the site provides free and premium services that will help you launch and enhance your career over time.

Integrated theoretical focus.   Rather than covering topics through a broad range of theories, we will explore all topics rhetorically and hermeneutically (a big word for interpretation). This approach allows you to understand the speech communication tradition as it applies to designing and understanding contemporary communication artifacts (e.g., business letters, email, blogs, and websites). You will also learn how to use rhetorical theory to

Communication majors and rhetorical critics make good search engine optimization strategists, which is an important career in today's social networking environment. (Image © Marco Rullkoetter, 2012. Used under license from Shutterstock, Inc.)

improve communication in the workplace and provide consulting services in a variety of contexts, such as résumé writing, search engine optimization, technical writing, and social networking.

Focus on skills improvement. Because of the integrated theoretical focus, the course can focus on applying one theoretical model (interpretive rhetoric) to all forms and forums of business and professional communication. It is important for you to learn a variety of communication theories and how to test them. This book, however, was written with the assumption that this knowledge is covered in other courses. The chapters therefore focus on knowledge and skills development rather than upon theories that promote certain skills. Unlike other books that only discuss concepts; this book emphasizes applying rhetorical techniques to a variety of business and professional artifacts. It also includes a list of useful resources for skills and knowledge development. In addition, there are several guides and tutorials available to students on the companion site.

Belief in students' motivation for continued learning. This book was written with the assumption that students are motivated to learn and enjoy exploring topics on their own terms. As such, the book does not include end-of-chapter questions and scenarios. Each student's skills and desires are likely to differ. After reading a chapter, think about how the material is applicable. Because it is assumed you will want to continue to learn, chapters offer a list of "continuing education" resources (e.g., books and articles). More resources are available online.

Web 2.0 Focus. The theoretical approach to this book reaches all the way back to pre-Socratic thoughts. The practical focus, however, is on preparing students to work and communicate in contemporary workplaces and markets. This requires not only a focus on how to communicate through traditional websites, but on how to utilize Web 2.0 to interact, collaborate, and share ideas in "virtual communities" that integrate social media and user-generated technologies. While not all of the technical specifics can be covered in this text, you can find additional useful links to resources and tutorials online.

Conclusion

This introduction outlines some of the rationale for this book, which will hopefully motivate you as we embark on this semester together. In a sense, it is a rhetorical argument that points out the benefits of this book and your course. It also suggests how you can approach reading and learning. Taking charge of your career as a working professional, consultant, or businessperson requires improving communication skills and technical understanding of ever-changing technology. This book accounts for the demands on contemporary workers in dynamic business environments, and it assumes that a slower pace of content delivery facilitates better learning.

References

Flynn, J., Valikoski, T.-R., & Grau, J. (2008). Listening in the business context: Reviewing the state of research. *International Journal of Listening*, 22, 141–151.

National Intelligence Council. (2008). *Global trends 2025: A transformed world* (NIC publication No. 2008-003). Washington, DC: U.S. Government Printing Office. Retrieved from www.acus.org/files/publication_pdfs/3/Global-Trends-2025.pdf

Norander, S. (2008). Surveillance, discipline, resistance: Carly Fiorina under the gaze of The Wall Street Journal. *Communication Studies, 59*, 99–113.

Port, M. (2011). *Book yourself solid* (2nd ed.). Hoboken, NJ: John Wiley & Sons.

Robinson, J. (2010, March). Email is making you stupid. *Entrepreneur Magazine*. Retrieved from www.entrepreneur.com/article/204980

Smith, W. P., & Tabak, F. (2009). Monitoring employee e-mails: Is there any room for privacy? *The Academy of Management Perspectives*, 23, 33–48.

The best and worst jobs. (2011, January 5). Retrieved from http://online.wsj.com/public/resources/documents/st_BESTJOBS0104_20110105.html

The bumbler from BP: How CEO Tony Hayward is making the Gulf oil-spill disaster even worse. (2010, May 18). *Newsweek*. Retrieved from /www.newsweek.com/2010/05/18/the-bumbler-from-bp.html

Surowiecki, J. (2004). *The wisdom of crowds*. New York: Doubleday.

Weick, K. E. (1993). The collapse of sensemaking in organizations: The Mann Gulch disaster. *Administrative Science Quarterly*, 38, 628–653.

Weick, K. E., & Roberts, K. H. (1993). Collective mind in organizations: Heedful interrelating on flight decks. *Administrative Science Quarterly*, 38, 357–381.

Unit 1

Writing and Design Fundamentals

Image © Lithium 366, 2012. Used under license from Shutterstock, Inc.

Chapter 1: Approaching Business and Professional Communications Rhetorically

Chapter 2: Planning and Crafting Professional Communications

Chapter 3: Designing, Distributing, and Evaluating Professional Communications

This unit introduces rhetorical concepts necessary for preparing, crafting, distributing, and evaluating professional and business communications. At the conclusion of this unit, you will understand the rhetorical tradition, be able to apply rhetorical concepts and techniques to the production of effective business communications, and understand the basic techniques used to give and receive feedback. The foundational concepts introduced in Chapters 1–3 can be applied to the construction and interpretation of multiple types of rhetorical artifacts. In practical contexts, such as the workplace and consulting scenarios, applying the concepts you learn in this unit will improve internal relationships, enhance information security, and boost computer-mediated interactions among organizational stakeholders.

Chapter 1

Approaching Business and Professional Communications Rhetorically

Image © Elena Elisseeva, 2012. Used under license from Shutterstock, Inc.

Starting Point

Let's imagine that you've just graduated and are looking for a job. You would prefer a well-paying position, but you know that you can't be picky in the current economic climate. You'll be happy to find a good entry-level position with a quality company. You search **www.monster.com** (and similar job search sites) to find the latest available positions. Based upon your degree in communication studies, previous employment experience, and skills, you decide to search for positions in marketing and sales, public relations, training, and recruiting. You know that you can't rely on online advertisements alone, so you go to your university's career services department and seek its advice. You even make a few phone calls to family friends, who may know of a company that is currently hiring recent college graduates. After several weeks of searching, you find a few noteworthy jobs. However, one posting, for a "Tasting Room and Wine Coordinator," appeals to you in particular:

> Our growing winery is searching for an energetic, engaging, upbeat, creative self-starter . . . to join our team in the tasting room and to coordinate wine club activities while contributing to local and regional marketing efforts. Responsibilities include retail wine sales, merchandise ordering and stocking, creating fun and engaging events for our wine club, fulfilling all wine club orders, maintaining our reputation as a fun and friendly winery, and most importantly HAVING A BLAST AT WORK![1]

You like wine. The location is optimal. A sales position fits your initial search criteria. Coordination requires communication skills, so your knowledge will be useful to the small company. Because the advertisement also includes a note that applicants "must like dogs . . . especially those which are needy and slightly overweight," you conclude that the owners must be fun and friendly.

By crafting a solid résumé (and perhaps due to some luck), you score a phone interview. Therefore, you begin to prepare how you're going to respond to interview questions. You even write down a few questions that you plan to ask during the interview. You know from the advertisement that you'll need to be "energetic," "market the company," and "meet with clients." In short, you know that you're going to need to show you are personable and can be persuasive. You wonder, "How am I going to convey these things in a phone interview? What evidence (i.e., examples of prior experience) will I point to as a way to support my claim that I am the best candidate for the job?"

This brief imaginative exercise begins to illustrate what many people intuitively understand—*searching for and obtaining a job is a rhetorical process*. For example, you use a set of criteria to make a judgment about which job is the right fit. You evaluate your knowledge and work experience to determine how to use these parts of your life to persuade the interviewer. You mitigate the negative interpretations of your gaps in experience by highlighting other things you believe will be credible and convincing.

Employers also must use rhetorical devices to persuade the best individuals to apply and to dissuade unqualified individuals. Companies try to highlight those aspects of the job that are likely to appeal to applicants, hoping that the impact of other, less-attractive factors will not limit the candidate pool. A small winery in rural mountain town may not be able to pay its employees as well as a large, city-based brewery. However, by claiming that "[you will] contribute to the growth of an emerging brand all while having a kick-ass time in a dynamic, fast-paced industry,"[2] the small winery just may sway you to change your initial compensation requirements. In short, just as applicants seek to persuade a potential employer to hire them,

---

[1] This is from an actual job advertised by Two Mountain Winery, which is located in Zillah, WA. The post was downloaded from **YakimaHelpWanted.com** on October 12, 2010. The full job posting is presented in the chapter *Crafting and Sharing a Curriculum Vitae.*

[2] Ibid.

a potential employer seeks to influence applicants. Understanding various persuasive tactics is therefore *valuable*—both in the financial and general sense—to individuals looking for jobs and companies trying to recruit and maintain talented people.

Of course, employment searches are not the only activity where rhetoric matters to businesses and professionals. All communication within business and professional settings requires the use of symbols for conveying meaning and for understanding. In this sense, all business and professional communication can be described as rhetorical. Though we can treat communication in any context as the purpose of rhetoric (Foss, 2008), this text focuses on improving your use of rhetoric within business and professional situations. This includes enhancing your ability to construct and critique business-related *artifacts* (e.g., documents and conversations). Becoming a better rhetorician and rhetorical critic will enhance your success in any profession and prepare you to begin a career as a communication consultant and trainer. You will be more capable of assisting other professionals to communicate better in the workplace. Today there is a significant and highly profitable market for life coaches, publicists, and communication training and development consultants.[3]

To apply an interpretive frame of mind to the study and practice of business and professional rhetoric, we first need to define rhetoric and establish the criteria by which we will evaluate the efficacy of such communication. This chapter introduces the criteria through which each chapter's material will be explored and evaluated using an integrative theoretical approach. It explains how to practice rhetoric ethically in rhetorical situations and to interpret business and professional artifacts.

Defining Rhetoric in Professional Communication

Over the years, scholars have defined rhetoric in a variety of ways. Its most basic definition describes it as the use of symbols to communicate. However, many everyday connotations of the word rhetoric are negative. The term is often associated, for example, with empty or flowery talk that is tantamount to sophistry—i.e., "subtly deceptive reasoning or argumentation" (**www.merriam-webster.com**). Frequently, we hear calls for "less rhetoric, more action." For example, in an article reporting a dispute between Boeing and the National Labor Relations Board published in *The Huffington Post*, reporter Christopher Corson argues, seemingly without self-awareness of his own use of rhetoric, that "we need to get past rhetoric and look at what the case is really about" (2011, para. 1). In reference to the slow process out of the Great Recession, which began in 2008, *Wall Street Journal* Economic Editor David Wessel writes the following: "it's time to end the rhetoric and find a solution" and "it will take more than soothing rhetoric to get businesses hiring again" (2010, para. 7). Even within academic circles, the rhetorical tradition has had somewhat of a tumultuous history. Dating back to at least the fifth century B.C., scholars have not only debated its definition, but have argued about its menacing nature. Today, speech communication scholars overwhelmingly consider it an important *techné* (special craft) that is essential to the construction and understanding of our social world.

---

[3]Visit the Bureau of Labor Statistics *Occupational Outlook Handbook* to search for industry outlook and growth, salary and wages, and other relevant information about the growth of consulting professions (**www.bls.gov/oco**).

One of the earliest debates to define rhetoric as a techné appears in Plato's *Gorgias*.[4] Interestingly, this dialogue also provides one of the first examples to demonstrate rhetoric's importance to professionals. The conversation takes place at a dinner party hosted by Callicles, in which the "most elegant feast" is followed by a verbal "fray" between Socrates and Gorgias. Socrates asks Gorgias to defend "with what particular things rhetoric is concerned" (Lamb, 1925, 449d). At one point in the conversation, Socrates asks Gorgias to explain what sort of advice a rhetorician is able to give those who are skilled in, for instance, construction or military affairs. Gorgias' brother is a doctor, so he responds with an example that draws from his experience shadowing his brother and other physicians visiting disobedient patients. Gorgias, an impatient observer, asserts his advice as a consultant. As he notes, "when the doctor failed to persuade him [the patient] I succeeded, by no other art than that of rhetoric. . . ." Gorgias then goes on to claim that "there is no subject on which the rhetorician could not speak more persuasively than a member of any other profession" (Lamb, 456b–c). Although Gorgias leaves out the role of a doctor's knowledge and credibility as

Contrasting times: statue of Socrates in a contemporary city. (Image © Nick Pavlakis, 2012. Used under license from Shutterstock, Inc.)

important to suasion, he highlights that consultants skilled in persuasive oratory and writing can help professionals learn to communicate more (com)passionately with their clients and customers.

Plato, who was not overly friendly to rhetoric, constructs the dialogue in a way that Gorgias does not fully defend its efficacy. Nevertheless, Gorgias' example demonstrates the usefulness of knowing how to use rhetoric to one's advantage in professional situations. In modern times, such circumstances could include teaching customers how to use and maintain equipment, encouraging employees to contribute to their communities, or resolving a conflict between an employee union and management.

To approach business and professional communication rhetorically, we must require of ourselves what Socrates required of Gorgias: ". . . to find out . . . what is the function of [this] art, and what it is that [it] professes and teaches" (Lamb, 1925, 447c). In other words, to use rhetoric sophisticatedly as a techné, we need to specifically define it. We must also develop a method for approaching professional communication rhetorically. The business communication approach we use in this book draws from the interpretive and narrative perspectives.

---

[4]Unfortunately, this dialogue limits rhetoric's domain by suggesting a somewhat negative view of it as "flattery" and a mere "knack" (Lamb, 1925, 463a-b). Nevertheless, it is an illustrative example and an important dialogue to know as a rhetorician.

A Definition of Interpretive Rhetoric

According to Aristotle, "Rhetoric is an ability, in each particular case, to see the available means of persuasion" (Kennedy, 2006, p. 14). This definition is particularly useful to interlocutors and critics interested in taking an interpretive approach to developing and analyzing business and professional communications. Three parts of the definition are particularly useful:

1. "Ability." As an "ability" (or "faculty," as it is often translated), rhetorical skills can be cultivated and improved through education and training.

2. "Particularity." Because rhetoric occurs in "particular cases," speakers, writers, and critics must study, in addition to analyzing the arguments and meanings embedded in messages, the context and intended audiences of communication. Rhetorical scholars often refer to the context of communication as the "rhetorical situation." The rhetorical situation, defined more thoroughly in its own section below, is the circumstances that "call forth" a rhetorical response. In crisis communication, for example, the rhetorical situation is the crisis. Researchers and consultants taking an interpretive approach accept that we can never fully know all of the constitutive elements of a rhetorical situation, the intentions of a speaker, or the (possible) interpretations of audiences. But understanding several of these elements improves interlocutors' argumentation and interpretation.

3. "Means of persuasion." Speakers, writers, and audiences must be able to "see the available means of persuasion." In other words, we need to be trained in persuasion in order to appeal to audiences (hence the need for communication courses). For Aristotle, the three available means of persuasion are *ethos* (appeals to speaker credibility), *pathos* (appeals to audience emotion), and *logos* (appeals to audience reason). The appropriate means of persuasion will change from one rhetorical situation to another.

Aristotle described an audience-focused approach to rhetoric, and he seemed to suggest that the interaction between communicator and audience define the rhetorical situation (Bitzer, 1968). His definition privileges a systematic approach to rhetoric that seeks to persuade an audience—it does not capture the role of *interpretation* in a shared and ongoing *process of enacting* and responding to multiple *rhetorical situations* simultaneously. However, in today's global and technologically mediated business environments, a definition and theory of rhetoric that attends to the simultaneity of argumentation and interpretation, to the process of enacting phenomena, and to context-specific rhetorical situations is likely to be more useful. A hermeneutic approach to rhetoric provides such an approach. (*Hermeneutics* is the study of the practice and theory of interpretation.)

Hermeneutical rhetoric realigns the relationship between interpretation and production of rhetoric (Leff, 1997). It can be defined as the process of *understanding* the circular way in which rhetoric constitutes rhetorical situations (such as business contexts) and how rhetorical situations call forth a particular type of rhetoric (such as business communication). As Hyde and Smith (1979) note, "the [basic and fundamental] function of rhetoric is to 'make known' meaning both *to oneself and to others. Meaning is derived by a human being in and through the interpretive understanding of reality. Rhetoric is the process of making-known that meaning*" (italics in original; p. 348). Rhetoric is, in other words, simultaneously an interpretive and persuasive activity.

During an interview, applicants and interviewers rhetorically (re-)enact the *rhetorical situation* of interviewing, and reinforce interviewing norms (they engage in what rhetorical theorists call *imitatio,* that is, imitation). Although you may have your own interesting approach to the interview process, it is not likely you can stray far from the socially constructed meanings of "proper interview techniques" without repercussions. What is more, the interview is co-constituted by the practices of the interviewer. The interview may be pleasant or difficult based on the approach of the interviewer. If she or he does not perform as expected, then the interview may not go well. We are never in full control of a communicative situation. Others will engage in their own rhetorical and interpretative processes, so we must adapt. Due to pressures to conform to social norms, it is likely you'll always experience one of the common types of interviews (e.g., structured, behavioral, or hostile interviews).

Hermeneutical rhetoric denotes an orientation toward rhetoric that sees it as both engaging in the production and interpretation of reality. It requires acceptance of the argument that the world is socially constituted using symbols that arise from and are accounted for in our everyday social practices. Paradigmatically, interpretive rhetoric requires rhetors (both speakers and writers) to adopt a belief that social practices are reproduced through a strong impulse to imitate (e.g., it is best to write a résumé consistent with employers' expectations) and that it is possible to understand the world from a subjectivist (personal) point of view.

A Definition of Narrative Rhetoric

Rhetoric approached from a narrative point of view often begins with the assumption that we are *homo narrans*, or story-telling beings. Like hermeneutical rhetoric, this approach is more of a paradigm for thinking about rhetoric. The narrative approach argues for an alternative conceptualization of Aristotelian *logos* (i.e., logical arguments derived from true or probable claims), which has predominated Western conceptions of science for centuries. As rhetorical theorist Walter Fisher notes:

> In the beginning was the word, or more accurately, the *logos*. And in the beginning, *logos* meant story, reason, rationale, conception, discourse and/or thought. Thus, all forms of human expression and communication—from epic to architecture, from biblical narrative to statuary—came within its purview. At least that was the case until the time of the pre-Socratic philosophers, Plato, and Aristotle. As a result of their thinking, *logos* . . . was transformed from a generic term into a specific one, applying only to philosophical (later technical) discourse. (1985, p. 74)

If we broadly define *logos* as communication that persuades, we can then ask what kind of communication is most persuasive. Narrative theorists argue that we are motivated most by stories, by plots, and by the flow of ideas that have beginnings, middles, and ends. They also argue that we do not always evaluate arguments based solely on rational appeals (Aristotelian *logos*); rather, we evaluate rhetoric based on whether claims seem coherent with our previous and imagined experiences. What this means is that you should hone your storytelling skills. Your résumé should appear logical (e.g., chronologically organized dates), but it should tell a story about you. Do not just list a bunch of random jobs or skills. Your challenge is to make the story of your skills come alive with cohesive points that will appeal to your specific audience. What sounds great to one potential employer may dissuade another.

Even if we do not deliberately set out to tell a story, we (re-)enact familiar storylines in our everyday speech and practices. These stories are often predictable. Some of them compete with one another. For example, when we talk about entrepreneurs, they often predictably emerge as (stereotypically male) heroes who, through sheer determination, arise from humble or difficult beginnings to obtain wealth (Bruni, Gherardi, & Poggio, 2004; Johansson, 2004). Small town entrepreneurs may not be as heroic, but they are still described by politicians as magicians who take risks with courage, caution, and fire in the belly (Nicholson & Anderson, 2005). We believe that entrepreneurs will spawn enterprises that will resolve economic woes. Not surprisingly, many individuals are motivated, despite the fact that failure rates supersede success rates (Shane, 2008), by the prospects of self-employment. The appeal of the narrative of entrepreneurship seems to overcome the rational decision to avoid investing money in something that is statistically likely to fail.

Those who approach rhetoric in the narrative tradition would not be surprised by the fact that people seem to start businesses underprepared for its laborious and financial demands. As Fisher (1978) notes, "*humans as rhetorical beings are as much valuing as they are reasoning animals*" (italics in original; p. 376). What Fisher is suggesting here is that we do not always need good reasons to be persuaded; we often just need to emotionally value that which we pursue. Stories within organizational and professional settings tend to push us strongly toward myth and ceremony rather than norms of rationality (Meyer & Rowan, 1977).

The Value of Interpretive-Narrative Theoretical Orientations

By adopting a rhetorical approach in general and "narrative" and "interpretive" approaches in particular, we are adopting a specific worldview. There are at least four reasons why an interpretive and narrative rhetorical approach to business and professional communication makes sense: 1) better understanding of the meaning of rhetorical artifacts in your professional life, 2) improved ability to deal with uncertainty and to be more persuasive, 3) greater appreciation of the concealing nature of rhetoric, and 4) increased professional flexibility.

First, by taking a narrative-interpretive approach, you will better understand the importance of integrating various rhetorical artifacts into a comprehensive narrative. For example, we will discuss the résumé. As a technical document, it does more than persuade others to hire you. In terms of a narrative approach, it can be understood as a story in the grand narrative of your professional life. We also assume that the person who reads your résumé is reading other applicants' résumés and, therefore, is constructing a narrative about the particular applicant pool. Since corporations also have their own stories that make up a comprehensive company narrative, you ought to write a résumé in a way that appeals to its particular storyline.

Through the narrative-hermeneutical approach, we learn to persuade by understanding others' stories. This amalgamated approach to rhetoric, therefore, is both rhetor and audience centered. In the following chapters, you will learn to explore artifacts in order to gain intelligence that helps you understand others' stories. You will also learn to adapt and tell your own story in a way that fits with others' narrative expectations. Finally, you will learn how to integrate messages in a way that builds upon narratives within professional environments.

Second, a narrative-interpretive orientation will better prepare you to handle ambiguity and uncertainty. Narratives join disparate messages into a comprehensive meaning system. Rhetors use rhetoric not only to persuade, but also to advocate for a particular reality. Rhetorical critic Barry Brummett writes,

> Humans are necessarily involved in sharing and manipulating messages to give and gain meanings about experience. But what experience means is not by any means agreed upon. The ambiguity is a feature of the essential rhetorical nature of reality. Ambiguity generates conflict and disagreement about meaning and a constant striving to resolve these divisions. This striving is rhetoric; while rhetoric may be defined in many ways and on many levels, it is in the deepest and most fundamental sense of the *advocacy of realities.* (1976, p. 31)

A comprehensive and ongoing story is always more effective at shaping others' understanding of a rhetorical situation. This partly explains why businesses are increasingly interested in integrated marketing communications (IMC). Through IMC, organizations seek to coordinate and integrate all marketing-communication tools and media into a seamless program that maximizes messages' impacts on internal and external stakeholders. Integrated communication helps companies develop specific identities and brands. Similarly, individuals can integrate their résumés, online social presences, and ways of speaking to create a personal brand or identity. Consistent messages allow rhetors to better manage how others perceive them personally and professionally. One outcome of IMC, therefore, is reduced ambiguity and uncertainty about others' interpretations of your (or a company's) narrative.

Third, narrative and hermeneutical approaches, as noted above, assume that rhetoric does more than persuade. According to these paradigms, rhetoric reveals, constructs, and describes our world for us. Consistent with other subjectivist approaches to rhetoric, narrative and interpretive approaches require an appreciation of the fact that our communication constrains our ability to see other possibilities in our social world. Kenneth Burke provides one of the best descriptions of this concealing and revealing effect of rhetoric. As he notes, "[Humans] seek for vocabularies that will be faithful *reflections* of reality. To this end, they must develop vocabularies that are *selections* of reality. And any selection of reality must, in certain circumstances, function as a *deflection* of reality" (1969, p. 59). A good example of the revealing-concealing feature of rhetoric is in the way organizations advertise weight-loss products, dietary supplements, and exercise programs. When companies pitch these products, or we talk about our diets, there is an underlying narrative of consumption. For example, people frequently ask what they can eat, or what special product they can buy to help them reduce their weight or live a more healthy life. What we deflect by using this consumerist rhetoric is a language of reduction and conservation. Overeating and weight gain is already correlated to consumption and multitasking (Hamilton, Vohs, Sellier, & Meyvis, 2011). Perhaps people would live healthier lives by simply purchasing less and doing less. In short, the rhetoric of consumption conceals the vocabulary and everyday talk we need to promote anticonsumption.

Fourth, the narrative-hermeneutical approach to rhetoric can assist you in becoming a more flexible, ethical, and culturally sensitive professional. As mentioned above, rhetors must analyze the rhetorical situation in which they find themselves. By trying to understand others' beliefs and modifying their argument to be more favorable to their listeners' points of view, rhetors invite change in personal and audience worldviews. This type of approach requires bias; however, it also requires flexibility (the etymology of bias means "slanted" rather than "rigidly straight"). By seeking first to understand and then to be understood, rhetors privilege others' ideas over their own. An orientation to communication that considers how others' stories converge with your story will likely make you a more tolerant person. An open-minded and flexible ethic will assist you professionally. Among other things, you will be more likeable.

Rhetoric is not limited by the fact that it is symbolic. According to the narrative-interpretive approach, rhetoric is itself action. Through rhetoric, we enact the (professional) world we inhabit. Table 1.1 summarizes the various definitions of rhetoric.

Table 1.1   Key concepts and definitions of rhetoric

Rhetoric	
Basic definition (Aristotle)	An ability, in each particular case, to see the available means of persuasion.
Hermeneutical rhetoric	The process of revealing and concealing meaning in and through an interpretive understanding of reality.
Narrative rhetoric	A paradigmatic approach to rhetoric that presupposes that humans are fundamentally story-telling beings; persuasion is achieved through (emotional) appeals embedded in stories.
Rhetorical criticism	
Foss definition (2008, p. 6)	"A qualitative method that is designed for the systematic investigation and explanation of symbolic acts and artifacts for the purpose of understanding rhetorical processes."
Cheney & Lair definition (2005, p. 60)	"The description, interpretation, analysis, and critique of organized persuasion—and, by extension, identification."
Classes of rhetoric	
Deliberative	Used in decision-making and politicking (future-oriented).
Forensic	Used to pass judgment regarding prior actions (past-oriented).
Epideictic	Used to assign praise and blame, promote and celebrate values (present-oriented).

(continues)

Table 1.1   Key concepts and definitions of rhetoric *(continued)*

Classical appeals

Ethos	Credibility of a speaker or writer as determined by the audience. Established by demonstrating good sense, competence, character, and use of credible data.
Pathos	Appeal to emotions in order to create a particular disposition in the audience (e.g., fear or boldness). Best when accompanied with appeals to reason (*logos*).
Logos	Word, story, reason, discourse, thought, etc. (Fisher, 1985). Logic appeals embedded in arguments (Aristotle).
Illustrations/Examples	The supporting evidence used to prove a sensible argument based on situational factors.
Syllogism	An argument with a major premise, minor premise, and conclusion.
Enthymeme	An argument with either a major premise or minor premise and conclusion.

Rhetorical situations

Basic definition (Aristotle)	The context in which we communicate. Rhetor addressing a specific audience, with a specific text, and in a specific environment.
Bitzer definition (1968, p. 6)	"A complex of persons, events, objects, and relations presenting an actual or potential exigence which can be completely or partially removed [by applying discursive constraints]."
Cheney & Lair definition (2005, p. 62)	"'Corporate' or organized bodies addressing multiple audiences, including one another, through multiple means, and in an elusive search for stable identities, within an exploding/imploding university of communication."

Additional concepts

Kairos	Opportune moment; the moment within a rhetorical situation in which an argument will become substantiated and believable to an audience (Aristotle).
Techné	A special craft or art that is oriented toward understanding through doing.

Using Rhetorical Criticism to Understand and Improve Business Communications

Now that the overall theoretical approach used to approach business and professional communication in this book has been outlined, let's look at the key concepts that are central to the application of this theory. This section discusses *rhetorical criticism*, a particular method for working through the interpretation and construction of professional communication artifacts. (In some of the following chapters, you will learn how to apply this method.) While the term "method" is typically applied to scientific inquiry, such as experiments or survey research, we are going to use the original meaning of the word as a way of teaching and learning. Method was derived from the Greek combination of the words *meta-*, which means "after," and *hodus*, "a travelling, way."[5] Method, in this sense, means to follow a communication phenomenon or artifact as it is used socially. We are interested in the study and design of professional communication and business-related artifacts (e.g., résumés, websites, and letters).

Rhetorical criticism can be defined in two useful ways. The first definition is from a recommended textbook, *Rhetorical Criticism: Exploration and Practice* by Sonja Foss:

> [Rhetorical criticism] is a qualitative method that is designed for the systematic investigation and explanation of symbolic acts and artifacts for the purpose of understanding rhetorical processes. The definition includes three primary dimensions: (1) systematic analysis as the act of criticism; (2) acts and artifacts as the objects of analysis in criticism; and (3) understanding rhetorical processes as the purpose of criticism. (Foss, 2008, p. 6)

The second definition is more specific to organizational communication and pinpoints one of the main purposes of rhetoric in professions—increased *identification*: "*Rhetorical criticism is the description, interpretation, analysis, and critique of organized persuasion—and, by extension, identification* (italics in original; Cheney & Lair, 2005, p. 60). Identification is a process that refers to the commitment to a particular identity. When people use a product because they think it represents their core values, for example, they are engaging in a process of identification with that product. Similarly, as you build a professional identity vis-à-vis the personal narrative you construct, you seek identification from potential or current employers. You want them to see you as a valuable contributor to their organization. Similarly, companies want employees to identify with their core values, so they become stewards of the organization's mission.

Although rhetorical criticism is primarily used to develop academic theories or typologies about communication, in this book we will use it to analyze and to create professional artifacts. We also use it to improve everyday professional practices. The approach to criticism used in this book, which is part of the activity of "invention" in the basic artifact construction process, described in Chapter 2, begins with the identification of the class of rhetoric, draws upon the use of the five canons of rhetoric, and applies the classical appeals to seek maximum persuasive effect.

---

[5]To discover meanings of words, visit **www.etymonline.com**.

A business team deliberating. (Image © Stephen Coburn, 2012. Used under license from Shutterstock, Inc.)

Classes of Rhetoric

Aristotle identified three types of rhetoric for specific occasions: deliberative, forensic, and *epideictic* (demonstrative).[6] *Deliberative rhetoric*, which is chiefly future-oriented, is the type of rhetoric that we engage in when we make (political) decisions. Boardroom meetings, for example, are places where one would likely observe the use of deliberative rhetoric. You may also engage in *intrapersonal deliberation* before making a decision regarding whether to deny or accept your boss's request. When you write a letter that invites an organization's stakeholders to a focus-group discussion, the letter is likely to provoke deliberation, which will then appear in the meeting as arguments for or against a decision. (Note that this is why we often describe meetings as deliberations, or say we need more time "to deliberate.")

Forensic rhetoric is the type of rhetoric we engage in when we pass judgments regarding actions that have occurred in the past. Though this type of rhetoric typically occurs in the court of law—and there are professional reasons one may find themselves in court (e.g., as an expert witness)—it is also used in a variety of nonlegal situations. For example, as rhetoric that seeks a "just resolution," managers often use forensic arguments when they mediate disputes among coworkers. If you should ever be accused of doing something in the workplace, you may issue

[6]See Kennedy (2006).

an *apologia*, or defense of your actions. Crafting a business letter to stakeholders that seeks to explain a company's nonculpability in an accident—which could eventually be used in court—clearly requires a different style and form of delivery than a letter congratulating a retiring employee.

Epideictic rhetoric is the type of rhetoric that does not require us to engage in immediate action. In this sense, it can be describes as present-oriented. Aristotle noted that this rhetoric is primarily concerned with assigning praise or blame. Organizational communication scholars have also described this rhetoric as the type used by companies and people to "celebrate values" and engage in "self-promotion" (Cheney & Lair, 2005). Eulogies, a type of speech that praises a person or thing, are common within business settings. For example, if you have to write a toast for an employee's ten-year anniversary, then you will engage in epideictic rhetoric. Such speeches also present an opportunity to reinforce the company's commitment to core values. If you are a manager, you'll likely use the opportunity to simultaneously seek employee identification with the company. Lee Iacocca, a former president and CEO of Chrysler, was a master at this type of rhetoric (Seeger, 1986). Public relations specialists often have to deal with crises. While such campaigns are often marked by a defensive (forensic) tone, it is not uncommon to hear a tone of concern and care seeking to appeal to people's memory of the company's history of success. During the Gulf oil spill of 2010, for example, British Petroleum ran a series of advertisements that included the testimony of locals praising the company for its response. This epideictic rhetoric appeals to emotions and seeks identification with the rhetor. Finally, customers' feedback and appeals for refunds or retribution are likely to be primarily marked by both forensic and epideictic rhetoric.

The above examples highlight why it is important to identify classes of rhetoric. Identifying the class of rhetoric used by a speaker or writer, as well as the type of rhetoric a particular rhetorical situation requires, will help you produce and interpret rhetoric more judiciously. Identifying a class of rhetoric will help you decide which tone and method of delivery are appropriate. Forensic rhetoric will often require more formality and documentation of delivery, whereas epideictic rhetoric, depending on message content, may use a variety of tones and delivery methods. But identifying the class of rhetoric is only the first step in using rhetorical criticism to develop better messages and responses. Don't forget to think about context. If you work in a customer services department or run your own company, for example, it is critical to understand the different rhetorical styles used to respond to positive and negative reviews.

Websites like **www.angieslist.com**, **www.yelp.com**, and **www.ripoffreport.com**, which are growing in popularity, allow customers to publish reviews of companies' services. Knowing how to respond to the particulars of business communication requires analyzing and producing messages adhering to the canons of rhetoric.

The Five Canons of Rhetoric

Between Aristotle and Cicero, the rhetorical process has been classified into five parts: *invention, arrangement, style, memory,* and *delivery.* Today, rhetoricians use these canons in slightly different ways than those intended by Aristotle and Cicero. Due to their adaptation, however, these five key principles remain remarkably useful for interpreting and constructing various types of speeches and documents. This section gives a general introduction to these key concepts, and the following chapter more thoroughly describes how to use each canon in business communication. Table 1.2 provides an overview of the definitions and key elements that make up each of the canons.

Invention refers to the sources of ideas (inspiration) and the adaptation of information to the audience. For example, the excerpts from the sample job advertisement at the beginning of this chapter invite a fun and quirky cover letter and résumé. By demonstrating in a cover letter that you are a fun *and* professional individual could go a long way in persuading the managers of the vineyard to invite you for an interview. If applying to companies that seem to use more traditional approaches and tones in their advertisements, then adapt your cover letter and résumé so that it appeals to such companies. A conventional résumé may be more helpful in making a case that you will fit with a more conservative organizational culture. When you read or design a press release, identify the motivation of the message. Is the release for advertisement, crisis management, or enhanced corporate identification? When you ask these types of questions or try to appeal to others' sensibilities, you are engaged in the process of invention.

Arrangement, often referred to as "organizational pattern," deals with the organization and structure of ideas that are best suited to the topic and intended audience. When you use bullet-points to list key ideas, for example, you are engaged in the process of arrangement. When you read something and say, "This does not make much sense," you are pointing to others' poor use of arrangement.

In most cases, organize ideas in a highly structured format. The basic format of most written and verbal communications includes an introduction, a body, and a conclusion. An introduction always includes some type of thesis statement and preview. A thesis signals to readers and listeners the purpose of the rhetoric and a preview provides a brief outline of the body of a presentation. (It also helps rhetors stay focused when developing artifacts.) By highlighting key points and ideas in an organized manner, individuals can better understand claims and evidence. Though teachers always emphasize the need for having a thesis, preview, and other outline elements, it is a concept that many people do not seem to grasp. However, adhering to these formats is essential for improving your organizational skills.

Arrangement is vital in business communication. Speaking and writing with structure allows others to more easily follow the logic of arguments. Avoiding the use of this canon could affect professional success, so hopefully you'll be more inclined to take its purpose seriously. Even the simplest of business communication (e.g., a text message) requires the sender to think about arrangement.

Style is the specific use of language and other symbols to express ideas. This is the canon that deals with issues regarding a rhetor's tone, choice of words, use of figures of speech, grammar, and so on. This canon also encompasses the use of colorful words that appeal to people's senses and understanding of the world. The use of metaphors, analogies, and similes, for example, help make difficult concepts more understandable.

Speakers and writers use style to convey meaning *and* to influence receiver reasoning and emotion. Business communicators typically want to strive for simplicity and aim for conciseness

Table 1.2   Canons of rhetoric

Canon	Key concepts
Invention (*inventio*) The process of adapting topics to rhetorical situations and discerning *what* to say (inspiration). Common techniques used in the invention process include brainstorming, conducting primary research, and analyzing artifactsand audiences.	• Recognizing purpose of rhetorical situations and *kairoi* • Identifying appropriate class of rhetoric • Searching for "common topics," or *topoi* - Identifying relationships, comparisons, circumstances, and testimony that will resonate with audience • Identifying *stasis* point—i.e., the point at issue in a debate (Is the debate concerned with definitions or facts?), or the inciting incident of a rhetorical situation (When does an issue become an issue or at what point is it resolved?) • Developing arguments and strategies that draw upon the appropriate persuasive appeals • Understanding desired outcome from rhetorical effort and establishing best method for obtaining specific results

Arrangement (*dispositio*)
The process of organizing rhetorical artifacts (e.g., speeches or written texts). Arrangement builds upon invention and is concerned with making decisions Introduction, body, conclusion about how to pattern an argument.
	• Writing an outline
	  - State purpose, identify thesis
	  - Provide preview
	  - Introduction, body, conclusion
	• Choosing stock patterns
	  - Topical
	  - Problem-solution
	  - Cause-effect
	  - Etc.
	• Choosing structure to internal arguments (must support thesis)
	  - Narrative (examples)
	  - Inductive/deductive
	• Locating appropriate place to use appeals
	  - Ethos is typical to the introduction
	  - Logos is often emphasized in the body of a rhetorical artifact
	  - Speakers and writers leave a lasting impression (conclusion) by appealing to audiences' emotions (pathos)

(continues)

Table 1.2 Canons of rhetoric (*continued*)

Canon	Key concepts

Style (*elocutio*)
The process of developing the artful expression of ideas. Style addresses *how* something will be said. Style is not a superficial or supplementary part of the process; it establishes the mood of rhetorical situations.
	• Determining which symbols and figures of speech will be most appropriate and effective. For example:
	  - Identifying biases and using them strategically
	  - Using appropriate analogies, similes, and metaphors
	  - Demonstrating cultural sensitivity and using gender-neutral pronouns

Memory (*memoria*) The process of memorizing parts of communication artifacts in order to succeed at extemporaneous recall. This is more central to the oral tradition, though it is a useful concept for developing artifacts that are easier to remember (e.g., lists).	• Developing strategies for recall of important key facts and ideas • Practicing a presentation several times • Obtaining feedback on written artifacts from trusted readers, who can comment on the writing fit for intended audience • Creating mnemonic devices (e.g., repetition and acronyms) that are useful aids for both speaker/writer and audience
Delivery (*pronuntiatio*) The process of delivering messages. Though this canon is concerned with actual performance, it is connected to other canons, especially invention. One must decide how to enhance an argument through delivery, how to increase the power of an appeal through kinesthetic movements, timing of delivery, and so on.	• Selecting method of delivery (verbal or written; see also invention) • Determining appropriate medium for delivery (podcast, commercial, website, text message) • Deciding aesthetical concerns (e.g., what color of paper) • Controlling environmental and contextual elements (e.g., appropriate lighting and microphone for webcast) • Using visual aids to improve delivery and enhance understanding • In spoken forums, controlling kinesthetic movements in order to appeal to audience

in their verbal and written communications. By choosing words carefully, using them correctly, and avoiding a significant number of grammatical errors, speakers and writers gain credibility and reduce the potential for confusion. By using the active voice, personal pronouns, and inclusive language, a speaker can gain credibility and sound confident. By using repetition and parallelism (i.e., arranging words and phrases in similar forms), speakers and writers can create a lasting impression among readers and listeners. They also should use language that is culturally sensitive and gender neutral and that doesn't include stereotypes.

Style aids in increasing influence and identification. As a critical listener and reviewer of others' rhetoric, decide the degree to which others' stylistic choices will influence your opinion. When complaining about the tone of a speaker or the grammar in a written message, interpreters are most often pointing to the canon of style. This does not mean, however, that the argument is necessarily bad.

Memory, often described as "the forgotten canon," is central to the oral tradition. It entails practicing a speech until it can be artfully delivered with a minimum reference to notes. By drawing on the canon of memory, speakers become more confident. Practice helps reduce performance anxiety and ensures successful delivery of information. Memory improves with practice, so forming a habit of preparation will increase your ability to remember details. The canon of memory promotes the use of various mnemonic devices (e.g., mind maps, poems, word associations, and acronyms). Using mnemonics can help rhetors remember names or details about important stakeholders, which can be important when greeting or introducing someone. Combining the canons of arrangement and style with a focus on memory can make documents and presentations easier for readers and listeners to remember, and can lead to productive and positive outcomes. For example, write your résumé and cover letter with lists and repetition. These devices are effective instruments for inducing memory recall and maximizing the narrative effect (Browning, 1992; Page et al., 2006; Ziegler, 2007), so search committee members may recall your application over others' submissions.

Delivery is the canon that deals with the nature of a message's presentation. This includes, among other things, vocal and kinesthetic behaviors and the use of visual and auditory aids. Speakers and writers must also consider which medium is most appropriate and effective for message delivery. For example, a Facebook or Twitter comment is inappropriate for sending news about layoffs, though it may be a good way to distribute links to updates regarding the layoff process. Email may be appropriate to share a list of what colleagues need to bring to a meeting, but it may be less efficient if used for deliberation in place of the meeting (Bordia, 1997). A phone call may be suitable in some circumstances, but to avoid nonessential banter, record and send a voice mail—an underutilized communication medium. Delivery also includes considering the meaning conveyed in and by a particular medium. For example, in many Asian countries, the presentation of a business card is more formal than in Western countries. Simply accepting a business card without commenting on its design or the title and position of the person is considered impolite. In the United States, business cards serve the primary purpose of distributing contact information; quickly pocketing a card given to you is more acceptable.

Using the five canons of rhetoric to interpret business-related messages will help you gain a better understanding of the usefulness of various business documents. In addition, by

Delivery is important, but it is only one of five canons. (Image © Yuri Arcurs, 2012. Used under license from Shutterstock, Inc.)

applying these canons to the construction of messages, you will become more effective in producing oral and written communications. When analyzing and crafting communication with the five canons, use persuasive appeals effectively and identify these appeals when others use them.

Classical Persuasive Appeals

As previously mentioned, the three persuasive appeals as described by Aristotle are *logos*, *ethos*, and *pathos*. This section describes each of these more thoroughly. Though each appeal is described separately, they are not mutually exclusive. Rhetors draw upon all appeals, often simultaneously; however, effective communicators accentuate certain appeals depending on the rhetorical situation.

Logos. *Logos*, as noted above, is "story, reason, rationale, conception, discourse and/or thought" (Fisher, 1985, p. 74). For Fisher, arguments are best constructed by using inductive reasoning, a type of reasoning that draws probable conclusions from individual instances. Illustrations and examples provide the proof (evidence) that the argument is reasonable. Aristotle, however, used the term *logos* to refer to appeals embedded in arguments directed at the audience's reasoning on a topic (i.e., logic). His approach is deductive, which is to say that a conclusion logically follows a set of premises or hypothesis. Aristotle differentiated between two types of arguments: the *syllogism* and the *enthymeme*. A syllogism is composed of a three-part argument that consists of a major premise, a minor premise, and a conclusion. Syllogisms move from a general stipulation to a specific instance. The classic example of a syllogism is as follows:

Major premise: All men are mortal.

Minor premise: Socrates is a man.

Conclusion: Therefore, Socrates is mortal.

Syllogisms are presented as absolute, which often lead to *fallacies* (erroneous reasoning). By using words like *all, every, most,* and so on, speakers and writers overgeneralize. In business and professional communication, therefore, it is usually best to avoid using these types of terms. For example, without proper evidence (e.g., statistical data) to verify a claim that *every* employee wants a pay increase, you run the risk of losing an argument in favor of better working conditions. If a manager can find one person who does not want a pay increase, then the argument weakens and you lose credibility. Supporting arguments with sound evidence—whether by statistics or personal accounts—can improve the persuasiveness of claims.

Arguments often cannot be supported in their entirety. There are many interpretations of any situation. This is why Aristotle suggested that the second type of reasoning, the enthymeme, was particularly useful in argumentation. An enthymeme is a syllogism presented as a probability rather than as an absolute. Qualifiers like "should" or "ought to" present ideas as tentative and flexible. By not sounding so resolute in communications, you can change your opinion as more information about a situation becomes available. Give yourself some flexibility by using less emphatic language. The difference been "always" and "sometimes" is huge.

In practice, enthymemes state either a major or a minor premise, but not both. For example, one can move from major premise to conclusion: "Energetic and happy employees are more productive; I should increase your profitability." Alternatively, one can move from minor premise to conclusion: "I am usually energetic and happy, so I should increase your profitability." By making the claim that you are energetic and happy, the implied assumption is that energetic and happy people make better employees (interestingly, the accuracy of this claim is actually debatable; see Zelenski, Murphy, & Jenkins, 2008). Since the major premise is unstated in this claim, it is an enthymeme.

Understanding how to construct and interpret arguments based on sound reasoning will increase your persuasiveness. Learning to analyze others' use of logos improves decision making because it reduces the likelihood of being persuaded by false claims. What is more, people who can provide a rhetorical explanation about why they rejected an argument appear more thoughtful.

Ethos.   *Ethos* is characterized by the credibility of a speaker or the source of data. When receivers of communication evaluate a speaker's, writer's, or company's competence, character, and goodwill, they are questioning ethos. Communicators who have the best interest of the receivers of the communication in mind (even when delivering negative news) will likely be considered credible. A communicator can also gain ethos by establishing his or her knowledge on a topic. He or she can point, for example, to an educational degree as evidence of professional qualification. Ethos can be drawn from the credibility of sources. For example, at times a company may want to highlight that the source of information is independent testing, academic research, or a nonpartisan agency.

Although ethos deals with having the proper authority to speak on a topic and citing relevant, valid, and appropriate evidence to support a claim, there are also subtle ways to establish goodwill through business correspondence. Sound more sincere, for example, by writing, "I am struggling to understand" instead of "What *you* said doesn't make sense."

As an evaluator, rhetors often point to others' use of ethos when they offer support. A letter of recommendation, for example, points to examples of a candidate's character and prior work experience and education. These claims seek to create an appeal toward the subject's ethos. To argue against a person's candidacy, examples draw attention to the subject's lack of skills or experience. This is an attempt to devalue a subject's ethos without sounding personal. If the letter writer's opinion is strongly valued (i.e., his or her ethos is considerably strong), then his or her opinions will be taken seriously. Build your professional credibility so that your rhetoric is considered valuable.

Pathos.   *Pathos* is an appeal to the emotions of the receivers of the communication. Stories may be persuasive, but those using vivid language and powerful words are more likely to invoke emotions. Aristotle identified anger and calmness, love and hatred, fear and confidence, kindliness and unkindliness, pity and indignation, and shame and shamelessness as the primary ways to arouse emotions in audiences (Kennedy, 2006, pp. 17–18). Pathos is effective in itself, but it should often be balanced with logos. Without such a balance, rhetors run the risk of sounding like demagogues or propagandists. While you want to appeal to your company's stakeholders by swaying them with emotional pleas, be cautious about overusing words and phrases that incite emotion without causation. Appealing to emotion can have unintended consequences: What appeals to one group may alienate another.

As you analyze others' use of language and consider your particular stylistic approach to crafting business communication, consider what language will inspire and what language will detract from your primary purpose or argument. As you engage in the production and analysis of business and professional communication, focus on the use of the classical appeals. The more effectively you use these approaches, the more persuasive you will be to potential employers, current employers, or other organizational stakeholders. The more capable you are at recognizing how others use these appeals, the more effective you become at mitigating the influence others have upon you.

Rhetorical Situations and *Kairos*

Rhetors must understand rhetorical situations if they are going to use rhetoric effectively. Similarly, effective evaluation of rhetoric requires understanding of *kairos*, or timing.

Rhetorical situations.   As noted earlier, *rhetorical situation* is the context in which we communicate. It has been defined in other useful ways. Aristotle defined rhetorical situation as a single rhetor (speaker or writer) addressing a specific audience, with a specific text, and in a specific environment or setting. The simplicity of this definition makes it a useful tool for rhetorical analysis. For example, a manager (rhetor) wants to inform employees (audience) about new policies and procedures. She or he therefore creates a list of the specific changes (text) and delivers it by email or at a meeting (context). The rhetorical situation is defined as this single episode of sharing information. We can analyze whether the list was well designed and easy to read and understand. We can imagine or verify the impact on the audience. We can validate whether email seemed to be the best medium for delivery. Aristotle's definition of rhetorical situation, however, is too simplistic for the narrative-interpretive approach to rhetoric in business communication.

Bitzer's (1968) definition of rhetorical situation aligns better with the narrative and interpretive traditions. According to Bitzer, "Rhetorical situation may be defined as a complex of persons, events, objects, and relations presenting an actual or potential exigence which can be completely or partially removed if discourse, introduced into the situation, can so constrain human decision or action as to bring about the significant modification of the exigence" (p. 6). In other words, rhetoric is used whenever there is a problem (exigency) that needs to be resolved. Rhetoric will sway people to solve the problem by changing and altering their practices that are believed to be the source of the problem. Bitzer notes that a rhetorical situation consists of three elements: *exigence*, *audience*, and *constraints*. The constraints include both 1) the parameters of the problem, which you hope to alter, and 2) the parameters established by a rhetor to focus an audience. In our sustained example, employee practices must have created an exigency that management felt could be addressed by changing policies. The manager is providing a list to try to ensure that employees will adhere (or be constrained) by these policies. If management is correct, then employee adherence to the particular policies will resolve the situation that initiated the creation of the rhetorical artifact. Bitzer's definition highlights the need for paying greater attention to the context and environment in which particular rhetoric is used, but it also emphasizes a focus on audience and text. When a manager shares a list of new policies, it is important to consider why management believes it needs to alter its existing policies (something a consultant would do).

The list of new policies, of course, may create new problems. A group may feel targeted by a policy, or employees may not be able to complete tasks without violating the new policies. In others words, an audience is not homogenous. In fact, the list addresses multiple audiences. In time, the policies may need to be altered to better fit established practices. In short, there are multiple interpretations of the text, and these interpretations change over time. Given the diversity of employees and department functions, management may need to create multiple types of messages and rhetorical artifacts to obtain compliance to new policies.

Since we often conceptualize corporations as human-like entities that communicate (e.g., we say "Coca-Cola issued a press release"), we can look at rhetorical situations as the institutional environment created by companies' shared and often competing discourses. Cheney and Lair's (2005) definition of rhetorical situation, therefore, is particularly useful for a narrative-interpretive approach to business and professional communications: "'Corporate' or organized bodies addressing multiple audiences, including one another, through multiple means, and in an elusive search for stable identities, within an exploding/imploding university of communication" (p. 62). This definition complements the narrative-interpretive approach. It underscores our need, as communicators, to think about multiple audiences, to use rhetoric to produce, maintain, and analyze identity, and to consider the concealing and revealing nature of communication. A representative of a company using this definition will think about communication more cautiously. As the narrator of your professional identity, consider how your personal rhetorical artifacts (e.g., résumé, Facebook and LinkedIn profiles, and behaviors at conferences) create a comprehensive story about who you are as a professional.

Regardless of which definition seems to make the most sense, remember that no single rhetorical situation applies to all business communications. There are innumerable rhetorical situations that require a rhetorical response and countless ways to respond to them. Since rhetoric itself creates rhetorical situations, responses can exacerbate current exigencies or create additional need for rhetorical replies. In short, we live in a world of innumerable rhetorical situations, and you will be faced with many in your professional career. So learn to use rhetorical criticism, rhetorical canons, and persuasive appeals to carefully craft artifacts. This will increase your rhetorical prowess in any situation.

Kairos (pl. kairoi). *Kairos* is the timeliness of delivery; the concept denotes the role that right-timing plays in deliberation, speech, and action (Sipiora & Baumlin, 2002). It is "a passing instant when an opening appears which must be driven through with force if success is to be achieved" (White, 1987, p. 13). For Aristotle, kairos is the moment in a rhetorical situation in which an argument becomes substantiated and believable to an audience.

Crises present unique rhetorical situations that require strategic use of classic appeals. (Image © Norman Chan, 2012. Used under license from Shutterstock, Inc.)

Successful business communication often requires recognizing an opportune moment to deliver a message. For example, salespeople who pitch products at tradeshows, in shopping centers, and late-night infomercials must "execute what in pitchman's [sic] parlance is called 'the turn'—the perilous, crucial moment where he [or she] goes from entertainer to businessman [sic]" (Gladwell, 2000). Entrepreneurs must anticipate what products and services others will desire in the future (often by listening and persuading). Job seekers must recognize the dreaded instant when they can nonchalantly (or directly) bring up salary and benefits during the interview process. Negotiators need to pause when there is an opportunity to relieve tension, perhaps through humor, to reduce the chances of an impasse.

The concept of kairos was central to the *Sophists*, a group of teachers in pre-Socratic Greece who set up their own schools to teach rhetoric to citizen-orators (often for a substantial fee). Isocrates and Gorgias were among the most famous. Sophists were, in some regards, a group of consultants or life coaches who taught others to use the tools of rhetoric to live a life of excellence. Though sophism, thanks to Plato, was condemned (hence the term "sophistry"), there is something to be said about teaching others to use rhetoric to improve society and improve career prospects—that is, to help others become *sophisticated*. That's why this book emphasizes the importance of communication consulting. Knowing how to identify and when to use kairos requires practice, and perhaps a little intuition.

Concerning business, kairos can be defined as the recognition of rhetorical opportunities that enhance profit and professional prospects. The proper use of rhetorical methods (classes, canons, and appeals) ought to increase your chances of creating or taking advantage of opportunities (think again of great salespeople who create a demand for their product). In the following chapters, you will learn how to use a variety of writing and speaking techniques in such a way that you will achieve kairos in many different types of rhetorical situations.

Conclusion

After spending a fair amount of time with professionals who negotiate the dual roles of experts and entrepreneurs (e.g., accountants, attorneys, private investigators, doctors, and mechanics), one typically finds that they need help with some part (or many parts) of the "business side" of their enterprise. While they may do fine work, they often miss opportunities to communicate this to key constituencies. By learning to think about business and professional artifacts rhetorically, you will learn to avoid mistakes that lead to lost business. Consultants can use a rhetorical approach to help multiple clients deal with issues related to communicating in various marketplaces. By approaching document writing, website optimization, and internal business communication as responses to rhetorical situations, you will improve your or your clients' chances of influencing various audiences.

By now you should appreciate the need to engage in rhetorical criticism of professional communications and should have a general sense of how to do so. Hopefully, you now see that rhetoric is more than just mere persuasion (e.g., it is a narrative that shapes our worldview) and you understand the method (or way) to evaluate and craft persuasive business and professional artifacts. As discussed in the chapter, rhetors first identify the class of rhetoric (deliberative, forensic, or epideictic) a particular situation requires. Second, rhetors evaluate the messages based on their use of the five rhetorical canons (invention, arrangement, style, memory, and delivery). Similarly, rhetors use these five canons to construct their own presentations and documents. Finally, rhetors decide how best to deploy rhetorical appeals for maximum effect and to evaluate others' (ethical) use of such appeals. There are no absolute rules you can follow to guarantee rhetorical success. Rhetoric is a craft that requires the artful use of general practices and rules that work in particular circumstances. The following chapters teach the principles of effective business messages and correspondence using the rhetorical tradition so that you will become more effective at expressing and promoting information and ideas.

Continuing Education: Recommended Texts and Resources

- *Rhetorical criticism: Exploration and practice* (4th ed.) by Sonja K. Foss. ISBN: 978-1577665861.

    This textbook outlines a descriptive procedure of rhetorical criticism. It provides ample examples of studies using rhetorical criticism.

- *Public relations writing: A rhetorical approach* by Michael Kent. ISBN: 978-0205595440

    Although this book overlaps with some of the content in this text, it specifically addresses PR writing. It also provides different examples and discussions about rhetoric and its use. As a complement to this book, students will become more proficient at writing for public audiences.

- *Community action and organizational change* by Brent Faber. ISBN: 978-0809324361

    This book demonstrates how to write in a narrative style. One of the chapters in the book describes how Faber, working as a consultant, helped re-narrate the importance of a local cemetery, which saved it from privatization.

- *Rhetoric: An historical introduction* by Wendy Olmsted. ISBN: 978-1405117739

    This unique book introduces rhetoric by describing the social context in which it emerged within ancient Greece and Rome. Students interested in the rhetorical tradition and post-graduate study in communication will find this book informative.

- *Nonsense—Red herrings, straw men, and sacred cows: How we abuse logic in our everyday language* by Robert J. Gula. ISBN: 978-0975366264

    An excellent resource on fallacies. Explains a variety of ways people fail to make convincing arguments in everyday speech and correspondence.

References

Bitzer, L. (1968). The rhetorical situation. *Philosophy and Rhetoric, 1*, 1–14.

Bordia, P. (1997). Face-to-face versus computer-mediated communication: A synthesis of the experimental literature. *Journal of Business Communication, 34*, 99–118.

Browning, L. D. (1992). Lists and stories as organizational communication. *Communication Theory, 2*, 281–302.

Brummett, B. (1976). Some implications of "process" or "intersubjectivity": Postmodern rhetoric. *Philosophy & Rhetoric, 9*, 21–51.

Bruni, A., Gherardi, S., & Poggio, B. (2004). Doing gender, doing entrepreneurship: An ethnographic account of intertwined practices. *Gender, Work and Organization, 11*, 406–429.

Burke, K. B. (1969). *A grammar of motives*. Berkley: University of California Press.

Cheney, G., & Lair, D. J. (2005). Theorizing about rhetoric and organizations: Classical, interpretive, and critical aspects. In S. May & D. K. Mumby (Eds.), *Engaging organizational communication theory & research* (pp. 55–84). Thousand Oaks, CA: Sage.

Corson, C. (2011, May 9). Less rhetoric and more of the law in the NLRB's Boeing action. Retrieved from www.huffingtonpost.com/christophcr-corson/post_2018_b_859201.html.

Fisher, W. R. (1978). Toward a logic of good reasons. *Quarterly Journal of Speech, 64*, 376–384.

Fisher, W. R. (1985). The narrative paradigm: In the beginning. *Journal of Communication, 35*(4), 74–89.

Foss, S. K. (2008). *Rhetorical criticism: Exploration and practice* (4th cd.). Long Grove, IL: Waveland Press.

Gladwell, M. (2000, October 30). *The pitchman: Ron Popeil and the conquest of the American kitchen*. Retrieved from www.gladwell.com/2000/2000_10_30_a_pitchman .html

Hamilton, R., Vohs, K. D., Sellier, A.-L., & Meyvis, T. Being of two minds: Switching mindsets exhausts self-regulatory resources. *Organizational Behavior and Human Decision Processes, 115*, 13–24.

Hyde, M. J., & Smith, C. R. (1979). Hermeneutics and rhetoric: A seen but unobserved relationship. *The Quarterly Journal of Speech, 65*, 347–363.

Johansson, A. W. (2004). Narrating the entrepreneur. *International Small Business Journal, 22*, 273–293.

Kennedy, G. (2006). *On rhetoric: A theory of civil discourse* (2nd ed.). New York: Oxford University Press.

Lamb, W. R. M., Trans. (1925). *Plato's Gorgias*. (W. R. M. Lamb, Trans.). London: W. Heinemann.

Leff, M. C. (1997). Hermeneutical rhetoric. In W. Jost & M. J. Hyde (Eds.), *Rhetorical and hermeneutics in our time: A reader* (pp. 196–214). New Haven, CT: Yale University Press.

Meyer, J. W., & Rowan, B. (1977). Institutionalized organizations: Formal structure as myth and ceremony. *The American Journal of Sociology, 83*, 340–363.

Nicholson, L., & Anderson, A. R. (2005). News and nuances of the entrepreneurial myth and metaphor: Linguistic games in entrepreneurial sense-making and sense-giving. *Entrepreneurship Theory and Practice, 29*, 153–172.

Page, M. P. A., Cumming, N., Norris, D., Hitch, G. J., & McNeil, A. M. (2006). Repetition learning in the immediate serial recall of visual and auditory materials. *Journal of Experimental Psychology. Learning, Memory & Cognition, 32*, 716–733.

Seeger, M. W. (1986). C.E.O. performances: Lee Iacocca and the case of Chrysler. *The Southern Speech Communication Journal, 52*, 52–68.

Shane, S. A. (2008). *The illusions of entrepreneurship: The costly myths that entrepreneurs, investors, and policy makers live by*. New Haven, CT: Yale University Press.

Sipiora, P., & Baumlin, J. S. (Eds.). (2002). *Rhetoric and kairos: Essays in history, theory, and praxis*. Albany: SUNY Press.

Wessel, D. (2010, October 7). Economy needs treatment, not fights on diagnosis. Retrieved from http://online.wsj.com/article/SB10001424052748704689804575535894001985742 .html

White, E. C. (1987). *Kaironomia: On the will-to-invent*. Ithaca, NY: Cornell University Press.

Zelenski, J. M., Murphy, S. A., & Jenkins, D. A. (2008). The happy-productive worker thesis revisited. *Journal of Happiness Studies, 9*(4), 521–537.

Ziegler, J. A. (2007). The story behind an organizational list: A genealogy of wild land fire-fighters' 10 standard fire orders. *Communication Monographs, 74*, 415–442.

Chapter — 2

Planning and Crafting Professional Communications

Image © Elena Elisseeva, 2012. Used under license from Shutterstock, Inc.

Starting Point

"Writing today is not a frill for the few, but an essential skill for the many."
~ The National Commission on Writing (*The Neglected "R,"* 2003)

Successful salespeople and entrepreneurs are often personable and usually good conversation-alists. Compared to writing, however, conversations are easy. While people may notice some-one's awkward statement or improper use of a word, conversations do not receive the same scrutiny as writing. If someone misspeaks or gets confused, there are many opportunities to clarify. Since language cannot be seen during a conversation (and to some degree during a speech), there will be no confusion between "your" and "you're," "there" and "their," or "employer's" and "employers." When reading or delivering a speech, however, misspelled words can become distracting to readers or cause a rhetor to misspeak. In turn, this can lead to a loss of credibility or increased work and business expenses. For example, if you are a loan officer and need to obtain financial information from an applicant regarding his or her previous employer (singular), but you send an email asking the applicant "to forward your previous *employers'* (rather than employer's) financial statements," the typo could create unnecessary additional work or delays. If the applicant believes you meant employers (plural), she or he could request records from several organizations. Such a mistake may seem inconsequential; however, when compounded with similar outcomes from others' poor writing, the financial costs due to productivity loss add up quickly. According to ProLiteracy, a national and international adult literacy organization, poor writing skills and illiteracy cost U.S. businesses, based on data obtained from the U.S. Department of Labor Statistics, more than $225 billion annually in lost productivity ("The Impact of Illiteracy," 2010). A survey of 120 major U.S. corporations conducted by the National Commission on Writing (2004) concluded that two-thirds of salaried employees have some writing responsibilities, and businesses spend up to $3.1 billion teaching remedial writing classes to these employees. Writing mechanics, punctuation, and grammar clearly matter.

The simplest mistake in punctuation can change the plausible interpretations of information, which at times can be humorous (e.g., Let's eat Veronica!), but at other times disastrous. Lynne Truss, a self-described punctuation stickler, who has no problem with taking out a permanent marker and fixing a mistake on a public sign, provides several examples in her best-selling book, *Eats, Shoots & Leaves*, of the deadly consequences of a misplaced a comma. Her story is "of the fateful mispunctuated telegram that precipitated the Jameson Raid on the Transvaal in 1896" in South Africa (2003, p. 11). Truss narrates the story of the "fiasco" as follows:

> The Transvaal was a Boer republic. . ., and it was believed that the British and other settlers around Johannesburg (who were denied civil rights) would rise up if Jameson invaded. But unfortunately, when the settlers sent their telegraphic invitation to Jameson, it included a tragic ambiguity:
>
> > It is under these circumstances that we feel constrained to call upon you to come to our aid should a disturbance arise here the circumstances are so extreme that we cannot but believe that you and the men under you will not fail to come to the rescue of the people who are so situated.
> >
> > As Eric Partridge points out in his *Usage and Abusage,* if you place a full stop [a period] after the word "aid" in this passage, the message is unequivocal. It says, "Come at once!" If you put it after "here," it says something more like, "We might need you at some later date depending on what happens here, but in the meantime—don't call us, Jameson, old boy; we'll call you." Of course, the message turned up at *The Times* with a full stop after "aid" (no one knows who put it there) and poor old Jameson just sprang to the saddle, without anybody wanting or expecting him to. (pp. 11–12)

A goal of communication is to convey meaning. Poorly constructed sentences, improper grammar, punctuation problems, and typos obfuscate ideas and cause confusion. It is important to master new technologies and understand how to use persuasion effectively, but it is also important to learn the proper use of the mechanics of English (or any other language), because not doing so can blunt the effectiveness of technology and persuasion.

Writing and speaking well in business and professional contexts requires specific focus on the canon of style—that is, elements of punctuation, grammar, word choice, syntax, and so on. As an employee, manager, entrepreneur, or consultant, you will increase opportunities and reduce costs by taking grammar seriously. Learning to edit, provide feedback, and teach others to construct well-written messages (and other business-related artifacts) will improve your own writing. Businesses need good writers and editors, especially as social networking and microblogging becomes more important to business success. These forums are public, which means that what you say and how you say it will affect your current and future career prospects; businesses are increasingly doing social media background checks (Preston, 2011). In short, your professional success is partly contingent on your ability to write well and your willingness to improve your writing skills through continuing education.

This chapter focuses on applying the canons of rhetoric to the basic writing process, with an emphasis on writing and proofreading documents. You will first learn the four basic steps of the writing process, which correspond to the canons of rhetoric presented in Chapter 1: 1) Prepare and Research (Invention), 2) Organization (Arrangement), 3) Write (Style), and 4) Complete (Memory/Delivery). Then, you will learn about the specific concerns and dynamics of writing, speaking, and evaluating. Last, you will learn pragmatic skills to improve punctuation and style.

The Basic Artifact Construction Process

Regardless of the information you need to convey or how you need to convey it, you will save yourself a lot of time and frustration by following a basic writing process. This four-step process, described with slight variations in books on effective writing, is a proven approach that aligns well with the canons of rhetoric. By adhering to the four steps for the construction and evaluation of all communication artifacts (see Figures 2.1 and 2.2), you will clearly, efficiently, and effectively convey your message. Although following such a methodical process may seem tedious, it soon will become routine and help simplify your writing tasks.

Step 1: Prepare and Research (Invention)

The first step in developing effective communication follows the canon of invention (see Chapter 1). Before beginning to write or speak, understand the rhetorical situation. For example, you will respond differently to a customer's complaint than to a satisfied customer's testimonial. The exigencies are different, so the "best possible arguments" (available means of

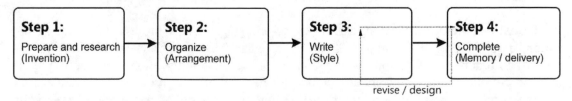

Figure 2.1. The four-step artifact construction process.

Summary of the procedures in the four-step artifact construction process

Step 1: Prepare and research
- Consider rhetorical situation
- Identify audience
- Establish purpose
- Establish what you know (brainstorm)
- Conduct primary or secondary research
- Select the medium
  - Written media
  - Oral media
  - Visual media
  - New media (e.g., electronic, portable, interactive)

Step 2: Organize
- Establish purpose (thesis / rationale)
- Choose rhetorical approach (direct, indirect, invitational, confrontational)
- Select organizational pattern that limits scope
- Create a purpose-driven outline

Step 3: Write
- Integrate message with storyline (point of view)
- Select appropriate style and tone
  - Seek conversational tone
  - Simple and concrete style
  - Use active voice
  - Use appropriate words and sensitive language
- Construct sentences
- Construct paragraphs
- Use quotations, paraphrasing, and citations
- Write effective introduction and conclusion

Step 4: Complete
- Check for general comprehensibility and possible interpretations (look for hidden meanings)
- Look for flaws in argument (fallacies)
- Check structure (sentences, paragraphs, etc.)
- Check clarity of sentences
- Check for ethical issues
- Eliminate grammatical and mechanical problems
- Check design and production errors
- Highlight important details
- Distribute

Figure 2.2. Four-step artifact construction procedures.

persuasion and topoi) and stylistic choices will vary. Similarly, letters soliciting new clients require a different approach than letters thanking customers for their continued use of services or products. Speeches to uninformed audiences require rhetors to deliver content differently than they would to more informed audiences. By understanding the rhetorical situation and purpose *before* crafting your communication, you will develop a much more effective rhetorical argument—one that achieves its purpose. While every type of correspondence will require personal touches and the use of situation-specific appeals, there are widespread standards for letter formats. It is useful, therefore, to learn and employ these standard formats and stock patterns to produce concise, specific correspondence—whether it is positive or needs to be negative. Later chapters cover these stock formats. This chapter introduces the general process.

Consider the rhetorical situation(s).   Within business and professional contexts, situations requiring formal verbal or written correspondence are diverse. Customers and suppliers will communicate with you, and the content of their communication will require you to respond. Similarly, you may feel that a company's description of its products or service is misleading. The choice to seek a partial or full refund or discontinue service will change your rhetorical style. Similarly, you may have been satisfied with the service you received from a company and want to share your impressions. If you are an entrepreneur and hope to develop a closer relationship with a supplier, you may write a more formal letter directly to the company to praise its operations. If you are a satisfied customer of a chain restaurant, you may post a review on Facebook, Angie's List, or Yelp. Your colleagues may have disagreements that increase workplace hostilities and you may feel bound to mediate the conflict. A problem or crisis may require your professional association to respond, and you will be asked to contribute to the dialogue in some way. All of these are exigencies that need a rhetorical response. The specifics of the rhetorical situation help determine the appropriate rhetorical process.

By considering the constitutive elements that give rise to particular rhetorical situations—such as the problems and circumstances, key stakeholders affected, and time available to respond—*before* responding, you will, among other things, be ready to use the most appropriate class of rhetoric (forensic, deliberative, or epideictic). You will also be able to anticipate the limitations of your arguments and the resistance your communication will face. Some considerations regarding the rhetorical situation are the physical conditions and barriers to effective communication and the events that precede and follow particular rhetorical responses. The following additional procedures all deal to some degree with elements of the rhetorical situation.

Identify audience characteristics.   When creating communication that responds to a specific rhetorical situation, you are likely to know details about the audience or recipients of communication. In some instances, such as advertising, the audience must be assumed. Whether designing communication for a specific or assumed audience, it is important to conduct an audience analysis and consider the possible ways in which specific audiences may interpret your rhetoric.

Audience analysis is an important part of the research and development process; it helps focus the purpose of the communication. It is necessary to understand the audience's areas of interests (What motivates the audience?), capacity to act (How much authority do the recipients of the communication have?), and willingness to change (How far can an audience be pushed intellectually, emotionally, etc.?). These factors will influence your rhetorical approach. For example, you do not need to spend as much time providing a detailed overview of your company's corporate philosophy if the audience already is very familiar with the company. If you are using the corporate philosophy as a basis for your decision, however, you may want to spend a few minutes explaining it to the audience. If you anticipate that recipients of news are likely to be excited, consider when and how to provide important details they could miss because of their excitement. If you are addressing a hostile audience, adjust your tone and consider the placement of negative information in order to facilitate a more effective communicative transaction.

Take some time to consider the following audience criteria:

- Age
- Education level
- Skills

- Language
- Cultural beliefs and customs
- Background knowledge
- Needs and interests
- Socioeconomics

Some techniques for determining audience characteristics involve doing background research, interviewing the audience, asking others about the audience, surveying the audience with forced-choice or qualitative questionnaires, and obtaining data from secondary sources (e.g., demographic information from the U.S. Census Bureau).

The above list is not comprehensive, but it does identify some of the more important factors that affect the ability of interlocutors to accept the content of a rhetorical artifact. For example, slow your rate of speech and consciously improve enunciation when leaving a voice-mail for someone who speaks English as a second language. When contacting someone in writing who may have a limited or fixed income, provide various ways for him or her to contact you (not everyone has an Internet connection or unlimited talk and text). For example, contact him or her by mail (for added customer service, provide a self-addressed stamped return envelope). Changing your communicative strategies to fit an audience and the rhetorical situation improves rhetorical effectiveness.

In some cases, rhetors need to conduct a more comprehensive analysis or hire public relations specialists to understand an audience better. In other cases, rhetors may generalize or

Adapting to your rhetorical situation and audience will improve your ethos. (Image © Igor Karon, 2012. Used under license from Shutterstock, Inc.)

gain details by analyzing the communications of the person with whom they are communicating. If, for example, you are responding as a business owner to an angry-toned online review of your company, ascertain details of the customer by conducting a rhetorical analysis of the artifact. The underlying motivations and assumptions of the expressed problem may be latent. An upset customer may state that he or she wants a refund, but what he or she really wants is respect. Reading "between the lines" can better ensure that the unstated needs or desires of the complainant are addressed.

Establish purpose and approach.   You may know what the purpose of your communication is before you thoroughly consider the rhetorical situation or analyze the audience. For example, you may have received a negative review on **www.yelp.com** or some other review site, and understandably want to defend your store's reputation. However, it is important to avoid writing a rushed response (it is, after all, asynchronous communication). Remain flexible and adapt your rhetoric after analyzing the rhetorical situation and the audience. A thoughtful pause will allow you to observe (and use) all the *available means of persuasion*. After some consideration about the Yelp post, for example, you may realize that any response really must address two audiences—the customer who posted the review and the public (possible customers). Thus, the purpose of communication shifts from defensive to invitational. Ask the customer to give your company another opportunity to impress him or her. Your communication with the person who posted the review probably should be private (e.g., through email or by phone). In response, offer an apology and, if appropriate, invite the person to give the store another chance. Include a (partial) refund, and a coupon for a future purchase.

To address the Yelp community (i.e., other potential customers) post a message that explains that you accepted responsibility. Persuade Yelpers to visit the store (with a discount, perhaps) to obtain first-hand evidence about the quality of the establishment and service. In short, motivate Yelpers to decide for themselves the accuracy of the review (by politely challenging the ethos of the reviewer). In some cases, the reviewer may remove the initial post and provide a positive review that reflects a commitment to customer service. In other cases, customers may come to the defense of companies, especially if they strongly identify with products and services.

The *general purpose* of all business messages is to inform, to persuade, or to entertain. The general purpose guides the elements used in the correspondence. If the goal is to persuade, consider strengthening the power of claims with concrete evidence. The *specific purpose* states what the rhetor hopes to accomplish with his or her message. State this purpose explicitly in the form of a *thesis*, which sets parameters for a specific artifact and articulates how the problem will be resolved. In the preceding example, the general purpose is to persuade potential customers; the specific purpose is to get Yelpers to come to your *fun and friendly* store in order to form their own opinions. When writing a response, begin by stating something like the following:

> We're bummed that this Yelper did not have a positive experience. We are currently communicating privately with her to resolve the problem. We know we can do a better job and are willing to prove it [thesis]. So give your eyes a break and come on down to our store [how to respond]. We want to show you that this person's

experience is the exception to the rule. Say "Yelping rules" when you enter the store today or tomorrow [insert dates], and we'll give you a fresh-baked cookie and a 15% discount on any one item in the store (no exclusions).

Note that this example is written in a conversational manner, which many social media experts recommend. It also demonstrates a *direct* and *invitational* approach to communication.

Based upon audience needs and the specific purpose, choose among four writing approaches. The optimal approach is determined by the *sequence of claim* (direct-indirect) and *tone* (invitational-confrontational). See Table 2.1 for combinations of strategies used to deal with each type of correspondence. Keep in mind, though, that there is no one simple formula. You typically want to deliver negative news in an indirect manner; however, get straight to the point, even if the news is unpleasant, when sending a message to a colleague. These approaches can also vary by degree. For example, you can be primarily confrontational while still leaving an opening for future dialogue (invitational).

Establish what you know and need to say. Before conducting research, consider what you already know about the topic. When working in a group, identify collective resources and stock knowledge, contributed by each individual member, before beginning research. The following list provides a few techniques that may be useful for identifying what a group already knows.

- **Brainstorming.** This is one of the most popular and useful ways for generating ideas, organizing ideas, and solving problems. It is an activity that can be done in groups or individually. It involves listing a free-association of ideas without initial criticism. All ideas are initially considered acceptable and "hitchhiking"—using one idea as a springboard for additional thoughts—is encouraged. The purpose of brainstorming is to stimulate creativity. Though brainstorming generally involves listing ideas, and the process should not be impeded by rules, it is important to establish some ground rules before beginning a brainstorming session with others. The following are some typical guidelines groups use for brainstorming:
  - All ideas are welcome, and the more the better. (Designate a reasonable time limit for idea generation.)
  - A note taker should write down ideas.
  - Do not allow criticism of ideas during the initial "storming" phase. Write down everything.
  - Once a comprehensive list is generated, discuss the ideas. The goal in this step is to analyze each idea for *relevance* and to discard redundant concepts. If necessary, break the larger group into teams to discuss ideas and to work to reduce the list. Establishing communicative ground rules is important (e.g., not allowing speakers to be interrupted and limiting discussion time).
  - Group concepts together in some kind of logical order. For example, ideas that best address the purpose of correspondence, ideas that can be linked together as claims and

Table 2.1 Communicative strategies and audience type

	Indirect approach	*Direct approach*
	Audience type: Uninformed, less educated, apathetic	**Audience type:** Sympathetic, interested, pleased
Invitational	**Strategies:** • Focus on capturing attention and interest of audience. • Stress "likability" and develop strong empathetic ethos. • Arrange body of message logically using a topical approach. • Close by requesting engagement and dialogue.	**Strategies:** • Start with main idea and pleasant news. • Use motivational stories, project an easy-going attitude, and focus on emotional appeals. • Reinforce message through positivity. • Stress commonalities with audience. • Clearly tell audience what you want them to do. • Close with cordial comment, create opportunity for future dialogue, or request specific action.
	Audience type: Hostile	**Audience type:** Critical and conflicted
Confrontational	**Strategies:** • Begin with a neutral statement and stress areas of agreement. • Buffer negative news or opposition with a cordial transition (e.g., We appreciated your enthusiasm, but. . .). • Address opposing views with a positive tone. • Give reasons to justify rejection, use euphemisms to indirectly imply the bad news, make positive suggestions. • Don't expect major changes. • Close cordially and, if possible, avoid soliciting action.	**Strategies:** • Present strong arguments and support them with specific evidence. • Use refutation pattern to address opposing views. • Begin by specifically addressing the issue. Avoid using buffers or other language that can be confusing. • If requesting action, be specific about directives. • Anticipate an emotional response.

evidence, and so on. Clustering ideas together can provide a starting point for creating an outline or solution.

■ Brainstorming can be fun, and it can generate better ideas than working alone. Individual contributions during group activities are not always equal; some members may be shy about sharing ideas while others may dominate the conversation. Existing conflicts and political maneuvering may manifest during brainstorming activities, leaving some group members unheard. Encourage input and discourage interruptions. Because brainstorming is frequently used, participants may treat it as routine and useless. Explaining the objective of the activity may inspire group members.

• **Nominal group technique.** This group technique is somewhat similar to brainstorming, but instead involves a more structured agenda that allows everyone to contribute more equitably. This approach is useful when dealing with controversial topics, as it promotes an orderly process (McShane & Von Glinow, 2000).

■ Participants work alone and write their ideas in a manner similar to brainstorming. Unlike brainstorming, however, the topic may be more refined. For example, the group can be presented with a particular problem and be instructed to come up with possible solutions.

■ Each member then reads his or her ideas aloud, one idea at a time (i.e., in a round-robin fashion), and without criticism or discussion. The ideas are recorded in a way that all participants can see the ideas (e.g., flip chart or by projection). This continues until all ideas are shared.

■ The listed ideas are then discussed and clarified; however, the facilitator does not allow evaluative comments at this point. The participants discuss the ideas until they all understand the meanings. If there are too many ideas to discuss, the facilitator or the group can work together to consolidate or remove redundant ideas.

■ The group then ranks and orders ideas by importance or effectiveness. Secret ballot is typically the most effect. The results are tabulated and presented to the group, demonstrating the best (or preferred) ideas.

• **Clustering.** This technique is also referred to as mind mapping. Use this approach as a stand-alone activity, or use it to explore ideas generated during brainstorming. Figure 2.3 demonstrates the way in which clustering is useful technique for recording and organizing ideas. To cluster or map, begin with a blank sheet of paper or flip chart and think of the key terms that best characterize the topic, thesis, or main argument of a message. Then think of subtopics that closely relate to the main topic. Draw circles around the subtopics and draw a line that shows a relevant connection. Continue this process, linking subtopics to additional (sub)topics, until you have generated enough ideas. The resulting map of clusters should help focus your research and organize the content. This technique is especially helpful when creating larger documents. There are a variety of free mind-mapping resources and tools online—for example, **https://bubbl.us, www.mindmapping.com, www.thebrain.com**, and **www.gliffy.com**. Gliffy is particularly useful for generating a variety of diagrams, including flow charts, organizational charts, and fishbone diagrams.

Figure 2.3. Cluster map from an idea-generating session. (*Image © maigi, 2012. Used under license from Shutterstock, Inc.*)

- **Question-answer chain.** This technique works backward from the anticipated questions of the audience to relevant answers (claims and evidence). For example, you could anticipate that an audience will want to know why a project is delayed. Write down all the relevant answers (reasons). Next, look at each answer and think about the additional questions each may generate. Then, answer these questions. Questions you cannot answer will require additional research. Continue this process until you find a good starting point for beginning correspondence and answer all the questions.

- **Journalistic approach.** Journaling is an idea-generation strategy that involves asking *who, what, when, where, why,* and *how* questions about unorganized ideas. The purpose of this technique is to help rhetors discover new information and ideas. When applied to brainstorming sessions, this technique reduces content overload.

- **Storyboarding.** This technique involves recording yourself with a voice recorder as you talk through ideas. Play back your monologue and identify key points. Then work to tighten your message. Continue to play back the message indefinitely until you obtain a concise and clear message. Doodling is a variation of this approach, which is useful when you need to construct messages delivered through conversations (especially conflicts).

- **Repurposing.** You've probably heard the expression, "Don't reinvent the wheel." This applies to most business writing. *Repurposing* (also referred to in technical writing situations as "boilerplating" or "single sourcing") involves the copying and converting of existing content and documents into another document or medium for a different purpose. Repurposing is particularly useful when deciding how to organize ideas. Look at others' work to generate ideas, but be cautious about ethical and legal issues, such as plagiarizing or violating copyright. Part of your research should include identifying quality document formats. In the workplace, it would be somewhat foolish not to use colleagues' work as a guide. Repurposing saves time. Once a quality standard letter is written, it should be used as a template (i.e., basis for a form letter) for future correspondence. Also, borrow from company resources. If you need to create a brochure for your company, some of the main ideas may already exist on the company website. Be sure, especially if you are using content-sharing websites like **www.istockphoto.com**, **www.shutterstock.com**, **www.legalzoom.com**, **www.templatemonster.com**, and **www.docstoc.com**, to read and understand the terms and conditions.

- **Other techniques.** Other techniques that you can use to generate ideas are *buzz sessions, idea writing, role-playing, flowcharting, fishbone diagramming, focus groups,* and *interviews.* These techniques, as with all of the above, can also be used as both problem-solving and research devices.

Provide supporting evidence for claims and arguments. At times, personal experience is very powerful. At other times, supporting evidence from neutral or external sources will provide greater ethos. Gathering data from other resources requires additional research. Establishing what you know in advance will save time during the research process. Instead of researching broadly, focus your search toward finding data to support a particular claim. (Ethically, remain open to the possibility that you may need to change a position.) Poor focus is a significant time-waster in the research process. Knowing what data to obtain and where to look will lead to fewer distractions. There is a lot of content online, and it's easy to get sidetracked. Following irrelevant links is a bad research habit—it reduces work productivity. The less focused your thoughts about a topic, the more time you will spend chasing interesting but unrelated ideas.

Conduct primary or secondary research.   Sometimes you will need to obtain evidence to support your claims. To evaluate others' claims you may have to do some additional research on a topic. The need for more data, information, and supporting materials will require primary and secondary research.

Primary research.   Primary research is the gathering of first-hand data using a variety of *qualitative* and *quantitative* methods. In qualitative research, emphasis is placed on directly observing, describing, and interpreting phenomena. Ethnography, shadowing, interviewing, journaling, rhetorical criticism, and focus groups are commonly used types of qualitative research. Quantitative research emphasizes the use of numerical (statistical) measurement. Typically, data are gathered through surveys, questionnaires, and experimentation; however, data can also be collected through qualitative means and later quantified. For example, a focus group can be qualitatively interviewed and the data obtained from the interview sessions can be coded and quantified (e.g., how frequently the consumer group mentions a particular practice). Similarly, questionnaires may ask qualitative questions rather than forced-choice answers.

Primary research is conducted in a variety of ways and in various setting. For example, consumer ethnographers—much like anthropologists who study ethnic cultures and ceremonies—now spend significant time studying shopping behaviors *in situ*. Data obtained from observing shopping practices over time and in consumers' natural habitat (e.g., a shopping mall) can provide different, if not richer, understanding than data collected by survey. The Internet has provided more ways to conduct primary research. For instance, discussion groups can be monitored and the content thematized. Skype can be used to conduct virtual interviews and focus groups. Second-life meetings can be explored ethnographically. Email and list servers can be used to request and distribute information (e.g., links to surveys).

Online services and other technologies have made conducting and analyzing primary research easier. For example, online data can be collected with premium survey services like **www .surveymonkey.com** and **www.zoomerang.com**. Digital recording devices, digital transcription kits, voice recognition and transcription software (e.g., Dragon speech recognition software by Nuance) have made collecting and preparing data for analysis much easier. Data analysis software, such as SPSS (quantitative) and ATLAS.ti (qualitative), accelerate the analysis of data. Despite all of these advances in technology, the costs of conducting primary research remain high.

Properly conducting primary research requires a significant time commitment and a large capital investment. What is more, there are risks when conducting primary research. In some instances, you may need to seek institutional approval. For example, most universities require their Institutional Review Board (IRB) to approve research conducted by students or faculty. To obtain some government and nonprofit grants, researchers must acquire an ethics review of research protocols through an independent and certified board, such as Institutional Review Board Services (**www.irbservices.com**). The U.S. Department of Health and Human Services' Office for Human Research Protections (**www.hhs.gov/ohrp/index.html**) provides excellent information on requirements and protocols that must be followed for research conducted with agency grants. These protocols are a good benchmark to follow when preparing research for grant approval; subsequently, this is also helpful information for learning about the ethical standards required of researchers conducting experimental research on humans and animals. Chapter 8 discusses primary research methods in more detail.

Secondary research. Secondary research is the gathering of information and supporting materials that already exist. These data are organized in an accessible form, such as a research article indexed by a search database. Examples of secondary research include others' primary research findings, ideas, or information. Using secondary data not only saves time and money, in some circumstances the data may be more credible than one's own primary research. For example, research published in scholarly journals has typically undergone a double-blind review process that demonstrates peer approval (consensus that it is good research). Data obtained from the U.S. government may be richer in details and less biased by ideological interests than research specifically conducted by a partisan think tank.

Sources of secondary research include books, articles, periodicals, reports, blogs, websites, audio and video recordings, podcasts, films, brochures, annual reports, correspondence, "Tweets," and so forth. In fact, any physical and symbolic data can be used as a source of both primary and secondary research. Nevertheless, information cited by more credible sources are more useful and influential.

The Internet has made gathering data from secondary sources relatively easy but also potentially problematic. For example, not all information on the Internet is *relevant*, and some useful information cannot be found on the Internet. Easy-to-find information is hardly the qualifier for useful information, though there is an increasing tendency for rhetors to use only data that they can quickly find with a search engine. Keep in mind that search engine algorithms sort information based on cached websites (see Cambazoglu, et al., 2010), end-user search patterns, and apparent relevancy. Pertinent information, therefore, may be hidden by servers (especially those that are password protected) because that data is not transparent (i.e., cached) by the search engine "web crawlers." What is more, previous searches affect future search results. This is problematic because, to paraphrase Kenneth Burke (see Chapter 1), any selection of reality is also a deflection of reality.

Consequently, it is important to develop a search strategy that involves using sources other than those found through popular search engines (e.g., Bing) and popular informational sites (e.g., Wikipedia). These may be good starting points, but you also want to use library catalogs to locate books, online databases and indexes (e.g., EBSCOhost's Academic Search

Research skills are transferrable, so spend some time in your university's library. *(Image © l i g h t p o e t, 2012. Used under license from Shutterstock, Inc.)*

Premier), and reference works (e.g., encyclopedias, dictionaries, bibliographies, atlases, handbooks, and statistical sources). In addition to these library-based resources, use research tools provided by search engines (e.g., Google Scholar, **http://scholar.google.com**) or go directly to a site that aggregates specific types of information (e.g., the U.S. Bureau of Labor Statistics). Table A.1 in appendix A provides a list of resources that are useful when conducting business research.

Before beginning a search for information, remember this: *you will save a lot of time if you prepare a strategy that is specific to the information you are seeking and stick to it*. Do not distract yourself with frivolous searches. If you are uncertain about where to begin your research, contact someone, such as a librarian, who may know the best source for the type of information you are seeking. A brief conversation with others can help

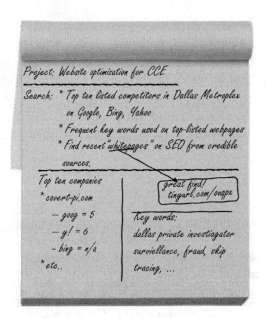

Figure 2.4. Sample research notes.

direct your search. One way to remain focused during the research process is to write a strategy on a notepad and keep detailed notes about what you find in each search (see Figure 2.4). Consider utilizing an Internet browser's "bookmark feature," an often-underutilized tool, for organizing notes and search content for a project, class, or subject of interest (see Figure 2.5). If you use this feature, be sure to map out a filing strategy (e.g., alphabetically, numerically, or topically) in order to relocate sites more quickly.

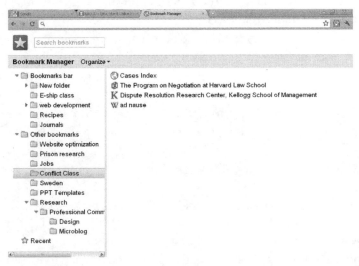

Figure 2.5. Example of Bookmark Manager in Google Chrome.

Research checklist, reminders, and tips.

✔ Be ethical. Among other things, check with the Institutional Review Board or ethics officer before conducting primary research. Seek others' permission before beginning research that could disrupt their work or environment.

✔ Know your personal or business resources. Do you have the time and money to complete thorough research and properly analyze data? Do you have access to the proper databases to conduct secondary research?

✔ Set parameters. Know what method and procedures are going to produce the best outcomes.

✔ Be specific. When conducting secondary research, limit your searches by using key terms (e.g., "primary research" instead of just "research") and Boolean operations (AND, OR, NOT). Typically, the "advanced search" feature of search engines and databases will assist you in this process. If you are looking for anything with the variation of a particular word, use asterisks to maximize search outputs. For example, to find articles with the key words "ethnographer," "ethnographers," "ethnography," and "ethnographies," type "ethnograph*" and the engine will search for all these variations.

✔ Try several search engines and databases to get varied results, but remember that algorithms suggest results based on a variety of factors, including previous search history and sites paying for listings.

✔ Use search aggregators to initially maximize search results (e.g., **www.dogpile.com**, **www.metacrawler.com**, and **www.metasearchengine.com**.

Evaluate sources by asking the following types of questions:

• Is the resource relevant and easily obtainable?

• Who created the resource? Are the authors credible and will the intended audience respect the source of information?

• Does the source of information disclose how data were collected? Does the source provide enough transparency for the data's accuracy to be verified?

• Do the authors of the information avoid fallacies and use a convincing (well-written) style?

• Is the information published through a legitimate process and credible publisher? For example, is the information peer-reviewed? Is the publisher of a book a reputable company?

• Are the purpose, scope, and political positions of the author and publisher fully disclosed?

• Is information presented in a cogent and professional manner? When looking at a website, for example, look to see if the site appears professional, up to date, and forth coming (check the "About us" page to learn about the authors).

• Can you provide a strong argument and support your choice to use a particular source? Are you willing to defend the reputation of the source information?

Select the medium.   When preparing for your research, be mindful of the medium you plan to use to distribute your message. The medium will partly dictate the aspects of the invention process. Research results, however, may determine which media will better reach an audience.

When choosing the medium, consider the advantages and disadvantages of using each type. Match the richness of the medium to the intended communicative function. For example, email can be very effective for generating ideas but is less effective as a tool for deliberation (Bordia, 1997). Factors to consider when choosing a medium include formality, access, urgency, cost, and an audience's social presence (e.g., immediacy, psychological proximity, intimacy, familiarity, and preferences). As suggested by Daft and Lengel (1986), within organizational contexts, one should weigh the *advantages* and *disadvantages* and *synchronous* and *asynchronous* nature of certain media along a *medium richness continuum* (see Table A.2 in appendix A).

Step 2: Organize and Outline (Arrangement)

Developing the ability to organize and outline messages will increase your persuasiveness in both oral and written presentations. In addition, arranging thoughts into a pattern and creating a plan saves time. An outline functions as a map of thoughts and keeps rhetors from getting lost during the writing process (this helps prevent wasting time composing unnecessary material). Outlining, like preparation and research, can be tedious work; however, thorough outlines limit superfluous thoughts and assists rhetors in getting started after a break from writing. When speaking extemporaneously, as is often the case in interviews, an outline will help you memorize key ideas in advance and keep you focused during a response. Prepare an outline in advance and write down points you want to cover. When asked a question to which you do not have a quick response, take a few moments to organize your thoughts into a pattern (typically a list) *before* speaking.

Organizing and outlining do not only benefit the writer and speaker. Readers also appreciate well-organized messages. Outlines and organizational patterns provide audiences with "signposts" to follow. Signposts and transitions assist an audience by helping them understand the logical flow of an argument, which in turn helps them to accept a message (the organized thoughts develop stronger ethos). Well-structured content also saves readers and listeners time. They don't have to struggle to follow an argument, wade through irrelevant information, or seek out additional sources to fill in missing ideas. Good organizational skills will likely enhance your professional possibilities; people will be able to understand your ideas, will see you as clear thinker, and will consider you as a careful interlocutor.

If you thoroughly worked toward fulfilling the demands of Step 1 (invention), developing an outline is easier to accomplish. Being a good organizer requires understanding your purpose (or thesis) and the main points to support your message. If you already have a sense of the claims you want to make, organizing is a rather simple process. The following sections focus on techniques you can use to organize and outline your ideas in a manner that *limits scope* and keeps your *message purpose-driven*.

Choose an organizational pattern that limits scope. The first thing to do when outlining is to choose an organizational pattern that is most effective for the artifact's content. There are various types of organizational patterns; the most common format arranges information topically.

Topical arrangement. Also frequently called a *categorical* pattern, a useful way to organize content is based on themes or clusters of ideas. For example, suppose you want to outline the benefits of social networking to a group of managers. So long as you have evidence to support the claims, you could focus on *creativity*, *productivity*, and *profitability*. Though these concepts are not mutually exclusive, you will avoid repetition and confusion by discussing each separately. In the conclusion, or along the way, you can explain the relationships among each category. However, any evidence you find while conducting research that supports the conclusion that social media improves organizational creativity would be itemized under "creativity." Once categorized, rearrange content to make an order that is more relevant to the audience's needs or interests. When speaking to an audience of entrepreneurs, you could first speak about productivity and profitability, and then add that social media also improves creativity.

Chronological (temporal). This type of pattern orders the main points sequentially. Use chronological patterns to describe events that occur or happened over time or to order serial actions and tasks, such as instructions used in product assembly manuals, customer service protocols, or recipes. It is possible that the topics used in the previous example—creativity, productivity, and profitability—could also be sequential. Perhaps you have evidence suggesting that companies that have increased profitability focused first on enhancing *creativity*, which in turn lead to increased *productivity*, which then improved *profitability*.

Spatial. If the purpose of a message is to describe or explain the physical arrangement of a place or object, then it is useful to arrange points in order of their physical proximity, relational characteristics, or direction relative to each other. For example, in a real estate brochure of a particular house, it may be helpful to describe the specific details of each room in the order that people are likely to move when viewing a house. Visually, points can be listed inside a diagram of the house. If pitching a proposal for a new facility, spatially describe the features of the building, as demonstrated below:

Thesis: The Chicago-based plant will be a state-of the-art facility that will reduce carbon emissions and energy costs simultaneously.

    I.   Upon entering the campus, visitors will immediately notice the large number of trees, which will function as a natural cooling environment for the plant.

    II.   When entering the building, visitors will see many of the ecological-friendly features; however, it is the hidden features, such as the EcoRock

   drywall by Serious Materials, which are offsetting carbon emissions and
   reducing the cost of heating and cooling.
  III. Making their way to the plant floor, visitors may notice that the windows are coated with heat-absorbing glazing that adjusts to sunlight, reducing the energy needed to cool and heat the building.

The list would continue. Notice that the descriptions are arranged spatially; however, the outline does not necessarily emphasize this fact.

Causal (cause-effect). Some messages present information that seeks to explain relationships that are outcomes of particular events. One of the best ways to organize data in these types of messages is by cause and effect. In such outlines, rhetors list multiple causes for a single effect or a single cause for multiple effects. For example, you may want to explain the many *causes* for customer loss in a division (Example 1). Alternatively, there may be many *effects* of lost customers (Example 2).

Example 1: Many causes for customer loss

 I. Cause 1: Increased competition

 II. Cause 2: Poor service response times

 III. Cause 3: Few subscription choices offered

 IV. Effect: 12% reduction in customer subscriptions during Q1

Example 2: Many effects of customer loss

 I. Cause: 12% reduction in customer subscriptions during Q1

 II. Effect 1: Increased employee furloughs and dismissals

 III. Effect 2: Decreased profits and shareholder value

 IV. Effect 3: Decreased revenue expenditures in research and development

Problem-solution. When using this pattern, there may only be two main points. The first is the problem (defining what it is) and the second is the proposed solution (the way to overcome the problem). You may need additional points to, for example, refute a proposed solution. With this pattern, propose a single solution to resolve several problems or a variety of solutions for a single problem. Speakers and writers often combine their points in a pro-con pattern.

Pro-con. Use a pro-con arrangement to compare and contrast the benefits and limitations of particular ideas. This approach invites the audience to consider the benefits and costs of a particular option. They then accept or reject the ideas based on the evidence provided. The following example combines the problem-solution and pro-con patterns to evaluate the decision of a small business to offer employee health benefits.

I.   *Problem.* Business has grown considerably and has excess capital for rein-vestment in human resources. Employees do not currently have health insur-ance benefits.

II.   *Solution.* Provide health insurance benefits.

    a.   *Benefits of offering health insurance (pro).*

        i.   Employees will have increased personal security.

        ii.   Employee retention and productivity will likely increase.

        iii.   Company will benefit from "goodwill" publicity.

        iv.   . . . .

    b.   *Concerns of offering health insurance (con)*

        i.   Not all employees desire health insurance; some would rather have a pay increase.

        ii.   Increased expenditures that are not easy to adjust, especially if current market conditions change.

        iii.   Difficult to forecast five-year capital needs due to volatility of insurance prices.

        iv.   . . . .

There are a variety of other organizational methods, such as the circular, star, wave, and spiral patterns. These patterns are less frequently used, but you may benefit from researching these and other organizational patterns. As the above examples demonstrate, a decision to use a particular arrangement is based on the purpose of a message and the contents of the supporting ideas and evidence. A house's features, for example, can be described spatially, especially if the document is to be used by potential buyers as they wander through a house. However, features of each room can also be listed topically.

Create an outline that keeps you purpose-focused.   The organizational pattern is embedded in the body of the basic writing format (not in the introduction, or conclusion). The general approach to outlining is something with which you ought to be already familiar. However, many people skip the outlining process and begin writing a draft without one. Application cover letters, letters of recommendation, reprimands and reviews, responses to inquiries for information, speeches describing new product lines, and so on are easier to write with an outline. Figure 2.6 is a skeleton of a useful outline style.

It is best to use this basic approach every time you begin a project. Over time, you will develop a habit of organizing your thoughts, even when speaking extemporaneously.

A good outline will be *unified*, *coherent*, and *balanced*. Each point, whether main or subordinate, will focus on a single idea and be roughly the same length. Typically, a message will have between two and seven main points. Points should reflect the main purpose of an artifact (the thesis) and should be declarative statements rather than passive thoughts. To help readers and listeners see the link between a main point and the thesis, rhetors need to explicitly state or imply the link. In rhetoric, this link between data and a claim is called the *warrant*. Headings and points of an outline should have *parallel structure*, or be alike in function and grammatical form.

An outline functions as a blueprint or map of main ideas and supporting evidence. Although many create a bullet-point list of ideas in the outlining process, its usefulness is solely an out-

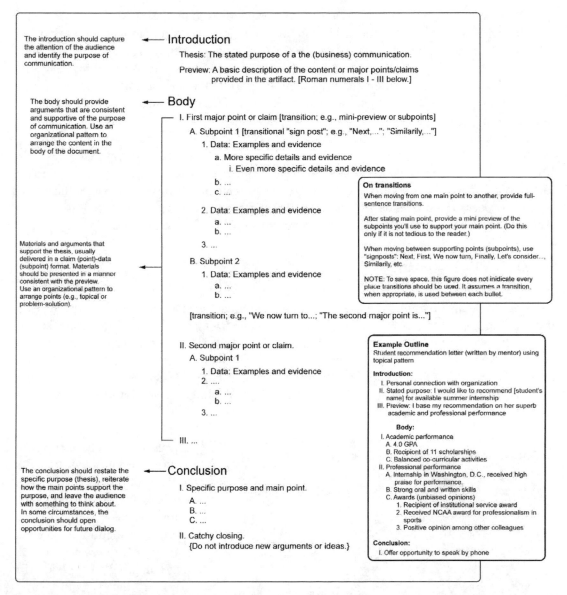

The introduction should capture the attention of the audience and identify the purpose of communication.

Introduction

Thesis: The stated purpose of a the (business) communication.

Preview: A basic description of the content or major points/claims provided in the artifact. [Roman numerals I - III below.]

The body should provide arguments that are consistent and supportive of the purpose of communication. Use an organizational pattern to arrange the content in the body of the document.

Body

I. First major point or claim [transition; e.g., mini-preview or subpoints]

   A. Subpoint 1 [transitional "sign post"; e.g., "Next,..."; "Similarily,..."]

      1. Data: Examples and evidence

         a. More specific details and evidence

           i. Even more specific details and evidence

         b. ...

         c. ...

      2. Data: Examples and evidence

         a. ...

         b. ...

      3. ...

Materials and arguments that support the thesis, usually delivered in a claim (point)-data (subpoint) format. Materials should be presented in a manner consistent with the preview. Use an organizational pattern to arrange points (e.g., topical or problem-solution).

   B. Subpoint 2

      1. Data: Examples and evidence

         a. ...

         b. ...

[transition; e.g., "We now turn to...; "The second major point is..."]

II. Second major point or claim.

   A. Subpoint 1

      1. Data: Examples and evidence

      2. ....

         a. ...

         b. ...

      3. ...

III. ...

The conclusion should restate the specific purpose (thesis), reiterate how the main points support the purpose, and leave the audience with something to think about. In some circumstances, the conclusion should open opportunities for future dialog.

Conclusion

I. Specific purpose and main point.

   A. ...

   B. ...

   C. ...

II. Catchy closing.

   {Do not introduce new arguments or ideas.}

On transitions

When moving from one main point to another, provide full-sentence transitions.

After stating main point, provide a mini preview of the subpoints you'll use to support your main point. (Do this only if it is not tedious to the reader.)

When moving between supporting points (subpoints), use "signposts": Next, First, We now turn, Finally, Let's consider..., Similarily, etc.

NOTE: To save space, this figure does not inidicate every place transitions should be used. It assumes a transition, when appropriate, is used between each bullet.

Example Outline
Student recommendation letter (written by mentor) using topical pattern

Introduction:
I. Personal connection with organization
II. Stated purpose: I would like to recommend [student's name] for available summer internship
III. Preview: I base my recommendation on her superb academic and professional performance

Body:
I. Academic performance
  A. 4.0 GPA
  B. Recipient of 11 scholarships
  C. Balanced co-curricular activities
II. Professional performance
  A. Internship in Washington, D.C., received high praise for performance.
  B. Strong oral and written skills
  C. Awards (unbiased opinions)
    1. Recipient of institutional service award
    2. Received NCAA award for professionalism in sports
    3. Positive opinion among other colleagues

Conclusion:
I. Offer opportunity to speak by phone

Figure 2.6. Outline format (skeleton structure).

come of a rhetor's outlining prowess, and it is not the only style available. Other kinds of writing devices, such as boxes and fonts, can emphasize structural levels of ideas and evidence. When using a word processor to outline and write, be sure to utilize formatting tools, such as rulers and tabs, to create editable and transportable documents (Microsoft offers a variety of tutorials online at **http://office.microsoft.com/en-us/training-FX101782702.aspx**).

Developing a strong outline requires much consideration. Decide which information you gathered in step 1 is relevant, what evidence from your research is likely to support a main point, when to present and justify an idea, and how to present ideas so that readers' or listeners' interest will be maintained. If you choose an invitational rather than confrontational approach (revisit Table 2.1), organize points so criticism is blunted. With an outline, you can "play around" and move ideas until you feel comfortable with the flow of arguments—something that is not easy to do once you have written all the content. In short, outlining is as much a decision-making process as it is a useful device for writing and speaking. With a strong outline, rhetors are less likely to make argumentative fallacies (explained in step 4).

To save time and improve rhetorical skills, break from bad habits and always begin by outlining thoughts *before* writing. It is not easy to outline. It is often a frustrating process. The difficulty in developing a good outline, however, is precisely what makes it useful—it forces you to think about what you are going to write or say. Remember, however, to treat the outline as an in-process document. Once you feel like you have developed your thoughts and produced a useful outline, it is time to begin generating content for the artifact.

Step 3: Write (Style)

Quality writing draws upon the canon of style, which includes choosing the appropriate words and tone. Style also includes the use of writing techniques, such as storylines, points of view, grammar and punctuation, as well as the use of secondary materials. With an outline at their side, rhetors can focus more attention on style as they write and develop documents and speeches. Style is *how* one uses language to express substantive arguments. Whether the purpose of the communication is to entertain or explain complex ideas, good writing expresses ideas intelligibly, meets the stylistic expectations of an audience, and builds credibility for rhetors.

Learn the canon of style, because professionals spend a significant amount of time writing. (Image © Yuri Arcurs, 2012. Used under license from Shutterstock, Inc.)

Integrate with storyline. When you begin to write, first decide how to integrate your communication with the appropriate personal, organizational, or institutional storyline(s). As mentioned in chapter 1, we are *homo narrans*, or storytelling beings. We often describe scenarios in the structure of a story—that is, with a coherent beginning that introduces a sympathetic or antagonistic character with a challenge to overcome, a middle that develops the plot and the specific complications and successes of characters, and an ending that describes the moral of the story or how the situation was resolved. For instance, to entice people to sign up for a weekend retreat, tell a positive story of previous excursions. To describe a difficult day at work, provide specific details that involve various characters (e.g., the antagonistic customer). If the purpose of the story is to discourage others from messing with you, the story may end with your describing how you denied a customer what she or he wanted. The point here is that we like to tell and hear stories. Thus, storytelling is an effective way to organize many business messages—from advertisements to employee training videos. Stories help personalize the message and make readers contemplate causes and consequences in ways that more conventional business writings, which typically uses an *impersonal point of view* and relies more heavily on writing aids like lists and figures, do.

Whether a message is structured as a story or is more conventional, it should integrate other messages perpetuated with the ongoing storyline. It would not make much sense, for example, to develop an image as an edgy consultant and then produce boring and conservative brochures. As an employee of a business trying to build a family-friendly image, however, curb your edgy attitude. In short, maintain a consistent storyline across various messages that fit your audience. Storylines are institutionalized over time. Audiences will expect that you will write or speak in a manner consistent with their expectations. If you are engaging with a particular group for the first time, rely on audience and rhetorical analysis to determine the storyline. Tap into an organization's storyline by mimicking or repurposing senior colleagues' work.

Although there are a variety of storylines one can follow, consultant and author Annette Simmons, founder of Group Process Consulting, has identified six common storylines worth telling: 1) "who I am" stories, 2) "why I am here" stories, 3) the "vision" story, 4) "teaching" stories, 5) "values-in-action" stories, and 6) "I know what you are thinking" stories. Although the titles of each of these story types are self-explanatory, her book *The Story Factor* is recommended for additional reading. Her prose offers useful reminders like the following:

> People don't want more information. They are up to their eyeballs in information. They want *faith*—faith in you, your goals, your success, in the story you tell. It is faith that moves mountains, not facts. Facts do not give birth to faith. Faith needs a story to sustain it—a *meaningful* story that inspires belief in you and renews hope that your ideas indeed offer what you promise. (2006, p. 3)

Regardless of whether you choose to use a storytelling approach, you'll have to choose what point of view to present ideas and information.

Establish point of view.   Point of view (POV) is the relationship writers and speakers have with the information they are presenting. It is important to select a POV that is audience appropriate. Seek to convey your message in a way that establishes and maintains shared meaning with an audience. POV is reflected in the use of the *personal pronoun*.

First person:	*I* am interested in the communication jobs currently advertising on **www.bright.com**.
Second person:	*You [they]* should apply for the communication jobs advertised on **www.careerbuilder.com**.

Apply for the communication jobs currently advertised. [Note: In this instruction, *you* is an implied pronoun.]

Third person: *He [she, we]* should apply for the communication jobs advertised on **www.career-hound.com**.

Many people are uncomfortable using the pronoun "I," especially in professional writing. The first-person pronoun, however, is often the better choice—it indicates that the writer is a responsible participant.

Awkward: It is understandable that the proposal needs to be revised.

Improved: *I* understand that *my* proposal needs revising.

To avoid the use of "I," rhetors often refer to themselves in the third person by using *one* or the *writer*. As the following examples demonstrate, this tends to produce less concrete, confusing, and impersonal sentences.

Awkward: By this time, *one* would expect the application for credit to be approved.

Improved: By now, *my* application for credit should be approved.

Awkward: *This writer* believes that the necessary forms were submitted.

Improved: *I* submitted all the necessary forms.

In some circumstances, such as in company reports, when the subject matter should be emphasized over the writer or the reader, the personal POV should be avoided. In these cases, the *impersonal POV* is used.

Personal: I received several complaints from conference participants about your hotel concierge services.

Impersonal: Several conference participants have complained about their experience with concierges.

Note that in the personal example above, the tone is accusatory. Using an impersonal approach and avoiding the use of the second-person pronouns (you, your) can mitigate conflict. Grammatically, remember that pronouns change for case, gender, number, and person.

Select appropriate tone and voice.   Tone, as highlighted in the previous example, is often controlled by the use of POV. When someone uses "I" when referring to a problem, she or he accepts responsibility. Similarly, using "we" can often make an audience feel part of a solution. By shifting between pronouns, an author can reflect personal opinion while simultaneously signifying the position of a larger organization:

I understand stockholders' frustration over the reduced dividend; however, *we* must also make investments in our employees' futures.

The use of "I" suggests that the identification with the stockholders is a personal position of the writer, not necessarily the company's opinion. However, the use of "we" suggests that the decision to reduce dividends is based upon consensus, not the writer's discretion. The tone of the message, by creating identification, works to improve the credibility of the author. Writers and speakers can make other choices regarding language and voice that will improve both ethos and pathos and establish shared meaning. These include using active or passive voice properly, avoiding biased language, and choosing expressive and concrete words.

Choose between active and passive voice.   The active and passive voice affects the tone and quality of a message. In a sentence using a*ctive voice*, the subject of the sentence performs the action expressed in the verb.

- Our supervisor *suspended* Sally. [In this case, the supervisor is acting upon Sally.]
- Consultants *conducted* a survey to capture employee moral.

    The subject (consultants) performs the action (conducted a survey).
- Supervising the R&D team reminds me of the television show Better Off Ted.

    The practice (supervising the R&D team) performs the action of reminding the author about the television show.

In a sentence using passive voice, the subject receives the action. The passive voice combines a form of the helping verb to be with another verb (usually in the past tense).

- The employee ethics seminar was missed by <u>over half the staff</u>.

    {to be + verb}

The action performs upon the subject (over half the staff), which means that this sentence is passive (indirect).

- *Active voice:* Over half the staff missed the employee ethics seminar.

- The emergency protocols were initiated by <u>the chemical engineers</u> just in time.

    {to be + verb}

- *Active voice:* The chemical engineers initiated the emergency protocols just in time.

Grammatically, the passive voice is correct. At times, particularly when trying to avoid an arrogant or accusatory tone, it is a valuable construction. For example, it may be better to say, "I was frustrated by the situation" rather than "You frustrated me," or "Quarterly profits were above analyst expectations" rather than "I raised quarterly profits above analyst expectations." A problem with the use of passive voice is that it often creates awkward, wordy, and vague sentences. The active voice is typically clearer and more passionate.

Avoid cultural insensitivity and biased language.   Language defines and creates culture, so language choices matter. Using colloquialisms, jargon, or culture-specific terms can distract (or confuse) an audience and lower your credibility. Writing or speaking in a culturally insensitive manner can create barriers to listening and unnecessarily reduce the power of an argument. When stating a personal opinion, for example, most European-Americans use specific examples and evidence to support their positions. Some cultures, however, view expressed personal opinions as impolite. Being sensitive to culture does not mean, however, that you need to prescriptively follow cultural expectations, avoid asserting yourself, or devalue your own culture. Instead, take cultural sensitivity into account by noting differences and by fusing one's own cultural identity and practices with others' cultural identities and practices. Cultural sensitivity is not "political correctness"; it is making a conscious effort to be considerate of language barriers, opinions, beliefs, and other cultural practices so that they do not become unnecessary barriers to expression and understanding. Unless they are part of a hostile audience, people will generally respect that your rhetorical style will be different due to your race, class, gender, sexual preference, nationality, and so on. They will also appreciate, of course, any effort you undertake to be inclusive of their worldview and practices.

Biased language is any language that uses stereotypes or unfounded, negative expressions that demean or exclude people based on identity-based markers, physical or mental attributes and abilities, religion, socioeconomic status, and so on. Besides being unethical, biased language can lead to the rejection of important ideas. Often rhetors unknowingly use sexist or prejudicial language, especially when speaking. The following are a few common examples of bias and alternative, more inclusive, approaches.

- When gender is nonspecific, do not use the generic pronoun "he." Doing so unnecessarily restricts the person or persons in question. Instead, use *she and he*, *she or he*, or *they*. In academic or professional documents, avoid the problematic punctuation of *s/he, she/he,* or *(s)he*.
  - Whenever possible, avoid using singular pronoun constructions. These often become awkward and clumsy. Instead, use the plural pronoun to reduce wordiness and increase clarity.

Singular pronoun:	A new employee cannot begin his or her job until he or she receives security clearance.
Plural pronoun (better):	New employees cannot begin their jobs until they receive security clearance.

- Sometimes it is possible to avoid personal pronouns altogether.

Pronoun:	Each truck driver must weigh his or her freight before departing.
No pronoun:	Truck drivers must weigh freight before departing.
Pronoun:	Instructors must submit their grades by Tuesday.
No pronoun:	Submit all grades by Tuesday. (The context implies an understanding of who should act.)

- Do not use sexist language when generically describing organizational positions or social roles. For example, do not refer to managers or engineers as "he," administrative assistants as "she," or a stay-at-home parent as "she." Doing so unnecessarily establishes a sexist hierarchy or insinuates social inequality.

- Replace out-of-date language with contemporary terms.

Instead of . . .	Use
mankind	*humanity, people, or humans*
man-made	*synthetic, manufactured, or machine-made*
foreman	*use supervisor or manager*
man the phones or man hours	*staff the phones or staff [worker] hours*
saleswoman or salesman	*salesperson*
businessman	*business owner, businessperson, business executive, or entrepreneur*
waiter or waitress	*server*

- Sometimes it is necessary to distinguish gender. In such cases, it is important to maintain parallelism.

Instead of . . .	Use
ladies and men	*ladies and gentleman or women and men*
man and wife	*husband and wife or partners* (which can be used to describe any type of intimate or formal relationship)
Mr., Mrs., Miss, and so on	*full names*

- Avoid inserting adjectives that unnecessarily point to race, class, gender, and such (i.e., the context does not warrant their use), as this rarely conveys useful information and almost always reinforces stereotypes.

Instead of . . .	Use
the young engineer	*the engineer*
woman doctor or male nurse	*the doctor* or *the nurse*
the black student	*the student* (Note that absent a particular context you wouldn't likely say *the white student*.)
my gay colleague	*my colleague*
the Latina CEO	*the CEO*

- When the context warrants mentioning a specific attribute of a person, deemphasize the attribute by avoiding the use of an adjective. Instead, change the sentence structure to emphasize the primary function of the person.
  - Instead of *disabled employee*, use *employee with a disability*
  - Instead of *mentally challenged customers*, use *customers with learning disabilities*

- If possible, choose alternative words that more accurately describe a group or captures the institutional concerns.
  - Instead of *at-risk students,* use *traditionally underserved student populations*
  - Instead of *minorities,* use *underrepresented constituents*

There is a time and place where using categorization is appropriate. When writing an Equal Employment Opportunity commission report, categorizing applicants and employees by race and sex is necessary. There are also situations in which audiences expect, for better or worse, problematic language choices to be used profusely. Comedians, for example, are professionals whose work is to communicate humor. Some use biased language as irony or parody. Others have created an edgy image by using derogatory and explicative language as part of their on-stage performances. Certainly, the use of such language, even as parody, is worth critique. The point of this example, however, is that rhetorical situation should dictate language choices, not rigid rules.

Nowadays, within the United States, people are aware of the need to be "politically correct." However, nongenuine attempts at being culturally sensitive undermine democracy. It is best to develop your character as someone who takes culture and identity seriously. Respecting culture and identity also includes appreciating the ways in which people are different. Rhetoric allows us to engage in dialogue about why others are different and why their practices may be fascinating, frustrating, or, at times, erroneous.

People can become overly conscientious about offending others, which often leads to socially awkward interactions where one person mutes their personality in favor of performing "social correctness." You needn't fret about making mistakes, as most people are generally forgiving. In writing, rhetors have the benefit of editing their work, and when speaking they can always apologize. The great thing about becoming culturally sensitive is that it gets easier over time with a little effort. Eventually, choosing more inclusive words and phrases will become habitual.

Choose words that are expressive and concrete. Sometimes writers and speakers seem bombastic. When people complain that an author uses unnecessarily complex words, we should be suspicious of the person making such a claim. There is a significant chance that he or she either does not appreciate the nuanced meaning of words or is too lazy to build his or her vocabulary. Sometimes a less common word carries more power or clarity than a lengthy description. For example, one could say, "When it comes to discussing colleagues, the employee is extremely talkative." It is not clear what "extremely talkative" means, as it could have a positive or negative connotation. It would be much better to say, "On the topic of other managers' leadership styles, the employee becomes garrulous." Garrulous is defined as excessive talk on trivial matters. It is now clear that the author has a somewhat negative opinion of the employee's talk on a specific topic—leadership styles. Note also that "on the topic" is clearer and by using the word "becomes," there is a slight nod to the fact the employee in this example is not always overly talkative. "The employee likes to gossip about colleagues" is

Use expressive words and, in most situations, be positive.
(Image © Sergej Khakimullin, 2012. Used under license from Shutterstock, Inc.)

another possibility without using a big word, but the word "gossip" also has a negative connotation.

Writers and speakers should always seek *conciseness*—that is, use fewer words to express thoughts. For example, abstractions like "old," "a lot," "good," "thing," and so on are uninspiring. To improve the rhetorical effect of messages, create imagery by using more colorful and descriptive terms. In order to produce clear and vivid images, sometimes it is necessary to add words.

Abstract:	We need to resolve our city's poor transportation system.
Concrete:	Our city has an inadequate number of buses and metro lines to satisfy commuter demands.
Abstract:	Our company offers a lot of great benefits.
Concrete:	Our company offers premium health insurance, paid vacations, biannual bonuses, and free parking.
Abstract:	We're facing an uphill battle to get through this difficult time.
Concrete:	This recession will challenge our profitability.

Notice that the concrete versions reduce possibilities for confusion. In addition to constructing sentences with more descriptive words, also choose technical terms carefully, such as average, median, and mean; biannual and biennial; and phenomenon and phenomena. Using jargon, idioms, analogies, and metaphors can be effective too, so long as you take into consideration the audience (e.g., nonnative speakers may not understand idioms). In general, try to maintain a plain style with an active voice. Read broadly and have a dictionary nearby to maintain and use vocabulary well.

Construct sentences and paragraphs.   Consider how you will use the above techniques before writing, and be mindful of these issues as you construct sentences and paragraphs. To improve stylistic writing choices, purchase Strunk and White's *The Elements of Style*.

Sentences.   Sentences are the primary building blocks of thoughts. In English, sentences are generally composed of verbs, nouns, pronouns, adverbs, adjectives, prepositions, conjunctions, and articles. The most basic sentence only requires a subject (noun or pronoun) and predicate (verb or helping verb). Sentences are classified according to structure, intention, and stylistic construction.

Structure. There are four types of sentences: simple, compound, complex, and compound-complex. A *simple sentence* contains only one (independent) clause. A simple sentence can be as short as one word (e.g., "Go!," "Run!"). However, simple sentences usually include a subject and predicate. Because they only contain one clause, all of the following are simple sentences (the subject is underlined once and the predicate verb has a double underline):

> Hire! (The subject, you, is implied.)
> Managers hire.
> The managers hired aggressively.
> Just this quarter, management hired 25 new employees.

A *compound sentence* consists of two or more independent clauses (or simple sentences) connected by a comma or semicolon and a coordinating conjunction (e.g., *and, but, or*) or conjunctive adverb (e.g., *therefore, accordingly, furthermore*).

- *Two simple sentences:* Google AdWords is an effective way to advertise. Local businesses should also advertise by radio.
- *Compound sentence:* Google AdWords is an effective way to advertise, *but* local businesses should also advertise by radio. [comma with a coordinating conjunction]

A *complex sentence* contains one independent clause and one or more dependent clauses, often separated by a comma, that express a subordinate thought. The complex sentence, unlike the compound sentence, contains clauses that could not stand on their own.

- *Two simple sentences:* My manager invited me to attend the executive retreat. I am nervous about going.
- *Compound:* My manager invited me to attend the executive retreat, and I am nervous about going.
- *Complex sentence* (example 1): Although my manager invited me to attend the executive retreat [dependent clause], I am nervous about going.
- Note that if you tried to put these two clauses into simple sentences, the first would be an incomplete thought. This is one way to identify a dependent clause. "Although my manager invited me to attend the executive retreat [incomplete sentence]. I am nervous about going."
- *Complex sentence* (example 2): As a bonus for my participation in the aggressive hiring campaign [dependent clause], my manager invited me to the executive retreat.
- *Complex sentence* (example 3): Productivity and profits will increase [independent clause] since we hired the right people [dependent clause].

A *compound-complex sentence* consists of two or more independent clauses plus at least one dependent clause.

- Hiring is essential to our long-term growth strategy [independent clause]; with the right people [dependent clause], we will improve the quality of our products and services [independent clause].

If you are not a strong writer, try to avoid complex and compound-complex sentences. These sentences increase opportunities for error.

Intention. Sentences should have a clear purpose and typically declare information, interrogate, command, or emphasize. The following examples illustrate each type of expressed intention.

- *Declarative sentence.* Used to convey information or state facts.

   "The distribution system is not ready yet."
- *Interrogative sentence.* Asks a direct question.

   "Is the distribution system going to be ready in time?"
- *Imperative sentence.* A statement that issues a command.

   "Please send me proof that you are going to make the deadline."
- *Exclamatory sentence.* An emphatic expression. In a sense, it is a declarative sentence that is stated with emotional force.

   "The distribution system is not ready yet!"

Stylistic construction. Convey emphasis and meaning in a sentence stylistically. Depending on how it is constructed, a sentence can place more or less emphasis on a particular idea. For example, structure a sentence by placing the major point at the beginning, or delay the main idea by presenting subordinate ideas first. Consider the following examples and note the slight difference of emphasis in each.

- We are selling Division X in order to focus on our core competencies. [emphasizes action]

   To focus on our core competencies, we are selling Division X. [emphasizes reasons]
- (Note: The subordinate clause is underlined.)

   The cost advantage of manufacturing in China is dissipating, <u>due to increased shipping costs.</u> [This is the most emphatic statement due to the placement of the subordinate clause at the end.]

   <u>Due to increased shipping costs,</u> the cost advantage of manufacturing in China is dissipating. [This statement is moderately emphatic.]

   The cost advantage of manufacturing in China, <u>due to increased shipping costs,</u> is dissipating. [This statement is the least emphatic because the subordinate clause is treated as a *parenthetical statement*.]

Modifiers can also be use to emphasize particular points. However, be careful that you convey the appropriate meaning and do not misplace them.

- He was the manager.

   He was *just* the manager.

He was the *just* manager.

- He managed to *barely* get a good deal with such a *wily* group of salespeople. [confusing modifiers]

He *barely* managed to get a good deal with such a group of *wily* salespeople. [better]

Combining stylistic construction with the artful use of modifiers can emphasize points and create interesting narratives.

- To assist conference planners, who needed to sign contracts with aggressive vendors, an attorney was hired. [less empathic]

An attorney was *promptly* hired to assist conference planners, who needed to sign several contracts with aggressive vendors. [more emphatic]

As you improve your writing skills, playing with sentences becomes fun. In a way, shaping sentences to capture what you want to say is an exciting game. As discussed in Chapter 1, rhetors are never fully in control of the message. People will interpret what you say and write based on their own subjectivities. However, part of the fun is to make writing work for you, not against you. The more you understand the power of a sentence, the more you will want to mold them. Due to time constraints, writers rarely get an opportunity to craft the perfect message (if that is actually possible). However, planning and avoiding procrastination will allow you to spend more time editing sentences, making them interesting, persuasive, and less likely to be misinterpreted.

Paragraphs. Form paragraphs by combining several related sentences that deal with a single topic. Paragraphs help readers by providing logical and visual breaks. Typically, paragraphs will follow an outline exactly, with each new paragraph formed by your outlined points and subpoints.

Elements of a paragraph. There are three main elements of a paragraph: the topic sentence, supporting sentences, and bridges.

- *Topic sentence.* This sentence contains the synopsis of a paragraph. It is usually most effective as the first sentence, but can be strategically placed in the middle or at the end of a sentence. As a précis, it contains the paragraph's main idea, purpose, or summary. Here are two examples of topic sentences:
  - The rise of realty television cooking shows, as you note, has generated increased interest in specialty foods; however, we feel that current regional market conditions would not support a retail store specializing in spices. [The remainder of the paragraph would provide evidence supporting the conclusion.]
  - Before we begin your investigation, we will need the following information and documents. [The details of the information and the documents are then described.]

It is sometimes useful to place a topic sentence at the end of a paragraph for emphasis. However, writers often incorrectly place their topic sentence at the end of a paragraph. We have a tendency to *arrive at a point* rather than *argue a point*. One helpful writing strategy is to determine if the last sentence of a paragraph is better at the beginning. Note that in the following example the last sentence (in bold), though technically okay, would function better at the beginning of the paragraph.

- We offer excellent health care for employees and their families. For the past 50 years, we have financially supported community events and sponsored several local charities. Following a recent flood in Fargo, where one of our factories is located, we suspended production and paid our employees to participate in pre-flood protection and post-flood reconstruction efforts. In short, **our company is an integral part of the communities we serve.**

- *Support sentences.* These sentences support and develop the topic sentence. In the previous example, all of the illustrations regarding why the company is integral to the community constitute the supporting sentences.

- *Bridges.* Each sentence in a paragraph should carry over the idea of a topic and be parallel in form. There should also be a bridge between paragraphs. Bridges are *transitions* and *signposts,* such as key words that are repeated (e.g., "We should develop a new sexual harassment *policy.* Such a *policy* would. . ."), enumerated (e.g., first, second, third), conjunctions (e.g., and, yet, also), or conjunctive adverbs (e.g., accordingly, furthermore, next, similarly, still).

Important mechanics of paragraphing.   There are three important mechanics to consider when writing paragraphing—length, unity, and coherence.

- *Length.* A paragraph should be long enough to adequately address the topic sentence and should deal with that single topic. If you find yourself transitioning into a new idea or point, start a new paragraph. Also, create a new paragraph when you want to contrast information or ideas previously presented, when readers need pause in a lengthier thought, or when you are moving between major sections of the paper (e.g., introduction, thesis, body).

- *Unity.* When every supporting sentence develops the topic sentence, the paragraph has unity. As noted, a paragraph should focus on a single topic. The focus of discussion should not change between the starting and ending points of a paragraph.

- *Coherence.* Coherence is the joining of ideas in a logically connected way. A paragraph should be parallel in form and maintain a particular point of view, tone, grammatical tense, and so on. Achieve coherence by using bridges, grammar, and punctuation effectively.

  - *Paragraph lacking unity and coherence:*

    Recently my friends and I went on a seven-day cruise. The company we chose was *Paradise Lines.* The boats are majestic, and offer plenty of fun activities. The quality of buffet food leaves a lot to be desired, but there are delicious entrées in the premium restaurants. Many passengers seem to enjoy the on-shore activities sponsored by the *Paradise,* but if you are adventurous and explore on your own you'll pay a lot less for the same activities. The on-board pools need to be better maintained and security is poor. One passenger we met said his wallet was stolen by cleaning staff. But this should not stop you from getting out and enjoying the on-board dance club. A winter trip on *Paradise Lines* is much better than spending one's vacation in Chicago.

- *Unified and coherent paragraph:*

  For winter vacationers tired of taking shore-side trips to cold northern cities like Chicago and New York, a seven-day cruise with *Paradise Lines* is a great alternative. The boats are majestic. There are plenty of on-board activities, such as three different dance clubs, and the food is scrumptious. What is more, there are plenty of highly recommended on-shore excursions and activities led by boat staff. However, if you are more adventurous, you can explore port cities on your own. My friends and I give *Paradise Lines* a rating of 7 out of 10 stars. Despite a few minor issues, such as dirty on-board pools, winter in the tropics makes these modest concerns acceptable.

Careful paragraphing is essential for presenting ideas in an organized manner. Hastily written and poorly constructed paragraphs confuse readers and make fantastic ideas convoluted. Good paragraphing makes writing and revising a paper much easier. It also makes memorizing and delivering speeches easier. The best way to craft quality paragraphs is to have a strong working outline and to refer frequently to it for guidance.

Quotations and citations.   Of course, not all sentences or thoughts will be your own. Sometimes people say things worth repeating verbatim. Another's voice or research findings will lend support to your arguments. Often people want to be able to look up the source of information or need a good starting point to locate others' work. To satisfy these needs, writers and speakers use direct and indirect quotations and cite their sources.

Quotations.   *Quotations* are an effective way to support a point or to let others make a point for you (perhaps because they said it better or are more credible). A *direct quotation* is an exact copy of a someone's text or comments. They are effective when rewriting the material would diminish the power of the idea. Typically, use direct quotations sparingly, and include only those that are relevant to a point. If rhetors over-quote others' work, their creativity and originality may be questioned.

Mark direct quotations by using quotation marks or indented block text. Offset them from the rest of the text with a comma, colon, or period. When using a style manual, such as the *Publication Manual of the American Psychological Association*, *The Chicago Manual of Style*, *The MLA Style Manual*, or *The Associated Press Stylebook*, follow the manual's formatting requirements. (If an organization or publisher does not stipulate the use of a particular style, choose one to use as a guide.) The following rules are common across most style manuals:

- *Deletions and omissions*. Use three ellipsis points (. . .) to show omission of material within a sentence and three points and a period at the end of a sentence (. . . .).

- *Inserting materials.* Use brackets [ ] if you need to add words to make a sentence unified or parallel or need to insert a clarifying comment or note.
- *Quotation within a quotation.* If you are quoting an author who has quoted someone else, it is custom practice in U.S.-American English to use single quotation marks to denote that inner quotation ("This is an example of 'quoted text' within a quote.").
- *Noting original author errors or objectionable material.* If the original work has typos or uses biased language (for example), place the expression *sic*, enclosed in brackets, next to the error ([*sic*]).
- *Punctuation.* In U.S. English, commas and periods *always* go inside quotation marks. Semicolons and colons *always* go outside of quotation marks.

An *indirect quotation* is the paraphrased version of an original text. When using another's thoughts without citing him or her directly, do not enclose these thoughts in quotations. You typically introduce an indirect quote with the word that.

- Sharron shouted, "Everyone needs a . . . [expletive deleted] vacation." [direct quotation with omission and explanation]
- Sharron, probably due to frustration, noted that everyone deserves a vacation. [paraphrased]

Citations. Often quotations and paraphrases come from printed or published materials. When drawing material from these sources, it is imperative to document sources by providing in-text citations and some kind of reference list, works cited list, footnotes, or endnotes. You may also want to cite sources merely as reference, for example, when you want to point your audience to similar or contrarian arguments. Follow the guidelines of the specific style manual preferred by a publisher or organization (e.g., *APA Manual*). These sources are the authority on writing style and are now widely available online. Citation manuals differ regarding how to reference sources; however, follow these tips and practices to avoid plagiarism:

- When using a direct quotation, always provide the author's name, the title of the work, the page number where the quotation is located, and the year published.
- Paraphrase as often as possible.
- When in doubt, cite the source of material.
- Use a reference manual to guide your decisions. If possible, mimic the referencing (and writing) style of a senior colleague's published work.
- Refer to The Purdue Writing Lab, which provides an excellent online resource for students and practitioners, including the APA, MLA, and Chicago Style reference guides.

Citing sources is not as difficult as it may initially seem. Students are unnecessarily intimidated by the process—or too lazy. It only requires a minimal effort to use a reference guide. Identify a manual you feel comfortable using and use it! Over time, you will memorize the guidelines, which in turn will improve your confidence. When an instructor or trainer asks you to use a particular guide, use it! When someone gives you feedback on your paper regarding the citation of material, do not ignore his or her comments. Use them to break bad habits.

Introduction and conclusion. Every document and speech must have an opening and closing. Because these differ by the type of correspondence (e.g., novel, routine, or electronic) and length (e.g., concise or extensive), strategies and examples of each are provided in later chapters. Irrespective of the type and length of correspondence, the following strategies should be considered (but not necessarily included), as they will increase readers' interest and improve clarity.

Introduction.

- State the objective, thesis, or problem early in the introduction.
- Establish the scope of the message or document. For lengthier communications, provide a description of the materials to be discussed (and excluded). This will help readers decide if the information is relevant; readers will be more interested if they know that the material is pertinent to them. If the topic is too simplistic or too difficult, they will lose interest in an argument or become frustrated. This could end future opportunities for rhetorical engagement.
- Provide background information or a historical overview of the topic.
- Summarize previous discussions on the topic and suggest how your material fits with the ongoing discussion. You may also summarize, in the form of an abstract, the materials presented in the document.
- Use institutionalized persuasive hooks, such as telling an anecdote, providing definitions, quoting other materials, highlighting shocking statements, or forecasting positive or negative outcomes. If used appropriately and sparingly, these techniques tend to capture audiences' interests. Any hook used, however, must be relevant and consistent. Telling a funny story or providing an obscure quote and then writing or speaking in a dull manner is likely to aggravate rather than motivate an audience.

Conclusion.

- Tie the main ideas together and make a final, significant point or suggestion.
- Summarize the topic, document, or speech by reviewing and highlighting the main points and outcomes.
- Provide a specific implication or prediction. Be sure this is consistent with your argument.
- When appropriate, provide the audience with additional ideas to consider.
- When desired, specify what kind of actions the audience should take.
- If possible and appropriate, provide an opportunity for future correspondence or dialogue.

Authors typically write linearly, which means that they construct a rhetorical artifact by producing the introduction before writing the body and the conclusion. This is fine, so long as the outline provides thorough guidance. Upon completing a document, however, it is necessary to revise the introduction and conclusion so that they remain unified with the body. By revisiting the introduction and conclusion, you may identify a better way to grab an audience's attention or realize that you need to alter the preview so that it is consistent will the main points.

Step 4: Complete (Memory and Delivery)

Upon completing the construction of the rhetorical artifact, it is time to revise and then distribute the document. This step combines the rhetorical canons of memory and delivery. Memory is the "forgotten canon" and applies primarily to oral delivery. The canon of *memoria* is the discipline of recalling the arguments of a speech; however, it also includes the practice of having a breadth of knowledge on topics. Rhetors skilled in the canon of memory are able to improvise, answer questions, and refute others' arguments. As a writer or speaker, create a memorable artifact by stylistically constructing points in a manner that enable an audience to recall points later.

Broadly, this step is the point in artifact construction when rhetors make revision and publication decisions. To revise a rhetorical artifact, consider the written document from the perspective of the audience. To do this effectively, distance yourself as a writer by taking a break between writing and revising. Depending on the type of document, it could be a couple of hours (e.g., an important email or a letter of recommendation) to a few months (e.g., a research manuscript). Taking this break makes your editing more objective.

Mainly, you want to check for general comprehensibility and clarity of arguments, hidden meanings, and structural issues. Table 2.2 provides useful tips on writing and revising, which will make both processes less exhausting. When revising any artifact, ask yourself the following questions:

- Has the original purpose of the artifact been fulfilled?
- Does the document address the intended audiences' needs?
- Has the thesis been supported with appropriate points?
- Have the main arguments been thoroughly supported with credible evidence?
- Does the supporting material relate logically to the main idea?
- Is there a unifying idea that throughout the artifact?
- Does the introduction clearly focus the topic and capture readers' or listeners' attention?
- Does the conclusion provide a summary of ideas or give proper directives for future action?
- Do individual paragraphs have clear topic sentences?
- Are sentences constructed well?
- Does the word order in sentences seem logical?
- Are verbs usually in the active voice?
- Do word choices seem appropriate for the purpose and audience?
- Have you used and cited secondary materials correctly?

Table 2.2 Writing and revising tips

Writing tips

- *Find a good starting point.* Many people often end a writing session by finding a good stopping point. They then plan to begin work on the artifact the next day from a fresh point (e.g., a new section). One of the hardest parts about writing is getting into the mood. Often rhetors are unaware what they are going to write in the next section, so they end up staring at a blank screen for some time. If the project does not have a deadline, other activities, such as watching television, will be more motivating. Writer's block can be frustrating and discouraging. Finding a good starting point means knowing what one will write the next session. This permits the author to get quickly into the writing groove.

- *Write all the time.* When working on an artifact, it is best to work on it bit by bit. Setting aside writing time and getting into a disciplined habit will help you produce a document with less stress. Also, avoid taking lengthy breaks between projects. Constant writing practice will help you develop, maintain, and sharpen your skills.

- *Keep it simple.* Often writers try to put too much into a single artifact. Shorter speeches and written documents are much easier to produce.

- *Improve your skills one habit at a time.* Don't try to break all of your bad habits at once. Identify a particular problem area and be conscientious of it as you write a document. Once you break one bad habit, focus on another.

- *Be okay with criticism.* To improve rhetorical skills, be open to learning from your mistakes. Listen to proofreaders or proof listeners. As a rhetor, you want an audience to adopt your point of view on a particular topic. However, they may not find your argument compelling. Figure out why by listening to their criticism. Be comfortable with criticism, and be open to changing your position too.

- *Don't be afraid to make mistakes.* All writers make mistakes. Don't become paralyzed by the fear of making one. You may not be the best speaker or writer, but chances are you're not the worst.

- *Read and listen!* One way to improve your rhetorical skills is to learn from others. Read artifacts not just for content, but also for style. Listen to great speakers and mimic some of their techniques.

Revising tips

- *Revise more than once.* Give yourself enough time to make multiple revisions. As you make each pass, focus on a difference set of problems.

- *Revise along the way.* When writing larger documents, return to the writing process by revising what you wrote the previous session. Waiting until the entire document is complete to begin revisions will make the revision process tedious and likely increase incoherence between sections.

- *Read your draft aloud.* Hearing sentences helps rhetors identify awkward statements.

- *Revise on a hard copy, especially when revising grammar and punctuation.* It is easier to identify mistakes on a hard copy than on a computer screen. Even if the final document will be in single space, edit the document with double-spaced lines. This leaves space for editorial comments. (Tip: Save paper and ink by formatting your paragraph spacing to 1.5 lines, print double sided, and print using draft mode.)

One way to ensure a thorough revision is to obtain a proofreader to review your writing and a "proof listener" to evaluate your speech. It is important to give these individuals directions regarding what you hope to obtain from their feedback. Also, make them feel comfortable giving you comments. Specify whether you want them to focus on larger structural issues and layout or to correct grammar, punctuation, and style. In organizational settings, you may write and speak collaboratively; this requires a slightly different process and use of technology. In addition to grammatical issues, look for flaws in your arguments (i.e., fallacies) and eliminate grammatical and mechanical problems.

Check for argumentative fallacies.   Craft a rhetorical artifact carefully. Arguments should be sound and not contain flaws in reasoning. When evaluating others' writing and speeches, analyze their arguments systematically. Whether constructing or evaluating, be aware of *rhetorical and logical fallacies.* For an argument to be valid, ideas and premises (the assumptions upon which an argument rests) have to be linked together logically, claims about social and natural phenomena need to be supported by empirical evidence, and appeals need to be void of mischaracterizations and improper emotions. Often when rhetoricians speak and write, they draw upon erroneous conclusions or fail to provide proper supporting evidence. Sometimes evidence is selective or applied illogically (e.g., saying science cannot be trusted and then later using scientific findings to support an argument).

Rhetoricians run the risk of losing credibility or appearing *irrational* when their communication is logically inconsistent or when they appeal to emotions too frequently. Learning to articulate thoughts by avoiding fallacies or using them strategically (e.g., knowing when to appeal to emotion alone) can significantly improve the effectiveness of your communication. Recognizing fallacies in others' communication, and pointing them out, can undermine others' credibility without resorting to personal attacks (i.e., *ad hominem* fallacy). For example, reveal to your customers that a competitor is missing evidence to support its claim about services—and don't expose yourself to similar criticism. Familiarize yourself with types of fallacies (see Table A.3 in appendix A.)

The best way to learn about fallacies is to take a philosophy course in logic and an argumentation course. An excellent text and resource is Robert Gula's *Nonsense: Red Herrings, Straw Men and Sacred Cows.* Table A.3 provides a comprehensive list of some of the most common types of fallacies found in everyday business communication.

Eliminate grammatical and mechanical errors.   Having checked for broader issues in previous revisions (e.g., organization and structure, tone, and fallacies), search for grammatical and mechanical errors. Ask another member of a team, a colleague, or a friend to review your document. If you have only time for one revision, focus on both proofreading and copyediting simultaneously; however, the best approach is to revise any work at least twice: once looking specifically for broad issues, then looking at grammatical issues.

Regardless of the type of rhetorical artifact (e.g., written report or speech), proofing is essential. Typos, misspelled words, and lengthy sentences in a speech outline can cause rhetors to misspeak or unnecessarily hesitate during delivery. Grammatical errors in an email can cause confusion and lead to additional emails as recipients seek clarification. While grammar and spell checkers are helpful aids for writers, they can make writers lazy or overconfident. Microsoft Word, for example, can identify stylistic issues (e.g., passive voice), but it rarely offers any solutions for making the sentence active. Furthermore, it cannot identify nuances, such as whether a sentence is emphatic enough. Spell checkers miss typographical errors that result in legitimate use of English words (e.g., "pubic relations" instead of "public relations"). Some checkers are becoming "smart," learning from users. However, if you mistakenly add a misspelled word or grammatical construction to a custom library, you will continue to repeat this error, forming or perpetuating a bad writing habit. The best way to avoid mistakes is to continue learning. Revisiting a writing manual from time to time will help you form and maintain good writing habits.

When proofing print copies, use standard proofreaders' marks (see Figure A.1 in appendix A). These marks allow you to make notes about changes with just simple notation. Too many notes on a single page makes incorporating changes difficult. Standard proofreader marks make communicating easier for authors and editors. Instructors, however, need to point to both grammatical and structural issues and often must do so in electronic documents or technology that does not allow track changes (e.g., when using Blackboard, Moodle, or Facebook). Instructors also do not want to copyedit a document; instead, they want to point to problem areas for self-guided learning (e.g., singular and plural confusion and passive voice). They may develop, therefore, their own marking and feedback system. Table A.4 in appendix A provides a sample handout of shorthand notes used for instructional notation.

When possible, proofread on a hard copy. (Image © Joanne Harris and Daniel Bubnich, 2012. Used under license from Shutterstock, Inc.)

Follow the advice in this chapter to improve your writing, from construction to revision. There are nine specific habits, however, frequent in student and professional writing, which, if identified and changed, will produce better artifacts.

1: Break up lengthy sentences. Often long sentences

would be clearer if written as two or more sentences. Writers have a tendency to want one sentence to do too much. Simple sentences make artifacts easier to read and understand, reduce wordiness, and decrease grammatical and mechanical mistakes.

2: Delete hedging sentences.   Writers often want to qualify a sentence by using an expression that points to a transition in thought (e.g., apparently, arguably) or a clarification of position (e.g., "It is my opinion that. . . ."). However, these qualifying words and phrases are frequently used unnecessarily. Be prudent when using them and look for those that may have crept into your document during the writing process.

> **Instead of this:** *It seems that* our forecast was off so *there appears to be* a chance we'll modify our quarterly estimates.
>
> **Write this:** Our forecast was incorrect; we'll probably modify our quarterly estimates.

3: Purge slow starters.   In addition to hedges, writers also tend to start sentences with "it is" or "there are." Slow starters delay the point and create unnecessary verbiage.

> **Instead of this:** *It would be* appreciated if you could send the files immediately. *There are* six of eight customers who seem to be unsatisfied with the new specifications.
>
> **Write this:** Please send the files immediately. Six of eight customers are unsatisfied with the new specifications.

4: Delete unnecessary phrases.   Another way to make writing more concise is to eliminate unnecessary sentences and passages. When trying to explain a difficult idea, writers often provide more examples than needed or repeat the same point with slight modification. Only include the minimal number of necessary examples. Sometimes rhetors combine words when there is a one-word equivalent.

Instead of this:	**Write this:**
in the event that	if
on the occasion of	on
due to the fact that	because
until such a time that	when
in the near future	soon

5: Eliminate repetition.   If someone says, "*Enclosed herein* are the documents you requested," she or he has used a redundant expression. If something is enclosed, it must be "herein." Here are some other common examples of unnecessary repetition.

Instead of this:	Write this:
each and every	each
absolutely essential	essential
ascend up	ascend
repeat again	repeat
collect together	collect
surrounded on all sides	surrounded
blend together	blend

6: Avoid passive voice.   Several of the above examples also use passive voice unnecessarily. Recall that sentences written in the passive voice focus on the receiver or product of an action and include a form of the verb "to be" and the past participle of a verb. This style inherently requires more words and often creates a noncommittal tone. By simply recasting sentences in a more active voice, rhetors write with greater clarity and sound more confident.

Instead of this:	It *has been noted* that you are having trouble with your new purchase.
Write this:	I noted that you are having trouble with your new purchase.

7: Impose parallelism.   Express similar ideas with the same grammatical structure. Parallel structure makes reading and listening easier. Repeating words, phrases, clauses, sentences, and sections in similar form helps audiences recognize related ideas of similar importance. Note that the list in this section is parallel, with each numbered point beginning with a verb in the same tense (delete, impose, avoid, maintain, etc.).

Instead of this:	Our company *sells artisan breads* and *is providing classes* to aspiring bakers.
Write this:	Our company sells artisan breads and provides classes to aspiring bakers.

8: Maintain singular-plural agreement.   A writing habit that challenges even the best writers is singular and plural agreement. Do not use the singular form of a verb or noun in one part of a sentence and a plural form in another.

Instead of this:	The bittersweet flavor of youth—its trials, its joys, its adventures, its challenges—are not soon forgotten.
	In my "Intro to Environmental Regulations" class, a list of local issues were passed around for each student to put their name down. . . ."
Write this:	The bittersweet favor of youth—its trials, its joys, its adventures, its challenges—is not soon forgotten.
	In my "Intro to Environmental Regulations" class, a

list of local issues was passed around for each student to put his or her name down. . . ."

9: Verify apostrophes are correctly used.   A common punctuation mistake is the missing or misused apostrophe. Use an apostrophe when needed, and place the darn thing in its proper place.

Instead of this:	Write this:
the childrens' game	the children's game
three employees letters	three employees' letters
my brother-in-laws money	my brother-in-law's money
Adam and Steves' excellent film (they made it together)	Adam and Steve's excellent film (they made it together)
Amber and Maya's articles (they wrote separate articles)	Amber's and Maya's articles (they wrote separate articles)
three G4's	three G4s
the 1990's	the 1990s
its raining money	it's raining money
the money is stored in it's rightful place	the money is stored in its rightful place

In addition to these tips, it is imperative to continue improving your writing by reading. You will learn how to write better by mimicking excellent writers. Continue your education by taking courses or reading books on writing.

Conclusion

This chapter explained the four-step writing process: preparing, organizing, writing, and completing. Whether preparing a speech or a report, a thorough outline will save time. Mastering the use of grammar and improving your vocabulary improves ethos among audiences. As noted in the introduction, the slightest mistake in punctuation can cost a business a significant amount of money (e.g., up to $225 billion annually in lost productivity; The impact of illiteracy, 2010) or invite catastrophe (e.g., the Jameson Raid).

Heed the advice in this chapter, and you will continue to develop and improve your rhetorical and technical writing skills. What is more, learning to write well can be financially remunerative. For example, you can become a writing coach. Writing and speaking well are sought-after technical skills that are becoming increasingly valuable to organizations.

Now that you are prepared to write well, the next concern for producing effective business and professional communications is adapting the content to specific processes of writing, speaking, and evaluating. In the following chapter, you will learn techniques and practices that will help you design, distribute, and evaluate graphical, written, or spoken rhetorical artifacts. Because improving these elements often requires working well with others, some of the chapter focuses on giving and receiving feedback.

Continuing Education:
Recommended Texts and Resources

- *Eats, shoots & leaves: The zero tolerance approach to punctuation* by Lynne Truss. ISBN: 978-1592400874.

   This witty and fun book demonstrates how to use punctuation well. It is a must read for anyone serious about improving technical skills and observing style in action.

- *Grammar girl: Quick and dirty tips for better writing*: A blog by Mignon Fogarty. **http://grammar.quickanddirtytips.com**.

   This site includes a series of blog entries and podcasts that are useful for those seeking short lessons on improving their writing. In addition to the blog, Fogarty has produced best-selling books. These are available on the site.

- *The elements of style* (4th ed.) by William Strunk, Jr. and E. B. White. ISBN: 978-0205609023.

   This classic book is a short and brilliant read that explains essential writing concepts in brief and linear entries. There are excellent examples of each element. The book is inexpensive and can be used as a guide for a concept-by-concept approach toward improved writing.

- *Qualitative communication research methods* (3rd ed.) by Thomas R. Lindlof and Bryan C. Taylor. ISBN: 978-1412974738.

   This book explains how to conduct a variety of primary communication research from qualitative perspectives.

- *The story factor* (2nd ed.) by Annette Simmons. ISBN: 978-0465078073.

   This is a highly readable book written by a business communications consultant. It suggests that storytelling is the modus operandi for business success. It outlines six stories one must learn to tell and provides illustrations of each. It is certain to improve your use of the narrative outline and the canon of style.

References

Bordia, P. (1997). Face-to-face versus computer-mediated communication: A synthesis of the experimental literature. *Journal of Business Communication, 34*(1), 99–120.

Cambazoglu, B. B., Banachowski, S., Junqueira, F. P., Cui, B., Bridge, B., Plachouras, V. . . . (2010). A refreshing perspective of search engine caching. *International World Wide Web Conference Committee.* Retrieved from EBSCO. doi:10.1145/1772690.1772710

Daft, R. L., & Lengel, R. H. (1986). Organizational information requirements, media richness and structural design. *Management Science, 32*, 554–571.

McShane, S. L., & Von Glinow, M. A. (2000). *Organizational behavior*. Boston: Irwin McGraw Hill.

The impact of illiteracy. (2010). Retrieved from **www.proliteracy.org/page.aspx–pid=345**

Truss, L. (2003). *Eats, shoots & leaves*. New York: Penguin.

National Commission on Writing (2003, April). *The neglected "R": The need for a writing revolution*. Retrieved from **www.collegeboard.com/prod_downloads/writingcom/ neglectedr.pdf**

National Commission on Writing (2004, September). *Writing: A ticket to work . . . or a ticket out, a survey of business leaders*. Retrieved from **www.collegeboard.com/prod _downloads/writingcom/writing-ticket-to-work.pdf**

Preston, J. (2011, July 20). Social media history becomes a new job hurdle. *The New York Times*. Retrieved from **www.nytimes.com/2011/07/21/technology/social-media -history-becomes-a-new-job-hurdle.html–_r=1**

Simmons, A. (2006). *The story factor* (2nd ed.). New York: Basic Books.

Chapter 3

Designing, Distributing, and Evaluating Professional Communications

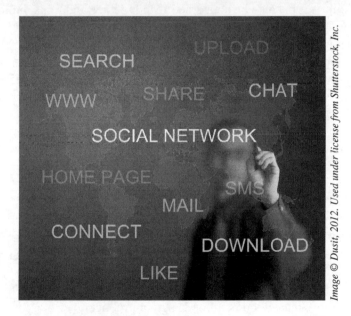

Image © Dusit, 2012. Used under license from Shutterstock, Inc.

Starting Point

The following quote is from Jason Fried's "Get Real" column, which is published by *Inc. Magazine*: "What's bad, boring, and barely read all over? Business writing. If you could taste words, most corporate websites, brochures, and sales materials would remind you of stale, soggy rice cakes: nearly calorie free, devoid of nutrition, and completely unsatisfying" (Fried, 2010, para. 1). Fried offers several examples of boring business writing. He also offers examples of exciting business writing, like Woot's response to a question on its FAQ page: "'Will I receive customer support like I'm used to?' . . . No. Well, not really. If you buy something you don't end up liking or you have what marketing people call 'buyer's remorse,' sell it on eBay. It's likely you'll make money doing this and save everyone a hassle" (para. 8).

A second example Fried (2010) provides is Saddleback Leather Company's crafty introduction to its commitment to quality:

> You know how when a magician exposes to the world how other magicians trick people, all of the other magicians get mad at him for spilling the beans? Well, I'm about to spill the beans and ruin it for all of those companies trying to trick you into buying their not so high quality leather. . . . You're about to learn what to look for and what to look out for as you shop for your next leather piece. By the way, if I soon die by a chopstick to the neck, you'll know why. I'm a marked man. (as cited in Fried, para.11)

Although Fried makes a great point about writing uniquely, business writers also need to think more about sprucing up their documents with better aesthetics (i.e., layout and design). Be serious about content, but also be concerned with typeface and fonts, bullet styles, pictures, colors, shapes, contrasts, and so on. Similarly, when speaking, consider performance choices, such as staging elements (e.g., lighting), sound effects, body movement, use of voice, and so on.

Once the content of a message or document has been constructed, rhetors turn their attention to matters of design, distribution, and evaluation. This chapter, in a sense, is a continuation of step 4 (memory and delivery) of the construction process. This chapter discusses how to improve written rhetorical artifacts by applying design elements. It also reflects upon the benefits and limitations of certain design decisions. Second, it covers special issues related to the distribution of written materials and oral presentations, such as cost of printing and delivery. Finally, it introduces techniques to improve our evaluation skills—including giving and receiving feedback.

Design

As an entrepreneur, consultant, or employee of a small company, you will likely have to lay out the content of messages and add design touches to artifacts. Even in a large company, some communications, such as memos, will not be sent to a production team. When design and production of a document are outsourced to another department or a team of professionals, you will need to proofread the document for design or production errors. Speaking the language of a designer is helpful when explaining a vision and correcting errors.

Layout and design elements improve the effectiveness of messages and influence audience perceptions of document content. The appropriate use of page design, typography, graphical elements, bullets, text boxes, and so on make complex information more accessible. They also make mundane communications more appealing to read. There are a variety of design programs available for purchase; however, for everyday communication among professionals, using the often-underutilized tools already available in productivity suites, such as Microsoft Office or OpenOffice, are sufficient. Being more thoughtful regarding the placement of text and visuals on a page, and using appropriate elements that are consistent with the purpose, context, and audience expectations, will enhance the performativity of a document.

Good design should improve readability, which means design features should be restrained, consistent, and balanced. *Restrained design* is simple and uncluttered. Certainly, there are situations where one wants to create a feeling of disorder and chaos; however, most business and professional documents are created to convey an idea or information efficiently. Using design elements strategically and sparingly is crucial. *Consistent design* is structured and ordered. Within a single document, there should be a recognizable pattern. It should be intuitive to readers and assist them in recognizing important information, breaks, details, and so on. For example, bold typeface can highlight keywords or headings. Across documents, consistency helps readers recognize the source of information. Repetitious use of similar logos, colors, symbols, and lines (e.g., thickness and color) provide readers with a consistent visual cue, allowing them to recognize the source of information without having to read a word. Typically, rhetors should use the same page setup (e.g., margins and tabs). *Balanced design* provides a sense of parallelism. Although balance is often subjective, typically one wants readers to feel like text or visuals belong in no other place on the page.

Presentation aids, which include objects, models, pictures, graphs, charts, video, audio, or multimedia, whether used in a written text or by speakers as props or illustrations, also need to be created with an eye toward design. The design and use of presentation aids for speeches is addressed later in this chapter (see the section Distribution as well as the section Presentation Aids in Chapter 6). This section addresses general design issues for written text: document formatting, typography, and embedded objects.

Document Formatting

The following section describes the most common features of document design and specific design considerations related to each of the following topics: 1) layout, 2) white space, 3) margins, tabs, and justification, 4) headings, 5) headers, footers, and notes, 6) lists, 7) columns, 8) color and shading, and 9) typography.

Page layout.   *Page layout* involves the combination of typography, embedded objects, and other design elements on a page. Page layout is determined by available technology, accessibility to design software, printer capabilities (or access to large printers), budget, and company or client policies. Creativity may be constrained, for example, by company policies requiring employees to use templates, which are commonly used in larger businesses to maintain consistency.

Make page layout decisions *before* beginning a project. In this regard, design decisions are part of the invention process. In most cases, decisions regarding page layout will not affect the content of a message. There are some circumstances, such as space limitations or the opportunity to present some content visually rather than textually (e.g., a picture or table is often more helpful than stand-alone text), that can lead to changes during the completion stage.

Once text and other content are generated, determine the following: document size (e.g., standard letter, A4, or

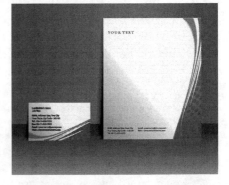

Templates and standardized design elements facilitate consistent and efficient distribution. (Image © Redshinestudio, 2012. Used under license from Shutterstock, Inc.)

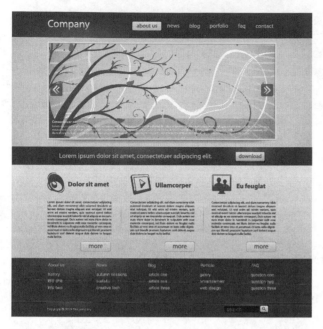

Figure 3.1. Sample "dummy document" for a webpage.
(Image © Slamer, 2012. Used under license from Shutterstock, Inc.)

legal paper) and orientation (portrait or landscape); height and width settings (inch, metric, or pixels); margin settings; colors and fonts for headings, subheadings, text, and, textbox borders; shading; and alleys (also called *gutters*—the space between columns). Having a plan and sticking with it will make reformatting elements much easier. For larger or collaborative projects, create and distribute formal written guidelines to help maintain layout consistency. Among other things, this will make the consolidation of information much easier. As a default, use a style manual.

Often designers plan complex documents, such as brochures and websites, by creating a dummy document (see Figure 3.1). This is a simple mock-up of the document that includes blocks of *lorem ipsum* text[1] and shaded boxes with textual cues for the recommended placement of visual objects. Typically, the dummy is sent to professional designers. If you are in charge of design, use the actual pictures and text; however, create a thumbnail sketch before writing. This will help you visual the final product.

White space.   *White space*, which is not necessarily white, is any space free of text or visual objects. White space visually frames content by providing contrast, which allows readers to see information as units. It provides rest stops for the eyes. White space is a crucial element in type design; it gives characters and images form. It is also important in writing; without whitespace, it is impossible to distinguish one paragraph from another. Properly used, white space can make text and objects perform as desired. For example, it can direct readers

---

[1]*Lorem ipsum* text is filler text, which has been used in typesetting since the 16th century. Graphic designers made it popular in the 1960s. Although the text seems random, it actually is derived from a passage in Cicero's text *On the Boundaries of Good and Evil*: *"Neque porro quisquam est qui dolorem ipsum quia dolor sit amet, consectetur, adipisci velit..."* Translation: "There is no one who loves pain itself, who seeks after it and wants to have it, simply because it is pain. . ." There are plenty of *lorem ipsum* generators on the web. The most commonly used filler is as follows:

> Lorem ipsum dolor sit amet, consectetur adipisicing elit, sed do eiusmod tempor incididunt ut labore et dolore magna aliqua. Ut enim ad minim veniam, quis nostrud exercitation ullamco laboris nisi ut aliquip ex ea commodo consequat. Duis aute irure dolor in reprehenderit in voluptate velit esse cillum dolore eu fugiat nulla pariatur. Excepteur sint occaecat cupidatat non proident, sunt in culpa qui officia deserunt mollit anim id est laborum.

For more information on *lorem ipsum* text, visit the site **http://lipsum.com**.

from one section to another or make content stand out. White space, given its function, is perhaps one of the most important parts of a document. As you lay out the content of a document, use the "print preview" function or print a document as a PDF to see how the content will display when downloaded or printed.

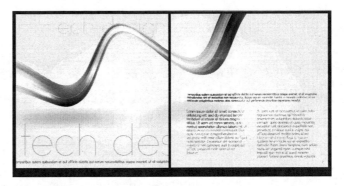

Margins, tabs, and justification. *Margins* define the white space at the boundaries of a page and between columns. The customary

White space can lead to sleek-looking and more readable documents. (Image © Ozerina Anna, 2012. Used under license from Shutterstock, Inc.)

margins for most documents are 1 inch (2.5 cm) on all sides for an 8.5 × 11 sheet of paper (standard letter size). When using letterhead or other custom paper, the margins may be adjusted to accommodate preprinted graphics. The best way to ensure that margins are accurately formatted for regular and custom paper is to create a template for these particular documents. The rulers, which are located at the top and at the left of most design and word processing software, are an often underutilized tool. The ruler marks off the width of a page based on the selected paper size and highlights the set margins. Rulers allow users to change the document margins when they need to change the position of all paragraphs in the document. (This can also be done using the "page set up" or similar menu feature.) You can also use rulers to change paragraph indentations and to set, edit, and clear tabs. Table 3.1 provides a reference guide for common tab features. There are a variety of video tutorials available online at **http://youtube.com** that demonstrate their functions. Some useful tutorials are listed on the textbook's companion site (**http://procommunication.me**).

Tabs are used to set text parameters, which then allow writers and designers to use the keyboard's Tab key (◇) consistently. Use paragraph indentation tabs to change the position of paragraphs, for example, to insert a long quotation or to establish consistent white space at the beginning of each paragraph. It is easy to set and adjust tab stops on the toolbar. A frustration of résumé consultants is that clients use the spacebar to align text, especially decimals, in lists (see decimal tabs in Table 3.1). Unfortunately, this takes more time and does not produce consistent print results.

Justification affects the appearance of text at the margins. There are four ways to arrange lines of text: justified, left-justified, right-justified, and centered. Justified margins are common in professionally produced publications, such as newspapers, books, and magazines. Newsletters commonly use full-justified margins because text is held within textboxes or narrow columns that need alleys (space between columns of vertically aligned text). Full-justified text is vertically flush with the margins on both the left and the right. Though full justification often creates a more polished look, it typically does not work well in everyday business documents, such as letters and memos. In order to compensate for disparate word count, word processors must

Table 3.1 Common tab and margin features

Ruler feature	Explanation
	The top marker controls the starting position of the first line in a paragraph.
	The bottom marker positions the subsequent lines in a paragraph. This is commonly referred to as the "hanging indent."
	The right indent marker positions the wrap point of text at the right-hand side of paragraphs.
L	The "left tab stop" sets the start position of text that runs rightward.
⊥	A "center tab stop" sets the position of text in the middle (it keeps text centered).*
⌐	A "right tab stop" sets the end of the text. This feature is useful for setting leaders.*
⊥	A "decimal tab stop" aligns numbers around a decimal point. Regardless of the number of digits, the decimal will always be in the same place. (This is how to get numbers 1–9 to align with larger numbers.)*
	*To set these tabs in Microsoft Word, first set the left tab by touching the ruler with your mouse. Then double-click the tab, which will open a "tab" window.

insert irregular spaces between words in each line of text to make them flush. This uneven spacing creates whitespace between words that is uncomfortable to read.

Left-justified margins, also called "ragged-right" margins because the text breaks unevenly on the right, are better suited for everyday business documents. Spacing between each word is evenly distributed and the right-hand margin has white space for eyes to rest. Using ragged-right for short-length sentences within documents (e.g., quotations and column-arranged text) may have the opposite effect. It can make the text disorienting.

Right-justified (or ragged-left) and centered text are less frequently used in everyday business documents. Typically, these justifications are used for headings and page numbers. Ragged-left may appear when text is taking a more contemporary look, needs emphasis, or is written in a language read from right to left.

Headings. Following the organization of your outline, headings provide readers with visual cues of section themes. As with style in general, follow the guidelines of the suggested or required style manual. If no style manual is suggested, choose one. This will lead to a standardized guide that you can consult, especially when heading levels become complex. Whether you are producing a formal or informal document, keep your headings parallel and use different typefaces and type styles to distinguish heading levels. Try to use five or fewer heading levels (e.g., bold, italic, capital letters, underline, and so on). To contrast between headings and the body text, try inserting extra space or use boldfaced sans-serif typeface (e.g., Arial or Helvetica) for the headings and a serif typeface (e.g., Times New Roman) for the body.

Headers, footers, and notes.   *Headers* and *footers* appear at the top and bottom of each page, and are gainfully used in templates and large documents. In templates, stock content, such as the company logo and contact details, can be inserted into headers and footers to standardize every page. In large documents, such as reports, headers and footers are used to nest page numbers, relevant dates (e.g., when the document was written), document name or file path, topic, author, and so on. Context will determine what information is relevant. Do not clutter the header and footers with too much information, as this is vital white space. In most word-processing software, writers can insert headers and footers under the "insert tab" on the menu bar or ribbon.

In research reports, footnotes or additional comments are often inserted into the footer. In some instances, particularly when the information is less pertinent, include these notes at the end of the document. Notes can be formatted the same as regular text (e.g., justified, indented, double-spaced, and bold). To insert endnotes and footnotes, select the "citations and bibliography" group under the "Reference" or "Insert" tab listings on the menu bar or ribbon.

Lists.   Any serial information, even in paragraph form, is technically a list. Typically, a list is designed as indented and prefaced by vertically stacked numbers or bullets. Lists that are stacked and offset from regular body text create valuable whitespace.

Sample magazine layout with two-column text. (Image © yienkeat, 2012. Used under license from Shutterstock, Inc.)

Lists are useful rhetorical devices that draw upon the canon of arrangement. Lists also draw upon style by highlighting or summarizing key information or by itemizing sequential steps. For hierarchical or chronological lists, use numbers. For general information or less hierarchical information, use simple bullets. To maintain consistency and to avoid numbering errors, create lists by using the tools available in software programs. Due to the often hierarchical nature of lists and the attention that they draw, within organizational contexts, they are politicized (see Browning, 1992). What one chooses to list (or not) and what one lists first, even if unnumbered, is often interpreted as more important. In contemporary rhetoric, many rhetoricians who take a narrative approach are leery of lists. They see them as favoring Aristotelian logic over story and narrative (e.g., O'Banion, 1992). Stepping outside this interesting debate, use lists to make the design of documents easier to read and understand. Readers are accustomed to seeing them. Maintain an interpretive approach by considering the ramifications of lists and construct ethical narratives when creating lists.

Columns. Columns can improve the readability of text by shortening lines. A single-column text, the standard for most documents (e.g., letters), is useful when at least a 10-point typeface is used. Any typeface that is smaller than this will require readers to strain to follow words. Text that is ragged-right and double-spaced is also often best prepared in single-column. The two-, three-, and four-column structure is best suited for small typefaces with single-spaced lines, though the three- and four-columns should be reserved for documents printed in landscape. A benefit of using a two-column structure is it reduces eye fatigue. Readers do not have to scan across a long line of text. In order to ensure that columns look balanced, avoid widows and orphans. A *widow* is a single word on a line at the top of a column. An *orphan* is a single word at the end of a column.

Color and shading. Color choices are becoming increasingly important as tablet computers and other smart devices enable users to read documents without having to print them. Color printing on paper has generally been expensive; in the digital age, however, color can now play a more prominent role in style and design. Color, when used appropriately, can draw attention to important information and make layouts visually appealing. When adding color, consider the appropriate balance of *screening* (shaded areas on a page) and the effects of different screen resolutions. Colors can clash or appear different on various devices. Color choices should be strategic and contextual. A current fashion is to highlight digital text in pastel colors, but this is not suited for all audiences. Restrict the use of color to three to four neutral colors (e.g., blue, gray, and black). Apply colors consistently. Use ample whitespace, even if it is color, to provide a visual break between embedded objects and text. Color and shading (screening) can emphasize information or set off sections in a document.

Typography. *Typography* is the technique of arranging type, though there is a fascinating art and science behind typesetting and type design. The **Wikipedia.org** entry on "typography" and the entries on "font" and specific typefaces (e.g., "Arial" and "Helvetica") provide history and fun reading about the aesthetics of typeface. For continuing education, read David Jury's book *About Face: Reviving the Rules of Typography*, which offers a beginner's introduction to the principles and theories of type design. Until recently, typography was a specialized occupation; however, due to computerization, "typography is now something everybody does" (Jury, 2002, p. 152). Though we are surrounded by it, we often do not pay much attention to typeface.

Typography is big business and it is political. Monotype Imaging Holdings Inc., a U.S.-based type foundry, for example, is traded on NASDAQ-GS under the symbol TYPE. The documentary film *Helvetica*, recommended for continuing education, illustrates both the business of type design and its politics. Helvetica, for example, is described both as a universal and socialist typeface by its supporters and as the typeface of capitalism and the Vietnam War by its haters.

The sans-serif typeface Helvetica (circa 1957) is named after its country of origin, Confoederatio Helvetica, i.e., Switzerland. (Image © Fedor Selivanov, 2012. Used under license from Shutterstock, Inc.)

Unless you are a typographer, chances are you interchangeably use the word *font* and *typeface*. Technically speaking, a *font* is a specific member of a single typeface style. For example, Arial regular, Arial bold, Arial italic, and Arial bold italic are four different fonts, but a single typeface. *Typefaces* are differentiated by their distinctive characteristics. There are a variety of typefaces, which are categorized into families. Roman type, the most broadly used, is subclassified into serif, sans serif, ornamental, and script types. Table 3.2 describes each type and how they may be used.

In addition to choosing the appropriate typeface, decide what size and style is best. Often these choices are determined by final design and production issues, artifact type, audience, and in-text emphasis. For example, a large document printed in 10-point font should use a regular serif style. Serif typefaces are easier to read in small print. However, digital or online documents should use a sans serif style because they display better on screen. Typically, professional documents should always be written in a standard typeface (e.g., Bookman, Times Roman, Arial, or Helvetica). Signs seeking a sleek appearance may appear better in sans serif typeface. Generally speaking, avoid using more than two typefaces in any document and limit your use of fonts.

In most regular business artifacts, use 6-point font for parenthetical notes, like document revision dates, file location paths, and internal directives (e.g., "Blue copy: Manager"). Use 8-point font for footnotes and captions. Use 10- to 12-point font for body text and 14-point font for headings. Stylistically, use capital letters to emphasize important headings or words, but use them sparingly. Words and sentenced written in all capital letters, especially in emails and text messages, can be interpreted as aggressive. *Italics can emphasize material or slow readers.* **Boldface** is useful for headings and for emphasizing words or important material. Of course,

Table 3.2   Roman typeface examples

Type family	Typeface name and example	Uses
Serif: Named for the features at the end of letter strokes	Times New Roman Book Antiqua Bookman Old Style Lucida Bright	Body of text, especially for small-sized characters and older-style documents. Printed materials, such as books, newspapers, and magazines are best printed with serif types.
Sans serif: This literally means "without serif" (i.e., the features at the end of strokes are absent)	Arial Helvetica Calibri Comic Sans Lucida Sans	Body of text, especially in electronic media (e.g., websites and digital books). Serifs often create problems with resolution, as they become pixilated if the text is too small. Sans serif is useful for headings and large print (e.g., signs). These typefaces supply more whitespace for easy readability.
Script: Imitates handwriting and calligraphy	Bradley Hand ITC Brush Script Freestyle Lucida Handwriting	Fancy documents, such as invitations, brochures, posters, menus, etc. Too many words are hard to read (e.g., long letters or brochures). Often used for aesthetic design, titles, posters, short words, and headings. Script is not good for body or websites because it is hard to read and they are not universally available.
ORNAMENTAL: NOVELTY / DECORATIVE	STENCIL MATISSE ITC Harlow Solid Italic	Documents for special occasions, such as invitations, labels, signs, and so on. Limited use. Requires significant white space. **Note: Unless you print a document or create a PDF of it, a font may not be displayed appropriately on another person's computer.**

these are just recommendations. Your decision to use a specific typeface and font style should be context appropriate. Here is yet another reason to do a thorough audience analysis. If you know that members of an audience have problems with their vision, use larger fonts. If appropriate, stick to a style manual, such as MLA or APA, which have directives for selecting and using fonts.

Embedded Objects

Sometimes text can be enriched with visuals, such as photographs, drawings, illustrations, and graphs. When adding these to a text, create a multimedia document. Most electronic devices support multimedia, so enrich documents in a variety of ways. For example, enhance interactivity in basic text documents by inserting hyperlinks that take readers to a different place in-text or to online content. It is now possible to embed audio and video into PDFs, blog posts, and websites. Be mindful, however, when embedding hyperlinks and objects into documents, presentation aids (e.g., PowerPoint), and so on. When you transport or share these documents, the embedded links to a multimedia object may break. Cloud computing will resolve some of these frustrating issues (see chapter 8).

With today's smartphones, mundane media, such as posters, packaging, tickets, advertisements on vehicles, and so on, are now interactive. URLs (website addresses) can be embedded in Quick Response (QR) code images, which are two-dimensional codes that can be read by smartphone cameras (see Figure 3.2).

When embedding an object into a text, consider factors such as location (its emphasis), size, pixilation, and printing. Readers tend to notice visuals before text, and they pay greater attention to larger objects than smaller ones. The relative importance of a visual, therefore, should be considered when making choices regarding emphasis. One of the challenges of visuals is resizing and printing. Poorly designed or specific-sized images appear pixilated (i.e. distorted) when resized. Typically, any visual that will be embedded into a document should be produced with at least a 300 dpi (dots per inch) resolution. Whenever possible, use vector graphics, which utilize algorithms that allow images to be resized without becoming pixilated (technically, they are resolution [dpi] independent). Vector images are better for printing because they adjust to printers' settings (i.e., they are WYSIWYG). In computing, WYSIWYG is an acronym for "What You See Is What You Get"—what appears on screen is how it appears in print. The creation and editing of vector images, however, requires higher technical skills and more advanced computer programs (e.g., Adobe Photoshop). When limited to creating files as JPEGs or GIFs, create them in the size they will be embedded into a document or printed. Also keep in mind that if a document is printed, a hyperlink must be transparent. For example, if you write "follow this link," a common practice in online blogs, the link will not appear if the article is printed. For this reason, it is useful to provide the web address: **http://somelink.com/article**.

Figure 3.2. QR code for this book's companion website (use your smartphone to go the website).[2]

Organizationally, objects can be placed in text, closest to a corresponding reference, or collected in one place (e.g., at the end of a document). Placing objects, particularly explanatory ones (e.g., graphs), closer to the material it references is most effective. In-text tables and figures also provide visual breaks and less annoyance (readers don't need to go back and forth among pages). Before placing images in the

[2]You can embed this into your website or blog with the following html code:

```
<img src="http://qrcode.kaywa.com/img.php?s=6&d=http%3A%2F%2Fprocommunication.me"
alt="qrcode" />
```

text, consider formatting concerns, such as boundaries and borders. Be sure to provide figure and image titles and captions.

The quantity and complexity of multimedia will increase production time and costs, require greater creative and technical skills, and increase opportunities for technical problems (e.g., compatibility issues). Fortunately, there are a variety of websites and free and premium software packages on the market that make creating and embedding objects for multimedia easier. With modest investments, people can now produce graphics, audio, and video that used to require professional expertise, studios, and expensive equipment. Table 3.3 provides a list of useful websites and software programs.

Distribution

Distribution of written messages, especially in more traditional forms, is obvious. Fold the letter, if appropriate, put it in an envelope, purchase postage, and send it along. Well, that's only partly true.[3] There are a few general issues that you ought to consider, typically in advance of production, regarding distribution of written, electronic, and oral messages. This section focuses primarily on oral delivery, an often under-practiced form of distribution. Since most presentations require presentation aids, or could be enhanced with their use, this section also covers issues related to the production and design of presentation aids. Social media has created additional methods of distribution, but has also raised some concerns, so issues related to this medium are addressed.

Factors Influencing Message Distribution

Both written and spoken messages need outlets. Nowadays, thanks to social media and other forums, rhetors can distribute messages in a variety of formats. Oral communicators not only have new venues in which to present, such as Ignite gatherings (see **www.igniteshow.com**), but they have new media channels for distribution. Formal and informal oral communications can be recorded on digital devices and distributed across the Internet as podcasts. Written communications similarly have old and new channels of distribution, such as printed text, email, blogs, PDF, e-book, and so on. Nevertheless, many of the concerns of the past still apply. Just because you can easily produce and distribute oral or written communications electronically, does not mean that you always should. It is important to consider a variety of factors, often at the stage of invention, regarding the optimal method of distribution: 1) rhetorical impact, 2) cost, 3) time, 4) availability, and 5) security and privacy. Because social media is gaining in popularity and comes with its own specific issues, this section concludes with a discussion specific to social media.

Rhetorical impact.   Delivery is an important canon of rhetoric. A formal business letter is less personal than a handwritten note, and a spoken presentation may allow you to express important emotion that is lost in written form. Some audiences prefer to listen, others prefer

---

[3]For readers less familiar with how to appropriately fold a business letter and use technology, such as mail merger features in word processing programs, you can find links to tutorials at **http://proCommunication.me**.

Table 3.3 Useful software and sites for producing multimedia object and documents

Media type	Content (online)^F	Editing/production software^O
Pictures, photos, illustrations, and images	stock.xchng (www.sxc.hu)^F www.istockphoto.com^{RF} www.pond5.com^{RF} www.shutterstock.com^{RF} www.corbisimages.com www.gettyimages.com	Inkscape^O OpenOffice Draw^O Raven^O SVG-edit^O Adobe Illustrator CorelDRAW ImageBot Microsoft Expression Note: All of the above programs can create vector-based images.
Audio	www.partnersinrhyme.com^F www.allmusiclibrary.com$^{F, RF}$ www.ibaudio.com^{RF} www.istockphoto.com^{RF} www.productiontrax.com^{RF} www.shockwave-sound.com^{RF} www.sound-ideas.com^{RF} www.neosounds.com	Audacity^O WavePad Sound Editor^O Adobe Audition Adobe Soundbooth Creative WaveStudio DJ Audio Edit Logic Pro Sound Forge Wavosaur
Video	www.stockfootageforfree.com^F www.artbeats.com^{RF} www.istockphoto.com^{RF} www.revostock.com^{RF} www.thoughtequity.com/video^{RF} www.gettyimages.com	Apple iMovie^O Microsoft Movie Maker ^{O} Wax^O Adobe Premier Elements Apple Final Cut Pro Corel VideoStudio Pro CyberLink PowerDirector Sony Vegas Movie Studio VideoPad

^{F}Free. There may be restrictions to use, so be sure to read the terms and conditions.
^{RF}Royalty free. Can purchase digital content a la carte or by subscription and use in perpetuity (usually in a single document).
^{O}Open source (freeware), shareware, or free with operating system. There may be restrictions to use or software limitations.

to read. Some may only have access to print, while others will only seek information distributed through social media. Delivery method, in other words, "says something" about the rhetor and the message. Choosing an inappropriate method of delivery can make rhetors appear out of touch, irresponsible, thoughtless, wasteful, hasty, or cheap. Distribution depends on the context, so do a thorough audience analysis and understands the rhetorical situation.

Methods of delivery are important to the process of persuasion. If you know your message is better suited to a particular medium but that your audience is resistant to this medium, you may need to coax members to adapt. People were initially afraid to make purchases and communicate sensitive information online. Today, it is largely an accepted mode of commerce and communication. The sustained efforts of many companies to coax customers to accept email delivery of statements, for example, has lowered expenses and made distribution of communications much easier. Remember that some messages, such as thank you notes, will feel even more personal due to the abundance of digital communication.

Cost.   Cost may not be a factor when writing a single business letter or when searching for a job. However, it will become a concern when producing artifacts that use multimedia, require mass distribution, or are lengthy. In addition to financial costs, be mindful of the environmental and social impacts of information distribution. Sometimes using recycled materials or choosing the "greener route" may be more expensive but may improve ethos with a particular audience. (Unfortunately, certain audiences may find environmental-friendly paper and distribution methods pretentious.) Often promotional materials are poorly manufactured and useless to those who receive them, so determine through audience analysis whether there are more thoughtful ways to promote your products and services. Such consideration about cost-related issues will not only save landfill waste, it also reduces human resource efforts at the production, distribution, and reception stages. Does a customer really want to read a lengthy report? Does a boss want to interpret a cryptic text message? Choose a method of distribution that consumes the least amount of resources while still achieving the purpose of a message.

Time.   Consider issues related to time at each stage of the writing process, especially at the distribution stage. How fast does information *really* need to be distributed? If information must reach audiences quickly, choosing electronic distribution may be the most effective method. If the message needs to reach multiple and diverse audiences, it may be necessary to take extra time to produce messages that can be distributed through a variety of media. Avoid the temptation to present all information as urgent. A message sent by overnight delivery with the knowledge it won't be immediately read by a recipient is a waste of money.

Don't forget to consider the role of kairos (opportune time) when delivering messages. Integrated marketing communication seeks to create the conditions necessary for messages to be most influential. For example, a company may entice participants to a special program by distributing by mail an elegant-looking letter, and then follow this communication with an electronic letter, Facebook post, or Tweet.

Availability.   Choose a method of distribution that will maximize the availability of content; be mindful, however, of security and privacy issues (see the next point). Although social media is becoming more popular, not everyone can access it easily. Being inconsiderate of others' technological capabilities may suggest that you are insensitive. Within an organization, you may want to store information on servers; however, keep in mind that large files may not be accessible by people working remotely.

Security and privacy.   In 2010, when WikiLeaks began distributing confidential diplomatic cables sent by various U.S. governmental embassies (Howard, 2010), it was a reminder that organizations with significant security protocols still are exposed to theft risks. Although social media is challenging the concept of privacy, people still get offended by distribution of personal information through public forums. In some states, such as Illinois and Massachusetts, it is illegal to record people without their consent. Doing so is a Class 1 felony. Should an interviewee, for example, consent to a recorded interview but not distribution, and this file is leaked or accidently uploaded to the Internet, the person who recorded the audio could face time in prison. Thus, it is crucial to obtain customers' permission to use personal statements or photographs in web-distributed videos. People expect that personal information and financial data will be well protected. For messages containing sensitive information, organizations should have policies regarding access and distribution. Password-protecting documents is one means of enhancing security; however, opening documents in locations with unsecured WiFi connections can expose the message to theft. Protecting external and internal communications is covered in Chapter 8; however, always be mindful of the security and privacy issues related to message distribution. Printed documents can be misplaced or photocopied. Electronic documents can store viruses and are easy to redistribute via the Internet.

Issues specific to social media.   All of the above concerns apply to social media. However, there are a few additional and more specific considerations worth noting. Chief among these issues is the need to maintain a social presence when using social media. People do not expect or want constant updates through more traditional distribution channels (e.g., mail or

Electronic privacy and security issues are of increasing concern to both small and large organizations. (Image © kentoh, 2012. Used under license from Shutterstock, Inc.)

telephone). However, followers of social media often do. If you plan to create a social media presence, it is important to interact with "followers" in a manner consistent with social media norms.

When distributing messages through social media, monitor peer-to-peer interactions and comments. Customers sometimes do businesses a disservice by creating an atmosphere that does not reflect the desired business image. Although there are additional risks to social media, such as protecting others' privacy, creating and maintaining profiles is often free. Therefore, one major benefit of social media communication is reduced marketing expenses.

If used appropriately, companies can outsource some of their customer service and support to end users. When an Apple iPad user, for example, has a problem with the device and turns first to a Wiki, where other end-users have posted fixes, Apple saves time and money on technical support. They also benefit from increased customer identification—end users like to contribute as "expert users."

There is still limited research on social media. It is difficult to say, for now, exactly what mix of social media is most effective or which mediums are best for particular types of messages. Anecdotally, there is a sense that Twitter may be more appropriate for promotions and short updates, LinkedIn for self-promotion and creating a professional identity, and Facebook for soliciting new customers and engaging with loyal ones.

Be cautious about who you allow into your network. For example, accepting every LinkedIn request may create confusion among potential clients about your areas of expertise. To develop an expert profile, make decisions that optimize your profile (see Chapter 9). Your friends may not be in the same profession as you are, so ask them to follow you in Facebook and reserve your LinkedIn account for those associated with your profession.

A recent white paper shows that customers use search engines and social media differently by industry (see "Online Marketing Opportunity Report," 2010). For example, in the insurance industry, search engines are god, with over 70% of users searching for relevant information through these channels. Blogs and social media account for a paltry 20% and 10% of traffic, respectively. In the nonprofit sector, however, over 80% of traffic filters through social media, 12% through blogs, and just 8% through search engines.

When delivering formal presentations, write for the ear and use an appropriate method of delivery.
(Image © Monkey Business Images, 2012. Used under license from Shutterstock, Inc.)

Oral Delivery

In addition to the concerns listed in the previous section, oral delivery requires some other considerations and practice. To become an effective public speaker or television pundit, you must get familiar with the different technologies, paces, and speaking styles used in these forums. Improving your ability to craft effective outlines is part of this course; however, training in specific techniques appropriate for different venues is beyond the scope of this book. Continued education and training will hone your oratory skills. College-level public speaking, debate, and voice and diction courses provide excellent training grounds for improved oral communication. The following advice and instructions are important to utilize when speaking in any venue or situation. They should improve your overall effectiveness when delivering messages orally.

Write for the ear.   While preparing a message that will be delivered orally, choose words and construct sentences carefully. In oral delivery, listeners get one opportunity to understand a message. They do not have the luxury of returning to a comment to think more deeply about its meaning. If rhetors speak unclearly, use complex words, or are insensitive to audience attributes, they work against themselves.

To make a speech easier on the ears, use familiar words, short sentences (avoid complex syntax), strong transitional statements, and repetition. Although you may think that a speech will sound methodic and dull when restating points or listing seriations like first, second, third, next, last, and then, audiences appreciate the step-by-step construction. The speech needn't be boring; use inclusive and culturally sensitive language to draw the audience into the message. Strive for a delivery that is natural. If a speaker sounds enthusiastic, and he or she appears confident (all of which is achieved through ethos and practice), the audience will likely find a speech worthwhile. In addition, using the appropriate method of delivery and controlling body and voice makes speeches come to life.

Use appropriate methods of delivery.   Four basic delivery styles are used by speakers to deliver messages: delivery by manuscript, delivery by simple outline or notes, delivery by memory, and delivery without practice. Each style requires a different type of outline and affects performance.

Delivery by manuscript.   Speaking from a manuscript, or teleprompter, is appropriate when a speech must be delivered verbatim or when there is little time for practice. Executives and politicians, for example, often have to deliver messages that require nuanced use of words and precise details, and they often do not have time to practice speeches several times. A speech delivered by manuscript is also useful because the transcript is available for immediate release. Speakers with severe speech anxiety can deliver by manuscript.

A speaker's focus on written text restricts eye contact and body movement, which can be interpreted in a variety of ways by an audience (you are untrustworthy or a poor communicator). When reading a script, speakers may deliver content in a manner that is too fast or too monotone. The best way to avoid these problems is to practice. By reading the manuscript several times in advance, speakers can memorize some of the content and break from the script, and their eyes become trained to relocate where they left off. Practice helps identify places where props or nonverbal cues can be added and words and phrases that require additional vocal expression or a slower rate of speech. Among other things, practices give rhetors time and opportunity to add notes to the outline, often in brackets. These are useful reminders of performance choices (e.g., [look at audience], [long pause], and [prop 1 here]).

A few tricks of the trade may improve your delivery by manuscript:

- Print the manuscript in 14- to 16-point Arial font (black) on a dull, white, or light-gray paper. Softer colors cause less eye strain. If delivering the speech on a stage with overhead lighting, a darker hue will absorb some of the light and reduce shadowing.
- Use a highlighter (various colors) to help provide visual cues and to help your eyes locate sections of the outline.
- Print only on one side and use page numbers to avoid confusion. Do not staple pages. To assure pages will not get disorganized (or blow away), put them into a three-ring binder.
- If you skip content, let it pass, especially if it does not seem to cause much consternation in the audience. The audience is unaware of what is written in your manuscript. In instances when a speech transcript or outline is distributed in advance or to the press afterward, note this fact at the end of the presentation, add a footnote to the speech transcript, and, if necessary, issue a press release that recognizes the incongruence between the audio and written version of the speech.

Delivery by simple outline. When delivering a shorter message or when content is familiar, use a key-word or phrase outline. This is often called speaking *extemporaneously*. This outline is usually similar to the outline created in the second step of the rhetorical process (arrangement). As with writing, the outline needs to be expanded for the speech. Provide notes, such as citations, quotes, or paragraphs of more complex data to ensure effective use of style and proper delivery. Delivering from a simple outline allows speakers to exhibit a conversational approach while nonetheless being well prepared and practiced. (Typically, these are the types of speeches you practice and deliver in public speaking courses.) Outlines or notes may be written or typed on 8.5 × 11 sheets of paper, note cards, or any other aid. Use whatever method makes you comfortable. Delivery by simple outline provides the security of recall without the restrictions of a manuscript. Simple outlines allow speakers to improve eye contact and stage mobility.

A few tricks of the trade may improve your delivery by simple outline:

- As mentioned, print the notes or outline on any device you are comfortable using. Avoid the temptation of using a laptop computer or tablet as your makeshift teleprompter, as these devices often require you to scroll through text and also increases the risk of technology failure.
- Use a wireless lapel microphone whenever possible to free your hands. Carry your notes if you think you may need to consult them while away from the lectern.
- Practice your delivery, which includes your stage or room movements. If possible, practice once in the actual space you will deliver your message. For longer presentations, deliver five minutes of the speech to get comfortable with the space and technology.
- If you are on a stage high enough so the audience will not see the floor, use tape to block your movements.

Delivery by memory. Technically, only a speech that is delivered completely by memory is called an *oratory*. Today, however, oratory is used almost synonymously with public speaking. It is these types of speeches that the ancient Greeks adored (hence the canon of memory), and many of their speeches were not short. Fortunately, unless you are a motivational speaker or your professional work is within the context of theater, comedy, or other staged performance art (e.g., you are a magician), it is unlikely that you will have to deliver a lengthy speech from memory. However, there are a variety of contexts in which delivery by memory is appropriate, such as eulogies, toasts, and introductions.

Delivering a speech from memory does not produce a more natural style; it can be very awkward, especially if the speech is longer than a few minutes. When delivering content from memory, it is hard to sound enthusiastic. The brain is working hard to recall information, so it is nearly impossible to maintain eye contact. Delivering content solely by memory can lead to delivery problems. If a speaker has a mental lapse, he or she has no device to assist in recall. This can lead to an uncomfortable silence or, worse, failure to complete the delivery of the message.

If you must deliver your speech by memory, try these two tricks of the trade:

- Chunk information into clusters (by topic is useful) so that you can memorize a section at a time. This can also prove handy if you forget a section. You can recall another cluster and then abandon or return to the other cluster later.
- Use visual, kinesthetic, or auditory mnemonic devices, anything that helps maintain focus on information recall.

Delivery without practice. A speech that is delivered without practice is called *impromptu*, which means "spontaneous" or "unpracticed." In business and professional contexts, there are many instances where one may have to speak impromptu, such as job interviews or as a respondent to another's presentation. Sometimes bosses unexpectedly ask for updates about progress on a project. In these cases, it is possible to anticipate such requests and, therefore, you should have some sense of what you will say if called upon. These are the rare circumstances when it is appropriate to speak without practice. However, one does not want to speak spontaneously if given time to prepare and practice; this lessens rhetorical ethos and could lead to significant professional repercussions. Even if a boss suddenly asks you to speak, don't be caught by surprise. Before attending any meeting, think about what you might say if called upon.

Impromptu speaking is uncomfortable for many people. They often fret about what they will say. However, most interactions with others require such unpracticed speaking. Conversations with friends, for example, are impromptu. Thinking in these terms should help reduce speech anxiety. Public speaking becomes easier with experience, so don't avoid situations to practice.

Here are a few tips that will help you become more confident in your impromptu speaking abilities.

- Take (or ask for) a few moments when requested to deliver comments without notice so you can collect your thoughts. If asked to speak suddenly or asked to respond to an unanticipated question (e.g., during an interview), the other person will respect your need for this time. There are only a few situations where a few seconds of "thought time" would seem inappropriate (e.g., live television).

- Organize your comments using a stock organizational pattern (topical arrangement is usually effective). If possible, write your points down before speaking. (This may reflect positively upon you during a job interview. You will appear prepared and interested.) Use your outline to help guide your response.
- Read. The more knowledge and information you have on topics, the more interesting things you'll have to say.

Control voice and body in delivery.   Body and voice are the design elements of oral delivery. Just as bolding and italicizing words can add emphasis in written documents, an uptick in volume and a decrease in tone can emphasize a spoken word. Using fingers to list items can help listeners see that speakers are moving from one point to another, just like a serial list in print does. In short, body and voice are powerful tools, so learn to use them. Part of practicing a speech is not to become perfect, but to master the content and performance elements. Practice provides an opportunity to hear what sounds awkward and gives a sense of how much time the talk takes. When using voice in delivery, be mindful of volume, pitch, rate, and articulation.

Volume.   The loudness of a speaker's voice is probably the most important element of delivery. Speak too softly, and the audience will not be able to hear. If an audience does not hear the message, then the speech is a failure—the objective cannot be achieved. Speak too loudly, and the audience will hear but will focus on this fact rather than the message. Regardless of whether rhetors use a microphone, they must sustain a volume slightly louder than a normal conversation in large venues. When delivering a message in a round table discussion, focus group, interview, and so on, a conversational volume is more effective. A slightly lower volume can provide a sense of sincerity. Determining how loud to speak is a subjective decision; however, pay attention to an audience's nonverbal feedback. If listeners look uncomfortable, try lowering your volume. If they lean forward, try increasing your volume. When in a television or radio studio (or situations involving the use of equipment), ask for feedback from the sound technicians. Generally, determine and change volume based upon 1) the size of the venue, 2) the number of people in an audience, 3) the type of equipment, and 4) background noise.

Pitch.   Pitch is the degree of lowness and highness of a tone. Technically, pitch is determined by vibrations (frequency). Varying pitch (*intonation*) helps to gain and maintain audience interest. Without pitch variation, speakers are *monotone*. Audiences associate pitch with enthusiasm and mood. Pitch should match the particulars of a message—a more somber topic may require a lower pitch. An uptick at the end of a sentence indicates a question. For example, "He's one of a kind" is a statement. As a question, say "He's one of a KIND?" The uptick in pitch signals a question.

Rate.   Speaking rate is the speed at which a speaker executes the articulatory movements required for speech production. Like pitch, the rate sets the mood. A slow rate can indicate thoughtfulness, genuineness, or somberness. A fast rate demonstrates enthusiasm, excitement, or happiness.

The desirable rate of speech is a subjective assessment, which should be determined and adjusted by the context and feedback of the audience. As a general rule, slower rates help draw attention to important content and faster rates suggest content does not require lengthy deliberation. In some contexts, such as job interviews, speaking quickly is a sign of insecurity or nervousness.

Gain confidence by adjusting your rate of speech through practice. One way to practice a formal presentation is to choose a paragraph of text and read it aloud. Adjust your rate until you feel comfortable. Practice with friends or colleagues and solicit their feedback. To learn how to control your rate of speech in interviews, practice interviewing with a colleague or friend, or record yourself and play back your responses. Also, listen to others' interviews and read the transcript when available. When speaking in a large venue, go slowly to compensate for amplification feedback.

Adults typically produce an average of 270 words per minute during conversation and can comprehend approximately 300 words per minute. (Children speak and listen at a slower pace, so know your audience.) Oral readings (e.g., audio books and podcasts) should have a rate of approximately 160–180 words per minute; the typical public speech occurs at approximately 120 words per minute (Shiplee & McAfee, 2008).

Articulation.   Articulation is defined as the formation of clear and distinct sounds in speech. It is demonstrated by the proper emphasis on vowels and syllables. Improving articulation requires practice. In addition to pronouncing words correctly, speakers need to properly emphasize vowels and syllables. Ensure audiences can hear whether you mean affect (aah-fect) or effect (ee-fect). Be sure not to say "uh-fect" in any case. Avoid adding filler words, such as "um" and "uh." These will not only distract your audience, but will make it harder for you to articulate. If you find you are often misheard or people complain that you mumble, try varying your pitch and go slower. These will automatically improve parts of your articulation. In any case, try to overcome articulation problems through practice.

Sometimes articulation is impeded by oral or periodontal issues. A cleft palate, speech impediment, or orthodontic device may restrict articulation. Speakers should address these issues directly and invite the audience to feel comfortable. Avoid unnecessarily creating conditions that induce articulation problems, such as drinking too much alcohol before speaking. As a listener, do not pay so much attention to a speaker's articulation; rather, pay attention to the content. Counting how many times someone says "um" is not evidence that you're special; it is evidence of poor listening skills and somewhat rude.

In addition to voice, use the body. The primary components of body in delivery are eye contact, facial expression, gestures, and staging.

Eye contact.   Maintaining eye contact with an audience invites them into the dialogue. It is one way to close the interpretive gap and create an inviting atmosphere. Eye contact is generally considered to be a sign of confidence. Holding a gaze on someone shows emphasis on a particular point as represented by the person (be sure not to stare too hard or you may come across

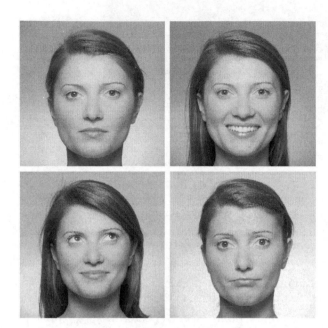

Use your body to convey additional meanings. Facial expressions, for example, can often convey more than words. (Image © Kalim, 2012. Used under license from Shutterstock, Inc.)

as creepy). In small audiences, make a point to make eye contact with everyone. In large venues, scan the audience. In an interview, be sure to maintain eye contact as much as possible.

Facial expression.   Smiling is an effective way to build rapport and to appear friendly. A nice smile invites others to listen. Other facial expressions convey happiness, fear, anger, and surprise. Be cautious of controlling facial expressiveness too much. Overdoing it makes speakers appear insincere or fake.

Gestures.   As previously mentioned, using fingers to itemize a list helps audiences hear and visualize the content. Gestures emphasize details, such as height (e.g., stating "she was tall" while raising a hand high above your head) and assist with metacomments (e.g., saying "she told me off" while extending a middle finger—only if audience appropriate). Gestures add emotional meaning (e.g., pounding a fist on the podium).

Only use gestures that you are comfortable using. If you plan to use gestures that build upon each other (e.g., listing items), practice so you do not skip points. The audience will learn the visual prompt and may get lost without it. Do not be shy about using gestures in more intimate situations. In a job interview, for example, use gestures to appear relaxed or excited.

Staging.   Moving around the stage and among the audience makes speakers less "talking head" and more "moving awesomeness." Posture and fluidity of movement will be judged by the audience, so practice. Slouching makes speakers appear sloppy or weak. Standing straight and moving freely helps speakers appear relaxed and uninhibited. Be sure not to be exclusionary. Moving to only one side of the stage or room can demonstrate preferential treatment. Also, keep in mind that as you move, people may end up behind you, making it hard for them to hear you.

Now that you have a general sense of how you can use your body and voice to add meaning to oral communications, practice honing these skills. While practicing, focus on the message, time your delivery (always prepare to speak under the time limit), and emulate realistic conditions. If you are uncomfortable with the technology, practice in advance and prepare for your surroundings. For example, if you are going to deliver a message in a webinar, practice speaking into a webcam. To practice, invite some of your friends or colleagues for a multiuser Skype chat.

Designing and Using Presentation Aids

Whether on stage, in a one-on-one interview, or communicating electronically, use presentation aids. Presentation aids are similar to embedded visual objects in written texts. In fact, the same presentation aids are used by business communicators in oral presentations and in documents. Presentation aids help listeners process and retain information, assist visual learners, convey information concisely (so don't pack too much content into a single presentation aid), and lend a professional image.

Presentation aids include props, images (e.g., pictures, diagrams, and maps), graphs, charts, video, audio, and multimedia. Visuals that are thoughtfully used in the proper context will help clarify and simplify a message. Listeners will be interested in the vividness of the aid and be motivated to discover the relationships between the visuals and the spoken content. For information that is complex and technical, presentation aids, especially handouts, are useful.

When speaking, present the visual components of your presentation by using a variety of technology—handouts, flip charts, posters, whiteboard or chalkboard, overhead transparencies, slides, audio files, and computer presentation software (e.g., Microsoft PowerPoint, Corel Presentation, OpenOffice Impress, or **http://Prezi.com**). Computer presentation software is often the default choice for those presenting to larger audiences. Unfortunately, it is not always the best option. For example, a whiteboard or flip chart may be better for a brainstorming activity, and a prop or model may help demonstrate a practice. It is slightly more boring to describe a practice on a projected PowerPoint slide than to demonstrate it. Regardless of the type or use, presentations aids should be simple—that is, to support, reinforce, or summarize content, not

When possible, spend some time getting comfortable with the room in which you will deliver a speech. (Image © Losevsky Pavel, 2012. Used under license from Shutterstock, Inc.)

Presentation aids can help explain complex information. Don't always rely on computers. Sometimes whiteboards and flip charts are rhetorically more efficient and effective. (Image © Andresr, 2012. Used under license from Shutterstock, Inc.)

present it—and maintain continuity. The same layout and design elements used to produce written documents—for example, color, typeface, and image style—apply to presentation aids.

When designing presentation aids, be mindful of purpose and usefulness. While Prezi is far more dynamic than PowerPoint, it is not always the better choice. Prezi uses a single canvas (instead of multiple slides), frames, and content clusters to organize main ideas, and zooming functions to help structure and emphasize points. The benefit of this design is that very small images can be embedded in larger ones and the flow of the presentation is not limited to vertical movement between slides. This creates a more stimulating presentation aid. However, Prezi follows a path, which makes it difficult to jump back and forth among content. To deliver simple text-based content that is linear, PowerPoint is more efficient and effective. Prezi also requires an Internet connection or Flash software, increasing the risk of technology problems.

Although people have become accustomed to citing sources of information in written documents, there is a consistent lack of references and citations in presentations. All materials borrowed from others must be cited. Failure to cite material in presentations is not only unethical, but can expose you to civil liability. Be sure to understand the end-user agreements you agree to when using royalty-free stock images.

Evaluation

Evaluation is important for improving your speaking and writing skills. Feedback can be solicited; for example, when a colleague asks you to review a report. Feedback can be unsolicited; for instance, when a conference attendee questions your claims or when your boss suggests areas in which you could improve your performance. Giving and receiving feedback honestly and productively requires disciplined effort. It is sometimes uncomfortable to give and receive unpleasant directives. Evaluating well, on both ends of the process, is an acquired skill that, with some effort and practice, becomes easier over time. This section provides some strategies for giving and receiving feedback openly.

Preparing Feedback

Being an effective evaluator requires preparation. Before sitting down to edit another's written work, get in the proper frame of mind and have the time to do a thorough job. Obtain, in advance, some direction from the person who needs assistance. Ask him or her to give you some guidance so that you do not waste time editing or taking notes on material that is not going to be well received or used. When you are providing editorial comments for educational purposes, focus on a specific grammatical rule or punctuation. This will keep the document from getting too messy.

Before attending a presentation or speech, read the materials sent in advance, and develop a note-taking strategy. For example, sketch an outline of content you hope will be thoroughly addressed. When these topics are addressed, fill in your notes in the appropriate white space. Things left unaddressed will remain blank. Questions can then be developed for the sections that are less understandable or raise concerns. Preparation helps evaluators anticipate what will be stated. This makes it easier for you to take notes and to analyze information. For written communications, a note-taking strategy, prepared in advance of reading, help evaluators stay focused. If the goal is to solely provide feedback on content, resist proofing and editing the document.

Improving Reading and Listening

Listening and reading are critical leadership skills that can be improved with practice. One of the biggest barriers to reading and listening well is lack of motivation. Disinterest in a topic leads to less attentiveness. Unfortunately, there is no "motivation serum" that makes people more mindful readers or listeners.

Caring about something is a matter of attitude and aptitude. One way to increase motivation toward content is to make it personally relevant. You may not be interested in listening, reading, or watching something on the topic of business and professional writing, but if you anticipate that you'll eventually need to write and speak well, then the content will become relevant. Aptitude, or the "natural" ability to understand or do something, also improves with exposure to information. At first, it may be difficult to understand a complex topic with which one has little familiarity. Remain open, however, to learning about the subject. It will become easier to understand over time.

In addition to motivational challenges, *selective attention* and distractions (noise) create barriers to listening and reading. Internal and external distractions, including being tired, using technology while reading or listening (checking your cell phone incessantly), room characteristics (it is too hot or cold), and preoccupation with personal issues (internal noise) lead to inattentiveness. Other factors that contribute to poor active listening and reading skills include arrogance and disrespect for the rhetor, programmed emotional responses due to ideological beliefs, ambushing (waiting for chance to interrupt), and listening solely for recall (e.g., to pass a test).

One reason we find ourselves easily distracted is that we can think three to four times faster than others talk. Sometimes the distractions are relevant—e.g., when a speaker makes a point about something interesting, and this sets off a series of thoughts on that particular topic. This is good; however, try to refocus as quickly as possible because the rhetor may quickly move on to other relevant points. You likely experience tangential thinking while reading. You read the words, but find you are thinking about something else. The best advice is to reread the passages.

If you want to become a good active listener or reader, try these handy tricks:

- *Paraphrase.* Get in the habit of restating what others have said or what you have read. Take notes that rephrase the material in your own words.
- *Express understanding*. In oral communication, when you consciously send feedback to the speaker, you are often drawn into the presentation.
- *Ask questions*. When you read or hear something, make a habit of raising questions about the material. Because we tend to ask questions relevant to our own interests, raising points of inquiry is an exciting way to create an attitude of caring. Also, listening with the intent of asking questions will force closer attention to minute details.
- *Play a game*. Doodling and playing little mind games that are simple and do not require much thought can help you stay focused, especially when content is boring. By remaining active, you stay alert, reduce sleepiness, and keep your mind from wandering.
- *Take breaks*. If possible, break up content so you do not read too much in a single sitting. If you can, step outside for some fresh air or to have a conversation between speakers. During presentations, give yourself a few moments to stop listening. This break will refresh your mind. Although you will miss some content, it is better to miss a brief episode than a lot of material due to mental exhaustion.

There are many reasons to be an active listener or reader, and many more strategies to use. Develop a process that works for you. The rewards for active listening include life-enhancing experiences, such as learning, being entertained, developing relationships, and coming across as a more interesting individual. Furthermore, effective listening leads to more engaging and intelligent conversations. It will improve your ability to make decisions. Among other things, effective listening prevents accidents.

Providing Constructive Feedback

Feedback is an important part of the active listening and reading process. No response is a type of feedback; however, not responding is not always an option. Managers, for example, must give feedback to encourage proper practices. Depending on the context, providing feedback can be uncomfortable. However, there are a variety of practices that can make giving feedback, especially negative or constructive feedback, easier: 1) stay focused on the purpose of feedback, 2) provide evidence and examples to support claims, 3) be honest and fair, and 4) be compassionate and work toward reconciliation.

Giving and receiving feedback is not easy. It is a rhetorical skill that requires training and practice. (Image © Yuri Arcurs, 2012. Used under license from Shutterstock, Inc.)

Stay focused on the purpose.   Understand the purpose of the evaluation effort. For example, providing feedback to employees should not be to justify punishments and rewards. If an employee is not performing well, the purpose of the feedback is to correct the practice, not to punish the person. When providing feedback on another's writing, the purpose of the comments may be educational—i.e., to improve writing proficiency—or to simply edit a business document. In the former case, the evaluator will likely point to concerns and ask the writer to identify the mistake and correct the problem. In the latter case, the evaluator may make corrections and ask the writer to be more mindful of writing mechanics in future communications. When invited to provide feedback, avoid the temptation to offer feedback that was not solicited. Doing so may generate animosity.

Provide evidence and examples to support claims.   Whether feedback is positive or negative, constructive feedback should always be descriptive and point to particular examples. For example, if an employee has demonstrated a high level of customer service, give him or her examples of particular instances. If you are helping a friend prepare for an interview, describe what you thought he or she did well and suggest areas for improvement. For example, you could say,

> I really like how you described your previous management experience as "rewarding" and then offered examples. Examples are always a good thing, and yours are rich.

When talking about a former boss, you said, "She was an *interesting* person." I think you meant she was *interesting* in a fun sort of way, but without an example that word choice could be problematic. "Interesting" can be interpreted as "odd" or "strange."

By providing specific and descriptive commentary, the individual receiving the feedback will be able to address specific issues. By being descriptive, evaluators are likely to present opinions that sound less judgmental.

Be honest and fair.   It is important to be honest and fair when giving feedback. Mitigating statements to buffer a person against criticism may seem like the nice thing to do; however, it can lead to confusion. Consider the following statement: "I wish we had more employees like you, but pay more attention to grammatical issues in professional reports." This is confusing because it is unclear whether the employee is being warned. In most cases, people selectively listen by focusing on positive comments. If a statement is mitigated with a buffer comment, the second part of the statement—that which is more crucial—may not be interpreted correctly.

Typically, the purpose of feedback is to help others improve. In addition to understanding the context, time the delivery of the feedback so that others will be open to listening to it, and avoid "sandbagging" a person by storing up negative criticism and then dumping it on him or her all at once. Focus on argumentative fallacies and other objective criteria rather than on subjective judgments.

Be compassionate and work toward reconciliation.   Giving feedback can be difficult; however, if you are compassionate and are willing to work through conflict toward integration (i.e., friendship, collegiality, and so on), chances are that any tension produced in the feedback process will quickly dissipate. Compassionate statements are demonstrated by speaking in the following way:

- Use "I" instead of "you" statements.
- Phrase the issue as a statement, not a question.
- Restrict feedback to what you know for certain.
- Provide both positive and negative feedback.
- Don't label, just describe the issue.
- Whether feedback is positive or negative, do not exaggerate.
- Understand the context and other constitutive factors. Situational factors may be to blame.

There are, of course, many other ways to demonstrate compassion. If you work within the interpretive frame of mind, you will be more self-reflexive and aware of your own limitations and questionable practices. Adapt to the person and situation instead of approaching feedback as a standardized process. If they feel the feedback is not just ceremonial, people will respect your evaluative ethos, even if they are at first reluctant to receive criticism about their work practices and products.

Receiving Feedback

When receiving feedback, avoid becoming arrogant or defensive. Prepare yourself to hear things that you agree or disagree with. Being boastful or becoming overconfident can be unappealing to the person evaluating your work, and it also can become a barrier to listening. Often the most important and critical feedback is embedded in mitigated phrases. This is one reason so many people are surprised when they suddenly receive news that they are underperforming and do not deserve a promotion or raise. The real feedback was embedded in the statement after the "but"—"Keep up the good work, but don't get too confident." Possible translation: "Yes, we know you are doing a great job and you deserve accolades, but you're starting to get arrogant and boastful."

Don't discourage feedback. If you hear things you do not like and become defensive, you will discourage future comments critical for improvement. Recognize that feedback usually sounds harsher than it is and that the evaluator may not have the best rhetorical skills. When receiving feedback, take deep and slow breaths to help your body relax. Use active listening strategies. Ask questions to clarify points, request specific direction to improve performance, and paraphrase what you heard. ("What you said was 'X, Y, and Z'; what I heard was '1, 2, and 3,' am I correctly understanding?") Acknowledge the valid points and agree with what you know to be true. Be aware that evaluators may not know how to give constructive criticism, so encourage them to practice the feedback guidelines noted above.

Conclusion

This chapter introduced you to elements of design for written communication, considerations regarding the distribution of artifacts with an emphasis on delivery, and some considerations about giving and receiving criticism. It is important to learn to write and speak well, as emphasized in the first two chapters; however, it is also essential to focus your efforts on improving your ability to design and deliver artifacts. In order to improve your and others' communications, it is necessary to gain confidence in giving and receiving feedback ethically and compassionately. This chapter outlined some tactics for accomplishing these objectives. (Chapter 7 provides a few more.)

Design and delivery decisions utilize the canons of style, memory, and delivery. A brochure that has a parallel and balanced layout will likely be more enticing than one that seems hastily pieced together. Even if the content is the same, the outcomes will likely be different. The well-designed brochure is likely to be visually appealing. If you deliver a powerful message in a monotone voice, the audience will be uninspired and fail to hear the power of the message.

The previous chapters, as with this chapter, sought to provide a foundation upon which the following chapters will be developed. Chapter 1 provided an introduction to narrative and interpretive approaches to rhetoric. Chapter 2 presented a thorough overview of the skills required to construct any rhetorical artifact. This chapter discussed the design, delivery, and evaluation of professional communications. These chapters are the skeleton upon which the meat of any type of business communication, whether spoken or written, hangs. All professional communications can be approached rhetorically and all can be improved by following the procedures and mechanics of the four-step construction process.

In the following chapters, the rhetorical process outlined in these first three chapters will be applied to specific types of business artifacts. Regardless of the type of communication you craft, the step-by-step construction process applies (revisit Figure 2.1). As you work through the concepts in the following chapters, maintain the interpretive frame of mind. Ask yourself how a communicative artifact or message should be crafted, designed, delivered, and evaluated to achieve its rhetorical purpose. The goal should always be to produce the opposite of what Jason Fried, as noted at the beginning of this chapter, suggested is common business writing. Instead of crafting "completely unsatisfying" artifacts "devoid of nutrition," use the strategies and skills developed in this unit to produce delectable and nourishing artifacts enticing to a variety of stakeholders.

Continuing Education:
Recommended Texts and Resources

- *About face: Reviving the rules of typography* by David Jury. ISBN: 978-2880467982.
    This book is an excellent introduction to the history and applied use of type. Unlike books that solely focus on the ins and outs of specific computer programs used in design, this book focuses on principles, theories, and examples. Due to its excellent examples, this book will improve your creative use of type and design.

- *Helvetica*, directed by Gary Hustwit. See **http://helveticafilm.com.**
    This film, part of a trilogy on design, provides a fascinating discussion about the politics of design. Watching it will help you gain a better appreciation of the use of type in communicative artifacts. It will likely also allow you to understand why typeface matters politically.

- *Confessions of a public speaker* by Scott Berkun. ISBN: 978-0596801991
    This highly acclaimed book, written by a dynamic professional speaker, provides relevant advice about mastering the art of public speaking. It offers personal accounts of mistakes made over the years, which are lessons about how to either avoid mistakes or be less fearful of them. The text is an engaging narrative, which offers another example of how to use personal narrative in business and professional communications.

- *Speaking clearly: Improving voice and diction with free pronunciation* by Jeffrey Hahner, Martin Sokoloff, and Sandra Salisch. ISBN: 978-0079259195
    If you cannot find a course in Voice and Diction at a university, then this book is good to have on your bookshelf. It includes a pronunciation CD-ROM that allows students to hear text examples. This book is great for advanced-level training and will improve the quality of your delivery.

- *The complete voice and speech workout: 74 exercises for classroom and studio use* by Janet Rodgers. ISBN: 978-1557834980
    This book is great for beginners and for those working solo. There are, according to the products description, "potent and empowering voice exercises by … master teachers." The book comes with a training CD.

- *HubSpot white papers*, see **www.hubspot.com/internet-marketing-whitepapers**
  If you are looking to enhance your technical skills in a variety of business-related topics (e.g., brainstorming, marketing, design, and so on), begin by reading the electronic white papers published by **www.hubspot.com**. The white papers cover a wide range of topics, particularly those relevant to internet business development and social networking.

- *Transcripts of speeches and interviews.*
  The Internet has made obtaining transcripts (and often audio) of contemporary and historic speeches and interviews easy. If you want to learn how business and political leaders, executives, and other relevant social figures engage in interviews and address large audiences, read transcripts. Of course, not all interviews or speeches are flawless, so these are excellent learning guides. Analysis of the transcripts will certainly by fruitful. *CNN* provides near-immediate release of all its shows. *American Rhetoric* is a great source for famous speeches. *Real Clear Politics* is a great source for public addresses from important contemporary figures (it is also a good source of political news and commentary). The links are as follows: **http://transcripts.cnn.com/transcripts**; **http://americanrhetoric.com**; **www.realclearpolitics.com/transcripts_speeches**.

References

Browning, L. D. Lists and stories as organizational communication. *Communication Theory*, 2, 281–302.

Fried, J. (2010, May). Why is business writing so awful? *Inc.* Retrieved from www.inc.com/magazine/20100501/why-is-business-writing-so-awful.html

Howard, A. (2010). What Wikileaks and Cablegate mean for open government. Retrieved from www.huffingtonpost.com/alexander-howard/what-wikileaks-and-cableg_b_788949.html

Jury, D. (2002). *About face: Reviving the rules of typography.* East Sussex, England: RotoVision SA.

O'Banion, J. D. (1992). *Reorienting rhetoric: The dialectic of list and story.* University Park: The University of Pennsylvania Press.

Online opportunity marketing report: Social media, blog, and search engine activity by industry. (2010). *HubSpot.com.* Retrieved from www.hubspot.com/internet-marketing-whitepapers

Shiplee, K. G., & McAfee, J. G. (2008). *Assessment in speech-language pathology: A resource manual.* Clifton Park, NY: Delmar Cengage Learning.

Unit 2

Crafting Business and Professional Communications

Image © Kurhan, 2012. Used under license from Shutterstock, Inc.

Chapter 4: Crafting and Sharing a Résumé

Chapter 5: Crafting Concise and Extensive Communications

Chapter 6: Crafting Electronic Communications and Presentation Aids

This unit applies rhetorical concepts to specific types of rhetorical artifacts and rhetorical situations. At the conclusion of this unit, you will know how to develop and manage your career, engage in the hiring process, write an effective résumé, and interview for jobs; you will know how to craft concise and extensive communications that convey positive and negative messages; and you will be mindful of the unique elements of crafting and engaging in computer-mediated communications.

Chapter — 4

Crafting and Sharing a Résumé

Image © kpcтyhka, 2012. Used under license from Shutterstock, Inc.

Starting Point

The résumé is a rhetorical artifact. It narrates a partial account of your professional identity, supplying evidence of your past experience, knowledge, and accomplishments in order to persuade others to respect you as a professional or potential employee. The résumé tells a story about your career; however, it is only one story in the larger narrative of your personal and professional life.

As a representation of just one small part of your work life, your résumé should not strive to fully represent your professional identity. This means two things. First, you must understand that the purpose of your résumé is to persuade a hiring committee to invite you for an interview. Other parts of the application process will allow you to demonstrate other aspects of your personality and skills. You do not have to put every job or position you've ever held into your résumé. Be selective; only offer information that is relevant to the particular organization you're sending your résumé. Write your résumé with the intended audience in mind. As you will learn in this chapter, this means adapting your résumé to each specific job posting.

Second, you cannot rely solely on your résumé to tell your professional story or, for that matter, land you a job. Social networking—both online and offline—is highly important. The résumé will help you obtain job leads and job interviews in today's competitive marketplace. Even as a working professional, you need to develop a consistent professional image and promote it—for example, as a fun and edgy accountant who gets financial results or as a compassionate public relations specialist who knows how to deliver persuasive messages to marginalized citizens. While your traditional résumé, as a list of professional accomplishments, is important, consider alternative methods and media to tell your personal and professional stories. You LinkedIn, Facebook, and Twitter accounts, your blog, and your personal website, as well as your offline community activities and conferences, provide a variety of outlets to build your professional image. But here's the rub: You have to develop and maintain a consistent message across these venues. With so many different ways to tell your professional story, it may be better to conceptualize your résumé as only one part of your *curriculum vitae* (see Box 4.1).

In short, it is important to think about your résumé as more than a single document of accomplishments. It is a small representation of an overall personal narrative (i.e., identity). It is just one part of your overall career portfolio and it is specific to your "personal brand." By thinking about it in this way, you should avoid using templates. Instead, work to craft documents that are expressions of your overall experiences in relation to your audience. If you are creative, then make this clear in your résumé and application letter. If you are more conservative, then this should be represented. How you present these personal orientations should change as you apply to different positions and companies. Each company is a different audience, each position a different rhetorical situation. Draw upon the canons of invention and style to produce a document that speaks to audience interests but is consistent with your overall message of your professional identity. Thus, the application letter and résumé, though drawing upon the same stock of information, experiences, and skills, will slightly change for each position to which you apply.

Box 4.1: The curriculum vitae (CV)

Curriculum vitae, Latin for "the course of my life," describes a résumé-like document that is used in select professions. When used as a documentation of one's professional work, it is generally referred to as "CV." A CV is longer than a traditional résumé. Unlike a résumé, which lists only one's work history and a few specialized skills, a CV provides thorough detail about a variety of industry-specific information. For example, in academic and creative circles, it lists publications and commissioned designs, and for doctors, attorneys, accountants, and other professionals, it lists continuing education and specialized training.

Although this chapter focuses on the process of obtaining a job, you must form the habit of keeping your résumé up-to-date and promoting your professional identity through social networking even while employed. Obtaining testimonials and recommendations and building a portfolio of high-quality work over time, instead of solely when contemplating a career move or facing unemployment, will help you stay prepared for employment contingencies and career moves. One longitudinal study conducted by the Bureau of Labor Statistics found that one cohort of baby boomers changed jobs an average of 11 times between the ages of 18 and 44 ("Number of Jobs Held . . . ," 2010). Not only do people change jobs, but they uproot themselves into new careers. The general sentiment among career planners and specialists is that people change their careers and professions several times during their active work life. Unfortunately, it is unclear exactly how frequently people do so. The U.S. Bureau of Labor Statistics, for example, "has never attempted to estimate the number of times people change careers in the course of their lives . . . [because] no consensus has emerged on what constituted a career change" ("National longitudinal surveys FAQs," n.d.). Despite the lack of strong statistics, sustained development of skills will strengthen your ethos when applying for jobs or making career moves. Having a strong résumé that reflects market-relevant skills requires a lifelong commitment to continuing education.

This chapter will begin by describing the employment search process, how to write a résumé and application letter, tactics that can be used during interviews, including responding to difficult or illegal questions, and additional employment considerations (e.g., negotiating salaries).

The Employment Search Process

This section focuses on the canon of invention, which is the most important rhetorical canon used to engage competitively in the hiring process. Understanding the occupational, professional, and institutional environment, using a directed search to find employment opportunities, and staying abreast of changes in a field by continuing your education and building a network will keep you competitive in the global marketplace.

Understanding Occupations, Professions, and Institutional Environments

As you begin to think about a career, consider what type of occupation is best for you, the professional requirements of specific occupations, and the pressures and changes caused by the larger institutional environment (e.g., government regulations and economic climate). In this book's Introduction, you were asked to spend some time thinking about the routine organizational activities you'd be happy performing. Some occupations are emotionally stressful, others are physically demanding, and some are both. Based on salary and benefits alone, some occupations may be overvalued and some many be underappreciated. Socially and organizationally, some occupations are recognized as more significant than others. It is important to understand what motivates you.

Professions are defined as vocations founded on specialized educational training. In some cases, consumers determine the qualifications by the quality of services provided. For example, anyone can be a yoga instructor; however, if an individual does not conduct sessions well, customers will go elsewhere. In some instances, organizations try to provide specialized training and certificates that over time become the de facto representation of legitimacy. For instance, the Yoga Alliance is a nonprofit organization that certifies training programs for yoga instructors. As a matter of law, however, yoga instructors are generally unregulated. Other professions, however, have specialized training programs that are tightly controlled by professional associations and regulated by states. The American Institute of Certified Public Accountants (which administers the CPA exam), tightly controls its profession by lobbying for laws that regulate and legitimize its work practices. Sometimes, professional associations advise and accredit college programs. Thus, understanding the professional requirements and the various associations that comprise a profession is important for developing a promising career. If you do not graduate from a legitimate college program, you may have difficulty obtaining a job.

The broader institutional environment is partly controlled by practitioners, professional associations, and the government, which place normative and coercive pressure on industries (DiMaggio & Powell, 1983). Part of this control limits profession accessibility. For example, although you may have a master's degree in criminal justice and have several years of experience collecting evidence as an insurance adjuster, you would not be able take the exam that would qualify you to be a private detective (an agency owner) in the State of Illinois. First, you would have to work for a private investigations agency as a full-time employee for at least a year. As the Illinois Private Detective, Private Alarm, Private Security, Fingerprint Vendor, and Locksmith Act of 2004 (225 ILCS 447/1510) stipulates:

> A person is qualified for licensure as a private detective if he or she meets all of the following requirements. . . . / Has a minimum of 3 years experience of the 5 years immediately preceding application working full time for a licensed private detective agency as a registered private detective agency employee. . . . / An applicant who has a baccalaureate degree, or higher, in law enforcement or a related field or a business degree from an accredited college or university shall be given credit for 2 of the 3 years of the required experience. An applicant who has an associate degree in law enforcement or in a related field or in business from an accredited college or university shall be given credit for one of the 3 years of the required experience.

These laws, often promoted by professional associations, are usually in place for good reasons. However, they create barriers to entry. When planning a career as a private investigator or information consultant, one could face unforeseen restrictions or legal problems if he or she does not research the professions thoroughly. If you know that you'll need a year of experience, interning with a private investigations company while in college could provide faster access into the profession. Research into the profession will also reveal which states have fewer regulations. For example, currently eight states do not require a license to be private investigator.

In addition to learning about professional associations and laws, become familiar with other institutional trends. Identify where openings for desired occupations are likely to occur, whether technological advancements and changes will render a career obsolete (at one time television repair was a lucrative occupation), whether positions are likely to be outsourced or eliminated, whether an occupation is dependent on other industries doing well, and, among other things, whether a job will require a significant investment in continuing education and training. The public's image of private investigators is that they follow cheating spouses. While some private investigators do specialize in surveillance on unfaithful mates, many others conduct business security analysis, locate missing persons, serve subpoenas, conduct witness interviews for civil litigation, research traffic accidents for insurance companies, conduct corporate espionage on their clients' competition, and assist in criminal defense cases. These are all highly lucrative areas of the profession but they require different skills, and some necessitate ongoing training and certification. At one time, providing background investigation searches was a profitable area of the profession. Easy and inexpensive access to online databases, such as **www.sentrylink.com**, has lowered the demand for this service within the profession. Today, many private investigators are enjoying an increase in workflow from insurance agencies. However, conducting accident investigation requires significant investments in equipment maintenance and training. Knowing this information helps people select the right types of internships and focuses skill development.

Some private investigators conduct third-party investigations for attorneys and insurance companies. Research into a profession reveals occupational opportunities and required skills. (Image © Rechitan Sorin, 2012. Used under license from Shutterstock, Inc.)

There are a variety of ways to learn about occupations, professions, and the wider institutional environment. Reading books and blogs written by professionals within the field is a great way to learn industry trade secrets and occupational frustrations. Browse professional associations' websites to identify trends, stay current with research or career developments, and learn about important seminars and networking opportunities. Explore the Bureau of Labor Statistic's *Occupational Outlook Handbook* (**www.bls.gov/oco**), which is available online, to gain thorough insight into trends within occupations, including salary information. Many state agencies, especially the Department of the Secretary of State and the Department of Professional Regulation (or equivalent), are great sources of information regarding the regulatory environment of a profession. Familiarity with regulations not only keeps professionals out of legal trouble, it saves them money. For example, there are a variety of private educational institutions offering certification programs in professions that either do not require them or do not recognize the certificate as valid. Knowing what counts as legitimate is therefore important. Of course, a practicing professional can tell students what education, knowledge, skills, and experiences matter in hiring decisions. (Refer to Table A.1 in appendix A for a list of useful resources that can assist you in learning about a profession.)

One of the best ways to learn about an occupation or vocation is to speak directly with a practicing professional. There are two common ways to do this: informational interviews and job shadowing. Although one can interview or shadow at any time during his or her professional career, students are regarded with less suspicion. Rhetorically, you can frame such activities as part of a learning experience. Use your time in school to engage with professionals. Professionals often enjoy speaking with students about what they do. By asking someone with tenure in the profession about its future, the challenges and opportunities of the profession, and what degrees and certifications matter, you will learn whether the profession or certain occupations within the profession are appropriate for you.

If successful, an informational interview is also an excellent way to make a connection and obtain job leads. Practice good business communication by preparing and practicing for the interview. Also, remain courteous and professional from initial contact (use appropriate artifact design and distribution) to final contact (send a thank-you note).

Shadowing entails accompanying and observing someone in a professional setting. Most people think of shadowing as a job training method. However, in recent years it has been used as an opportunity by people contemplating a career change (see Ferrell, 2010). Businesses specializing in job shadowing, such as VocationVactions (**http://vocationvacation.com**), mediate the relationship between shadowers and shadowees. By spending a full work day (or longer) with a professional, shadowers see what the job entails.

A benefit of shadowing is that it functions as an extended interview. As rapport builds, shadowees become more comfortable sharing information. As with all rhetorical situations, remain conscientious about communication. If a shadower is too intrusive or disruptive, or leaves a bad impression with the shadowee and her or his colleagues, he or she may limit future business or employment opportunities. If done correctly, however, shadowing is an excellent way to get recognized. Students who have engaged in shadowing have found it to be beneficial. Some have realized, for example, that the profession they once glamorized was not for them. Others find internships and jobs. Be careful, however, with being hasty in generalizations. You may have a glittering or negative experience, but a single case may not represent the whole of the profession.

Searching for Opportunities

Finding the right job, especially in a tough economy, can be a frustrating process. Simply applying to a large number of jobs and accepting the first offer is not an optimal approach to launching a career. You may get a job with a poorly planned search, but it may not be the ideal job. Appreciate the complexity of the process and remain diligent. Developing a thorough plan, searching broadly, beginning a search early, and behaving like a professional will improve your chances of finding a good job.

Develop a thorough plan.   A job search can take several months. It involves sorting through hundreds of position announcements in a variety of places to identify a select few jobs that fit your criteria and qualifications, contacting multiple people in dozens of companies, and writing or modifying a dozen or more cover letters and résumés. Keep all of your files and the details of each contact straight. If you do not, you risk losing important information, such as contacts, appointments, and deadlines. The following practical tips will assist you in your search.

- *Determine your search criteria in advance.* Reading through inappropriate job postings, attending unnecessary job fairs, and interviewing for the wrong jobs are not productive activities. You shouldn't be too picky when searching for your first post-graduation position or when you've been unemployed for a while; however, spending time reading irrelevant posts or following unnecessary leads takes time and energy away from finding relevant and optimal jobs. If you don't plan to take a job in Fairbanks, Alaska, because you want to stay close to home and live in Florida, don't waste your time or the company's money applying. Using the interview as an opportunity to "gain experience" is ethically questionable, and it takes time away from obtaining a preferred job. Write down realistic job criteria, which include location, salary, job responsibilities you are (or are not) willing to accept, and so on.
- *Itemize electronic folders and bookmarks.* You will likely spend most of your time searching for positions online. Decide *before searching* how you will organize content. Create a bookmark folder labeled "Jobs," then create a separate folder for each position (e.g., "Serious Materials: 3.20"; 3.20 represents the application deadline). Do the same for your application packages. Create a desktop folder called "Jobs," then create a folder for "Open positions." Save the files with deadline dates first so they appear chronological in a list (e.g., "3.20_SeriousMaterials"). Make two other folders, such as "Applied" and "Closed." Create a separate folder for each position. Keep the application deadline in the folder name. File your modified résumé, application letter, and other relevant information in each job's folder. When the position has been filled, move the entire

folder into the "Closed" file. Keeping records of the positions in this way makes it easier to reapply should another position open. Also, another company may advertise a similar position.

- *Use a separate manila folder, large envelope (e.g., 9″ × 12″), or both to hold information for each position.* A manila folder is useful because you can staple information, such as printed emails and business cards, to the flaps. However, you can also still hold loose items that may need to be presented at a later date. In a sense, this is a duplicate of the online content.

- *Design an information tracking sheet in Excel or a similar program.* Recommended columns include the following: Due date, Company, Contact, Job posting (URL), Initial contact (include relevant information), Application sent (the date), Follow-up (the date), and Notes. Decide how to track the information. Color coding the rows is one way to stay organized. For example, red rows are closed, yellow rows can indicate positions applied for, and green rows could indicate ones with approaching deadlines. The Notes column can also be used to code the status (e.g., 1 = applied; 2 = need to apply). This column may also be used write general updates, for example, "Spoke w/Yolanda (office manager) on 8/22"; keep track of delivery confirmation numbers if you mailed an application; and document online job application URLs if you filled in an application online.

- *Use more than one medium.* Do not focus a search strategy solely on online advertisements. Utilize your college's alumni association's job placement and advising center, look at bulletin boards around campus, search company websites, search job search engines sites (see the next section), attend job fairs, and so on.

The above list contains general suggestions. Ultimately, you should devise an organizing system that will make it easier for you to find and locate information when needed. Using good organizational principles, no matter what the system looks like, saves time and lowers frustration.

Search broadly.   Once you have developed a thorough search and organizational strategy, begin your search. Do not limit your search to one medium or a single location. Look for job fairs beyond ones your college or community hosts. Look at a variety of websites that advertise or discuss jobs and trends within and among companies. When searching online, expand the possibilities by using multiple search engines and job sites:

- **http://collegerecruiter.com**
- **http://communicationsjobs.net**
- **www.idealist.org**
- **http://indeed.com**
- **http://jobs.prsa.org**
- **http://jobster.com**
- **http://jobtarget.com**
- **www.linkedin.com**

Job fairs are used to screen candidates. If possible, attend other community's and college's job fairs to increase face time with recruiters. (Image © Piotr Marcinski, 2012. Used under license from Shutterstock, Inc.)

- **http://monster.com** (also try **http://college.monster.com**)
- **http:// opm.gov**
- **http://rileyguide.com**
- **www.simplyhired.com**
- **www.tweetmyjobs.com**
- **www.usajobs.gov**

In addition to using job search websites, target specific companies and look for "Employment," "Job Opportunities," "Work for Us," "Join Our Team," or similar links. Sometimes companies post advertisements only in these locations. Call your family and friends and probe for leads at their companies. Other strategies are available on the book's companion site (**http://proCommunication.me**).

Begin early.   Too often job seekers, especially students, wait to begin their job search until closer to graduation or departure from a job. This is way too late. Some jobs are advertised as much as a year in advance, particularly for cyclical or specialized positions. Companies attend job fairs in the fall to begin trolling for top candidates for anticipated summer openings. Some companies advertise positions in October and want to fill them quickly. If the right candidate comes along, however, they may be willing to wait until after fall commencement. Some companies attend job fairs all of the time, even if they don't have an immediate need for new hires. Recruiters keep on file candidates that make an impression and give these individuals first notice when positions do become available. Also, if you wait like most students do, you'll be competing against more candidates for the limited time and attention of recruiters. If you begin early, you can attend more job fairs and events, search through more ads, and get more advice and feedback on your résumé. What is more, if you attend multiple job fairs, you may see the same recruiters and gain more one-on-one time.

If you are a year or more away from actually applying for a job, get in the job search frame of mind. By looking through job advertisements now, you can recognize employment trends, determine what skills and knowledge seem to be most important for occupations, and learn to speak the language of the profession. By recognizing trends or desired skills, you can begin to close gaps in your experience and skills (e.g., by doing an externship, internship, or volunteer work), shore up your credit (since many companies now check credit reports), and take control of your online identity. Keep in mind that it takes time to do these things. Ensure time is on your side by beginning early.

Behaving like a professional.   Instead of just projecting a professional image by cleaning up your online profiles, it is a good idea to begin behaving like a professional. This means actually thinking about how you fit within a larger profession, how you will shape it, and what role you will play in the profession as an employee for a particular company. Employers want to hire people who can bring with them skills and knowledge that not only satisfy their hiring need but make them more competitive. This requires employees to have an understanding of industry trends and fresh ideas. Professionals stay up on the "conversations" in their field and understand how market trends affect it.

To learn more about a professional field, begin reading leading business periodicals and newspapers, such as *The Economist*, *The Wall Street Journal*, *Fortune*, *Entrepreneur*, and *Inc.*, and industry trade publications. Speak with a librarian to locate databases that index trade publications (e.g., *Business Source Elite*). Use CREDO*Reference* (**http://credoreference.com**) to identify a variety of summaries on best business practices. Many libraries provide patrons with free access to Credo. Stay abreast of developments and trends by following blogs or podcasts (check out **www.podcastalley.com** for a list of hot blogs and podcasts on a variety of topics in professional fields).

A profession that you may want to get knowledgeable about while you are in the job market, regardless of your own field of interest, is corporate recruiting. By reading corporate recruiting blogs and periodicals—e.g., *Workforce Management*, **http://thehrlibrary.com**, **http://fistfuloftalent.com**, and **http://hrcapitalist.com**—you will learn recruiters' desires, concerns, issues, annoyances, and so on. You can then use this information to avoid common résumé and interview pitfalls.

Continuing Education, Networking, and Counseling

Once you obtain a position, don't simply sit back and wait for retirement. In today's dynamic organizational environment, no job is safe from the prospects of outsourcing and downsizing. Relatively stable institutions, such as the U.S. Post Office and universities, are facing significant downsizing and outsourcing efforts (e.g., Leonard, 2011). Tenure-track academic positions are being replaced by temporary adjunct positions. Traditional teaching models are being displaced by online learning, which creates a platform for self-learning modules, video tutorials, and syndicated podcasts by authors. With the rise of doctorate degrees in China and India, taught in English, grading can be outsourced. Robots, already at work as physicians and pharmacy aides, may someday replace lab technicians working in the fields of forensic science, hematology, and academia ("Should we make way . . . ," 2009).

Your ability to remain viable, flexible, and mobile hinges upon the effort you invest in continuing education, networking, and counseling. Continuing education certainly involves staying up on trends in a profession, but also gaining additional technical skills. For example, learning a second, third, or fourth language, or continuing your studies at a university in a related or separate field, will keep you competitive. Continued educational efforts could qualify you for managerial positions overseas. If you continue your education at a university, you not only get a cost advantage over time due to inflation, you could be tapping into a company benefit (some companies pay for classes and advanced degrees). Most importantly, you won't have to spend much time in school if you change your career. You'll have fewer courses to take to complete the degree requirements. If you already have a communications or management degree, you could focus on accounting or some other closely related field that is more technical and likely to remain in demand. People talk about diversifying their financial portfolio; it is a good idea to diversity educational portfolios too. Research shows that individuals with higher levels of education are not only more likely to succeed as entrepreneurs, they are also more profitable (see Shane, 2008).

Networking is important before, during, and after the employment search process. Networking occurs wherever informal or formal connections exist. Your informal network of friends and colleagues needn't be forced; however, your professional and social network should be designed with some planning and care. A Facebook network may be comprised of a variety of folks, but your LinkedIn account should be built more strategically; some employers now contact people in your list even if you don't include them as a reference (Garone, 2009). Who you spend your time with at professional conferences should be different than those you spend time with during happy hour. Your social and professional networks, of course, are not likely to be mutually exclusive. People need to know, however, whether they are solely a part of either group to avoid conflict. Your friends don't want to feel used only when you need them, and a professional contact may not want you sending him or her random email messages.

You want to have your network in place before you need them. Some of your classmates will eventually move into important positions and be willing to bring you along. Young attorneys eventually make partner, so do some free work for them when they are just starting out. Socially conscious executives (or those looking for good public relations) do community service, so you should too. You never know who you will meet when serving lunch at a soup kitchen or building a home with Habitat for Humanity.

Always keep in mind that networking is about people helping each other. If you are only taking help, you will "burn bridges." If others seem only to be "takers," don't waste your time helping them. Even if they make it to a position where they can help you, chances are they won't unless it benefits them somehow.

Due to online social networking, some rules of the networking and recruiting game have changed. For example, you can join social media networks, such as Twitter, to find or share job leads. You can use Facebook to connect with like-minded people. If you use effective rhetorical practices, you may eventually establish enough rapport with people to meet in an offline environment. For example, if you are part of a network with a recruiter or employee of a company of interest, you can use your common interests to invite him or her out for coffee or beer. If you don't have a strong enough connection to do this, find out the locations and dates of important company-community events and try to introduce yourself to people there. These relationships could eventually lead to important job leads and references.

Finally, don't hesitate to get career or wellness counseling from time to time. People frequently check in with their financial advisors and doctors, even when their portfolios and bodies are in generally good health. Requesting the assistance of people who can help you deal with uncertainties, develop healthy strategies for dealing with stress, and provide advice on your career is a healthy way to deal with work and career challenges. When planning a career change, it is especially useful to seek guidance from someone who can help you obtain the tools and give advice that will smooth the transition. Practicing psychologists, career counselors at your alma mater, life coaches specializing in career transitions, or head hunters can be useful when you have problems at work or when you are looking for a change.

Use online social media sites to find people in a company or profession with whom you share common social interests. Invite them out for coffee or beer. Such informal meetings could lead to job opportunities. (Image © Deklofenak, 2012. Used under license from Shutterstock, Inc.)

Writing the Résumé

In this section, you learn to apply the rhetorical concepts you learned in Chapter 2 to write the résumé.

Rhetorical Situations

A résumé is not just a document sent for a job. It is a rhetorical argument that needs to respond specifically to each unique rhetorical situation. There are at least three purposes for writing and maintaining one or more résumés.

It is a *professional statement*. The résumé, in this situation, is a story that narrates who you are as a professional. It says, "*This is who I am* in relation to my professional peers." It helps others with similar interests find you. Describing your professional identity also helps to distinguish you from your peers.

It is a tool for *planning a career*. In this situation, use your résumé to help keep track of what you have accomplished or will soon accomplish (e.g., writing "anticipated graduation date"). Add items that you want to achieve, and it can serve as an itemized list of your goals. Get creative and write the full entry of something you plan to accomplish within five years. For example, create a position for "regional manager" and fill out the details of all the things you will have done as a regional manager. You can use the résumé, in short, as a motivational tool that leads toward self-actualization. In essence, this story can narrate the tale: "This is what I want to do." (Be sure not to confuse your actual accomplishments with your imagined ones.)

It is useful as a tool for *gainful employment*. In this résumé, which is the one you are likely more familiar with, you tell your audience, "This is why *you* need me." Notice the emphasis on *you*. This is not a story of why, in general, some company may want to hire you. It is written for a specific audience. As an employment tool, the résumé should be crafted as a response to a specific job opening. Translate your skills, knowledge, and experience into solutions for the employer. This means customizing your résumé and application letter for each application package.

An up-to-date résumé also reminds current employers about their employees' unique skills and experiences. It catalogs accomplishments and work completed at the company. Giving an up-to-date résumé to your manager or HR department can be a great way to keep decision-makers in the company informed about your relevance and importance.

Now that you know what purpose your résumé serves, apply the five canons of rhetoric to craft a document that contains the appropriate information. Because it is assumed that most readers are or will be job seekers, the following examples focus on finding a job. With a little imaginative effort, though, it should be easy to identify ways to practice each canon when using the résumé to show current employers how important you are to the company. For example, instead of using a position announcement as a guide, use the job description provided by your company.

Applying the Five Canons

In this section, you'll learn to apply the canons of invention, arrangement, style, memory, and delivery to the application process. This process includes evaluating the job description using the method of rhetorical criticism.

Invention.   As with any rhetorical artifact, spend time planning your approach to writing. This includes knowing unique arguments. Though you will certainly need to do some secondary research, including background investigation on the company and department to which you are applying, identify evidence you can include to support your argument that you're an optimal candidate. In other words, *know your skills*, *understand your audience*, and respond to the rhetorical situation by *analyzing the job description thoroughly*.

Know your skills and supporting evidence.   To identify what you will eventually put on your résumé, complete a "SWOT analysis." A SWOT analysis describes your personal <u>S</u>trengths and <u>W</u>eaknesses and, depending on the level of analysis you prefer, an assessment of the industry's, profession's, or company's <u>O</u>pportunities and <u>T</u>hreats. For example, you may have five years of experience working in the food service industry. If you apply for a management position with a restaurant, this is a personal strength. If, however, you know that there are people with 10 or 15 years of experience applying, or you're applying for a position in a non-food service industry, this fact may be a weakness. To conduct a SWOT analysis, consider following these steps:

1. Identify a specific professional or occupational field of interest.
2. Create a list of your *strengths*. List your skills and knowledge as well as your current and previous work, educational, and cocurricular activities. Also include your personal attributes and psychological characteristics that are considered positive (e.g., charismatic and motivated). This list should be generated by brainstorming.
3. Go back through your list and add specific details that demonstrate both how you obtained the skills and why they are relevant to the profession or company. For example, you may have "customer service experience" because you worked at Subway as a "sandwich artist." Specifically, however, you may have been given a special service award that would *demonstrate* that you are good at customer service. You may be an "experienced technical writer" because you've "written over 250 blog entries for small and large companies in the entertainment industry." Be sure to repeat this process for negative personal attributes and characteristics.
4. Mark items on your list that are relevant to your chosen field of interest or company, and rank them as most to least relevant.
5. Brainstorm a list of the skills, knowledge, and experiences required or preferred for entry or success in your field. Identify those that you can convincingly *demonstrate* as being part of your repertoire of knowledge or skills set. Items on the list that are important but which you do not convincingly posses point to your *weaknesses*. In addition,

honestly assess those personality traits and behaviors that could be considered negative in your profession (e.g., garrulous, nosy, and easily stressed).

6. Think about external trends and how they may impact your occupation or profession of choice. For example, are you going to need to obtain a master's degree? Because you do not currently have a master's degree, this is a weakness. But this is also a *threat* because it requires more time in school (an opportunity cost) and additional expenses. However, the location of a particular industry or corporate headquarter can be an *opportunity*. For example, if an industry happens to be centered in a city in which you want to live, this is an opportunity.

As you complete this exercise, consider both your short-terms needs (obtaining an entry-level position) and long-term desires (e.g., executive-level position or time for family). Be honest about what skills you have or will need to obtain to achieve your goals. You may need a Master's of Business Administration (MBA) degree if you aspire to be the manager of a bank; however, if you will be content working in the bank's customer relations department, you may not need it. A SWOT analysis of a profession is subjective. A threat to one person may be an opportunity for another. A weakness to one person may be an asset to another. Be serious, however, about context and trends. Certainly people without knowledge of how to read a financial statement can be successful executives, but success is more likely for those who can. If an industry is on the decline or saturated with high-quality candidates, these are threats to your potential for success.

The SWOT analysis is just one way to begin recalling your experiences and assessing your skills. If you haven't already done so, begin building a career portfolio. Set aside a box, drawer, or binder in which you can store all of your certificates and award, testimonials, work products (e.g., anything you've written in a professional context), or other relevant information (including articles in the media about your work and testimonials and references). Do the same for any electronic files and notes (be sure to back this file up). This information will undoubtedly be useful when you need to recall certain experiences, skills, or attributes. Maintain a bullet-point diary that lists and summarizes all of the items in your portfolio. This will make it easier for you to create customized résumés—just copy and paste.

Understand your audience. A résumé is a structured argument that uses a person's skills, education, employment history, and job qualifications as evidence. What is relevant evidence to one job search committee or recruiter may not be convincing to another, so you need to learn as much as you can about the individuals who are likely to review your résumé. Many recruiters and managers use the same social media that you do (e.g., Facebook, Twitter, LinkedIn), so you can learn a lot about them just from online content. Use a search engine to see if a recruiter or manager blogs about topics of interest or attends special conferences. As you conduct research about a profession, ask others what they consider important, and be sure to pay attention to popular conversations on professional websites. This will give you some insight into the trends of a profession and the needs of a company.

Most recruiters and managers are going to be very busy. Your résumé is not to get you the job, but to get you in the door. Appearing courteous of these individuals' time by avoiding unnecessary communication exchanges and keeping your résumé brief will send the message that you are conscious of their time—an unexpressed rhetorical argument with significant implications. A résumé should generate interest. It should not list everything you have ever done or flaunt all of your skills and abilities, just *some* of the relevant ones. A résumé will need to make an impression in about 30 seconds or less. If it does, it will be more thoroughly read with a handful of other applicants' résumés. Thus, you will want to keep your content short and make the document stylistically memorable. Today, your résumé may be screened electronically. This require a slightly different approach. One must consider using appropriate keywords strategically and creating a header with a summer of skills qualification. In some cases, it may even be appropriate creating a ASCII résumé (discussed later).

Analyze the job description.   Perhaps one of the best ways to know your audience and to keep a résumé and application letter relevant is to respond to the specifics of the job description. To analyze a job description, submit it to a rhetorical analysis. Recall, from Chapter 1, that rhetorical criticism is a systematic analysis of the symbols used in an artifact. Your analysis needn't be as thorough as one completed by an academic researcher, but reading into the job listing can elicit unique insights that become important. Appendix B demonstrates how a student used rhetorical criticism to transform a résumé and application letter into a specific argument. This appendix also shows the consulting process that transformed a client's first-draft résumé into a much better, though not perfect, document.

Figure 4.1, which is an unedited position announcement from a small vineyard in Washington, provides an example of a job description written by a small company for an entry-level position as a coordinator. This is a realistic opening for most first-time job seekers with a degree in communications or a related field. As a business document, the ad could use some minor work; however, it is generally written well and achieves the effect of promoting the business as a fun place to work and visit. (The company's website achieves this pathos as well; see **http://twomountainwinery.com**.)

As you rhetorically analyze the posting in Figure 4.1, make note of *patterns in word choices* as well as *descriptions that excite or concern you*. These provide clues that will help you decide whether the position is the right fit. This process will also help generate a list of questions to ask at an interview and give you material to include in a cover letter and résumé.

Patterns in word choice.   Notice, for example, that the position announcement uses the word "self-starter" twice. It would therefore be prudent to use the word "self-starter" somewhere in your résumé or application letter.

You can see that the advertisement mentions the word "sales" five times, but "marketing" only twice. Typically, a sales position is associated with establishing new clients through cold calls, travelling, retail interactions, and so on. Marketing is often associated with developing public relations or advertising campaigns. Though it is clear that social media management and advertisement design will be part of the position, the fact that the employee would only need

Great Opportunity with a Growing Company!!!

Tasting Room and Wine Club Coordinator

Our growing winery is searching for an energetic, engaging, upbeat, creative self-starter willing to take advantage of working freedom to join our team in the tasting room and to coordinate wine club activities while contributing to local and regional marketing efforts. Responsibilities include retail wine sales, merchandise ordering and stocking, creating fun and engaging events for our wine club, fulfilling all wine club orders, maintaining our reputation as a fun and friendly winery, and most importantly HAVING A BLAST AT WORK! Think you are just the person? We would love to hear from you. Please send a resume and cover letter to [redacted] Offering competitive wages, commission, and a FANTASTIC opportunity to learn and contribute to the growth of an emerging brand all while having a kick-ass time in a dynamic, fast-paced industry. We are interested in a long-term relationship--one-month stands need not apply.

Required Skills/Experience:
- Engaging, outgoing personality
- Great attitude
- Flexibility of mind, body, spirit, and work working hours
- Basic computer ad Microsoft Office skills
- Ability to do daily sales reconciliation. Yes, this means mathematics.
- Strong communication skills-both written and oral
- Willingness and ability to learn publishing program
- Ability to work in a fast-paced environment
- Ability to lift 40 pounds
- Impeccable organizational and planning skills
- Ability to be a self-starter
- Retail/sales experience a plus
- Must like dogs . . . Especially those which are needy and slightly overweight

Responsibilities
1. Tasting Room
a. Retail Sales
b. Daily Sales Reconciliation
c. Ordering, pricing, and maintaining inventory of gift shop items
d. Stocking shelves
e. Maintaining a fun and entertaining retail environment
f. Selling, selling, selling lots of wine

2. Wine Club
a. Relationship management with Club members
b. Club event planning
c. Shipment processing and fulfillment
d. Growing membership
e. Creating innovative and creative incentives for the members

3. Various Marketing Opportunities

Company Name: Two Mountain Winery
Location: Zillah
Available: Immediately. Full Time.
Posted: 10/10/10

Figure 4.1. An example of a job advertisement perfect for student graduating with a communications or other liberal arts degree. *(Copyright © 2010 by Two Mountain Winery. Reprinted by permission.)*

to have a "willingness and ability to learn" publishing programs suggests that the focus is more on in-person sales than creating advertisements and brochures. Other giveaways are the clustering of "retail" next to "sales" three times, and the last bullet point under responsibilities: "Selling, selling, selling lots of wine." If you do not have sales experience, this is obviously a weakness. Applicants should emphasize their sales or retail experiences in the application letter and résumé, or the application will probably receive less attention. Obviously, if a sales position does not appeal to an applicant, he or she should look for another job.

Other words, when taken together, also suggest a few things about the position. It seems that a lot of time will be spent interacting with customers and doing physical work. The emphasis in the position announcement is on "energetic" people who can work in a "fast-paced" environment [mentioned twice] and "lift 40 pounds." Responsibilities include "stocking shelves" and "Ordering, pricing, and maintaining inventory of gift shop items." In short, emphasizing any inventory management experience would be persuasive. It may not be intuitive to a potential employer that many McDonald's employees are responsible for cataloging inventory loss, so help résumé readers understand examples with descriptions. The advertised position seems to be more retail than corporate, so one had better like "working the cash register," or this position, based upon information in the advertisement, is not likely to be a good fit.

Comments that excite and concern. In addition to the comments in an ad that provide a general sense of what types of information to include in a résumé, look for statements that can be used to help you decide whether the position is right. These references can also help craft questions for further clarification during the interview stage. Note, for example, that there seems to be a tension between "freedom" and having a "kick-ass time" and "responsibility" and "fast-paced environment" (read: stressful). There are a lot of duties listed (perhaps too many?) and an undertone that the employee will be told to do many different things (and he or she better maintain a good attitude about it). Applicants may want to ask if the position has been previously filled or whether it is new. If it was previously filled, the emphasis on attitude may be written in response to the bad relationship the company had with a particular employee. By clarifying this point in the interview, applicants will gain context for their interpretation and decision-making. The former employee, if the company had one, certainly may have been a bad apple; however, she or he may have experienced burned out.

The emphasis on selling may mean that job performance will be evaluated solely on sales figures, even though there are other responsibilities that may make it hard to focus on this job function. If the position is being filled for the first time, be hesitant. Owners and managers may not have realistic expectations and they may not deal well with delegating responsibility. Of course, an interview can clarify these things. The hired applicant can also ask the company to clarify job performance review in the employment agreement in order to mitigate misunderstanding.

Certain adjective choices also should make applicants pause. One doesn't need just organizational skills, but *impeccable* organizational skills. The emphasis on "selling," "flexibility," and "impeccable" should make one wonder if there is a potentially hostile or micromanaged environment underlying the rhetorical façade of fun and freedom. Also, there may be differences of opinion between employees and owners. In co-owned businesses, especially, the owners may themselves disagree about what constitutes "urgent matters." This could lead to confusing directives or to getting trapped in a partnership feud.

There are many things to be excited about, of course, in this job description. The overall tone of the description is seemingly positive and the rhetor, most likely an owner or manager, seems to have an easy-going attitude and sense of humor. The posting emphasizes hard work, but also play (and wine). As noted in chapter 1, this job description should get candidates excited.

Having completed an analysis, draw upon what you initially found to help craft a résumé and application letter. For example, the references to self-starter, sales, the "needy dog," and personal ads provide the perfect set-up to grab the recruiter's attention:

- As a self-starter with six years' sales and marketing experience, a desire to establish a career in a rural location, and who loves any dog, especially needy ones, I think that you've met your long-term match.

During the invention stage, consider what media and format is best for the specific job announcement. You will likely have to produce your résumé in several formats and distribute it using multiple media. This chapter generally focuses on the production of the traditional printed résumé. Produce video résumé and website portfolios with a broad audience in mind.

Arrangement. After you know what content and materials you will use in the résumé, arrange the content. Fortunately, there are a variety of formats and templates to follow. You will be introduced to six types of résumés in this section. For first-time job seekers with limited experience, the most useful format is a combination of résumé types (discussed in the next section) that borrows elements from the chronological and functional organizational patterns. No matter the format, all résumés have a variety of elements in common. Some of these items, however, are disputed.

Common and disputed elements. Many items on a résumé are practical, like contact information. However, some items may not be necessary and, therefore, take up precious résumé "real estate." Résumé writing is more art than science, so résumé advisors often disagree about certain features, such as whether objective statements are needed. Generally, however, the following is the basic information you should include in your résumé:

- Header: your name, address, email address, and phone number.
- A strong profile section detailing the scope of your experience and areas of proficiency.
- Reverse chronological employment history emphasizing achievements over the past 10-to-15 years.
- Education (new grads may put this at the top).

It is ultimately up to you to decide what your résumé should include or exclude. Consider foremost how information will be perceived by an audience. To keep abreast of current trends in résumé writing, consider subscribing to the Résumé Writers' Digest (**http://rwdigest.com**). The résumés in Figures 4.2 and 4.3 describe the layout of some of these items. Appendix B provides a more detailed discussion of each of these items and contains additional examples.

Résumé formats. There are six commonly used types of résumés: chronological, functional, electronic, mini, interactive, and video. This section provides a brief explanation of when to use each type. The Internet is loaded with examples of each type of résumé. Figures 4.2 and 4.3 provide examples of chronological and functional (hybrid) résumés, respectively. They are real examples, and neither résumé is ideal. Ask yourself what works and does not work in each example and discuss this with your classmates. These résumés, along with the examples in Appendix B, were developed during consulting sessions. Each résumé went through several revisions before arriving at the state published here. Writing résumés is difficult. In the

Name Redacted
2100 W. Hill Lane
City, TX 12345
000-000-000 ext. 0000
Name.Redacted@Email.Com

Profile

Solid background in commercial insurance claims investigation, coverage analysis, and damage evaluation, with strong emphasis in arbitration, negotiation, dispute resolution and litigation management. Developed and led seminars and training courses for adjuster continuing education.

Experience

Liberty Mutual Group – Irving, TX
Technical Claims Specialist, 06/11 to current

- Review, analyze, and process complex claims consistent with policy and legal requirements.

Outcomes:

- Plan and conduct claims investigations to analyze and confirm coverage and to determine liability and compensability of damages
- Coordinate litigation activities associated with assigned claims to ensure a timely and cost-effective resolution.

Liberty Mutual Group – Irving, TX
Sr. Claims Consultant, 03/00 to 06/11

- Analyzed claims to determine company liability; made approval/denial decisions and negotiated settlements with claimants in accordance with policy provisions. Collaborated with insurance agents and policyholders to investigate claims and resolve claims issues. Provided technical guidance to team members. Analyzed claims data to identify trends in frequency and severity of losses. Managed team in absence of team manager.

Outcomes:

- Specialization in Commercial Trucking claims investigation, including cargo losses from March 2008-June 2011.
- Investigated and negotiated fair settlements on hundreds of files a year.
- Reviewed files for claims protocol compliance and issued payments up to $75,000 for loss payee and $25,000 loss expense.
- Completed 45-day case reviews to provide technical guidance of business-market protocols.
- Presented claims reviews to commercial market policyholders.
- Developed and presented topics regarding arbitration and negotiation training for the AL Business Market Claims.
- Developed and presented course material on cross-cultural communication and dispute resolution.
- Used property damage releases to limit loss exposure.
- Recipient of numerous awards for contributions to the success of the Dedicated Trucking Unit.

Page 1 of 2

Figure 4.2. Example of a chronological résumé, which is useful for people with significant experience. *(Copyright © 2010 by Erin E. Reprinted by permission.)*

Other relevant experience
Arbiter, Arbitration Forums, 12/06 to current
- Certified arbiter in property, med pay, special, and auto subrogation
- Work as third party neutral to resolve insurance subrogation disputes
- Utilize claims and legal knowledge to make decisions and arbitration judgments

Mediator, Arbitrator, ADR Consultant, 10/06 to current
- Work as a third party neutral to assist disputants in resolving their claims against each other
- Conducted over 43 mediations and negotiations at Southern Methodist University Center for Dispute Resolution
- Completed over 160 hours of training in mediation, arbitration and negotiation
- Completed course work in team building and executive coaching and dispute systems design for corporations
- Public speaker regarding Conflict Management and Alternative Dispute Resolution

Education
Southern Methodist University – Dallas, TX
Master of Arts, Dispute Resolution

University of Wyoming – Laramie, WY
Bachelor of Arts, Criminal Justice
Bachelor of Arts, Humanities/Fine Arts

Memberships
Southwestern Conflict Resolution Network
World Affairs Council, Member
American Bar Association, Section for Dispute Resolution

Prof. Licenses
Property & Casualty Adjuster
Texas Certified Mediator
Certified Life Coach

Figure 4.2.   Example of a chronological résumé, which is useful for people with significant experience. *(continued)*

<u>**Name Redacted**</u>   LinkedIn: tinyulrgoeshere   (000) 000.0000
                              Skype: Name1234   *name@someemail.com*

<u>Employment History</u>

2007 – 2010	**Resident Advisor**	Colorado Mesa University	Grand Junction, CO
2007 – 2010	**Project Assistant (Summer)**	McLane	Temple, TX
2004 – 2007	**Owner**	M.C. Mobile Entertainment	Park City, UT
2003 – 2007	**Shift Manager**	McDonald's	Park City, UT

<u>Education</u>

Colorado Mesa University – Grand Junction, CO   December 2010
Bachelor of Business Administration: Hospitality Management, GPA: 3.98
Considerable coursework in communication

<u>Areas of Effectiveness and Transferable Skills</u>

Sales / Management
- Performed every function of small business management, including writing a business plan, persuading a bank for a $6000 loan, forecasting sales, budgeting, and marketing. Sold business for substantial profit.
- Mastered the art of upselling and cross-selling while working for McDonald's. Completed two levels of the official McDonald's management training program in Denver, Colorado.
- Planned and implemented social, recreational, cultural, and educational programming for over 140 residents while overseeing employees and a facility budget; as well as policy enforcement, conflict resolution, and diversity issues in a college residential facility.
- Collected over $400,000 in overdue payments from the Army/Air Force Exchange Services and facilitated order delivery for Yum! Brands (Taco Bell, Pizza Hut, KFC) while working for McLane as a temporary, summer employee.

Organizing / Planning
- Balanced courses, co-curricular activities, full-time employment, and personal wellness to graduate in seven semesters with a 3.98 GPA.
- Scheduled events, coordinated activities, and delegated responsibility for a successful bicycle rodeo and helmet awareness campaign for children in Fruita, Colorado.
- Participated in the planning, development, and implementation of a large, regional conference for the Intermountain Affiliate of Colleges and University Residence Halls.

Communication / Public Relations
- Designed, coded (using CSS), and optimized multiple websites for three small businesses.
- Produced and distributed press releases, brochures, cards, posters, and social media messages as part of an integrated marketing campaign for a new venture.
- Completed numerous college speech courses, specifically in public speaking, marketing communication, and conflict resolution.
- Presented numerous leadership and management workshops to various organizations; was awarded overall best presenter for work at regional and national conferences.

Current Volunteer Work: Big Brothers Big Sisters; Humane Society

Figure 4.3.   Example of a functional résumé. Useful when rhetor needs to emphasize skills.

examples in Appendix B, look at the originals and revisions, along with some of the commentary to determine what seems to work and not work.

Chronological. A chronological résumé lists work history by date. Use this format when:

- You have an extensive work history.
- You want to highlight specific accomplishments related to specific jobs.
- You have held a single position for a long time (especially if it is impressive).
- You have technical, professional, and organizational *knowledge* relevant to the available position.
- You want to update sources.
- You are being recruited.

Functional. A functional résumé emphasizes transferrable skills and experience. Use this format when:

- You don't have an extensive work history, are changing careers, or have a gap in employment.
- You have held several positions or worked for several different companies over a short period of time.
- You have many broad experiences from a variety of sources.
- You are applying for a job that requires a *bricoleur* (a "jack-or-jane-of-various-trades").
- You have technical, professional, and organizational skills fairly relevant to the available position.

Note: A hybrid (or combination) résumé utilizes features of both the chronological and functional résumé (see Figure 4.3). The hybrid résumé is a great tool for most recent graduates who have limited work experience.

Electronic. An electronic résumé emphasizes either work history or transferrable skills. Use this format when:

- You are applying to a company that requests this format (or a company with older technology).
- You are applying to a large company or for a position with an anticipated large applicant pool.
- You want to highlight key words.

Note the following key considerations:

- Left-justify all information, including headings (do not center them).
- Eliminate bullets and replace with an ASCII characters (* or -).

- Avoid using tabs.
- Do not group too much information together.
- Insert spaces between headings.

Mini.   The mini résumé summarizes career highlights and qualifications. Use this format when:

- You are asked to provide a brief summary of qualifications.
- You are networking.
- You are seeking references and referrals.
- You want to provide more information than a traditional business card, but less information than a full-length résumé. (Note that when you use a table-tent style business card, the mini résumé can be listed on the backside of the card.)

Interactive.   An interactive résumé emphasizes skills, experiences, work products, and personal brand. Use this format when:

- You are applying for positions in "creative fields."
- You are a freelancer or entrepreneur.
- You want to exhibit your work.
- You want others to find you.

Video.   A video résumé emphasizes key points verbally and visually. Use this format when:

- You are applying for positions in "creative fields."
- You are applying to a company's request for this format.
- You want to advertise yourself.
- You feel like you will not be discriminated against.

It is likely that you will use a variety of résumé formats during your working life. Regardless of which format you choose, no one résumé will work for all positions. Applying for jobs can be exhausting, but avoid the temptation to use a template résumé and application letter. A résumé is a rhetorical artifact. It requires a strong argument based on your analysis of another's rhetoric (position announcement), audience analysis (employer), and rhetorical situation (desire to obtain a specific job). You must understand the situation and fitting response (invention), choose an organizational pattern that is suitable (arrangement), and use arguments that appeal to ethos, pathos, and logos (style). The latter point is addressed next.

Style.   As a written document, the effectiveness of a standard résumé is largely dependent on style. Drawing upon the classic appeals—which means being ethical, addressing anticipated concerns, and choosing the right words and phrases—will make your résumé more effective. This section provides tips that will help improve your résumé in all of these three areas.

Ethos.   A résumé should reflect your skills and abilities. Do not overstate what you can do or fabricate information. According to one study, nearly one of every two résumés have some kind of misrepresentation (see IOMA, 2006). Some applicants buy fake diplomas or hire firms who fabricate information and pose as legitimate references (see Chandrasekaran, 2004). This is no way, of course, to earn professional credibility. In today's social media environment, where many documents get shared online, a single instance of misrepresentation can be hard to eliminate. If you are unsure whether your creative descriptions are misrepresentations, seek advice from career counselors or other professionals in the field. A rule of thumb to follow: When in doubt—leave it out.

Pathos.   Your résumé should use words and phrases that evoke emotion and provoke inquiry. If you sound interesting, a recruiter will want to hear more and will request an interview. Write your résumé using the *simple and direct style* described in Chapter 2. Write in the first person when necessary, but generally avoid the word *I*. Overusing personal pronouns in a résumé creates repetitious and wordy documents. Also, reviewers may conclude that the applicant is a self-involved egomaniac. Instead, use action verbs, such as those in Table 4.1.

"Are you sure your resume is accurate?"

(Image © Cartoonresource, 2012. Used under license from Shutterstock, Inc.)

Table 4.1   Useful action verbs.

Accelerated	Earned	Launched	Revised
Accomplished	Edited	Lectured	Revitalized
Achieved	Effected	Led	Saved
Adapted	Eliminated		Scheduled
Administered	Enabled	Maintained	Screened
Advised	Energized	Managed	Served
Analyzed	Established	Mastered	Set up
Arranged	Evaluated	Met with	Simplified
Assembled	Expanded	Motivated	Sold
	Expedited	Negotiated	Solved
Balanced			Standardized
Billed	Facilitated	Operated	Steered
Blazed	Forecasted	Optimized	Strengthened
Built	Found	Orchestrated	Structured
		Ordered	Supervised
Carried out	Gained	Organized	Supported
Channeled	Gathered	Originated	Systematized
Collected	Generated	Oversaw	
Communicated	Graded		Taught
Compiled	Graduated	Participated	Tested
Completed		Performed	Trained
Conceived	Handled	Planned	Transformed
Conducted	Hired	Prepared	Translated
Contracted		Presented	Tripled
Controlled	Implemented	Produced	Typed
Coordinated	Improved	Programmed	
Counseled	Increased	Proved	Underwrote
Created	Influenced	Provided	Updated
Cut	Initiated	Published	Upgraded
	Innovated	Purchased	Used
Delegated	Inspected		
Demonstrated	Installed	Recommended	Won
Designed	Instituted	Recruited	Wrote
Determined	Instructed	Reduced	
Developed	Interpreted	Reinforced	
Directed	Interviewed	Represented	
Dispatched	Introduced	Researched	
Distributed	Invented	Resolved	
Documented	Issued	Reviewed	

Take time to craft unique statements that say something unique about you and capture the essence of what you've accomplished. For example, students in an entrepreneurship and communication course at the University of Montana did a service-learning project with the Prison Entrepreneurship Program (**http://pep.org**). They worked as business plan advisors for men incarcerated in a Texas prison. Some of the students served as liaisons for their three-person teams. From the following list of statements, they could choose or modify one to put in their functional résumés under a section "leadership skills" or "mentoring skills":

- Provided business plan advising to carefully selected and proven leaders with high potential for societal impact while serving as a mentor for the internationally recognized Prison Entrepreneurship Program.
- As team liaison, coordinated communication between multiple parties during a four-month project while volunteering for the nonprofit organization Prison Entrepreneurship Program.
- Mentored an at-risk individual as part of a team-based service learning project while attending the University of Montana. Main responsibilities included conducting business research and providing grammatical feedback.

Notice that in each of the above statements, with some variation, there is a simple formula:

- *"In situation X, I did Y (action), which led to Z (skill or accomplishment)."*

This formula is recommended as the underlying order for each bullet point.

As you craft a résumé, keep in mind that effective, not diverse, word choice is what really appeals to hiring managers. Instead of saying "assisted," for example, try to be more specific about what you did while assisting. If you helped a faculty advisor research materials on communication disorders using library databases, then say "researched communication disorders for an academic researcher." This is much more impressive sounding and illustrates a specific action that demonstrates your transferrable skills—you know how to research. Be sure to avoid the common résumé blunders described in Table 4.2.

Logos. Your résumé needs to make sense to potential employers. Following with the interpretive and narrative approach of this book, consider what included and excluded information reveals. For applicants with a gap between jobs, for example, it is going to be obvious if they provide dates of employment with each position. Be creative (e.g., write length of time with employers rather than range of years employed) or directly address the situation in the application letter. The following is a list of common concerns and how to address them.

- **Frequent job changes.** If the jobs are similar or related, group them under a single heading (e.g., restaurant experience). If the job changes are a result of circumstances beyond your control, add descriptors (e.g., layoff due to downsizing).

Table 4.2 Common résumé blunders

1. Being too focused on job duties and responsibilities. Focus on your accomplishments, not your prosaic activities.

2. Misusing or overusing words like ambitious, empower, motivated, leveraged, incubated, and facilitated.

3. Using an objective statement instead of headlines. Instead of "Highly motivated professional seeking entry-level technology position," write in bold font "Microsoft Certified Computer Technician."

4. Not making a hard sell in a summary or header section.

5. Not peppering the résumé with key words. Use the position announcement to create keyword density.

6. Providing a résumé that is too long or too short. If you have a lot of relevant experience, a two-page résumé is appropriate. If you are a neophyte, try to keep it to one page.

7. Using personal pronouns and articles. Instead of "I developed a new product . . . ," write "Developed a new product. . . ."

8. Listing irrelevant information. This should not happen if you think of your résumé as a rhetorical artifact.

9. Using a functional résumé when you have an excellent career history.

10. Referring to your references. Remember, everyone expects that you'll have references available when requested. You needn't write this.

11. Typos. It is not that people are so pretentious that they don't make writing mistakes themselves. But something as important as a résumé should demonstrate near-perfect writing.

- **Gaps in work history.** List relevant activities completed during these gaps (e.g., volunteer work). If the information could disclose information that is legally contentious (e.g., you were out of work while raising a child), try to avoid listing dates of employment and instead provide the number of years employed at each position.

- **Inexperience.** Focus on education and training and cocurricular activities that created relevant skills required to succeed in the position advertised. Use a functional résumé.

- **Over-qualification.** Focus on only those skills that are relevant to the position. Do not list degrees or certifications that are not required for the position.

- **Criminal record.** Leave this off the résumé; however, it may be required to list on a job application (and you are required by law to provide this information if asked). If you suspect a background check, then own up to your incarceration or probation in the application letter and focus on your rehabilitation. Gain connections through volunteer work and community service to obtain references (perhaps include a letter from a person with ethos—a police officer, a judge, or church leader). Contact people who have found gainful employment following similar circumstances.

The above list is not comprehensive, just enough to get you started. Keep current with résumé writing trends and adapt your résumé to fit the specific rhetorical situation.

Delivery/memory.   Applying this canon to the résumé involves its production and distribution. To print and mail a résumé, use professional résumé paper, place documents in a 9″ × 12″ envelope, and mail in a U.S. Postal Service priority flat-rate envelope.

Today, companies use a variety of application tracking systems, databases, and software to scan applicant materials and sort them based on predetermined criteria. It is more likely, therefore, that you will produce a variety of résumés in multiple media and submit them electronically rather than through the mail or by fax. Traditional résumés, like those in Figures 4.2 and 4.3, are still the most commonly used design; however, they are often submitted by email or uploaded to websites.

To maintain a consistent design when transporting and sharing electronically, submit portable document format (PDF) files. Newer versions of most office suites allow users to save documents in PDF. If your word processing software does not allow you to save as PDF, then find a computer at a public or university library that has a professional version of Adobe Acrobat installed, or download a free version of PrimoPDF (from **http://primopdf.com**). Some companies require résumés in a scannable format. In this case, produce a scanner-friendly résumé by including a keyword summary at the top of the document and avoid using special characters (such as bullets), lines, and more than one font. If you need to produce this type of résumé, search online for examples. Search for "plain-text (ASCII) résumés," which are designed specifically for online distribution. Typically, you will want to save ASCII documents with a .txt extension.

To create an *online résumé* (also referred to as e-portfolios or social media résumés), you will need to know something about web design. While being able to code websites in CSS (cascading style sheets) or HTML (hypertext markup language) is useful, there are a variety of webhosting companies that offer basic, user-friendly templates. Check out, for example, **http://visualcv.com**, **www.scribd.com**, **http://carbonmade.com**, and **http://issuu.com**. Some of these sites convert PDF files into portfolio-style magazines or create HTML text that can be used to embed these documents into other websites. Once uploaded, you can include links to your résumé or portfolio by including a hyperlink (URL) in any artifact (e.g., printed résumé, website, and business card) or social media. A web-based résumé can be single or multiple pages. Shorten links by using a URL shorteners, such as **http.//goo.gl**, **http://tinyurl.com**, **http://tiny.cc**, or **http://bit.ly**.

Once created, a video résumé can be distributed easily. Upload the video to sites such as **www.youtube.com** or **http://vimeo.com**. As with e-portfolios, once uploaded, use the automatic HTML code generators to create code that can be used to embed the videos into other sites, such as a personal webpage. Provide links to your video résumé on social media sites. Remember to be cautious about using video résumés, as these can reveal discriminatory information (e.g., age, race, sex, and body type).

Companies posting job advertisements will, of course, explain how to submit materials. Remember to always follow companies' directives. In the eyes of recruiters, no applicant is special until he or she is hired. Do not violate the rules of a job posting. If the advertisement states, for example, "no phone calls," then do not call the company. To clarify something, get creative. Seek advice from someone familiar with the company, a career counselor, or someone with extensive job search experience (e.g., a family member, friend, or advisor).

Writing the Application Letter

Much of the previous discussion also applies to the design and distribution of application letters. *Application letters* support and add to the résumé and require other specific considerations. The application letter, also frequently called a *cover letter*, is similar to a sales letter—you pitch yourself as the best candidate for the job. The application letter translates how skills, abilities, and knowledge, as described in the résumé, relate to the job. The successful application letter accomplishes four goals: 1) it specifies which position applicants are applying for and why; 2) it catches readers' attention and gets them primed and excited to read the résumé; 3) it indicates how the content described in the résumé matches the position advertised; and 4) it requests an interview and opens an opportunity for further inquiry.

Writing an application letter is easy. Use the position announcement as a guide. The application letter should address the items discussed in the job advertisement and, in most circumstances, repeat its language and tone. The three main sections of an application letter are the salutation and opening, body, and closing. Using the job description for the tasting room and wine coordinator in Figure 4.1, the following sections describe each part of the letter in detail.

Salutation and Opening

If the name of a specific individual is provided, write your letter directly to him or her. If no name is provided, check the company's website, social networking sites, and people in your network familiar with the company to see if you can find a name. If you are not certain to whom the letter should be addressed, use a generic salutation: "Dear Members of the Hiring Committee." Alternatively, you can use a subject line and leave out a salutation, or vice versa. In the subject line, include the position to which you are applying.

In the introductory paragraph, provide context by indicating how you heard about a position. If you do not have a subject line that provides the job title, name the specific job title or area. If you were referred by someone, be sure to mention his or her name. Show enthusiasm by explaining what prompted you to apply. Indicate that you know something about the organization. Be sure to provide a preview, which is the basic outline of the major points discussed in the letter. Drawing upon the job description for inspiration, the initial paragraph in the cover letter for the wine coordinator position could read:

111 Applicant Address
City, ST 12345
September 22, 20XX

Mathew and Patrick Rawn
Two Mountain Winery
2151 Cheyne Road
Zillah, WA 95953

Subject: Tasting Room and Wine Club Coordinator Opening

In an advertisement on Monster.com, you indicate you a looking for a long-term relationship with someone who would like to join your family business. As a self-starter with six years' sales and marketing experience, a desire to establish a career in a rural location, and who loves any dog, especially basset hounds and yellow labs, I think you've met your long-term match. I have enclosed my résumé, which highlights my relevant transferrable skills. I hope that my education, work history, and previous volunteer activities, which I briefly highlight below, will inspire you to invite me for an interview.

Obviously, the introductory paragraph, especially the preview, would change depending on the background of the applicant. Notice that the introductory paragraph does not mention that the applicant likes wine. This is wise for at least two reasons. First, it is likely that most applicants will mention this fact. The applicant will come across as unoriginal—just another applicant stating the obvious. Second, the applicant doesn't want appear to be a "lush." The introduction does, however, mention basset hounds and yellow labs. The company's website features these breeds, so it shows that the applicant did some research.

Body

In the middle paragraphs, organize content based on the preview. Be descriptive. Don't *tell* readers that you are qualified, *show* them with examples. Limit each paragraph to just one point, which is stated in a topic sentence. In some cases, create a list of bullets that are borrowed, with some modification, from the résumé. Indicate how you can make a contribution to the company and highlight your achievements. Refer to the résumé (only if you do not do so in the opening or closing), but do not summarize it. Continuing with our example, the applicant might write:

I recently graduated from the University of Montana with a degree in Communication Studies. The following are relevant courses that I can draw upon to fulfill the primary goals of the position: Public Relations, Persuasion, Advanced Public Speaking, Organizational Communication, and Entrepreneurship and Communication. To reconcile accounts and manage inventory, I will draw on my Management courses in Marketing, Finance, Accounting, and Inventory Control. To stay flexible in mind, body, and spirit while lifting 40 pounds, I will utilize my skills I picked up in cocurricular yoga classes.

My work experience includes two years as a part-time telemarketer for a large cellular company, three years' sales and marketing experience for a wine and cheese club gift store, and one year as a fundraiser and marketing assistant for a foundation. These experiences have prepared me for sales in a growing industry. I have learned techniques to stay motivated and, as a result, I have never missed a quarterly sales target set by my employers.

I have extensive volunteer experience, which demonstrates my willingness to be a self-starter. If you call the Humane Society of Western Montana and speak with Jane Doe, you will learn that I have a fun, engaging, and outgoing personality. I also volunteered with Big Brothers Big Sisters and the Zootown Arts Community Center, the latter of which put me in touch with sophisticated wine drinkers on a regular basis.

Notice that in this body, the topic sentence follows the format indicated in the opening paragraph. Each paragraph addresses a single topic and offers examples that are relevant to the position. In addition to drawing upon the job description, there are notes that indicate the applicant has visited the company's website. While the paragraphs border on the lengthy side, employers will see that the applicant made a significant effort to translate his or her experiences for readers. It is important to be concise, but it is more important to make connections for readers.

Closing

The closing is the shortest paragraph. In the final paragraph, request an interview. Include your phone number and email address so readers know how to contact you. If appropriate, indicate you are available for a Skype interview and provide your handle. If not discouraged in the job posting, provide an indication that you will follow up the correspondence with an email or phone call, for example, "If I do not hear from you by [date], I will contact you to check the status of my application." End with a positive statement and thank readers for their time. (Remember to proofread your letter carefully. Errors can give employers the impression you lack writing skills or that you are careless.)

The closing may sound a bit more business-like than the rest of the letter. You want to leave an impression that you are serious about the position. Figure 4.4 provides an alternative example and design.

I look forward to learning more about your company during an interview, which will give you an opportunity to observe my superb verbal communication skills. I can be reached by email (your.name@ymail.com), phone (000.000.0000), or Skype (SkypeUsername).Thank you for your consideration.

Sincerely,

Name

name@someemail.com   September 22, 20XX
(000) 000.0000
LinkedIn: tinyurl
Skype: Name1234

Mathew and Patrick Rawn
Two Mountain Winery
2151 Cheyne Road
Zillah, WA 95953

Dear Mathew and Patrick:

In response to the Tasting Room and Wine Club Coordinator position advertised on Monster.com (9.18.20--), I am submitting my résumé. I hope that my diverse employment history, education in hospitality management, and sales experience are sufficient for the available position.

As you will see on my enclosed résumé, I am a self-starter, entrepreneurial, motivated, and committed to long-term employment with organizations. I also enjoy working in fast-paced environments. Because I have completed a comprehensive management-training program with McDonald's (Denver, Colorado), I will bring a strong understanding of inventory management to your operation.

While receiving my degree in hospitality management, I worked two jobs and maintained a high grade point average. As reflected on my LinkedIn account and demonstrated by my co-curricular involvement in business associations, I have a large network of contacts with whom to develop a strong sales network.

In total, I have four years of business management, marketing, and sales experience. Some of my experiences involve:

- Managing a small business, including forecasting sales, budgeting, and marketing.
- Using upselling and cross-selling techniques to increase marginal profits on orders.
- Coding websites according to international (W3C) web standards.
- Optimizing company websites for improved search engine ranking.
- Writing press releases, brochures, cards, posters, and social media messages as part of an integrated marketing campaign for a new venture.

I would be happy to discuss my résumé and other qualifications in an interview at your convenience. Please telephone me at 000.000.0000, Skype me at Name1234, or email me at name@someemail.com. I look forward to talking with you.

Sincerely,

Full Name

Figure 4.4.   Example of an application letter.

Speaking: Conversations and Interviews

There are two situations that involve speaking about a résumé, each representing a different phase of the interview process. For lack of a better term, the first is "conversations." The second phase is interviews.

Conversations

When you meet with a recruiter for the first time, at a job fair, for example, engage in a brief conversation. It is important that you are prepared but seem at ease speaking extemporaneously. Don't be hasty; if possible, observe how others interact with recruiters before you approach them. This will let you know recruiters' preferred style of conversation. For example, do they expect a résumé immediately or toward the end of the conversation? When approaching recruiters, shake hands firmly while looking them in the eyes. Say your name and give them your "elevator pitch." This pitch is so named because it would be brief enough to get through it in the time it takes an elevator to go up or down a few floors. It is a brief introduction that highlights your objective. If, for example, you are interested in a specific job, the introductory paragraph for your application letter would be effective. It is likely, however, that you will not yet have written an application letter, so be sure to do your homework on the company, position, and profession. Write some notes and practice the brief, 30-second speech on your education, background, and career objectives. Recruiters use these initial interactions as part of the *screening stage*.

An effective pitch is brief, descriptive, and states something specific about the company (which requires only minor modification when speaking to representatives from different companies at a fair):

> I will graduate in May. I am looking for entry-level sales positions in the renewable-energy markets or with ambitious companies in other industries that will be able to utilize my degrees in organizational communication and biology. I have two years of summer internship experience with a large biodiesel company. I worked both in the lab as a technician and in the field as a sales representative, so I know a bit about products in this market. As my résumé indicates, I have strong communication and leadership skills. This will be valuable to a company like yours, which seeks [insert two or three points about a specific company].

Other situations in which you may find yourself engaged in conversations include follow-up calls, dinners, and other brief interludes during formal interviews. Always assume that your conversations are being evaluated. Before calling, figure out what you are going to say so you sound focused. During dinners, use proper etiquette and consider how your behaviors will be interpreted. When moving between offices or areas, use the time to ask questions about the company to show your interest.

Interviews

The employment interview is a formal meeting that involves an exchange of information between candidates and employers. The employer's objective is to hire a talented candidate who will fit culturally with the organization. The candidate's objective is to determine if the company is the right fit for his or her career goals and objectives.

The interview process follows three stages: screening, selection, and negotiation. During the *screening stage*, the organization filters out applicants who are not a good fit for the company. Of course, recruiters may have prescreened candidates during conversations at job fairs or other recruiting contexts. Screening can take place in a variety of places. For example, if you make an impression during the conversation or your résumé stands out, a recruiter may invite you back later in the day for a brief interview. Applicants may be screened by telephone or by Skype or another Voice over Internet Protocol (VOIP) program. Some large companies use computer-based programs that record responses to computerized questions (these aren't that common, though). Remember that time is limited in screening interviews, so keep answers short. While speaking by phone or by VOIP, find a location free from interruptions and, if video is used, sit against a blank white wall or sheet.

The *selection stage* helps organizations find the best candidates. Usually a small number of candidates are invited for a longer interview. If the position is mid- or high-tier, this process could take several weeks and involve multiple interviews. For most entry-level positions, however, these interviews consist of a half-hour to hour-long interview. During these interviews, show keen interest in the job, explain how your skills will be valuable to the company (use your experiences and knowledge as evidence to support your claims), listen attentively, and ask insightful questions. Prepare in advance for the interview by writing notes (e.g., speaking points) and questions, researching the company and backgrounds of individuals with whom you may speak, and practicing answers to anticipated questions.

The *negotiation stage* occurs after the company selects top candidates and is ready to make job offers. There may be one final review by top executives, but in most cases this is mere formality. Sometimes applicants receive a job offer on the spot or within a few weeks of the selection interview. At this point the company will try to impress upon an applicant the benefits of the organization. This is when an applicant should negotiate salary and benefits. While most people focus on salary, consider negotiating for other things that companies may be willing to consider, especially if they seem inflexible on salary. In place of salary, for example, negotiate for parking privileges, additional vacation time, start-up funds (e.g., money to purchase specific equipment for your needs), or a shorter probationary period.

Common types of interviews. There are a variety of types of interviews, each serving a different purpose. The *structured interview* involves asking a series of the same questions to each candidate. The purpose of this type of interview is to screen candidates by ensuring they meet the basic job criteria. Because the questions are standardized, anyone from the organization can technically conduct the interview and record responses. The process is somewhat more objective, since candidates' responses can be compared. Organizationally, these types of questions formalize the process and reduce the chance that recruiters will ask illegal questions.

Open-ended (unstructured) interviews involve asking question adapted to the situation, candidate materials, and previous answers and questions. These types of questions give interviewers an opportunity to better understand the candidate's claims in his or her application materials. Recruiters conduct a rhetorical analysis of the applicants' materials, then modify questions to address specific issues. Although this type of interview often feels more conversational and candidate-centered, responses should be focused, professional, and address organizational needs. For example, when asked to clarify experience on your résumé, answer by explaining how you can apply that proficiency for the interviewing company.

Panel and group interviews are not as common as one-on-one interviews, but they are frequently used by employers when a position requires a person to work with a variety of individuals in a department or team. Sometimes, such as in democratic organizations, hiring decisions require input from several individuals. In these types of interviews, several interviewers ask structured and open-ended questions. Try to connect with each individual and tailor answers to address the different perspectives of each individual. When answering, make eye contact with all the panelists, not just the person asking the question.

Behavioral interviews are a type of open-ended interview that involves questions that solicit responses that point to a candidate's specific experiences and practices. To answer behavior-oriented questions effectively, quickly summarize the situation and your actions, and then explain how your responses positively (or negatively) affected the outcome of the situation. To prepare, refamiliarize yourself with your work and educational experiences before the interview.

Situational interviews are similar to behavioral interviews except that the interviewers ask how an applicant would respond to a hypothetical work situation. Preface your answers by indicating that you would like to receive training or know the culture more. Then, explain how you might act by drawing upon your prior behaviors in a similar or relatable situation.

Working interviews involve actually engaging in some kind of job-related tasks. These types of interviews allow others to observe how you would actually perform on the job. For example, you may be asked to lead a meeting or make a presentation.

Stress interviews seek to place candidates in uncomfortable situations. From the hiring organization's perspective, this rare form of interview should only be used when there are bona fide occupational reasons for doing so. Sometimes stress is induced by asking candidates uncomfortable interview questions or creating an awkward situation that shows a candidate's responses and actions. If you start to feel like you are in a stress interview, do not be alarmed. Simply collect your thoughts and be confident in your responses and reactions, which should be easy once you recognize what the interviewers are doing.

Telephone, video, and Second Life. There are a variety of media, some previously mentioned, that are now used for interviewing. Because these contexts create unique situations, there are a few things to consider. When interviewing by telephone, find a landline. If you must interview by cell phone, find a location where you are guaranteed to have a quality connection. Interviewing with a phone that has bad reception can be frustrating for you and the interviewers. If you find that you are interviewing with a panel and they are using a speaker phone, do not be shy about giving feedback. Let them know you are having trouble hearing. They understand the limitations of their equipment. When interviewing by phone, dress and behave like you would if you were meeting face-to-face. This will improve your performance.

Seek a secluded area free from distractions. Large walk-in closets can be excellent places to do phone interviews.

If invited to interview by video, be sure to use a high-quality camera and an area with good lighting. Block all background objects by sitting against a bare wall or by hanging a white sheet. Test equipment in advance and restart the computer just before the interview to clear the computer's memory, which may improve the connection.

Some companies now conduct job fairs and interviews in Second Life. Familiarizing yourself with Second Life now may be useful to you in the future. More companies are likely to move toward this model. In 2009, Amazon.com, for example, hosted a job fair in Second Life. Create an avatar that is professional and representative of who you are. Store files that you might share in a manner that will make them easy to find and transfer upon request. For example, if a recruiter asks for a résumé, have it already uploaded to the Second Life shell and ready for transfer. To learn more about second life, visit **http://secondlife.com**.

Sample interview questions.   When asked questions, answer in a natural and conversational manner. When asking questions, do not be interrogative or hostile. In the tradition of good rhetoric, ask purpose-driven questions and interpret questions and answers contextually. For example, to find out what the position entails, ask, "What will be the candidate's primary job responsibilities?" If the answer is vague, it could mean that responsibilities have not been clearly defined. This could cause frustration for you on the job. Good questions are open ended (i.e., cannot be answered with a simply "yes" or "no") and better questions are almost always behavioral ("How have you evaluated employees in this position in the past?").

Questions you may be asked.

- Tell me something interesting about yourself.
- What courses in college did you like and not like? Why?
- What is your greatest weakness?
- What did you like (or not like) about your previous jobs?
- What are your major strengths and weaknesses?
- What opportunities or threats do you see our company (department) facing in the future?
- Describe a work-related situation that helped you learn a lot about yourself.
- Why did you choose the major that you did?
- How have your education and previous work experiences prepared you for this position?
- On your résumé, you mention "X". How do you see this translating to our company in general and this position in particular?
- What are your short-term and long-term occupational goals?
- Where do you see yourself five years from now?
- Do you work better with others or alone?

- Why did you choose this particular field of work?
- Why do you think you would like this particular job?
- What type of boss do you prefer?
- Why do you want this job?
- How do you like to spend your free time?
- What are your proudest accomplishments?
- Why are you leaving your current position?
- Why should we hire you?
- What salary and benefits do you expect?

Sample behavioral questions:

- Tell me about a time when you had to adjust to a classmate's or colleague's working style in order to complete a project or achieve your objectives.
- Tell me about a situation where you had to solve a difficult problem. What did you do? What was your thought process? What was the outcome? What do you wish you had done differently?
- What is your typical way of dealing with conflict? Give me an example.
- Describe a time when you put your needs aside to help a coworker understand a task. How did you assist him or her? What was the result?
- Tell me about a time when you missed an obvious solution to a problem.
- Narrate your response to a (recent) situation in which you had to deal with a very upset customer or coworker.
- Describe a situation where you worked as part of a team to achieve a result. What was your role in this?

Questions you may want to ask.

- How does your organization show it values its employees?
- What are the company's strategic plans for the next five years?
- What are the organization's/company's/department's strengths and weaknesses compared to its competition?
- What are the various ways employees communicate with one another to carry out their work?
- Could you describe your company's management style and the type of employee who fits well with it?
- What kind of work can I expect to be doing the first year?
- How much guidance or assistance is made available to individuals in developing career goals?

- Can you describe an ideal employee?
- How will you measure success for someone in this position?
- What is your organization's managerial philosophy?
- What systems or policies are available for assisting employees with career and professional advancement?
- What are the first tasks or issues that immediately need to be addressed by the person you hire?
- The last time an employee made a mistake, how did you respond?

Illegal questions. In almost all circumstance, potential employers cannot legally ask the following questions:

- What was your maiden name?
- Are you married?
- What is your race?
- Are you a member of an underrepresented group?
- Do you have physical or mental disabilities?
- Do you have a drug or alcohol problem?
- Have you ever been arrested? (In many states interviewers can ask if candidates have been *convicted*, but not arrested.)
- What country are you a citizen of?
- What language do you speak at home?
- Do you own or rent your home?
- Where were you born?

The above questions all violate the U.S. Equal Employment Opportunity Commission (EEOC) guidelines. Should you feel that questions during an interview were unreasonable or asked with the intention to discriminate, file a complaint with the EEOC (**http://eeoc.gov**) or an agency in your state that regulates fair employment practices. Be reasonable, however, because accidents do happen. Just because an interviewer asks these questions does not mean that he or she is being malicious. These questions often occur during "conversations" rather than formal interviews, and it is easy to understand why. Nevertheless, during any stage of the process, they are illegal.

If asked an illegal question, do not become angry. Answer it if you think it will not adversely affect your application. Deflect the question by politely asking if the question might be prohibited—"I'd like to answer that, but are you sure it's allowed?" Refuse to answer it by politely stating it is not something you feel comfortable answering.

If you choose to answer the question, consider your response carefully. Often the question is motivated by a desire to know something else, so see if you can answer "the question behind the question." For example, if you are asked "Did your parents go to college?" or "Did you grow up in [area of town]?", the interviewer may simply want to know if you have overcome adversity or he or she may be searching for something in common. Perhaps she or he thinks you too are a first-generation college student or thinks you may have grown up near a friend (given your accent). You could answer the assumed question behind the question or spin it to your advantage. "No, my parents didn't go to college. I should mention that I had to pay my way through school by working three jobs."

Keep in mind that there are some circumstances in which employers can ask some of the generally illegal questions. These questions must be verifiably bona fide occupational qualifications (BFOQ); that is, the answer to the question must reveal details that are specific to the job function. For example, the question "Can you lift 40 pounds?" could discriminate against people with disabilities. If the advertised position is for an office assistant in a legal office, this would not qualify as a BFOQ. However, if the position is for a baggage handler, it qualifies as a legitimate BFOQ. As an interviewer, it is always best to seek legal counsel before asking any questions that are likely to be protected by EEOC regulations.

Follow-up   After an interview (or during it), jot down pertinent information you obtained and keep notes that will help you compare job offers. Also, be sure to track the names of the individuals you make contact with during the screening and selection stages. As soon as possible after an interview, send interviewers and others thank-you notes in a brief letter or email. If it is context appropriate, be different by sending a hand-written note by mail in addition to an email. Typically, a note includes the following information:

- A reference to the job for which you interviewed.
- Your thanks for the interview and for the time dedicated to you. Mention individuals or groups who should also be thanked, or send a note directly to them.
- Something that you find attractive about the job. Mention that you feel confident that you can perform the job well.
- A follow-up to a question you said you'd respond to later (if applicable).
- An offer to provide additional information if requested.
- If appropriate, a withdrawal for consideration for the position. Mention that you may be better suited for other positions with the company, though.

If you are offered a job, accept the offer both verbally and in writing as soon as possible. If necessary, request an extension to consider other offers. Write a refusal letter or email as quickly as possible.

Additional Employment Considerations

There a few issues that deal with the employment process that are worthy of special mention: how to dress and appear during interviews, how to negotiate salaries and benefits, and how to resign. Unfortunately, there is no one approach that fits all situations, but the following are some rhetorical choices you should consider.

Dress and Appearance

Dress sharp and conservatively, even if the organization you are applying to may be informal. Show that you respect the process. Don't overdress, but look your best. While many books recommend a conservative look (e.g., blue and white), it is much better to wear a suit and other accessories such as a scarf or tie that represents you. It is not likely this will matter much and, if it does, then it may not be the type of place you want to work anyway. Avoid displaying a large amount of jewelry and piercings, unless this is an important part of your identity—in which case, be yourself. Tattoos are not as taboo as they once were; however, cover them up if they are not audience appropriate. Practice good hygiene and don't overdo it on perfumes and makeup.

Often students wonder about whether they should wear wedding bands. It's a silly thing to fret over. Do what seems ethical to you and will reflect your ethos. While dress and ornamentals do matter rhetorically, these are the least of your concerns. Although inappropriate dress or your appearance could have a slight impact on how other interpret your ethos, preparing for the interview and providing good responses will be much more important and memorable than your choice of dress. What really matters is whether you have the knowledge, skills, and experience and can convey this information.

Negotiating Salary and Benefits

Unless required by a job announcement, do not provide details in your application materials that are suggestive of your desired salary. As a standard practice, the opportune time (kairos) for salary negotiations is either at the end of an interview or after a formal job offer. In most circumstances, salaries will be either advertised with the job posting or will initially be extended to you by the company.

If you are asked to state your desired salary, it is often to see how well you know the industry. Always answer with a range rather than a specific number (e.g., $42,000 to $48,000), and suggest it is negotiable. It is always better to respond to a salary request and negotiate salary and benefits with strong arguments that are supported with strong evidence. Draw on data from the Bureau of Labor Statistics' Occupational Outlook Handbook to get salary ranges for the profession (**http://bls.gov/ooh**) and the Consumer Price Index (**http://bls.gov/CPI**) to adjust the salary to a specific location. Use online cost of living calculators to estimate how much you should be paid in comparison to your current location (e.g., check **http://salary.com**). You could say, for instance, "I am aware that starting salaries for someone in this occupation are approximately $34,000. Given my background and the cost of living, I would like to request $34,500 to $38,000. Of course, this is negotiable and I am willing to consider other benefits in lieu of salary."

If you need time to figure out a desired salary, try delaying the decision: "I am sure that your company pays a fair and competitive salary for a person with my qualifications," "I am ready to consider your best offer," "I need a bit more time to learn more details about the position before I express my desired salary," or "I currently have offers from another company but they have not provided me salary information. I would like to see what they offer me first so I can tell you; this will allow me to consider both offers equally."

Do not accept the first offer, even if it is tempting. If you have researched the occupation, you will know whether the salary is competitive. Consider other factors before you make a decision. For example, ask interviewers or check with current employees of the company to see if raises are frequent. In addition, obtain information regarding the standard percentage increase. A company that has been on a pay freeze may not be as appealing as a company that has consistently given a 4% increase, even if the salary is initially slightly lower. Also, consider opportunities for growth and advancement. Salary matters, but it is not the only negotiable and important benefit. As long as you always support your questions and arguments with data and evidence, people will respect your desire to negotiate.

Resignations

If you need to leave a position, maintain good relations with your supervisors by writing a thoughtful letter of resignation. If you are recruited by another company, give you current employer (if you wish) an opportunity to keep you. Follow the advice for writing and delivering negative correspondence by remaining direct and positive. Say something favorable about the organization, even if you are frustrated. Companies can change when people come and go. If an opportunity should arise to return to the organization, you don't want a letter in your file that makes you sound like a curmudgeon. State your intention to leave and give a date of your departure. If possible, try to provide some flexibility in your departure date, which should almost always be at least two weeks in the United States. Before departing on your final day, thank colleagues. Request an exit interview, whether it is formal or informal. The exit interview can provide you and your supervisor with critical feedback on your tenure.

Conclusion

This chapter explored the various stages of the interview process, as well as the multiple purposes for various employment-related documents. For example, the résumé is useful as both a career-planning tool as it is a job-seeking tool. Remember that the best applicants understand their rhetorical situation and practice good rhetorical skills by drawing upon the five canons. If you spend time developing a résumé and application letter that responds to a specific job advertisement and repeats its key words; if you prepare for interviews by doing research on the company, practicing responses to questions, and writing questions to ask in advance; and if you send a thank-you note after the interview that sounds sincere, you are going to significantly improve your chances of being hired.

Continuing Education: Recommended Texts and Resources

- *Acing the interview: How to ask and answer the questions that will get you the job* by Tony Beshara. ISBN: 978-0814401613

    This popular press book is a good resource with practical examples for responding to a variety of interview questions.

- *Interviewing: Principles and practices* by Charles Stewart and William Cash. ISBN: 978-0073406817

    This is the most widely used textbook for interviewing courses on college campuses. According to its description, "It incorporates the ever-expanding body of research in all types of interview settings, recent communication theory, and the importance of equal opportunity laws on interviewing practices. It provides the most thorough treatment of the basics of interviewing, including the complex interpersonal communication process, types and uses of questions, and the structuring of interviews from opening to closing."

- *The encyclopedia of careers and vocational guidance (15th ed.).* ISBN: 978-0816083138

    This reference volume is a great asset for choosing careers. It is also useful for consultants and career coaches. It is a bit pricy, so see a librarian to obtain a copy for your library or to borrow through inter-library loan.

- *"Headhunter" hiring secrets: The rules of the hiring game have changed . . . forever!* by Skip Freeman. ISBN: 978-0615346212

    This book has received significant praise among all types of professionals. It is a useful read for anyone looking to impress professionals in today's difficult job market.

- Résumé Writers' Digest | **www.rwdigest.com**

    This is an excellent resource for individuals interested in staying abreast of changes in opinion among professionals who read résumés for a living. It includes a newsletter that has plenty of useful tips that can be used by job seekers, human resource personnel, career counselors, and life coaches.

References

Chandrasekaran, A. (2004, March 9). Resumé fraud gets slicker and easier. USAToday. Retrieve from www.usatoday.com/tech/news/2004-03-09-resume-cheats_x.htm

DiMaggio, P. J. & Powell, W. (1983). The iron cage revisited: Institutional isomorphism and collective rationality in organizational fields, *American Sociological Review*, *48*, 147–160.

Ferrell, D. (2010, November 15). Test-driving your dream job: Oregon entrepreneur helps would-be entrepreneurs take their ideas for a spin before sealing the deal. Entrepreneur. Retrieved from www.entrepreneur.com/article/219305

Garone, E. (2009, October 19). Using LinkedIn for job references. *The Wall Street Journal*. Retrieved from http://online.wsj.com/article/SB125417485682447495.html

IOMA. (2006) How to ferret out instances of résumé padding and fraud. *Compensation & Benefits for Law Offices*. 06-06, 1 4–12.

Leonard, D. (2011, May 26). The U.S. Postal Service nears collapse. *Bloomberg Businessweek.* Retrieved from www.businessweek.com/magazine/content/11_23/b4231060885070 .htm

"National longitudinal surveys: Frequently asked questions." (n.d.). Retrieved from www.bls.gov/nls/nlsfaqs.htm

"Number of jobs held, labor market activity, and earnings growth among the youngest baby boomers: Results from a longitudinal survey." (2010, September 10). Retrieved from www.bls.gov/news.release/pdf/nlsoy.pdf

Shane, S. (2008). *The illusions of entrepreneurship.* New Haven, CT: Yale University Press. "Should we make way for the robots and leave the lab?" (2009, May). Retrieved from www.timeshighereducation.co.uk/story.asp?storyCode=406415&sectioncode=26

Chapter — 5

Crafting Concise and Extensive Communications

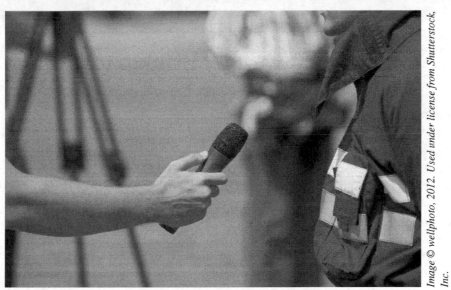

Image © wellphoto, 2012. Used under license from Shutterstock, Inc.

Starting point

Maureen Evans (@cookbook; **http://twitter.com/#!/cookbook**) is the author of *Eat Tweet*, a cookbook of condensed recipes that are delivered via Twitter. She also maintains the website **http://eat-tweet.com**. The following recipe, Tweeted on July 7, 2011, is an example of one of her recipes:

> Summer Tian: Brwn2onion/2T olvoil. Put in shallow bkgdish; lyr+equal eggplant&bellpep&zuke&tom/s+p/3T oil&h2o. ~2h@400F(top w foil if nec)

138 characters in length, this refreshing summer dish remains two characters under the 140-character limit imposed by Twitter. Amazingly, it is easy to read. To craft recipes this short, Evans developed her approach with strict parameters—for example, dishes that have relatively few ingredients—and a glossary of terms (see **http://cookbookglossary.pbwiki.com**). Producing concise communications, such as Twitter posts, requires an inventive effort and must often be complemented by more extensive communications.

This example demonstrates something unique about the times we live in. Text messages and Tweets are almost always 140 characters or less, so we've become relatively adept at crafting and interpreting detailed information with abbreviated words. A usually extensive artifact, such as a cookbook, is now concise. A company's policy guidelines, manuals, and other documents can also be developed and distributed via Twitter-style microblogs. Employees likely pay more attention to short passages delivered over a period of time.

Given the right type of messages and the right audience, extensive communications, such as websites or brochures, can use an abbreviated style. In some cases, you may want to develop a résumé in a 140 characters or less. Twitter can catalog your résumé, which you tweet over time, and it is a useful tool for posting recommendations, references, and links to knowledge, and it helps users develop potential leads (followers). As @jorganbrown notes, "LinkedIn is for people that I've worked with. Facebook is for people I knew in school and growing up. Twitter is for people that I want to know."

In today's social media(ted) and 140-character-or-less-fixated world, it may seem odd to cover electronic communication and social media discussions in separate chapters (as is the case in this book). Don't we write and speak both concise and extensive communications in virtual environments too? Sure, but given the focus on social media, it is important to dedicate a chapter to traditional artifacts—knowing how to craft a memo still matters. Businesses often use Twitter and Facebook to distribute links to information, which are often nothing more than PDF versions of more traditional-style communications, for example, a letter to customers.

Even if a rhetor has "mad skills" when it comes to social networking, at some time he or she will need to write concise and extensive communications in more traditional forms. The more traditional, everyday types of business artifacts range from brief media interviews and memos to symposium presentations and handbooks. Crafting and designing the documents in this chapter will help improve your grammar, punctuation, and style. It's great if you can write in 140 characters (or less) or speak in sound bites, but even these types of communication are predicated upon more extensive communications, such as strategic plans and talking-points, distributed by memo internally within an office. In this chapter, various types of oral and written, concise and extensive artifacts are explained and exemplified.

Applying the Five Canons

Chapter 2 covered the application of the five canons of rhetoric to oral and written communications. The choice to use a concise or extensive format of communication is partly determined by the rhetorical situation, which will be identified during the invention process. Regardless of artifact length, apply the canons of arrangement and style to the development of content. The length of information affects what information is included in a message as well as how this information is delivered. This section addresses some of the issues related to delivering information in both concise and extensive forms.

Invention

The invention process for artifacts, regardless of their length, is determined by the type of audience (e.g., sympathetic or hostile) and the desired effect (to invite or to confront). If these are known, then artifact construction can be approached in a more formulaic manner. Refer back to Table 2.1, which provides an overview of the types of communicative strategies that one can use when dealing with various types of audiences.

When crafting both concise and extensive artifacts, understand the audience and determine the optimal approach for delivery. Recall that kairos, or timing of argument delivery, is critical to whether audiences accept or reject ideas and information. For example, a spokesperson for a company that has just experienced a plant explosion, which is a rhetorical situation inviting negative correspondence, needs to pacify the audience in a brief news report. He or she would generally want to present positive news first (e.g., "nobody was injured, to our knowledge"), to express common interest with the audience (e.g., "we want to be assured that our community is safe"), to present facts and directives (e.g.,"the smoke is contaminated with dangerous chemicals and residents within 10 miles of the plant need to evacuate"), and to indicate there will be more information and opportunities for dialogue (e.g., "we will hold a press conference"). This approach is consistent with an invitational-direct approach, used when audiences are likely to be highly interested or invested in the information.

Table 5.1 builds on Table 2.1 by describing specific strategies one can use to approach messages that deliver positive or negative news. For example, if an audience is likely to be hostile to information in a letter, then it should begin with a neutral statement to buffer the negative news. When applicants are sent a rejection letter, for example, it begins with a statement regarding how many applicants there were (a neutral statement) and that many were highly qualified (a buffer statement). In closing, the rejected applicants are wished luck in their ongoing job searches. To understand the audience and purpose of a communication, do a thorough analysis during the invention stage and determine a specific purpose.

Arrangement

In concise correspondence, arrangement is not likely to be a major issue, but it is important nevertheless. A bulletin board posting that announces an upcoming meeting and lists the three topics to be discussed has an implied thesis (you are invited) and is arranged topically (e.g., there are three topics to be discussed and here is when and where we'll meet). The conclusion may also be implied by certain information (this benefits you), but sometimes it is stated (lunch will be provided, so here is another reason to attend). The design may not appear linear, but it is certainly focused.

In extensive communications, which are usually longer, the arrangement is critical to the development of ideas. The outline and pattern assists the rhetor and the audience with

Table 5.1   Approaches to positive and negative messages

Type of message	Approach	Process
Routine or Positive message	**Direct approach:** In almost all circumstances, it is better to be direct when crafting documents that are routine or positive. Common types of routine and positive business messages include: • Requesting information, action, recommendations, or adjustments. • Making claims or complaints. • Providing positive feedback. • Responding to routine requests, complaints, and positive feedback. • Writing letters of recommendations, congratulations, appreciation, or condolences. **Indirect approach:** Use when you want to be less emphatic or don't want to appear overzealous.	• State main purpose of correspondence and, if necessary, a preview of the points to be discussed or described. • Provide details and explanations to justify communication (use a list when possible). • Close with specific request and express goodwill. Note: When responding to routine or positive messages, be as brief as possible. Appendix C provides additional strategies when responding to claims. • Start with a polite comment, and then follow the process above.
Negative message	**Direct approach:** Use when firmness is needed, when audience anticipates or expects bad news (it won't be shocking), when situation is minor or routine, or when recipients prefer bad news first. **Indirect approach:** Use in emotionally charged situations, when audience is going to be displeased with news, or when recipients do not anticipate bad news.	• State bad news first. • Provide reasons for situation or rationale for decision. • Close with positive comment, statement of goodwill, invitation for future dialogue, or any combination that is suitable to the rhetorical occasion. • Begin with a buffer statement (see Appendix C for examples). • Provide reasons for the situation or rationale for the decision. • State bad news. • Close with a positive comment, statement of goodwill, invitation for future dialogue, or any combination that is suitable to the rhetorical occasion.

understanding and interpreting lengthy details. A report needs to be organized in such a way that the information is easy to follow. This often requires the layering of stock patterns. For example, there may be five main sections in a report (topical arrangement), and one section may be arranged chronologically (e.g., history of the company) and another by problem-solution (e.g., we face three critical challenges and these are our proposed solutions).

An outline, regardless of how brief the communication is, also makes crafting artifacts and engaging in verbal correspondences easier. It enhances the possibility of achieving desired persuasive outcomes. When presenting information in oral form, have a solidly arranged outline. Outlines make it easier for speakers to transition from one topic to another without confusing the audience.

Style

Recall that style is closely linked to the classical appeals ethos, pathos, and logos. If presenting brief oral communications in a television interview, for example, it is more important to present information that is simple and explanatory rather than poetic and descriptive. In short written messages, however, telling succinct stories, using other narrative techniques, and adopting poetic language is likely to be more effective at obtaining and maintaining audience interest. In brief oral and written correspondence, analogies, comparisons, and audience-specific jargon is useful. These devices aid in the delivery of complex or comprehensive ideas using fewer words. In longer communications, maintaining audience interest can be achieved through style, including design aesthetics. To reduce wordiness, direct communication is preferable to indirect approaches.

Regardless of the medium or length, style can cushion the impact of negative news or enhance the effect of positive news. Obviously, the shorter the communication, the less space or time one has to develop emphasis. In longer communications, telling a story may be possible and effective. In brief correspondence, a short analogy may be better than a detailed narrative account.

Use a direct approach for messages that are routine and positive, and either a direct or indirect approach when crafting messages with negative information (see Table 5.1). Direct and indirect approaches often do not affect the content of a message, just the delivery. For example, when delivering negative news, the direct approach opens with the bad news and provides reasons for a situation or decision; the indirect approach begins with the reasons behind the bad news and then gets to the problem. The direct approach is best when firmness is needed or when the negative information will not be shocking.

Memory/Delivery

Short messages take less time both to craft and read, and the content is easier to remember. This is one reason concise and brief communications are always preferable to extensive ones in daily business correspondence.

Choice of mnemonic and organizational devices is critical to the long-term effectiveness of messages. For short messages, use lists and acronyms to effectively deliver content that needs to be memorized or recalled at a later time. Mnemonic devices are also helpful in brief interactions involving verbal communication, such as for the media or job interviews. They help speakers keep information and facts straight and ensure that they cover the main talking points. These devices also help reduce complex ideas into memorable sound bites, something that is especially important in today's media-saturated environment. For longer documents, provide executive summaries, a table of contents (front matter), and an index of key words (back matter) to aid audiences.

Delivery method affects interpretation, so be careful what message your method of delivery might imply. Sending condolences electronically may be interpreted as insincere. Sending nonurgent information by overnight delivery may create an impression that the information requires immediate attention. Sales pitches, described later in the chapter, often come across as hurried. If a client wants or needs to feel special, a two-hour meeting at a classy restaurant may be preferable to a quick pitch. Knowing audience preferences is essential for choosing the proper delivery method and medium, so don't stint on the invention process.

In the following sections, types of concise and extensive communications are discussed and, in some cases, exemplified. Thanks to the proliferation of such documents on the Internet, it is not difficult to find useful templates and examples of each type. What matters most is the application of the canons to the specifics of rhetorical situations.

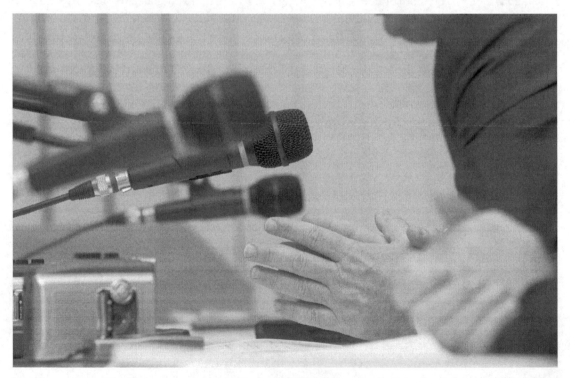

Public forums require both concise communications (question-and-answer sessions) as well as extensive communications (an expert's in-depth presentation). All participants, including the audience, should use the five canons of rhetoric to contribute to productivity. (Image © Picsfive, 2012. Used under license from Shutterstock, Inc.)

Concise Artifacts

Concise business communications are typically routine. They include, but are not limited to, letters, cover letters, memos, and press releases. Generally, the message informs or requests something (e.g., a recommendation, action, product, or adjustment). Whether written or spoken, brief messages should get to the point as quickly as possible.

Strategies for Crafting Concise Communications

Follow these strategies when writing routine concise business messages: state the purpose of the communication up front in a courteous manner, give evidence to explain or justify a request (if you make one), and end with a specific request and polite comment.

Be direct but courteous.   Unless conveying negative information, begin a message by immediately stating its purpose. For example, if requesting information, lead with your request. This will save the audience time and increase the chances that main points will receive the most attention. This does not mean that the tone should be abrupt. Don't demand action; instead, seek readers' and listeners' permission and invite them to respond. Soften the request with words like "please" or "I would appreciate." For example, in a letter or phone conversations, write or say: "*I would appreciate*, when convenient, that you send the following information to me:. . . . "

Rhetors can assume that an audience will generally comply with requests, so don't be pushy or use gimmicky language. Even when trying to persuade an audience, don't be forceful. Invitational rhetoric, which is a feminist and civility-oriented approach to persuasion, can be just as effective at obtaining consensus and action as more aggressive persuasion (Bone, Griffin, & Scholz, 2008). Using the available means of persuasion to get something does not require force or fallacious claims. In most circumstances, the opposite is true. Be polite, courteous, and reasonable, and you will often find a better solution through collaboration (see Chapter 7). Principled negotiators do not argue for their positions; instead, they generate options for mutual gain. What is more, they are not rough with people, but invite others to be hard on the problem (Fisher & Ury, 2011).

Sounding soft does *not* mean not articulating your main points. Use emphatic sentences but modify the tone of the statements to avoid sounding brazen. Be specific about wants and reduce mitigation. By being clear and specific in a soft tone, you reduce your audience's interpretive burden and increase the chances of being heard.

Provide evidence to explain or justify a request.   Once a request has been articulated, give evidence and reasons that support the appeal. Present this in an easy-to-read format, such as a bulleted list. Subsequent paragraphs or lists should explain needs. If you are asking for an adjustment in a bill, for example, provide evidence to support the rationale for the request. The rhetorical burden is to prove the suggested issue and that the proposed solutions are reasonable.

Whether making a request or providing information, help audiences understand how compliance with demands benefits them. In short, keep the message audience-focused and write in the "you" viewpoint—that is, write in a way that places the audience's interests and perspectives in the foremost position. Even if a rhetor feels he or she has been wronged, demonstrating how the solution benefits the audience will be rhetorically more effective. The "you" viewpoint does not necessarily mean that using words like "you" and "your." As noted in Chapter 2, sometimes it is best to avoid these words to avoid an accusatory tone and to maintain goodwill.

To organize the message so that it flows and avoids confusion, address the most important points first, omit needless comments and references, and present only one topic per point (refer back to the discussion of outlining).

Close with a specific request. The conclusion should include a specific request for action or provide directives in a courteous tone. Include any relevant deadlines as well as contact information if it is not obvious. In the last sentence, express goodwill and appreciation. Figure 5.1 provides an example of a letter requesting a refund that demonstrates all of these elements. If a similar communication is delivered orally, work from an outline. When speaking with a customer service agent by phone, for example, a prepared statement can ensure a calm focus and that all points are addressed. If meeting with the audience in person, deliver your comments, invite a response, and then, in closing, ask for a business card, thank the audience for his, her, or their time, and follow up with a quick email that summarizes the conversation.

Written Types of Concise Communications

After social media messages, you are likely to spend most of your life writing concise forms of communication. These most common types of concise communications are letters, cover letters, memos, press releases, forms, and brochures. Specific strategies for writing each are discusses below.

Letters. As illustrated in the sample application letter in Figure 4.4 and the request for a refund in Figure 5.1, letters, one of the most common types of brief correspondence in professional situations, should include the following sections: the heading, addresses, salutation, body, closing, and end notations (optional). Business letters are typically written to correspond with individuals less familiar with the rhetor, such as with external stakeholders of an organization. Although it is not necessary to print letters on cotton fiber paper or use letterhead, doing so communicates formality, respect, and authority. Letterhead and templates help maintain consistency and uniform results and promote a particular brand or image.

Word processing and other productivity software often includes templates. For example, Microsoft provides a large catalog of free templates (**http://office.microsoft.com/en-us/templates**). While these are useful, they may not provide the appropriate dimensions and spacing needed. However, you can adjust the dimensions of these documents, but it is important to learn how to write and format letters without these devices.

Style. If an organization specifies using a specific format for letters, use it. Otherwise, use either a *full-block style* as shown in Figure 5.2) or the *modified-block style* in Figure 5.1.

1234 Your Street
Your City, ST 00000
December 10, 2011

Shelly Shopowner
Hot Bottom Boutique
123 Main Street
Some City, IL 00000

Subject: GIFT CERTIFICATE REFUND

Dear Shelly Shopowner:

Despite these difficult economic times, I hope that your business is doing well. I was a frequent patron of your store and miss shopping with you. I moved to another state several years ago and was sadly unable to return to your store as I had hoped. I am writing to request a refund for a $100 gift certificate (enclosed), which has recently expired (December 5, 2011).

As you know, Illinois law (Illinois Rev. Stat. ch. 815, §505/2SS9.b) requires that gift certificates may not be subject to post-purchase fees or penalties and must, if unused and marked with an expiration date, be refunded to its holder, or the value turned over to the state (Illinois Rev. Stat. ch. 765, §1025/10.6). I hope that you will be willing to return the money directly to me, which will save both of us time.

I understand that you may need time to refund this money, especially during the busy holiday season. I am willing to wait until February 1, 2012, to receive this refund. Should you have any questions, please feel free to call me at a time that is convenient for you. I hope to return in the next few years to Some City, and I will be sure to stop by to check out your latest fashions.

Sincerely,

Happy Shopper

Happy Shopper
000.000.0000

Enc.: Gift certificate (copy retained)

Figure 5.1.   Example of a routine business letter: Requesting a refund.

In the full-block style, all information is aligned to the left. In the modified-block style, the return address, date, and closing are centered, while the rest of the content is left-justified. In some cases, depending on the layout of the letterhead (some organizations place information in the left, right, or bottom margin space), a specialized style may be required, which will be a variation on the modified-style theme. For example, only the date might be right-justified.

Ground Floor, 1 Y Place Road
PO Box 1234
City Name, Illinois   1234
ph. 000.000.000 | fax: 000.000.000
www.companyurl.whatever

10 December 2011

Attorneys at Law
Attn: Jane Pinkerton-Jones, Esq.
1234 Some Road
City Name, ST 12345

Dear Jane Pinkerton-Jones, Esq.:

I am pleased to submit our final report for the subcontracted field investigation, which we conducted on behalf of your client (Acme Insurance).

We began the investigation on December 6, 2011, and concluded it on December 9, 2011. We were able to document potential fraud and are happy to report that we came in under your client's budget (refund of retainer enclosed, check no. 01234).

Enclosed you will find an investigative report, which summarizes the specific details of the investigation, and the surveillance footage (DVD). As per your request, we are sending a duplicate directly to your client.

If you require me to attend a deposition, please contact our office assistant, Pam Johansson (000.000.0000), to schedule a meeting.

Thank you,

Dr. Stephanie Yeun
Insurance Fraud Specialist

SY/pj
Encs: Investigative Report; Surveillance DVD; Check #01234 (refund)
cc: Legal Department (for archives)

Figure 5.2.   Example of a transmittal/cover letter.

For a professional appearance, center the letter vertically and horizontally. Use the word processor's rulers and tabs to maintain parallel design. Try to maximize white space by using 1″ margins; however, adjust the margins proportionately to maintain consistency. Insert a space between each paragraph instead of indenting paragraphs. (For letters with very little content, increase the margins to give the letter a fuller look.)

Heading.   If using letterhead, you don't need to include the company's address. When not using letterhead, then the heading should be the first item in the document. Because the writer's name appears at the end of the letter, it can be excluded from the address block. Do not, unless it is aesthetically more appealing, abbreviate address information: spell out street, avenue, north, and so on. The standard is to use the letter-letter postal abbreviation for state names, but you can spell out the name of a state. The date the letter is written is typically placed under the author's address. Use the following style, without abbreviation, for dates: August 15, 20XX. (Note that in international correspondence, it is common to write the date as 15 August 20XX.) Right align the date to make it stand out or appear less crunched between the addresses. Alternatively, use the modified-style and center align the author's address (see Figure 5.1).

Inside address.   The recipient's full name, title, and address should be two to six lines below the date. This is determined by the length of the letter and style. For example, six lines of spacing may be more aesthetically pleasing when using the modified-block style. The inside address is always aligned with the left margin, salutation, and body text.

Salutation.   The salutation (greeting) goes two to three lines below the inside address and is always aligned with the body. Use any appropriate (abbreviated) professional titles (Dr., Professor, Prof., Ph.D., Esq., Senator, Major, etc.) followed by a colon. Whenever possible, avoid gendered titles (Mrs., Ms., and Mr.) and use full names instead (Dear Jona Smith:). When addressing multiple parties, use these variations:

- Dear Mr. President and Senator Dick Durbin:
- Dear Mr. John Smith and Mrs. Jane Cuomo-Smith:
- Dear Drs. Polouska and Myers:
- Dear Profs. Smith, Ahmed, and Czarniawska:
- Dear Colleagues [Members, Staff, or other suitable collective term]:

If addressing an unknown recipient in a large organization, try the following:

Dunkin' Donuts
150 Depot Street
Bellingham, MA 02019

Attention [or *Attn*]*: Customer Relations Department*
or
Subject: Inquiry about DD Perks Rewards Card

I recently obtained my DD Perks Rewards card and. . . .

Never use "To Whom It May Concern:"; it's long been buried as a useful format.

Body.   Begin the body of the letter two lines below the salutation (or any element that precedes it, such as a subject line). Use a single space between lines of text and double space between paragraphs. If providing or submitting additional forms or documents, indicate this in the body and provide an end notation of enclosures.

Closing.   The complimentary closing goes two lines below the body. Use a standard expression, such as *Sincerely, Sincerely yours, Yours sincerely, Thanks, Best regards, Best, Be well,* and so on. Always use "Sincerely" or "Thank you" when unfamiliar with the person. Capitalize only the initial letter of the first word of the expression and follow it with a comma. Note that the cover letter in Figure 5.2 provides a simple thank you. Nowadays, "Thanks in advance" is considered presumptuous.

Writer's signature block.   The writer's full name is aligned four lines below the complimentary closing. (Sign the letter in this space.) Single space and align additional information that is not included in the letterhead or body of the letter, such as title, contact information (telephone number and email), website, and so on.

End notations.   Place additional information and notes two to four lines below the writer's signature block (the spacing is determined by aesthetic preference). This is always left-justified, even if using a modified-block format. Reference initials, enclosures, and copies are the most commonly used end notations (all demonstrated in Figure 5.2). Reference initials are only necessary when a person other than the writer types the letter. The writer's initials are in capital letters, followed by a slash mark or colon, and the typist's initials are in lower-case letters. Enclosure notations indicate what materials are included in a package sent with the letter (e.g., an invoice or form). Note that one should include a reference to enclosed materials in the body of the letter as well. Here are some common forms of enclosure notations:

- Enclosure: Grade Report
- Enclosures (2)
- Enc. or *Encs.*

Copy and blind-copy notation tells recipients and reminds the sender that the letter is being sent to someone else. Use "cc:" for copy and "bcc:" for blind-copy notation (do not include the "bcc" information on the original, only the copies).

Continuing pages.   When a letter requires a second page or more, use paper of equivalent color and quality as the first page, but only use letterhead for the first page. The header of additional pages should include the recipient's name, the page number, and the date (see the following examples). If aesthetically appropriate, place the page number in the footer, centered with two dashes: - 2 -. Only use a second page if there are more than two lines of continuing text, otherwise, adjust fonts, margins, or other features to make the letter fit on a single page.

Cover letter (transmittal).   Transmittal letters are formatted similarly to other business letters. Since they are specifically written to accompany reports, they are more formal

Example 1:

Dr. C. Smith   [header]
Page 2
August 15, 20XX

Example 2:

Dr. C. Smith   [header]   2   [header]   August 15, 20XX

Example 3:

Dr. C. Smith   [header]
August 15, 20XX

                                                  -2-   [footer]

and direct. They apprise readers of a report's context and any information that may not be in the report, such as project due dates and contact information for inquiries. For example, the author of the report's contact information may be in the report itself, but the letter may tell readers to direct inquiries to the public relations department. Figure 5.2 is an example of a transmittal letter. Note that cover letters for faxes use a similar format to memorandum. You can find many templates and examples of cover letters online.

Memorandum (memo).   Memos are documents typically used for communication within a company, such as directives, instructions, responses to inquiries, and announcements. They can be just as formal as a business letter and can be used for more extensive messages (e.g., short reports or proposals). Memos follow a standard format, which includes *To:*, *From:*, *Date:*, and *Subject:* fields, which can be single-spaced or 1.5-line spaced. Figures 5.3, 5.4, and 5.5 illustrate these fields and the most common types of memos: informative, directive, and response. Also note that, unlike letters, a memo can include headings (in bold or underlined or both) in the body text, which can emphasize information and provide clarity of organization.

Email has largely replaced the function of memos, but writing a traditional style memo on company letterhead communicates formality and authority. Also, attaching a memo to an email

Ground Floor, 1 Y Place Road
PO Box 1234
City Name, Illinois   1234
ph. 000.000.000 | fax: 000.000.000
www.companyurl.whatever

Memo

To: Managers and Staff
From: Shaniqua Jones, Vice President
Date: December 12, 2011
Subject: Annual Bonus Increase

Beginning January 1, 2012, we will introduce the following modification in our company policy with regard to bonuses:

1) Managers who accrue the highest monetary value of executed contracts (total) will receive a bonus of $5000 at the end of the fiscal year.
2) 78% of any unused portion of an investigator's per diem or unused expense budget will be given as a bonus at the end of the fiscal year. The investigator with the highest level of return will receive a $1500 bonus.
3) Staff members who recommend cost-saving measures that are implemented will be given a $100 per-suggestion bonus, which will be distributed at the end of the fiscal year.

These bonuses will not affect or alter other bonuses. This policy adds to our already wonderful list of bonuses and benefits packages, which our employees have come to love.

We will have a meeting on December 20, at 10:00 a.m., to discuss this new program. At this time, we will also create a committee, which will be responsible for promoting this program and for developing other cost-saving programs.

Figure 5.3.   Example of an informative memo.

can be more effective in some situations. As an attachment, for example, the document can be saved more easily to employees' computers.

As with other business documents, especially email, learn the cultural practices of writing and distributing memos within companies. Learn who to copy and which order people should be listed (there are politics to such lists). If rank is not important within the organization, alphabetize recipients' names. Depending on the content of a memo or the context, one may need to initial or sign printed memos. This demonstrates acceptance of responsibility for a memo's contents. It is unnecessary to include initials in electronic memos, but if it is a scanned PDF copy, initials are placed on the original.

For additional pages, follow the same rules as for letters: use the recipients' names (or an abbreviated subject line), the page number, and the date in the upper left corner or across the page, as demonstrated in the examples in the section Letters).

Ground Floor, 1 Y Place Road
PO Box 1234
City Name, Illinois   1234
ph. 000.000.000 | fax: 000.000.000
www.companyurl.whatever

Memo

To: Customer Relations and Sales Team
From: W.B. Jones, CEO   *W.B.*
Date: May 27, 20XX
Subject: ACCP PROPOSALS

Following yesterday's meeting, it is clear that I need to be more direct about the process, schedule, and proposal due date. It is also clear that we need to do more research. However, we must be able to pitch our services to our client at the ACCP annual meeting, which will begin on July 8, 20XX.

Schedule
- Divide research into three subgroups and compile information (by June 6)
- Review possible solution proposals (by June 14)
- Write proposal (by June 20)
- Revise proposal (by June 25)
- Practice proposal and pitch at least five times (by June 30)
- Pitch proposal (July 8 - 10)

External consultants
We will be involving two external consultants, a freelance writer and small business consultant, and a document design specialist from FedEx Office, who will assist us in the document design process. Both consultants will join our team on June 20, and will assist us until June 30. It is imperative that we meet any deadline they impose.

I have enclosed several proposals that have been successful.

WB/pj
cc: Shaniqua Jones, Vice President

Enclosures: Sample Proposals

Figure 5.4.   Example of a directive memo.

Press releases.   A *press release*, also called a *news release*, is a communicative artifact crafted for an external audience. Press releases typically announce new products or services, policies, special events, changes, sponsorships, community programs, or information and updates related to ongoing events or crisis.

Press releases are effective devices for distributing information and for managing the external image of the company. For example, good news reminds a community about the importance

Ground Floor, 1 Y Place Road
PO Box 1234
City Name, Illinois   1234
ph. 000.000.000 | fax: 000.000.000
www.companyurl.whatever

Memo

To: Marageta Simpson, Process Manager
From: Mike Murphy, Accounts Manager
Date: August 14, 20XX
Subject: Re, Proposed Time Change to Daily Briefings

Purpose: This is a response to your request to move the daily briefings from 9 a.m. to 8 a.m.

Summary: This request is satisfactory, pending approval by W. B. Jones.

Discussion: W. B. Jones is not likely to have a problem with this change, so long as it does not lead to an increase in overtime pay.

Action: I have notified W. B. Jones's office assistance about this proposed change. We should be notified the end of the week. Until then, we should continue to meet at 9 a.m.

Figure 5.5.   Example of a response memo.

of a company. Even in times of crisis, a company can limit damage to its image and promote itself by demonstrating candor through a compassionate tone and by respecting stakeholders' desire to remain informed. Press releases can help pacify fears or get people excited about difficult changes. For example, the release can explain the long-term benefits of changes.

Press releases are useful for mass distribution, as they can be posted on company websites, sent directly to media outlets, such as newspapers, radio stations, and television studios, or sent through social networks. Some Internet companies, such as PRLOG (**http://prlog.org**), Wired PR News (**www.wiredprnews.com**), and PR Newswire (**http://ireach.prnewswire .com**), provide free and premium press release distribution, which are useful for companies seeking search engine optimization or that need to outsource distribution to a single source (e.g., a sole proprietor who cannot dedicate a significant amount of time to marketing efforts). Learning to write press releases will make you more valuable to your employer, and will enable you to provide consulting and writing services for small businesses.

When writing a press release, write in a clear and concise manner. Provide accurate information and definitions of important terms. Address the five Ws and one H of journalism: *who, what, where, when, why,* and *how.* Write the most important information first, as editors customarily cut a release from the bottom up if they need to make a release fit the space available for print. Many of the online services provide dynamic templates, which format content to a specific style with little effort. Figure 5.6 illustrates a basic template that can be followed when writing a press release.

New Release

<Company Logo or Letterhead>
Address | City, ST ZIP

Contact: Name of contact
Email: name@emailaddress.me
Phone(s): 000.000.0000

FOR IMMEDIATE RELEASE
or [RELEASE DATE: Month ##, ####]

HEADLINE GOES HERE
Subhead here

CITY, Date of release: Begin body copy. Paragraph 1: answer who, what when, where, why, and how.

Paragraph 2: Expand on who, what, when, where, why, and how. Add quotes, references, and sources throughout.

Paragraph 3: Expand further.

Paragraph 4: Expand even further.

#

About your company. This is where boiler plate information, such as when your company was founded, its mission, its community service activities, and so on goes. Include a company website address.

Figure 5.6.   Example of a press release.

If available at your university, take public relations courses to master the art of PR writing. Also read some of the books recommended in this chapter's Continuing Education section.

Forms.   Forms are used to gather information from respondents using a standardized structure, which makes data easier to process. Online forms are easiest to tabulate because respondents enter their own data entry and computerized programs consolidate the information. Although the rhetorical situation and audience should determine whether one uses printed, electronic, or online forms, a benefit of online forms is that they can offer response choices in limited space. This is achieved by using dropdown menus. Online forms also include text boxes, option ("radio") buttons, lists, and check boxes, which are aligned using tables and cells, just as in word-processing programs. Furthermore, responses collected electronically can present unique choices based on previous responses. This has a tendency to keep respondents interested.

Organizations processing large amounts of printed forms can use scanning devices. This equipment is now reasonably priced, so even small companies can buy them for a few hundred dollars. For example, The Neat Company's NeatDesk and Epson's WorkForce Pro are relatively inexpensive devices that scan business cards, receipts, forms, and other data and automatically populate information into designated programs such as Excel and QuickBooks.

Forms require significant planning and forethought (invention), and they should be arranged and designed in such a way that they are easily understandable. An effective form is easy to fill out and read, record, and interpret. Thus, be sure to consider how you want to provide instructions (typically at the beginning of the form or at the start of each section) and use design elements such as headings, labels, spacing, and fonts. Use *writing lines* or *writing blocks* (demonstrated in Figure 5.7) to help respondents understand where information goes.

Ensure that the information collected is the information needed. For example, if it is unnecessary to know the sex or race of respondents, don't include such questions. People are often uncomfortable providing this information and they take space away from more valuable questions. Choose response types that solicit the maximum amount of information with the fewest words possible. Decide, for example, between open-ended and close-ended questions (e.g., between multiple-choice or forced-rank responses). A course in communication research methods will likely improve your data-collection processes.

To design forms, use form-design software (e.g., Adobe's Acrobat X Pro), word-processing software, or markup languages (e.g., HTML5 or XML, which are introduced in

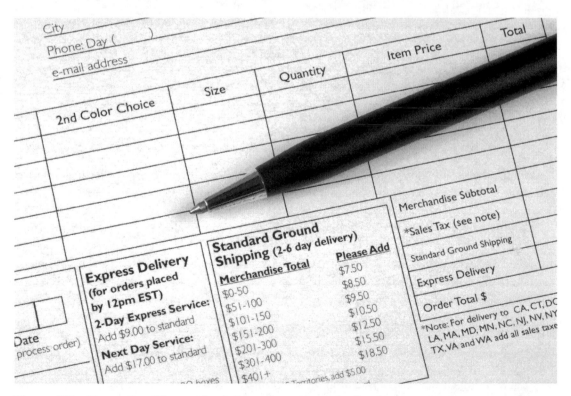

Figure 5.7. Forms simplify complex information and standardize data-entry processes. *(Image © JohnKwan, 2012. Used under license from Shutterstock, Inc.)*

Chapter 9). The best way to craft a form is to mimic one that has already been developed. Government agency forms are excellent models to follow (**http://search.usa.gov/forms**).

Brochures.   Brochures are an institutionalized form of external business communication. You have probably seen a fair share of both effective and ineffective brochures. While design and production is important, because this affects the target audience's interpretation of the material, a brochure's quality is determined more by its ability to achieve its rhetorical purpose: to inform or to persuade or to do both. Even if printing is limited to a basic printer (e.g., instead of multicolored print on glossy paper, you have basic black print on a standard sheet of colored paper), if the message is clear and readable, then the brochure will be effective.

Sales and informational brochures are the two most common types of brochures. A *sales brochure* is used to promote products for services. For example, a résumé consultant's brochure would describe his or her specific services. Although price information could be provided, it is recommended not to include details that are likely to change. *Informational brochures* are created to inform and to educate readers. For example, they can explain a change or disruption in service due to maintenance or describe the types of community services the company has been involved in (as means of promoting goodwill). Sometimes organizations create informational brochures simply to inform the public. For example, a town's fire department may create a brochure to describe ways to reduce the risk of fire in homes and offices.

Writing and designing a brochure.   When writing and designing a brochure, follow the canons of rhetoric. Determine the purpose, the target audience, and the context of the communication. Create a dummy document (see Chapter 3) that replicates the final design. This helps determine how many words will be needed in each section of the brochure. Determine if the brochure will need to be bifold or trifold (typically printed on 8.5″ x 11″ paper) or quadfold (typically printed on 8.5″ x 14″ paper). Figure 5.8 demonstrates a trifold design.

A variety of software programs on the market come with standard brochure templates. For example, Microsoft Office Publisher, which is standard in some versions of the Office productivity suite, provides many user-friendly templates. There are also a variety of free and premium template designs available online through Microsoft and third-party distributers. Gather sample brochures from other companies and organizations, especially competitors, to help stimulate thinking about how to develop an effective layout and design.

Figure 5.8.   Sample layout of a trifold brochure. *(Image © Redshinestudio, 2012. Used under license from Shutterstock, Inc.)*

Use parallel, unified, and appropriate style. If promoting something fun, such as a holiday vacation, use entertaining graphics and writing. Testimonials from customers and pictures of people having fun would capture this spirit. If, however, the brochure is about a serious medical topic, then images of professionals and less emphatic language would be appropriate. Brochures should complement other forms of communication used within and outside the organization. For example, colors and graphics in a brochure should match those of the company's website. Such continuity helps develop identification and promotes an organization's image and brand.

A brochure's design has four elements: the cover panel, the first inside panel, subsequent inside panels, and the back panel. The *cover panel* should capture the audience's attention and demonstrate or specify the brochure's purpose and intent. Keep the amount of text on the cover panel to a minimum. Use larger boldface fonts and graphics that attract readers. The *first inside panel* should again identify the organization and describe the purpose of the brochure. Use large boldface fonts as headlines and keep text to a minimum. Treat the first inside panel as an introduction and preview. The goal is to capture the audience's attention, identify who is likely to be interested in the content, and explain what the brochure is about. *Subsequent panels* should provide content that achieves the purpose of the message. For example, in sales brochures one may use images of products and descriptions. In informational brochures, list useful information supported by facts and other evidence. Use subheadings and lists to move readers along and to maximize white space. The *back panel* typically includes additional useful material, such as contact information, website addresses, citation references, and a special note to contributors of content or organizational supporters.

Printing and distributing the brochure. It is now easy and inexpensive to print professional-looking brochures. Mass customization printing websites, such as **www.vistaprint .com**, provide easy-to-use printing templates and services. Design a brochure using stock images that are available online, or upload a PDF version of brochures, posters, business cards, or other items and, at a fraction of the cost of years before, have the documents printed in small or large batch sizes. This approach keeps paper waste and costs low. One can print on a variety of paper styles (e.g., glossy or flat, heavy or thin paper).

Brochures can be mass mailed, displayed in such places as brochure racks and waiting rooms, and posted online as PDF files. If it is important to reach a wide audience, consider distributing brochure files through a variety of online venues, such as **http://issuu.com** and **http://twitter.com**.

Spoken Types of Concise Communications

Concise verbal correspondence is common in business and professional situations. Though the line between concise and extensive presentations can be difficult to draw, a fundamental criterion for concise communications is that it is either short (not longer than 30 minutes) or single-topic focused or both. For example, a sales pitch is typically short, but certain types of sales pitches can last for hours. Nevertheless, a pitch generally focuses on a single topic, for example, one product or service. Three common types of concise verbal communications are pitches, oral briefings, and question and answer sessions. Media interviews follow the same guidelines as oral briefings or question-answer sessions.

Pitches. A *pitch* is a short, prepared line of talk that attempts to persuade. In Chapter 4, for example, the "elevator pitch" described a pitch that attempts to summarize a person's job objective and qualifications in an attempt to persuade a recruiter to look more closely at his or her résumé. Two of the most common types of formal pitches used in business and professional situations are sales pitches and investor (angel) pitches. However, you may find yourself informally pitching ideas in meetings. All of the canons of rhetoric are used in this brief type of oral communication. Style, for example, is critical to evoking pathos, which is needed to inspire the audience to take action (e.g., give money). The canon of arrangement, however, may be one of the most important elements to pitching. When information and material is delivered, kairos is just as important, if not more so, than what type of information is delivered. Arrangement seems to significantly influence people's receptivity to a pitch (Aronson, 2011; Todd, 2009).

A persuasive organizational pattern that is effective in pitches is Monroe's Motivated Sequence, which was developed by Alan Monroe (1945). Its organizational pattern proceeds as follows:

- *Attention:* The rhetor grabs the audience's attention by narrating a detailed story or by providing shocking examples or statistics, essentially saying that there is a problem that requires a solution. The function of the attention getter is to make a strong impression and motivate the audience to listen.

- *Need:* The rhetor provides more evidence to support that the story, examples, or statistics provided in the attention step are significant. The rhetor offers a specific statement of the problem (makes it more concrete than in the attention step), provides illustrations that paint the problem as a significant issue for the audience, and points to testimonials, illustrations, and ramifications to show the magnitude of the problem. The function of this step is to get the audience *to feel* a need or want, not just think about its existence.

- *Satisfy:* The rhetor offers a solution (product or service) that will satisfy the need. It is important to give evidence, either by demonstration or explanation (e.g., testimonials), that demonstrates the proposal is a satisfactory solution to the need. The function of this step is to inform the audience how to fill the need or want.

- *Visualization:* In this step of the sequence, the rhetor works to intensify the audience's desire for the solution. This can be achieved by the positive method—focusing on how much better life is with the solution—or the negative method—how much worse life will be without the solution. In some cases, the rhetor may want to use a contrasting method—a combination of the positive and negative methods, which addresses negatives first and positives second. The function of this step is to get the audience to see the benefits of the solution by visualizing the outcomes (primarily benefits) that come by taking a particular action (e.g., buying a product and using it).

- *Action:* In this step, the final appeal to action is made and the rhetor makes his or her strongest appeal. In short, the speaker suggests, "it is either now or never." The function of the action step is to get the audience to actually take action, not just think about it. The goal of the pitch is to get the audience to accept an idea or buy a product or service.

Monroe's Motivated Sequence, demonstrated in the following pitch, can be summarized in a simple, memorable format: 1) "Hey! Listen to me because we (or you) have a problem!"; 2) "This is what the problem looks like."; 3) "I have a solution!"; 4) "If we implement my solution, this is what will happen. Or, if we do not implement my solution, this is what will happen."; and 5) "It's time to take action and implement my solution or accept the consequences."

Oral briefings.   A *briefing* is an act of giving precise instructions or essential information. Briefings are sometimes called *status reports*. Their purpose is to update management, clients, and other interested personnel on the progress of your or your organization's work on a project. In a briefing on the status of a project, for example, state what work has been done, what changes have been made in the work, and what work still needs to be completed. Most importantly, let the audience know whether or not the project is on schedule and whether there are any current or potential problems.

Technically, briefings can be written. Written briefings are often provided in memos and emails, so just follow the guidelines regarding oral briefings here and adapt it to written form. In written form, follow the rules and procedures for writing for the medium selected (e.g., memos or email). During meetings, employees, team leaders, managers, or committee officers are frequently asked to give status updates on projects and other important pieces of information. Because meetings are often scheduled, and information does not always apply to every person in attendance, keep briefings short. In fact, treat all communication in a meeting as a briefing, even if discussion is impromptu.

An example of an idea pitch

We're losing market share to our competition and are likely to face layoffs [attention]. Our sales are down by 3.5% for the year and accounting projects an additional 2% decline by year end; we must do something [need]. I've thought of a plan: Hire interns from University X and pay them on commission. I am willing to organize and manage the effort [satisfy]. If we don't act, our sales will almost certainly continue to decline and we'll have to lay off staff next year. With my solution, the students will get excellent experience, you'll not have to worry about the additional management burden, and we'll get increased exposure and an inexpensive temporary labor force. This worked at my brother's company, which was in a similar situation [visualization]. If we do nothing, we're in trouble. We have nothing to lose, so give me permission to try my plan. Just say "yes" [action], and I'll get to work.

Generally, briefings should be between one and five minutes in length. When information is more complex, the briefing should be accompanied by handouts that summarize information or provide visual aids (e.g., graphs, charts, or figures). The briefing focuses on selling the audience on the importance of the available information and how to read the handouts or website. For oral briefings, plan, organize, practice, and deliver using the performance strategies described in earlier chapters. Create a short outline and practice delivery, especially if you are notified in advance that you are expected to brief an audience.

When giving oral briefings via televised media, seek the assistance of the media crew before going on air. Ask them to look over talking points, if possible, and use their directives to improve performance. If given time to prepare, avoid speaking without practice.

Questions and answers (Q&A).   An important form of oral communication, which is often overlooked in business and professional communication, is asking questions and providing answers. As with any form of communication, use all the canons of rhetoric during a Q&A session. Asking effective questions and providing circumspect responses will help an audience appreciate that you are an eloquent and thoughtful speaker. Treat the opportunities for asking and answering questions with as much diligence as you do other forms of communication. The Q&A session is an important part of the interpretive process and can help speakers and audiences understand each other better. Unfortunately, most speakers treat question and answer sessions as secondary to the presentation by not giving much time to the activity and by underpreparing.

When asking questions, write or memorize the question. Before speaking, practice or visualize asking your question several times. Questions should be short and focus on a single topic. If it is necessary to ask a two-part question, inform the speaker and organize the question so the parts are clear. Be polite and invite the speaker to respond to only one part of the two-part question. This is important, because he or she may want or need to attend to other questions. If the two-part question is long, suggest that the speaker respond to the first part, and, if willing, give you an opportunity to ask a second question. Be fair to the speaker and to other members of the audience by staying on topic, by having looked at all the premeeting materials and presentation handouts, and by asking questions in as succinct a manner as possible.

A question-answer session is not an opportunity to argue or cross-examine a speaker. Avoid asking loaded questions and don't launch into a mini speech. If a question requires some kind of background explanation or argument, try to find a way to ask the question that would force the speaker to mention specific details. For example, if you disagree with a policy position of the speaker, simply ask, "Can you explain your rationale, with strong supporting evidence, for your position on policy X?." If the speaker is unprepared, she or he will reveal flaws in his or her arguments. You don't need to be argumentative to prove points. Audiences tend to protect speakers, even ones they don't like, so don't be aggressive. This will often have the opposite rhetorical effect—you could turn the audience against you.

Answering questions requires speaking extemporaneously. Of course, one can mitigate this by preparing in advance. Write down anticipated questions and practice responding to them. Having a mastery understanding of a topic and explaining the relationship the speaker has with a topic can help deal with difficult questions. One can, for example, decline to answer a question if he or she suggested to the audience that he or she is not an expert (perhaps just a spokesperson). When a member of the audience is asking a question, write details about the question to ensure focus during the response.

To effectively respond to questions, consider the rhetorical situation and behave accordingly. For example, remain standing if it is appropriate. Don't run away; give the audience an opportunity to ask questions. To be informal, sit down. In some cases, one can sit and still project formality. For example, there are times when teams or groups have a dedicated spokesperson. She or he may sit so that when questions are asked, the team member with expertise can stand and respond. It is not necessary for everyone on the team to stand or sit at the front of the room during a presentation. Doing so can lead to unanticipated problems. For instance, team members who are not speaking often appear bored and, if they look uninterested, the audience may become indifferent. Another common problem is the audience may target a specific team member or a more outgoing team member who is dominating the responses. When presenting as a team, be courteous to team members and the audience by adhering to time restrictions and redirecting questions to the appropriate team members.

In addition to being prepared and projecting an inviting attitude, consider doing the following during Q&A:

- Set parameters, such as a time limitation, a specified number of questions, or a specific topic of focus.
- Try to select questions from different parts of the room.
- Repeat the question before you answer it, so everyone can hear it.
- Answer the question clearly and move on.
- Signal when you will accept just one more question.
- Do not respond negatively to tough or critical questions.
- Practice answering questions as part of rehearsal.
- Approach the session as a dialogue and embrace the opportunity to clarify points.

Allow as many people as possible to ask questions. Politely deny the request to questions that are off topic or in multiple parts. (Facilitators or moderators can also do this on behalf of the speaker—"That seems a little off topic, perhaps we can address it at a later time.") Invite

Use the canons of rhetoric to improve Q&A sessions. (Image © AVAVA, 2012. Used under license from Shutterstock, Inc.)

people with complex questions to discuss the issue after the presentation. Remember that an audience always assumes that the speaker is in control, so, unless he or she enforces the Q&A rules, nobody will. Don't leave an audience frustrated over Q&A; this can have unintended consequences on the effectiveness of a message. When someone begins to launch into a speech, instead of asking a question, or asks irrelevant questions, contain the situation as quickly as possible.

Extensive Artifacts

Unless you choose a career as a technical writer, you are unlikely to prepare extensive business communications frequently. Thus, you can rely on templates and others' similar artifacts as a guide for producing extensive documents. Extensive business artifacts include various types of reports and proposals, plans, and multiple-part presentations. For example, a business plan for a new venture is an extensive artifact. The U.S. Small Business Administration (**http://sba.gov**) provides excellent information, guidelines, and examples that can guide you through the business plan writing process.

Whether written or spoken, extensive messages require significant focus on the canon of invention, particularly in the areas of primary and secondary research. It is the process of invention and the effort required to craft the artifact that makes it extensive. Although extensive artifacts are generally long, they don't have to be. Some extensive artifacts are short; however, extensive communications are considered as such because of the effort that goes into producing them. Recall from Chapter 2 that invention, particularly as it relates to research, is important to developing a clear understanding of an artifact's *specific purpose*. Is your goal to inform, to persuade, or to demonstrate? Do you want to identify problems and provide solutions, or do you want to compare and contrast proposed ideas? Knowing the purpose of the communication helps frame what to look for when conducting research.

To conduct effective research, plan your research process thoroughly (e.g., how will you save and organize data?), locate the data and information needed (e.g., consult a librarian), have the right tools and knowledge to process data and information, and apply your findings in a manner that is void of fallacies. Track your sources and cite them; this will build ethos by revealing the credibility of claims.

This section introduces various strategies for crafting extensive communications and different types of written and spoken extensive communications.

Written Types of Extensive Communications

In general, extensive written communications fall into three categories: plans, proposals, and reports.

Plans.   *Plans* are primarily decision-making tools. They commit individuals, departments, and organizations, and the resources of each, to specific activities in the future. They are often written by the intended audience in order to guide its actions. They may be shared with other internal or external stakeholders for informational purposes or to obtain feedback.

While plans often look similar to proposals in form, they do not aim to persuade the audience. In a sense, planning assumes that external stakeholders will only be able to make suggestions; only a plan's authors will have real authority over making changes. In short, the audience is expected to be compliant. Plans are useful tools for long-term planning and decision making.

Plans are an expression of rational administrative behavior (Simon, 1997/1948). Written plans and the process of creating and maintaining them forces individuals and teams in business and professional contexts to engage in a psychological process of thinking about the activities required to achieve a desired outcome. Planning involves forecasting problems and preparing solutions in order to guide actions when unanticipated issues arise.

The four most common types of plans are operational plans, tactical plans, strategic plans, and contingency plans. *Operational plans*, such as construction or project plans, can be categorized as single-use or ongoing. They are often used by managers or other organizational decision-makers to accomplish job responsibilities, which includes directing the practices of others. A *tactical plan* is often supported by the operational plan. It provides details about the specific practices required to achieve operational outcomes. An advertising campaign for a product is an example of a tactical plan. These plans often specify short-term and measurable goals that are implemented during phases of the strategic plan. *Strategic plans*, which are often set by the executives or top-level managers, are used for long-term planning. Business plans and 10-year plans for large organization are examples of strategic plans. These plans are developed in order to craft specific tactical and operational plans. *Contingency plans* are used to deal with crises, including both anticipated and unavoidable issues that often hijack the fulfillment of a strategic plan. A crisis communication plan to deal with fallout from a change in service is an example of a contingency plan.

Useful plans draw significantly upon known data that are outcomes of previous actions and performances. Historical data allow planners to identify main issues and challenges as well as benefit from examples of practices that worked to manage earlier crises. Research significantly shows that goals and practices outlined in plans should be realistic, specific, acceptable to the organization, and easily measurable (see Matthews & Draper-Watts, 2011; Nunamaker, Weber, & Chen, 1989; and Windischer, et al., 2009). K. Richmond Kemple (2002), in *Public Relations Quarterly*, provides a useful acronym—CLEAR—to use when writing effective strategic goals: Concrete, Linked to business objectives, Executable, Action-oriented, and Results-driven. For many businesses and teams, assessing outcomes remains one of the biggest challenges.

Plans often follow the basic type of structure as reports (discussed later in this chapter), but they may also be as short as a memo—for example, when stating a single operational goal and procedure. The best way to learn to format a plan is to model it on an existing one. Plans are readily available online. Part of the invention process should include identifying those plans that would be useful guides. For example, universities often post strategic plans online, the U.S. Small Business Administration, as well as several other organizations, offer business plan writing guidelines and examples, and various government agencies publish contingency and crisis management plans for public view.

The best plans are not those that have a fancy format, but are those that focus primarily on the practices of the canon of invention and are specific to the organizational or rhetorical situation. Simply copying another organization's plan is not only a form of plagiarism, it is not likely to be useful when making rational decisions or responding to real crisis. Many entrepreneurs, for example, may not have a formal written business plan; however, it is likely they have a strong and thorough understanding of their goals due to invention. Having a written plan, nevertheless, can assist decision makers. Written plans do not need to be long. Business consultant and serial entrepreneur David Ronick (2011) recommends writing business plans in presentation software like PowerPoint or Keynote because it forces the entrepreneur to keep it short. He notes that these concise plans are used by entrepreneurs to avoid big mistakes, to counterbalance emotions, to ensure everyone is on the same page, to develop a game plan, and to raise capital. Understanding your audience's needs is critical when writing an extensive plan, as it will help determine if a long or short plan is optimal. For example, if raising capital is the primary goal, a traditional business plan may not be as effective as a simple, one- to two-page statement that reports balance sheet and cash-flow projections (Lister, 2011). However, a traditional plan may be useful for long-term strategic decisions.

A plan represents an important rhetorical process—creation. "Planning" is not about the object (written plan) but the objective (thoughtfulness).

Proposals.   *Written proposals* are documents crafted with the intent to persuade. Proposals make requests for decisions or actions. Among other reasons, they may request decisions from internal stakeholders, such as managers, for funding, research and development, or building maintenance projects. They may also make requests of external stakeholders. For example, they may be written to obtain investments, grants, permissions, long-term contracts or purchase agreements, or a community's commitment or financial investment in a project.

Proposals may also be solicited or unsolicited. *Solicited proposals* are prepared in response to requests for goods or services. Like responses to position announcements (see Chapter 4), it is important to conduct a thorough rhetorical criticism of the request for proposal (RFP) or invitation for bid (IFB). (To learn how to write RFPs and IFBs, a type of written-request letter, it is useful to look at examples published online.)

RFPs typically solicit a solution to a defined need or problem. The procuring agency or organization is looking for the optimal solution. When responding to RFPs, use keywords and emulate the language, style, and tone of the procuring organization or agency. Also, identify exactly what the organization wants and respond to these specifics. For example, a company may want a community program to generate a specific type of response; it is the respondent's rhetorical burden to describe how these responses will be achieved and measured. Providing examples from previous successful campaigns is one way to provide evidence.

When responding to RFPs, follow the formatting requirements if they are specified or maintain the integrity of a template if the organization provides one. Often RFPs will specify the desired page length, margin widths, typeface and font size, paper color, binding requirements, numbering systems, headings, and necessary appendix attachments (supporting materials). Any proposal failing to meet the standard or requirements may be immediately rejected.

IFBs are more restrictive and detailed. They often already state the solution and product specifications. Procuring agencies seek only proof that the bidding organization can legally meet the performance standards, technical specifications, and time and cost frames. Typically, IFBs are issued by governmental agencies or companies that outsource manufacturing of products to third-party vendors. Like RFPs, it is important to follow the specified format requirements.

IFBs and RFPs are generally posted online through professional or industrial trade magazines or listservs. Subscribe to the appropriate distribution channels and bulletin boards and monitor databases that publish or catalog various types of proposals. Some useful online sources for government and corporate RFPs and IFBs or grants are The RFP Database (**http://rfpdb .com**), Foundation Center (**http://foundationcenter.org**), FindRFP (**http://findrfp.com**), **http://grants.gov**, Community of Science (**http://cos.org**), and the Federal Business Opportunities (**http://fbo.gov**).

Unsolicited proposals are submitted to a company or department without a prior request for a proposal. These are typically written for a company that has an identifiable problem that they may not have initially recognized. Often unsolicited proposals are written following a meeting or conference with a salesperson, in which the approached company or organization expresses some openness to purchasing a solution, product, or consultancy relationship. Following the initial meeting, the proposing agency conducts a study or needs assessment to determine whether a solution is viable and only then writes a proposal, formally pitching the product or service.

Whether a proposal is solicited or unsolicited, remember that these are legally binding once both parties have agreed to the terms and conditions. RFPs and IFBs promise the delivery of goods or services within a specific time frame and at a specific cost. Therefore, be realistic about your or your company's technical abilities and operational facilities. If working as a consultant on behalf of a company, understand a client's operations *before* writing or submitting bids and proposals.

When writing a proposal, it is your rhetorical goal to convince readers that they need what you are proposing, and that you are the right person or organization to provide the product or services proposed. Thus, draw significantly upon the classical appeals—ethos, pathos, and logos—to convince readers.

Ethos. Whether a proposal is for an internal or external audience, know your audience and purpose. Evaluators of proposals look for how well you answer their questions, how well you articulate your plan to achieve specified objectives, how much your financial bid presents a realistic proposal, and how well you explain the benefits of your products or services.

Readers will also look for the proper use of technical and professional vocabularies. The more you sound like you know the needs of the industry and profession and understand your strengths and weaknesses, the more credible you will appear.

Pathos. Appeal to readers' emotions by using vivid descriptions and by summarizing the benefits of outcomes in ways that allow the audience to get excited. Nevertheless, be cautious about overstating the case or by providing little support for claims. When meeting with representatives of a company for the first time, especially when trying to lay a foundation for acceptance of an unsolicited proposal, curb your enthusiasm. The expression "the faster they rise, the harder they fall" applies here. Salespeople may get a company excited about a new product or service only to have the engineers write a realistic and, therefore, less impressive proposal. If a company expects miracles, then anything less than that will be a real disappointment.

Logos.   Once you state your purpose and main points, stick to them. Wandering from the main points you are trying to articulate will not only confuse readers, it will lower your credibility. Cite relevant sources of information, including facts, statistics, and specific examples of comparative outcomes or accomplishments. These data will help convince readers that you can meet their needs and have a proven track record. If bidding on a new type of product or service, that is, one you have little experience with, focus on the details of the plan's process and implementation. Show through narrative rather than telling. A convincing story that includes descriptions of equipment and expertise is just as convincing as customer testimonials.

Proposals often require more than one level of approval, so take into account all potential readers. Remember that not everyone will have the same technical knowledge or time to read the document. So, like reports, use a clear-cut organizational pattern. Provide a glossary of complex terms, an appendix that summarizes complex information that is specific only to one particular audience (this way it does not convolute the text), use graphics and objects to help explain complicated concepts, and include an executive summary.

Proposals are often converted, with some modification, into plans, which guide the implementation of a solution or development of a product. Reports inform stakeholders whether a plan's objectives are achieving the proposal's specifications.

Reports.   A *report* is an organized presentation of information or analytical findings. *Informational reports* offer data, facts, feedback, and general information without analysis or recommendations. A newsletter, for example, is a basic type of informational report that often summarizes what's been going on in a business. It promotes the internal and external activities of employees. Other common types of informational reports include progress reports, activity reports, and trip reports. *Analytical reports* offer both information and analysis of data. Often these include investigative reports, trouble reports, white papers, and a variety of other formal reports. They are written both for decision-making and persuasion. They may be written for internal and external audiences and may contain information gathered collaboratively to pass along to upper-level management.

As with any type of business communication, understand the audiences' needs and the rhetorical purpose of the document. For example, informal newsletters can provide essential updates about the organization and build goodwill among employees. The kind of information provided and the tone of the presentation will be much different than a newsletter aimed at external constituents. The results of an investigation, however, should be written in a more formal manner and will likely include both information and analysis. However, if a client or manager does not expect or desire recommendations, then the investigative report can remain primarily descriptive.

Sometimes reports are more informal or short, such as trip reports, activity reports, and progress reports. In these cases, write and distribute the report in a letter, memo, or email. As is always the case, writing should be organized with a solid introduction and preview, body, and conclusion (which may include recommendations).

When reporting on major projects, such as the outcome of research activities, the end product is likely to be a *formal report*. Unless an organization has a specific style, follow the format described below. There are plenty of formal report examples available on **www.docstoc.com** for free. The following is a list of the typical elements to include in a formal report.

Front matter (in order of presence).

- **Title page.** The title page typically includes the report's title; the name, job title, and address of the person or company that commissioned the report; the name, job title, and address of the person, group, or company that prepared the report; and the date of submission. Sometime the title page is used as the document cover.
- **Abstract.** The abstract summarizes the content of the report. It should highlight the major points of the report so that readers can decide whether the report is pertinent to them.
- **Table of contents.** This should list at least the major sections of the report and their corresponding page numbers. A more thorough table of contents will provide summaries or subsections. The table of contents can function as a useful outline when preparing and writing the report. It will, in the end, look very different than a working outline, however. You can generate a table of contents with many word processing programs automatically if you tag the sections and subsections you want included in the table of contents.
- **List of figures.** All visuals, such as photographs, maps, charts, and graphs, should be labeled. If you have several figures or other labeled materials, create a table of contents for them. List them, along with the page numbers, on a separate page following the table of contents. Do the same for lists of tables and, if you prefer, a list of any other visuals you have labeled uniquely (for example, if you have both figures and photographs, you can label them differently).
- **Foreword.** This optional prefatory statement is written by someone other than the author(s) of the report. Within business settings, this is often a letter from the chief executive officer or project manager. Because they make a rhetorical pitch for the usefulness of a report's contents, forewords are very useful. In particular, they often summarize what parts of the report are likely to be meaningful to readers not directly associated with a project or give a preferred interpretation of its contents.
- **Preface (synopsis).** The preface is another optional introductory element. It is a statement written by the author(s) of a report. It usually announces the work's purpose, scope, context, and acknowledgments. It may even specify the intended audience.

Body.

- **Executive summary.** Long reports often begin the body of the report with an executive summary, which provides a complete overview or "mini" version of the report. This is intended for people who lack the time or need to read the entire report. Nowadays, the executive summary, or other parts of the text where appropriate, may include an *executive dashboard*, a type of graphical user interface that is designed, much like a car's dashboard with gauges and information panels (e.g., charts and graphs) that make information easy to read and more accessible. To learn more about these interfaces, check out the following dashboard software manufacturers: **www.domo.com**, **http://inetsoft.com/ products/dashboard_examples**, and **http://www-01.ibm.com/software/analytics/ cognos/products/.**

- **Introduction.** The introduction gives readers a preview of the report's overall contents. It fills in any contextual and background information that is necessary for understanding a report's contents.

- **Text.** This is the heart of the report. If you have a synopsis or executive summary, minimize any redundancy. The text should present the details of how an investigation or research project unfolded, what alternatives were explored, how problems were solved, and all the evidence supporting recommendations, conclusions, outcomes, and so on. Be sure to cite references to secondary sources and include any other explanatory footnotes that may be helpful to readers. Due to the longer length of reports, it is best to use as much of the narrative style as possible and to enhance content with visuals, such as tables,

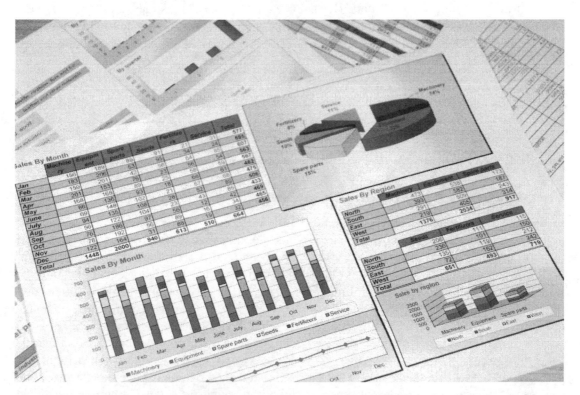

Use charts and graphs to make complex information more understandable and easier to read. (Image © Nataliiap, 2012. Used under license from Shutterstock, Inc.)

charts, graphs, maps, and so on. Be sure to use an appropriate organizational pattern, such as topical, problem-solution, or geographical.

- **Conclusion.** In the conclusion, summarize all of the content and interpret some of the outcomes for the audience. Provide information that may be useful, such as future studies and reports.

Back matter (supplementary materials).

- **Appendixes.** An appendix clarifies or supplements materials in the report. Sometimes appendixes provide additional information that is too detailed or too lengthy for body text. List appendixes in your table of contents and provide in-text references to them. Organize appendixes in a logical pattern.
- *Reference list and bibliography.* A reference list provides only those works cited in the materials. A bibliography lists all works consulted, even those that are not cited. Typically, bibliographies are provided because they provide readers with additional resources to consult.
- **Glossary.** A glossary is an alphabetized list of special terms used in the report and their definitions. These can be helpful to readers who may not have mastery of technical jargon.
- **Index.** An index is an alphabetical list of names, places, and subjects mentioned in the report. It cites the page numbers where discussion of each topic can be found. This helps readers find or relocate information. The index is always the final section of any report.

To print a report, use a professional printing service and, if the budget permits, use color and bind the materials together. Use Adobe Acrobat Pro to assemble documents, and use hyperlinks for the table of contents and all cross-references. This will allow readers to easily move between sections and referenced materials (e.g., figures). Finally, post reports on a website. Either provide a downloadable PDF version or embed the document into a website through services offered by publisher websites like **http://issuu.com**.

Verbal Types of Extensive Communications

In respect to the canons of rhetoric, there is little difference between concise and extensive verbal communications. The differences are in scale rather scope. It simply takes more time to plan, craft, practice, and deliver more comprehensive verbal communications. However, both long and short, detailed and less-detailed verbal presentations and speeches require the same amount of diligence and effort for invention, arrangement, style, and memory. Often, having more time to present is better than having less time. If you have a lot of information, make it tighter by writing it as a briefing and then develop the longer presentation. Usually extensive communications are prepared for events that cover special topics, such as conferences. Thus, the burden of presenting extensively on a topic is often shared among various participants, groups, and teams. Within the context of group gatherings, people may have more or less time to present. There are four general types of gatherings requiring extensive communications: forums, panels, colloquia, and symposia.

Forums.   A *forum* is a type of extensive presentation that involves speaking and listening to an audience. It is set up in the form of a public discussion. The entire audience is invited to participate. The discussion, often arranged as several short reaction speeches, is usually followed by a presentation or series of presentations on a topic or problem. Forums are facilitated by a moderator and follow a specific schedule. If time is short, sometimes written materials are delivered in advance and respondents, representing different stakeholder groups, are asked to prepare short presentations.

The purpose of a forum is to allow various speakers to present and support arguments, state positions, take issue with what has been said, clarify points, ask questions, answer questions, and respond to comments. Forums are often contentious events with an argumentative atmosphere. This ought to be encouraged, so long as people remain respectful, adhere to the established rules, and avoid *ad hominem arguments*—a type of fallacy in which a person attacks the person rather than the argument. A good forum ensures healthy democratic debate, not a good feeling. If people feel that they were represented and that their objections, views, and preference respected, they are likely to have a favorable impression of the forum, even if their ideas are not ultimately accepted. "Town hall" meetings, public hearings, and various plenary sessions are designed as forums. Due to simulcasting, which allows for the presentation of an event through multiple media, forum participants may be either physically or virtually present.

Forums can be contentious. It is important to respect speakers and moderators, but be assertive so your opinions are heard. (Image © Anton Gvozdikov, 2012. Used under license from Shutterstock, Inc.)

During the event, if speakers are not predetermined, the moderator will select speakers. If the venue is large, microphones are sometimes placed in the front of the audience. Speakers then line up behind the microphones. If the topic is contentious, sometimes two or more microphones are used and designated in specific ways (e.g., "pro" and "con"). The task of the moderator is to enforce speaking rules and to create a climate of fairness. For example, moderators can encourage people to speak up for an opposing view if one side has been particularly over-represented. The role of the moderator is a difficult one. As a speaker, therefore, it is important to respect the rules of engagement.

Forums often take on elements of the other types of presentation formats. For example, a panel of experts may present on a topic or a symposium-style series of presentations may be delivered before the discussion.

Panels. A *panel* is a presentation format that offers an opportunity for a group of experts (typically four, but up to ten) to discuss a topic, problem, or decision in front of an audience for approximately an hour. This is a discussion format that includes both formal and informal presentations and discussions among the various presenters. At times, the panel can be structured in more of a debate format, allowing panel participants to challenge each other during a cross-examination period. However, it is important that panel participants be mindful that the general purpose of a panel is to be informative to the audience, not an opportunity for confrontation among speakers. Moderators need to ensure that speakers follow rules and remain tactful.

An effective panel presentation involves designating a theme that is timely or addresses a niche topic of interest to the audience. Sometimes panels are imbedded in larger conferences and provide subtheme discussions on the larger conference topic. Panels are only effective if the panel members are selected, assigned, or invited with some forethought. By assembling a team that can present on various facets of a topic, and who are willing to work together, the audience is provided with a sensible, though dynamic presentation. The variation of speakers avoids monotony typical of long presentations.

Whether organizing or presenting on a panel, it is important to prepare. As an organizer, providing speaking details, rules, guidelines, technological capabilities, speaking order, definitions, the topic problem, potential questions and answers, and so on in advance, and ensuring that all of the promises are kept so there are no big surprises on the day of the presentation, will make a panel presentation effective. As a presenter, adhering to the rules is not only courteous to other speakers, it will be appreciated by the audience. Although the presentational burden is shared, participants rely on other presenters to deliver their material well. Thus, do not skimp on the canons of memory and delivery. Just because you know a topic well does not give you license to wing it. Collaboration means doing your part, even without the opportunity for advanced discussion with panel participants.

The planner also sometimes functions as the moderator. The moderator's role is to call the meeting to order, to describe to the audience the topic or problem, to explain the proceeding format to the audience, to introduce speakers, to keep time, and sometimes to summarize speakers' perspectives. Some panel formats invite an expert respondent to give feedback to panelists or take up a specific position based on the panelists' presentations. The panel format is not designed for direct interaction between the audience and panelists; however, following a panel discussion, sometimes there is a moderated question-and-answer session or a forum-style discussion. These are in addition to the one-hour typically designated to session presentations.

Colloquia. A *colloquium* arranges a presentation in such a way that a group of experts, typically three to six, discuss a problem or divergent views. More so than a panel, this format encourages a problem-solution structure and invites audience participation following presentations. The colloquium is more informal than forums and panels, with the moderator simply facilitating the discussion by selecting speakers and determining when to move on to another. The primary purpose of the colloquium is to identify, develop, and work through a particular solution to a problem, which is usually introduced by the moderator. The typical colloquium lasts between one and two hours.

Symposia. For the Greeks, a symposium was a convivial meeting for drinking, music, and intellectual discussion. Today, many academic and professional conferences could be described as symposia. In today's sense of the word, a *symposium* is any meeting or conference for discussion of a topic that encourages audience participation. It may include several panel discussions over a week, in which attendees participate as both panelists and audience in different scheduled sessions. By definition, however, a symposium can also be a single meeting in which a series of two to six well-prepared and polished speeches are presented in an uninterrupted fashion to the audience. These speeches may be brief, all presented in a single sitting, or lengthier, each presented in separate time slots. Speeches may be followed by a forum discussion or coffee breaks. Participants are encouraged to continue discussion during these times. The moderator introduces the session(s), addresses the important issues about the topic, introduces speakers, and provides closing remarks. For a symposium with multiple speeches occurring at different times during the day, the moderator may begin each session.

Conclusion

This chapter presented a discussion and examples of extensive and concise written and verbal correspondence. Although many of these types of communications are now distributed electronically, think of these everyday and traditional forms of communication on their own. Crafting traditional letters well and knowing how to properly engage in different types of group discussions will save you time, improve your professional image, and make you more persuasive and effective.

As people increasingly use electronic forms of brief communications, the more traditional look can be refreshing. By writing professional-looking documents and practicing good speaking habits, you will become known as a conscientious professional with whom others want to work. Also, you will form better writing habits that can easily be transported between virtual and nonvirtual communications.

You should always be thinking about and applying the five canons of rhetoric to any situation. While this chapter presents some standard formats and common ways of writing and presenting ideas that are worth emulating, always adapt to rhetorical situations. While a forum may be ideal for open dialogue, it may not work well if the topic is too contentious at the time. Thus, it may be worth muting the audience by using a panel without discussion or a symposium without forum discussions. However, if the goal is to stimulate ideas, breaking from or modifying all the more traditional formats discussed above may be worthwhile. For example, brainstorming sessions before panel discussions could give panelists more direction; miniforums in lieu of panels could encourage more participation from people uncomfortable with speaking in front of large audiences; or a creative or unconventional combination of the extensive presentation formats could lead to interesting outcomes, especially if the audience is looking for something different. In recent years, the concept of "unconferences" or "mashup meetings"—types of participant-driven meetings that try to break from more formal conventions and conferences—have become popular. In these types of meetings, participants brainstorm topics and then people who are "experts" join panels and speak extemporaneously. The "unconvention" breaks from the hierarchical structure of planned meetings to make them more democratic. Generally, planners and facilitators arrange the venue, establish a broad topic, and allow attendees to set the agenda on site.

Other things to consider are how you might present ideas stylistically, which is a subjective decision. It is difficult to know whether to be assertive or indirect, or to present ideas in a more conservative or playful tone. The situation and audience will partly determine this, but also your level of comfort. Certainly, an audience will appreciate if communication follows conventions, is deliberate, and demonstrates courteousness toward others. When presenting with others, consider the rules of engagement and stick to them. If there is a 10-minute limit for speaking, don't hijack the presentation by going longer. If there are several speakers, determine whether all group members will speak and whether all members will sit in front of the audience like a panel.

Designating a single spokesperson can be an effective way to ensure continuity of speech and to limit the exposure of a group's interpersonal conflicts. Often groups share in presenting ideas, but this can create awkward transitions due to lack of practice. If all members sit in front of the audience, some may project an awkward tension or boredom. If your group or fellow panelists look bored, the audience will begin to feel bored, creating a negative and downward feedback loop. Worse, some members or panelists may continue to prepare for their talk while another member speaks, creating distracting movements of paper as they make last-minute edits to their outlines. If you write a document that is just one part of a larger document or ongoing communication, or present on a panel, demonstrate respect by maintaining consistency, by being prepared, by staying within the specified time frame, and by looking interested.

Continuing Education: Recommended Texts and Resources

- *Public relations writing: A rhetorical perspective* by Michael L. Kent. ISBN: 978-0205595440.

    For students interested in public relations, this book will be very useful. Not only does it describe and illustrate the various types of public relations doc-

uments one is likely to write, it approaches the topic from a rhetorical perspective.

- *The social animal (10th ed.)* by Elliot Aronson. ISBN: 978-1429203166

  This book is a landmark text for the field of social psychology. It is written
  in a compelling narrative approach with substantial research. It lists and
  describes several interesting studies that can be used to improve arrangement of ideas, improve sales and marketing tactics.

- "The pitchman" by Malcolm Gladwell (originally published in *The New Yorker*).
  Available online: **www.gladwell.com/2000/2000_10_30_a_pitchman.html**

  This short article describes the art of the television pitchman. According to
  Gladwell, the most important part of a pitch is "the turn," where the pitchman turns from entertainer to salesperson.

- *The American jeremiad* by Sacvan Bercovitch. ISBN: 978-0299073541

  This book describes a rhetoric that is fundamentally U.S.-American. It suggests an approach that is rooted in the U.S.-American Puritan tradition that
  unites public and private life. Although the book is more of the literary tradition, business and professional communicators will find the approach still
  useful. First, the rhetor laments the state of society, predicts its downfall, and
  then suggests a way to progress out of such a state (usually the rhetor's solution or product). In his review of the book, Victor Turner notes: "American
  Jeremiad is truly a seminal book . . . the most illuminating study of the root
  paradigm of American culture yet written."

- *Inviting transformation: Presentational speaking for a changing world (3rd ed.)* by
  Sonja K. Foss and Karen A. Foss. ISBN: 978-1577667216.

  Invitational rhetoric offers a much different approach to rhetoric in that it
  suggests an approach that involves the audience without coercion. The book
  offers an analysis of a variety of speeches based on the process of invitational presentations, which is useful for anyone trying to find ways to communicate with diverse audiences.

- *Getting to Yes: Negotiating agreement without giving in* by Roger Fisher and William
  L. Ury. ISBN: 978-0140157352

  This book discusses a variety of strategies that can be described as a conjoin-
  ing of invitational and classical approaches to rhetoric. The authors suggest
  that positional bargaining is not as effective as principled negotiation, which
  is based on a five-step system (outlined in the book). This classic book is
  considered one of the most important on the topic of negotiation. They
  authors offer a variety of examples that are set in business contexts. Sales
  pitches and negotiations are likely to be much more effective if approached
  from the perspectives discussed in this book.

References

Aronson, E. (2011). *The social animal* (11th ed.). New York: Worth Publishers.

Bone, J. E., Griffin, C. L., Linda Scholz, T. M. (2008). Beyond traditional conceptualizations of rhetoric: Invitational rhetoric and a move toward civility. *Western Journal of Communication, 72,* 434–462.

Chandrasekaran, A. (2004, March 9). Résumé fraud gets slicker and easier. USAToday. Retrieved from www.usatoday.com/tech/news/2004-03-09-resume-cheats_x.htm

Fisher, R., & Ury, W. (2011). *Getting to yes: Negotiating agreement without giving in.* New York: Penguin.

Kemple, K. R. (2002). Setting CLEAR goals: The key ingredient to effective communications planning. *Public Relations Quarterly, 47*(2), 32–35.

Lister, K. The myth of the business plan. *Entrepreneur Magazine.* Retrieved from www.entrepreneur.com/article/220440.

Matthews, J., Draper-Watts, P. (2011). Deliverable objectives: Considerations for creating measurement plans. *Public Relations Tactics,18*(5), 12.

Monroe, A. (1945). *Principles of speech communication.* Glenview, IL: Scott, Foresman and Company.

Nunamaker, J. F., Weber, E. S., Chen, M. (1989). Organizational crisis management systems: Planning for intelligent action. *Journal of Management Information Systems, 5*(4), 7–32.

Ronick, D. (2011). 5 reasons you need a business plan. *Inc. Magazine.* Retrieved from www.inc.com/articles/201107/5-reasons-why-you-need-a-business-plan.html.

Simon, H. (1997/1948). *Administrative behavior* (4th ed.). New York: The Free Press.

Todd, A. (2009, Sept. 29). The sales pitch: Content is almost irrelevant. *BNET.* Retrieved from www.bnet.com/blog/sterling-performance/the-sales-pitch-content-is-almost-irrelevant/3317

Windischer, A., Grote, G., Mathier, F., Meunier Martins, S., & Glardon, R. (2009). Characteristics and organizational constraints of collaborative planning. *Cognition, Technology & Work, 11,* 87–101

Chapter — 6

Crafting Electronic Communications and Presentation Aids

Starting Point

Because email is user friendly, quick, and widely available, it has become a routine medium of exchange for both personal and business communication (Sumecki, Chipulu, & Ojiako, 2011). In early studies of email and its effect on business and organizational processes, researchers focused on its utility as a tool for organizational decision making (Mackay, 1988), cost reduction (Berghel, 1997), and communicative richness (Panteli, 2002). Research has shown that email, along with other forms of electronic communication (e.g., instant messaging), when used conscientiously, leads to gains in productivity and efficiency (Berghel, 1997; Huberman, Romero, & Wu, 2009; Sumecki et al., 2011).

In more recent years, however, many researchers and commentators have focused on email's darker side. For starters, its ubiquity has led to an ever-increasing volume of sent and received messages, which leads to significant business costs. Organizations spend upward to $17 billion per year to support the volume of email (Radicati Group, 2007; as cited in Sumecki et al., 2011). Employees experience "email overload" as they work to keep up with the pace of incoming emails, which arrive in an average of five-minute intervals (Jackson, Dawson, & Wilson, 2003). Email overload leads to increased workplace distractions, message fatigue, and a reduction in analytical processing. According to a Microsoft study, it takes the average employee approximately 15 minutes to refocus on an activity or project with the same level of pre-interruption intensity (see Robinson, 2010). These issues, of course, lead to lost productivity and financial loss (Sumecki et al., 2011). To top off this list of negatives, email and other electronic communication media are addictive (Fried, 2005). Email has blurred the boundaries between work and personal time, upsetting a healthy work-life balance.

Rhetorically, email can also be problematic. First, electronic communication often lacks proper contextualization (Ducheneaut & Bellotti, 2003), reducing its efficacy as a communication medium. Second, it is hard to set the proper tone of electronic communication. Recipients tend to misinterpret senders' tones, leading to an increase in conflicts (Correia, 2008; Turnage, 2007). Third, its efficacy is limited primarily to the epideictic class of rhetoric. For example, it is useful for making announcements and for gathering or distributing information, but it is not very effective—again partly due to misinterpretations of an interlocutor's tone—for deliberation (Santra & Giri, 2009).

In recent years, a variety of creative solutions to the problem of email have been developed. For instance, some companies have instituted policies that declare certain periods of time as email free. For example, Robinson (2010) notes,

> Intel is using Quiet Time at two of its sites. Other companies, including U.S. Cellular and Deloitte & Touche, have mandated less e-mail use, encouraged more face-to-face contact and experimented with programs such as "no e-mail Friday." The results often are surprising: employees build rapport with colleagues—and they save time. Co-workers can settle something in a two-minute phone conversation that might have required three e-mails per person. (para. 18)

Companies should develop protocols for writing, sending, and replying to email messages within the workplace, including the time frame in which a recipient should reply. Formalizing procedures and training employees how to use email can reduce employee anxiety and increase productivity (Fried, 2005; Robinson, 2010).

Technology has addressed some of the problems noted above. Based on use preference, email messages can now be filtered into specific mail folders as they arrive. For example, users can designate all email from a certain sender to be automatically filed into a folder that they check irregularly (e.g., messages from email lists). Spam, or unsolicited bulk mail messages, is now filtered or blocked relatively well by mail-hosting companies and programs.

From a rhetorical perspective, perhaps one of the most exciting products to enter the market in recent years is an application called ToneCheck (**http://tonecheck.com**). ToneCheck's algorithms "read and interpret" an email message before it is sent. The program, described by its developers as "the emotional spellcheck for email," warns users about the message's potentially problematic tone. While it may not stop all possibly misconstrued language, it helps senders catch something that they initially did not see as questionable. From a company's point of view, this program can be used as the first level of "reprimand," giving managers more authority to discipline or dismiss employees who use an improper tone with vendors, customers, or coworkers. The program can also permanently block messages with certain words, such as those that are discriminatory or profane. This software allows users to set at a variety of levels of filtration (see Wang, 2010). The best part is that it is completely free.

As this introduction suggests, email and other electronic communication can increase productivity—or decrease it. Technology is adapting and changing to keep up with the user demands, but the costs, benefits, and negative consequences of adopting technology must be considered (as part of the invention stage). This chapter explores various forms of written and verbal electronic communications, along with the potential benefits and consequences of adopting one form of communication over another. Because presentation aids used in the delivery of more traditional and routine messages are now designed and delivered electronically and digitally, the discussion of presentation aids is also discussed in this chapter. It is especially important to consider the design and use of presentation aids in electronic communications.

Applying the Five Canons

Applying the five canons to electronic communications, particularly in regard to arrangement and memory, is similar to their application to traditional forms of communication. However, as emphasized in other chapters, one must weigh the benefits and costs of distributing information through electronic media. For example, not all customers have equal access to the Internet, so providing customer service by Internet-based platforms only (e.g., instant messenger) may not be wise. Some customers may prefer to connect by telephone. The cost savings for online chat versus telephone chat, therefore, cannot solely be calculated in savings on equipment and labor costs, but also must account for lost customers who must (or prefer) to connect through more traditional media.

Part of the invention process is to determine whether electronic media is the delivery method that will work best for the intended audience or communicative situation and, if so, which particular electronic medium is preferable (e.g., instant messenger, blog, or video chat). Table A.2 in the appendix provides a summary of the advantages and disadvantages of the various types of communication media. As noted, electronic communication is a semi rich medium that does allow for some verbal and nonverbal cues. However, not all electronic media are the same. Instant messenger, for example, is largely a *synchronous* form of communication; however, it does not offer visual cues. In some situations, this can be good. For example, when working with a customer on a potential problem, the customer does not have to hold while on the phone while waiting for replies. This also allows more time for information processing on both ends. There is no feeling of pressure to do something, giving each side time to deliberate and think of alternative solutions. Video chat does offer the ability to see visual cues, but it may be an uncomfortable form of communication for people who are not familiar with it. It may also create additional distractions and pressure interlocutors to respond quickly, reducing information processing. Email is largely asynchronous, but because there are few verbal and non-verbal cues, messages can be easily misinterpreted.

Stylistically, rhetors must decide, among other things, how formal and informal to be with others. Some electronic media, such as instant messenger, are considered to be slightly informal; thus, creating a professional presence requires a more conscientious effort. As with face-to-face interactions, approaches may vary depending on individuals' prior communication and familiarity. If a customer is easy going and playful, for example, then a customer service representative may want to model the customer's rhetoric. However, the representative may still want to maintain a more formal tone to avoid confusion. Not surprisingly, given the wide array of what people consider to be professional communication when using electronic media, there is a propensity for businesses to regulate and monitor electronic communications in the workplace (Allen, Coopman, Hart, & Walker, 2007).

Length of message is also an important stylistic consideration that may drive the choice of medium. Because instant messenger, for example, is not the best medium for long messages, keep them short. Companies should formalize procedures for interaction and train users to methodically solicit information. Ready-at-hand stock phrases and hot keys based on a formal manual may be required to speed up instant messaging processes.

When designing presentation aids for electronic exchange, consider things like file size, compatibility, and effectiveness. These days, it is relatively easy to transfer files in most instant messenger programs. Users simply drag and drop files directly into the program window, which initiates the file transfer. But asking end users to open the files and look at them while describing what the information means is not easy when solely using the text function in instant messenger programs. Message recipients may not be able to move back and forth between windows very easily. Those with older computers may have insufficient memory. Consequently, their computers may freeze or operate slowly when moving among multiple open programs. Using voice chat may allow one window to be open while describing the visual aid. This eliminates the need to move between programs, but it may still slow a user's computer. As is the case when using any technology, but even more when communicating electronically, especially by text rather than voice, users may not fully understand how to use their programs, creating additional technical and operational issues tangential to the issues being discussed.

Several programs, such as Microsoft Lync (**http://microsoft.com/en-us/office365**), Cisco's WebEx (**http://webex.com**), GoToMeeting (**http://gotomeeting.com**), Mikogo (**http://mikogo.com**) and ShowDocument (**http://showdocument.com**), provide platforms for virtual meetings. Using these programs, presenters can engage in live video chat and also enable desktop sharing. This can be more effective then instant messaging for user-to-user consultations. These programs' real power, however, is in replacing live meetings and conferences. With desktop sharing, a presenter can project a series of visual aids, or even a prerecorded show, onto others' computer screens, or they can watch a live video. Either way "attendees" can view a presentation or demonstration live just as they would in person. These types of meetings, often called webinars, web conferences, or virtual meetings, can save money for companies and individuals who no longer have to travel to meeting sites and can even lead to more inclusive and effective meetings (Warkentin, Sayeed, & Hightower, 1997). These technologies, to varying degree and cost, allow people to demonstrate, present, and collaborate in virtual environments.

Visual aids, especially in computer-mediated communications, can range from more traditional handouts that are shared as PDFs, with presentation software (e.g., PowerPoint), or within online portfolios (e.g., **http://visuu.com**) to live webinars with dynamic video and voice. Although you should try to create useful *and* impressive visual aids, think creatively about other not-so-obvious visual aids, which are sometimes more effective. For live oral presentations, for example, using anything other than PowerPoint (or similar software) can be refreshing. Using an overhead projector is not only a classic move, but it can be much more effective for some things. Sketching a flow charts live (rather than presenting them as static on a projected slide) can help the audience keep pace with the speaker.

Simple presentation devices and aids in electronic communication can also make messages easier to understand. For example, long emails should provide a mini preview (or abstract) at the top of the message and use numbered paragraphs that correspond to the preview. Multiple-participant video chatting can be improved if everyone wears a name tag that is always visible on the camera. This way, participants can refer to others by name. Instead of live web presentations, audio can be layered over PowerPoint slides, then converted into a movie using production software (e.g., Microsoft MovieMaker, Apple iMovie, or Sony Vegas Movie Studio), and then uploaded online as a tutorial. This is a cost-effective solution that provides the opportunity to edit content in advance, giving more control over presentation outcomes. Another tool to consider using is screen-capturing software, which allows users to narrate what they are doing on a computer. This is effective for creating tutorials on how to do something with a computer or software. There are, of course, concerns that need so be considered when developing and using any form of presentation aid; some of these issues are addressed later in this chapter.

Written Electronic Communications (Concise to Extensive)

This section addresses various forms of written electronic communication, from the most concise to the most extensive. These include text messages, instant messages, email, and blogs.

Text Messages

A text message is a brief message, often called an SMS (for Short Message Service), that is sent and received from a fixed or portable device or network. Today, texting may also refer to sending and receiving Multimedia Messaging Services (MMS) messages, which contain image, video, and sound content.

One of the most common ways that people text is by sending messages to and from mobile phones; however, there are a variety of ways in which text messages can be sent and received. For example, a text message can be sent from Skype or other VoIP service to a mobile phone and vice versa. Businesses and organizations often use text messaging in their *direct text marketing* campaigns to alert customers of sales, to authenticate orders or transactions, and to disseminate information to customers and employees (e.g., notification of disasters or other threats, appointment reminders, and package tracking).

A text message can also be automatically sent by a bot (short for robot), which is programmed to respond to humans' or other computers' actions. For example, a bot may send a text message with an order number confirmation to a customer after he or she places an order on a website. Customers may request that updates, such as a flight's status, be sent to their mobile devices as text messages. The computer will then automatically notify customers when updates are available. Alternatively, humans can send text messages to automated systems. This is commonly used to order products or participate in advertising contests.

Important considerations regarding the use of text messaging and its benefits and risks to businesses and organizations are similar to those of instant messaging, so these are addressed in the next section.

Instant Messages

Text messaging is *asynchronous* (recipients may not immediately attend to the message) and frequently unidirectional. An alternative to text messaging is instant messaging (IM). Companies use IM more frequently than text messaging for employee-to-employee communication and for customer-to-employee communication. Together, SMS and instant messaging (IM) are overtaking and, in many cases, beginning to replace email as the preferred communication tool within companies (Moulds, 2007).

As an alternative to texting and email, IM can be used by employees to communicate with each another in real time. Meetings, especially those used for information gathering rather than deliberation, can be held in a "chat forum" in which all participants' IMs are seen instantaneously by other participants. As an alternative to phone calls, customer service and sales representatives use IM to communicate with current and potential customers. For example, when someone browses a webpage, he or she may receive an invitation to chat with a sales representative. More and more, IM capabilities are being embedded into other communication media, such as social networking sites (e.g., Facebook) and websites. Smart phones offer a variety of apps, short for application software, for instant messaging. Apps can enable users to access other messaging platforms with ease (e.g., Skype, Yahoo! IM, and ICQ). This will only further push companies and professionals further away from email.

There are a variety of premium IM platforms available for businesses, such as Liveperson (**http://liveperson.com**), WhosOn (**http://whoson.com**), and Meebo (**http://meebo.com**). These services give companies the capability to engage with customers and manage information obtained from these interactions in a variety of ways. In addition to basic chat, these IM systems provide *presence awareness* capabilities (e.g., when a sales associate is at his or her desk and available for chat), invitation request pop-up windows that appear to potential customers browsing a website, remote display of documents, video chat, and remote control of computers. These systems also gather a variety of analytics on customer and employee inter-actions, which can be used to make decisions, improve process, and train employees.

As with any type of business and professional communication, it is necessary to understand the risks and benefits of using SMS and IM and learn how to apply the canons of rhetoric to crafting such messages. For example, text messages can be effective ways to communicate updates. However, oversending messages can annoy recipients. By engaging with customers in a creative ways and by incentivizing messages, text messages can be very effective. For example, they can be used to encourage users to use **http://foursquare.com**, and when users check in with their friends, they can receive a discount. However, IM can be difficult to use because employees or customers may not be the best writers, creating miscommunication opportunities. The permanence of many things on the web could come back to haunt the com-pany. A frustrated customer can easily copy and paste text into a blog. Security is another major concern. Files distributed through IM can contain viruses. IM systems require an open portal to the Internet, which can be a doorway for hackers. Thus, running IM systems on sep-arate computers and servers is a wise choice. However, this requires duplication of technolo-gy; customer service representatives need access to two computer terminals.

A variety of tips are available for using IM for business and professional communication. The following list, provided by Microsoft (Enbysk, n.d.), is comprehensive:

1. DO: Adopt a user policy for instant messaging.
2. DON'T: Use instant messaging to communicate confidential or sensitive informa-tion.
3. DO: Organize contact lists to separate business contacts from family and friends
4. DON'T: Allow excessive personal messaging at work.
5. DO: Be aware that instant messages can be saved.
6. DON'T: Compromise a company's liability or your own reputation.
7. DO: Be aware of virus infections and related security risks.
8. DON'T: Share personal data or information through instant messaging.
9. DO: Keep instant messages simple and to the point and know when to say goodbye
10. DON'T: Confuse contacts with a misleading user name or status.

Email

Email is one of the most used forms of electronic business communication, but primarily by default—it was one of the first forms of electronic communication widely available and, there-fore, comfortable to use. Of course, email does have many benefits (e.g., quick delivery). But it also has a darker side (e.g., spam, viruses, and overuse). In the workplace, email is used to share electronic files and information both internally (e.g., among employees) and externally (e.g., with suppliers and customers). As noted earlier, email is being replaced by other elec-tronic mediums better suited for specific types of messages and contexts. For example, IM is much better when interlocutors need to engage in brief and synchronous conversations when verbal messages are not possible or desirable. Some email platforms are adapting to the changing needs of business. For example, Google and Yahoo! provide IM platforms within their Gmail and Y!Mail interfaces. Google introduced Wave, a real-time messaging platform, in spring 2009. Google scrapped Google Wave in 2010, citing lack of adoption. Arrington (2010) describes Wave "as part email, part Twitter, and part instant messaging." It allowed users to collaboratively write (as they can in Google Docs), share and embed files within a page, set meetings, play games, and begin an IM conversation on a specific line of an email message. (Messages could even be played back so people joining a Wave conversation late could see it progress.) Google Wave and, in many respects the concept of collaborative sharing, changes the framework of sending and receiving a series of emails in a "thread" and instead looks at email and forms of virtual communication as a conversation. Such developments break from traditional communication systems and reinvent them in the age of fast Internet computing. Wave, and programs like it, are amazing and will eventually revolutionize how we communicate electronically. However, people cling to what they know (e.g., many people still fax), and Wave was, as Arlington further notes, "just ahead of its time." Eventually, once people get more comfortable with the concept of "cloud computing" and really understand its potential, programs like Wave will become the standard. Many of Wave's features are being decoupled and used in other Google apps.

Email still has many advantages over IM and other virtual communication media. First, it is universal. Anybody can send and receive messages with an email address, regardless of system or host. There is no need to register for a new account, manage a profile, or invite others to join a new service. Second, email allows rhetors to craft formal message that require special formatting and tend to be longer. Third, email does not require instantaneous communication. So long as it is used properly, it can actually reduce interruptions.

Although it is easy to treat email as an informal medium, it should always, within professional contexts, be treated as any other type of business and professional correspondence. For internal communication, rhetors should follow memo guidelines. For external communication, rhetors should treat emails like letters. In other words, avoid the temptation of sending first drafts—proofread, copyedit, and revise!

Use plain text as much as possible when crafting and designing email messages. Although most email systems allow users to craft messages using a variety of fonts (italics and bold), sizes, and design elements, which are automatically converted into hypertext markup language (HTML), it is not recommended. These features may be blocked or displayed unpredictably in recipients' email systems. (Fonts larger than 12 point look unprofessional.) Instead, consider using the following design elements to add emphasis.

- **Use uppercase letters sparingly.** To emphasize a particular word or SHORT phrase, uppercase letters can be used. Using all uppercase letters in long passages is called "shouting."
- **Use asterisks.** In place of *italicization* or footnotes, use asterisks to achieve the intended effect.**

    **This note, placed at the end of the email, would correspond with the double asterisks.

- **Use intermittent underlines.** Indicate that something ought to be underlined by offsetting the text with intermittent underlines: _Business Communication for Professionals and Consultants: A Rhetorical Approach_. Recipients understand that italicization and underlining are not common in emails, so it is okay to use basic capitalization for titles of books, articles, and so on.
- **Attach figures and tables.** To provide information in a table or supply figures or photographs, send them as attachments. Be sure to reference them in the email. When attaching a large number of files, number them for recipient. When they save them to file, they will appear in the folder chronologically.
- **Use the em dash (—) to indicate a bullet list.** If a numbered list is not appropriate, use a double dash to begin a new item in a list.

    --**Item number 1**

    --**Item number 2**
- **Double-space between paragraphs.** So that messages do not look dense, keep paragraphs short. Double-space between paragraphs, and do not indent. Avoid a clunky look by writing a series of single-line paragraphs. If possible, create a list of ideas rather than paragraphs.
- **Keep response at top.** Most email systems are designed to automatically place responses at the top of a message thread. If an email system places messages at the bottom, or you accidently begin writing below a message, be sure to reformat the message before sending.
- **Quote specific references.** When replying to a specific point in another's email, quote only relevant parts (delete the rest of the content) and consider doing so on a point-by-point basis. Use the symbols < and > to distinguish quoted material from responses.
- **Use subject line appropriately.** If the email is a specific response to a message, then simply hit reply. The message will indicate it is a response with "Re:" (regarding). When changing the course of a message thread or to emphasize something of importance in the response, consider changing the subject line altogether or use brackets: "Re: Assignment #1 [Graded Submission Attached]" Many email systems organize the thread based upon the subject line, so altering it could begin a new thread. This could be beneficial in some situations and create organizational issues in others. So change the subject line with some forethought.

Figure 6.1 provides an illustration most of the design elements described above.

In almost all cases, avoid using background images and borders. These increase the email size and can make recipients nervous about opening messages—viruses can be embedded into image files. Many email systems automatically block images for this reason. To send an email as a webpage, code it correctly and check the message in a variety of browsers (e.g., Internet Explorer, Google Chrome, Mozilla Firefox, and Apple Safari).

Emails are never completely private and are never thoroughly deleted, at least not for a significant period of time after sending. Employers are legally allowed to read email messages, and they sometimes do so as a security measure (Smith & Tabak, 2009). Security software

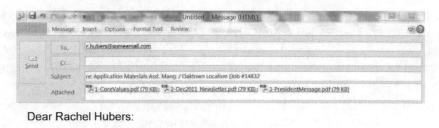

Figure 6.1. An example email.

programs, such as SpectorSoft's (eBlaster) can monitor computer use to the specific keystroke, which means that even if you change the message before sending it, what you originally wrote will be recorded. In some instances, mail logs may be subpoenaed by investigators or attorneys and presented in a court of law. Before pressing send, carefully consider how an email messages could be interpreted, whether the content is appropriate, and how you might feel if the content is made public. Table A.5 in Appendix A provides a list of common email mistakes and remedies.

Blogs

A blog is a journal-like website that allows writers, commonly referred to as "bloggers," to post (i.e., "to blog") commentaries, opinions, journalistic articles, press releases, catalogs of events, a list of thematized articles from across the web or "blogosphere," photographs, podcasts, art, music, and videos (vlog). Blogs are easier to personalize and update than a website, and often they invite active participation from the audience, such as requests for information, comments on posted materials, and reposting articles (creating linkbacks). Individuals and small businesses can choose from a variety of free and fee-based blogging services, such as WordPress (**http://wordpress.org**), Blogger (**http://blogger.com**), Movable Type (**http://movabletype.org**), and TypePad (**http://typepad.com**). For large organizations, medium-sized enterprises, or individuals who mass a large following (i.e., large monthly data transfer), for those who want a specific URL (e.g.,), or for those who want advertisement-free pages, upgrading to a premium hosting package or hosting company (e.g., Yahoo! Small Business or Network Solutions) is necessary. Blogs can be decoupled from a company's website or integrated into the site, the latter of which is a preferred method for website optimization (see Chapter 9).

Blogs can be internally or externally oriented, and in business and professional communication they can be used in a variety of ways. Typically, blogs present less formal narratives than the ones presented on websites. They are also less static than websites. Consequently, organizations and businesses can use blogs to achieve a variety of business goals, such as developing a sense of community among employees, distributing company news and updates to employees (or external audiences), attracting and retaining customers, providing useful information and tips for customers, promoting goodwill, soliciting feedback, facilitating crisis communication, recruiting employees and customers, increasing customer identification, and distributing press releases and newsletters (the blog may replace newsletters altogether). Individuals can use blogs to further develop a professional profile, typically by writing articles and commentaries about the profession or by posting links to important websites or articles relevant to a professional field. A blog is also an excellent way to develop a web resume or manage a portfolio.

Matters of invention: When writing and designing blogs, understand your audience(s). A blog should largely focus on well-defined group. Larger organizations are likely to maintain several different blogs and may even have on staff employees who blog, or they may hire freelance bloggers. Each blogger should focus on developing a personal style of communication and a specific voice and narrative. If ghost writing blogs, it is necessary to understand the desired image that the company wants to project. Although each author's voice and each blog's specific tone will differ, all blogs typically are designed to deliver new information quickly, cover topics that are part of an ongoing theme, and speak to audience interests. Blogs should encourage active participation of some kind. When blogging, be sure to define the purpose and stick to it.

Matters of style: Generally speaking, blog entries should be informal, in first person, and use active voice as much as possible. Be concise: Use contractions (e.g., "we've") and keep sentences short. Appeal to pathos: Use an active voice, write with emphasis, and use creative language. Consider design: As much as possible, use lists, word clouds, images, pictures, and layout and design elements, such as boldface fonts and ample white space. Pull content from other sources that will be interesting and provide hyperlinks to encourage interactivity with other blogs and websites. Get your audience to share blog entries throughout the blogosphere and Twitterverse.

- Tag content so that is easy to follow posts by topic or category of interest. Use a tag cloud so that users can see what the most salient topics of the blog (see Figure 6.2)
- Encourage sharing by using bookmarking and sharing services, such as AddThis (**http://addthis.com**).
- Do not post information that is confidential or proprietary to an employer, and be sure not to use copyrighted materials without acknowledgment or permission.
- Don't post attacks against others, especially colleagues, competitors, customers, or other bloggers. To challenge a point, use invitational rhetoric to invite dialog. (Unless, of course, that is the purpose and specific style, which may attract a specific audience.)

Figure 6.2. An example tag cloud of words commonly used to describing blogging activities. *(Image © Gilmanshin, 2012. Used under license from Shutterstock, Inc.)*

- Blog with a clear plan and purpose. To make a change to the overall theme of a blog site, inform readers so they are aware the change is deliberate.

- Post frequently. People who read blogs and engage heavily in social networking expect that material will be updated. If you plan to post updates periodically, then note this within the header of the blog page.

- Listen and learn from your audience. Part of the interactivity of blog requires that rhetors adapt to the audience. Check in with posts and reply directly on the blog, or privately if warranted (and an email address of the poster is available).

- Proofread before publishing a post. Check specifically for grammatical errors, typos, formatting errors, and layout features. Use the "preview" feature to see how content will look. When copying and pasting material from a word process document into a blog, there are often compatibility issues.

- Obviously, don't post anything you wouldn't want the world to see—forever (people may use screen capture and repost elsewhere).

Spoken Electronic Communications (Concise to Extensive)

This section addresses various forms of spoken electronic communication, from the most concise to the most extensive. These include voice messages (voicemail), teleconferencing, podcasting, and Second Life.

Voice Messages

Many people are accustomed to calling a number and receiving an option to leave a phone message. However, this does not mean people are good at leaving voice messages and, given the many features of voice messaging systems, this is an underutilization of the technology. Technically, answering systems that intercept calls and direct people can be labeled as a voice message system; however, this section covers specifically voicemail—the recording and distribution of a voice message by phone. While voicemail may seem somewhat archaic in the age of text messaging, IMing, and Tweeting, it is still popularly used among many older professionals. Also, many people still use voicemail because it is a standard feature with most cell phone plans. As more companies like Google (Google Voice), Microsoft (Microsoft Lync), Vonage, and Skype (now owned by Microsoft) expand their features and products in the Voice over Internet Protocol (VoIP) market, they are finding creative ways to unify communication, primarily by integrating voice communications, IM, audio, video, and web conferencing into a single platform. Voice messages are now automatically converted into text and emailed, phone calls can be switched to video conferencing using simple webcams, and so on. Learning to leave voicemail messages that are brief, that communicate important details, that are friendly to text recognition software, and that solicit a reply will increase productivity and improve responses (important for sales calls).

Like all forms of business communication, voice messaging is a skill that requires thoughtfulness and practice. In other words, plan and practice a message before the call, even if you expect the person will be available. Knowing what to say in the event that the person does not answer will keep you from getting caught off guard. Often people are inclined to hang up, think about the message, and call back. Don't do this. The person you are calling may be near the phone but busy, or on another line. Calling back is unnecessarily disruptive and may create an unnecessary sense of urgency. When leaving a message, be as brief as possible, and follow this simple formula:

1. *State your name and phone number.* **+** (State your title and occupation, if necessary.)

   Speak slowly and pause between sections of the number "618". . . "203". . .

2. *Give your message a headline and priority level.* **+**

   Indicate immediately what the message is about and whether you need an immediate response. Some phone voice messaging systems allow users to flag a message as priority, moving the message up in the list. Only use this function if the message really is urgent.

3. *Deliver your message in a clear, concise, and positive tone.* **+**

   Use a topical outline if you have more than one point, but keep it under one minute.

4. *End message with directive, restate name, and phone number.*

   Spell your name, especially if it is unique or difficult to understand.

Based on the above process, your message would sound something like this:

> "Hi, my name is Geetha Parameshwari, that's G-E-E-T-H-A, my number is "618-" . . . "000-" . . . "0000." I'm a customer service representative for Acme Widgets. This message is urgent. We need to know if it is possible to extend a warranty on one of your discontinued products. The current policy is set to expire in 10 days. Please call me at 618-000-0000. Again, this is Geetha, G-E-E-T-H-A. 618 . . . 000. . . 0000. Thanks, and have a great day."

In addition to following a thorough script, keep your tone positive and upbeat. Without nonverbal cues, the message may come across incorrectly (especially if the message is about a contentious issue). Maintain an even volume and pitch and enunciate. Always leave a message, not just a phone number and a demand to call you back. You're more likely to get a return call with specific details. Besides, it's the courteous thing to do for people who are already very busy. This gives the recipient an opportunity to prioritize your message and consider alternative response methods—perhaps you need information that is easier to deliver by email. To avoid "telephone tag" provide a time to call back or alternative contact directions (e.g., an email address).

Like email, voice messaging can take up a lot of time, both for the person making the call and the person receiving the call. Many large businesses have phone systems (commonly referred to as PBXs [private branch exchanges]) with a variety of features. Most of the new cloud-based telephony services, like Google Voice and Skype, as well as many cellphone providers, allow callers to pre-record messages and then send them as a voice message. This gets around the problem of having to ring someone. This is optimal if you prefer to leave a message by voice anyway, or don't want to speak with or disturb others. Also, these systems allow users to create distribution lists and blast messages to several mailboxes instantaneously (one can even set the distribution date and time). What is more, one can create internal and external greetings, record a name, and set vacation responses and so on, which assist callers and voice message recipients. With do not disturb functions, call forwarding, simultaneous ring, "skip to end of message," and a variety of other features, phoning can become a tool for effective and efficient communication. Like all communication media, however, the use of telephone messaging is only as strong as the individual user. Training, literature describing features, and commitment to the technology are vital to the successful use of voice messaging.

Teleconferencing

A teleconference, or teleseminar, is the live exchange of communications among several people who are linked by a telecommunications system. People connect with one another remotely using a variety of terminals. The most basic teleconference is the conference call, in which people connect with one another by phone. Often telephone interviews are conducted in this way. A panel of interviewers sit in a room and use a phone's speaker to listen in on a call and ask questions of the interviewee, who is in another location.

Nowadays, teleconferencing systems allow users to use a variety of media, including video, audio, and data services by several means, such as telephone, computer, radio, and television. Internet teleconferencing draws upon VoIP platforms, which allow users to share documents, stream video, and use screen image display (users get to see the presenter's computer screen, so PowerPoint, for example, can be used).

Although teleconferences can occur in a variety of ways, one of the most popular formats involves a live demonstration, seminar, or meeting that is then streamed to a remote location where another audience watches on a screen. Often both audiences have cameras and microphones. This type of teleconference allows speakers to see both the live and remote audiences on two screens. Another popular type of teleconference involves a live presentation that is then streamed as an audiocast or videocast across the Internet. Using a variety of media is called a simultaneous broadcast (or simulcast).

Videoconferencing systems need to be used purposefully. In most circumstances, setting up a teleconferencing system lies with a company's information technology department (system administrators), or conference planners. When considering the purchase or use of a teleconferencing system, consider the following (Sacco, 2007):

1. *How the videoconferencing system will be used.* Will it be used for simple face-to-face meetings between people? Is if for an occasional meeting? (If so, consider a basic VoIP

service or an integrated system [e.g., Microsoft 365].) How many locations will connect simultaneously? Will those locales be outside of your network's firewall? What equipment will correspondents use and how tech-savvy are users?

2. ***Know where the system will be used.*** Will the system be installed in a room that's dedicated to videoconferencing or will the system need to be mobile?

3. ***Know the budget.*** Purchasing and installing new videoconferencing systems can be costly. Customizing conference rooms and purchasing high-definition (HD) equipment can run into the hundreds of thousands of dollars. Even for small-time users, getting the latest gadgets can run several hundred dollars. Basic streaming can require an equipment upgrade or a subscription to a premium-level service that can utilize equipment features. (What good is an HD camera if you are streaming at standard definition?) Also, know what is going to be effective. Sure, broadcasting in both video and audio may be ideal, but a basic live audiocast, often much cheaper to do, may be just as effective. (Consider distributing visual aids in advance.)

4. ***Investigate various vendors.*** Know which vendors can provide the greatest level of service at the best price. Not all videoconferencing service providers can work with a company's pre-existing infrastructure. Also, not all companies' individual or small-business package levels are the same. Consider what functions you absolutely need and which you are able to forgo. Consider current equipment and future equipment purchases, as well as projected demand (the price difference between 100-attendee and 1000-attendee packages with GoToMeeting.com, for example, is significant). Companies to consider for large investments in videoconferencing systems, such as those that will go in conference rooms or multiple sites, are Cisco, Codian, Hewlett-Packard, and Sony. For individual users and small businesses, consider ACT Conferencing, Adobe Acrobat Connect, Elluminate, GoToMeeting, Microsoft Office 365, and WebEx.

5. ***Consider attendees' network capabilities.*** Not all sites or attendees are the same. Some may not have enough bandwidth or sufficient download speed, which could lead to access problems.

6. ***Prepare to work with firewalls.*** Companies likely have firewalls installed to prevent incoming and outgoing web traffic. Videoconferencing systems have to be given an open portal or they will be blocked. For small businesses and individual users, educating potential attendees can be a frustrating ordeal. Chances are that webinar listeners will have some kind of antivirus software that may block connections. People with little understanding of computers will not know that they have a firewall or may not know how to disable it. Fortunately, many companies now offer the option to stream the media through a webpage.

Teleconference presenters and attendees should follow these tips and etiquette guidelines to improve the overall experience:

- **Before the teleconference meeting.**
  - *Set clear objectives.* Know what will be accomplished in the session and communicate goals to participants.

- *Prepare an agenda or presentation and practice.* Establish ground rules for participation during the conference.

- *Distribute the agenda and relevant materials in advance.* Create a specific online site for the webinar or teleconference, which will also be the portal where the video or audio will be streamed.

- *Eliminate environmental distractions.* In a conference room, this is not likely to be a problem. For teleconferencing that occurs in a variety of locations (e.g., on a college campus), consider lighting issues and possible background noise. Boom microphones can pick up traffic noise outside of a building, so think about any possible noise and how it will sound. When teleconferencing into a meeting as a visible attendee, eliminate any background that could be awkward or distracting.

- *Adjust the equipment.* Make sure that everyone is visible and that microphones are working and in a location where everyone can be heard. The goal is not to have to adjust equipment, such as moving a camera, once the teleconference begins.

- *Arrive early.* As a presenter, arrive to a teleconferencing room early to test the equipment and to become comfortable using it. When on a private computer, reboot and close any unnecessary programs to increase processing speeds.

- *Choose speakers in advance.* If presenting to a remote audience, choose one person to facilitate questions at the remote site. If teleconferencing with several remote users, assign an order to speakers.

- **During the meeting:**
  - *Use a facilitator.* Appoint a meeting facilitator. Just like a "live" meeting, a videoconference meeting can get out of control unless somebody takes the job of traffic cop. The facilitator can also take responsibility for muting and un-muting the microphone and adjusting the camera. For collaborative computing (data conferencing), it is especially important that everyone knows who has control of the presentation. All others should be instructed to mute microphones.

  - ***Offer a quick practice session.*** Allow participants a brief "practice session" to become familiar with the equipment and setup.

  - ***Introduce everyone.*** As a presenter, acknowledge the live and remote audience(s). If the participants don't know each other, and the number of attendees is small, have them introduce themselves. Consider using nameplates or nametags to help people keep names straight.

  - ***Act normal and talk slowly and clearly.*** Treat the experience as if it were a face-to-face meeting. Look straight into the camera, use the speech strategies described in earlier chapters, and use natural nonverbal expressions. Cameras tend to pick up face gestures well, so don't think negative thoughts or roll your eyes.

  - ***Don't be distracted or hold side conversations.*** Don't work on other things or check your mobile devices regularly. This will distract others and, if the distractions are in the remote locations, the distractions may be outside the camera's frame (awkward!). It is not polite to disrupt speakers in live or virtual situations.

An example of a teleconference using a basic phone-in system. (*Image © Peter Hansen, 2012. Used under license from Shutterstock, Inc.*)

- *Limit movement.* As speaker, move, but not too much. Excessive movements are disruptive to remote viewers. If sitting, as is often the case when people use basic VoIP services, try to control body and head movements.
- *Wear conservative clothing.* Bright colors and patterned shirts can create unnecessary distractions, such as disorientation caused by a camera trying to adjust to different shades.
- *Don't talk over each other.* Again, have a speaking order and ask permission to speak. Establish rules for speaking. When not speaking, mute the microphone.

It should go without saying, but we often forget, that it is important to have a backup plan for a meeting or seminar. In the event of connection failures or equipment problems, people attending a remote meeting may become frustrated. If the conference is fee based, this can create accounting issues and upset customers. Communicating, in advance, the backup plan will help people feel at ease (for example, that the seminar will be made available for streaming or downloading at a later date). Also, when creating presentation materials, such as agendas, charts, Prezis, PowerPoint presentations, and so on, use large (e.g., 15-point), sans serif fonts. Serif and small fonts may be difficult to see, especially if these are projected behind the speaker rather than on a computer screen.

Podcasting

A podcast is a non-streamed webcast, which is prerecorded and distributed on the Internet or other platform (e.g., iTunes) by syndication. Podcasting is attractive because it is conversational and people tend to get more from listening or watching something than reading alone.

Podcasts can be either audio or video. Often podcasts are produced episodically and are the main feature, much like a blog post. In these cases, the podcast is part of a podcast channel. However, podcasts are also often produced to support other communications. For example, a podcast is often published alongside a feature story in large newspapers and magazines. The podcast, in such instances, is used to generate interest in the article. Developers of new services or products may talk about design features or updates that will inspire and motivate consumers. Podcasts are, of course, an excellent way to distribute recordings of teleconferences for playback.

The business and professional possibilities of podcasts are only limited to individuals' creativity. For eloquent speakers with something interesting to say, a podcast is the product. People are willing to purchase podcasts, much like other media content. Podcasts are a great way to promote written materials, as noted above. They can also be used to distribute company updates. Video podcasts, which can also be distributed via UGC sites like YouTube, and redistributed across multiple platforms (e.g., traditional webpages, others' blogs, and so on), can lower the cost of information distribution. Rather than printing expensive brochures, videos can be produced to show others how to use products or services. By encouraging customers to participate and collaborate in the production of tutorials and videos, they not only identify more strongly with a product or service (hello, repeat customer!), but they provide a free service that saves the company time and money on marketing and technical support.

Creating podcasts, in terms of the technical requirements, is relatively easy. Digital audio recorders are now widely available and inexpensive. Most personal computers and cell phones offer digital recording capabilities, capture audio in basic WAV (.wav) or MP3 (.mp3) file formats. These files can then be imported into a variety of free or premium audio editors, such as Sound Forge by Sony or Audacity (**http://audacity.sourceforge.net**). Refer back to Table 3.3, in Chapter 3, for a list of free and premium software. After editing the audio file, the file should be converted into MP3, the most universal and one of the smallest audio file sizes (ideal for electronic distribution). For distribution, the file is simply uploaded into the preferred distribution channel (e.g., iTunes, YouTube, blog, website, and so on). Once a stable URL is available, the file can be validated with a RSS/Atom validator, such as **http://feedvalidator.org** or **http://allpodcasts.com/Tools/RSSValidator.aspx**.

To stay up to date on all things podcast, check out **wwwpodcastalley.com.** For live radio in place of pre-recorded shows, check out "Shoutcast" sites: **http://broadcastat.blogtalkradio.com, http://streammonster.com, http://sambroadcaster.net, or http://nch.com.au/streaming.** To produce a television talk show, check out **http://make.tv**.

End users interested in following blogs, podcasts, and other frequently or intermittently updated material on the web use RSS (really simple syndication) or Atom feed aggregators to help organize content and notify readers of updates. Like a bookmark in a web browser, RSS and Atom help people to keep track of what is interesting on the Internet and to follow specific content. The benefit of validating a feed and using an RSS/Atom reader to follow others' content is that these programs send notification when new content is posted. There are a variety of feeders available, although most web browsers have add-ons available or already included (e.g., Firefox Live Bookmark).

Second Life

As note in Chapter 4, Second Life has been used by companies to conduct job fairs and job interviews (Athavaley, 2007). Second Life (SL) is an online virtual world (see Figure 6.3). It was developed by Linden Lab and was launched in 2003. SL users connect remotely by private terminals into a shared space, known as the grid, and interact with one another with avatars. Basically, using keyboards, audio, and mouse functions, users walk around and explore worlds. Although the world is virtual, profitable businesses have emerged (and failed) as people barter and trade various products and services. There are a variety of communities within SL, such as education, relationships, and competitive gaming. Professionally, SL has been used to host conferences, such as academic conferences and tradeshows. It can be used for training.

Figure 6.3. An example screen shot of a Second Life round table meeting. From http://information-literacy.blogspot.com/ by Sheila Webber. *(Copyright © 2010 Information Literacy Blog. Reprinted by permission.)*

Perhaps one profession that has embraced SL in interesting ways is education. Some educational communities are operated by universities, which offer distance-learning classes that take place solely in SL. Some courses are even offered in a hybrid format. In these cases, students meet in a traditional classroom space on campus and in SL. A variety of universities also offer hybrid courses that utilize an educational management system, such as BlackBoard and Moodle (an open-source competitor to BlackBoard). The benefit of Moodle is that it offers a SL platform called Sloodle (**http://sloodle.org/moodle**). These hybrid formats allow students and teachers to have a much more interactive experience. SL also is more dynamic than a class offered only in an education management shell, like BlackBoard.

As SL grows in popularity, users will continue to develop programs and tools to enhance the learning environment. For example, one of the most popular items used in SL is the MetaLab Whiteboard, which was developed by Annabeth Robinson, a Senior Lecturer in Digital Media at Leeds College of Art (**http://metalab.blogspot.com**). For more on SL, including links to interesting videos, visit this book's companion website or visit **http://secondlife.com** and **http://opensimulator.org**.

Social Networking and Collaborative Electronic Communications (Written and Spoken)

The above forms of electronic communication produce messages that mimic more traditional artifacts. For example, a text message is similar to a bulletin, email is similar to a memo or letter, and podcasts are similar to radio addresses. In recent years, a variety of new media have emerged that allow businesses and professionals to communicate in new and exciting ways. These media fit a general pattern toward a more integrated use of virtual spaces and networks, which allow interlocutors to collaborate using a variety of brief, extensive, written, and spoken communications simultaneously. The following list of written communication systems is not comprehensive, but does introduce some of the most fashionable platforms, many of which are used for purposes of integrated marketing communication and website optimization (see Chapter 9).

Microblogs

A microblog is a blog-like platform that allows users to share content and links to other content on the Internet. A distinguishing feature of microblog is the brevity of messages, which are often restricted to a specific number of characters (140 characters is the emerging standard). Twitter.com is one of the most popular microblogging sites on the Internet. Users, identified by a handle such as **@ProRhetoric**, post notes ("tweets") that include a variety of information. Businesses commonly post links to more extensive forms of communication (press releases), sales information, product launches, or notes of appreciation (and other *epideictic* rhetoric). One of the goals of Twitter is to disseminate information through user participation, which is called "retweeting." Because a retweet should provide context (i.e., additional characters are required), it is recommended that tweets designed for sharing are kept to 120 characters (see **http:// twittinsecrets.com;** Brown, 2011). Within organizations, enterprise microblogging applications can be set up on company intranets. These systems allow executives, manager, and employees to dissemination ideas and updates.

Interestingly, a language and organizational system emerged organically among users of Twitter and continues to evolve to this day. Knowing how to use microblogs effectively and staying on top of "Twitterspeak" is important. Here are just a few of the important symbols:

@username: A direct tweet sent to another Twitter user.

#: The "hash tag" allows Twitter users to group tweets by topic, making it easier to search particular conversations using Twitter Search.

RT: ReTweet, used to repost something that's already in the Twitter stream. Usually preceeded by "@[username]," to give credit to the original poster.

d: This is a direct message. It is similar to an email because no one else can see this. It will still be required to meet the character specifications (no more than 140 characters). When you input this, place a space between the d and the username (i.e., **d** [username]). If there

is no space (dusername) it will show up on your newsfeed, and this could be problematic.
t.co: This is the preferred and official tinyurl for Twitter links. Visit t.co to shorten URLs.

Social Networking Sites

Facebook is the most visited site on the internet (Nielson, 2011), so it is safe to assume that you are familiar with it. At one time, you may even have had a Myspace account. If you still do, don't tell your classmates. Using Facebook for personal reasons is much different than utilizing it for business. However, businesses are much more informal on Facebook and other social networking sites because they need to project a personality consistent with the tone of social networking sites. Facebook, for example, is an excellent way to connect with consumers and engage with them through promotions and sales, while LinkedIn is useful for connection with other professionals, promoting a company as a place to work, and establishing business to business connections (B2B). Google+ (**https://google.com/+**), a relatively late starter in the social networking scene, allows users to cluster individuals into circles. This is very useful for businesses and professionals who want to deliver messages within the same platform, but want to share content differently to different groups.

To get the most out of social networking, have a clearly defined purpose, an understanding of the desired effect of the communication, and the "culture" of each social networking site. Then, craft messages in a way that they join the ongoing conversations and practices of the community. For example, Facebook wall posts are generally used to provide information and updates.

There are a variety of other social networking sites that allow businesses to share ideas. Entrepreneurs seeking to raise capital should check out **http://kickstarter.com**. Nonprofits and philanthropists hoping to raise capital for projects, make donations, or network, should check out **www.idealist.org** or **http://kiva.org**. Journalists wanting to collaborate with others, share stories, and raise money for investigative reporting should check out **http://spot.us**. Craftspeople wanting to raise money and sell their products should head to **www.etsy.com.** To stay up on these crowdsourcing trends or to identify new and useful sites, visit and follow **http://crowdsourcing.org**.

User-Generated Content (UGC) Sites

User-generated content sites, abbreviated UGCs, encourage users to develop and distribute content to other users. Sites like **http://youtube.com, http://vimeo.com, www.flikr.com, www.wikia.com,** and **www.websitetoolbox.com,** provide platforms for hosting videos, pictures, wikis, discussion boards, and community question and answer databases. Although these are used heavily by individuals wanting to post and view silly videos, like "animals close-up with a wide-angle lens," as spoofed in *South Park* episode "Quest for Ratings" (season 8, episode 11), they are also useful for businesses (from sole proprietors to Fortune 500 corporations) and professionals. Businesses, for example, provide a variety of self-produced and customer-produced "how-to" videos. Other businesses use the sites for commercials, executive interviews and updates, or contests for advertising (e.g., Purina seeking to award the cutest dog video). During periods of crisis, videos, sometimes created by UGC posts, can be effective ways to distribute content, and wikis can be used to gather supportive testimonials from stakeholders. For example, when two Domino's employees uploaded a video in 2009 of them doing disgusting things to customer orders, Domino's President Patrick Doyle responded with his own video, assuring that anyone who searched "Disgusting Domino's People" would also see "Disgusting Domino's People – Domino's Response" (Fox, 2009). Although there is no reference to the crisis on Wikipedia.org today, Domino's did, at the time, miss a crucial opportunity to help manage its image. Pete Blackshaw, a brand strategist for Nielson Online, notes that Wikipedia is a "reputational broker" for mediating the relationship between external stakeholders and a company's brand (Gregory, 2009). During the crisis, there was a link on Wikipedia to the controversial video. What was missing, according to Blackshaw, was a link to Domino's video response:

> That's a crucial component of brand editing. Wikipedia's editors typically strike links to anything that smacks of propaganda, but says Blackshaw, 'I'd be surprised if Wikipedia pushes back. A response from a Domino's executive to a major controversy is fair game.' (as cited in Gregory, 2009, para. 10–11)

Domino's did, however, receive a lot of positive support from dedicated employees and customers, who reminded users that the company should not be punished for unpredictable and disturbing employee behavior.

Often, companies and individuals integrate UCG content into their social networking sites or traditional webpages (e.g., embedding video, which is hosted by Youtube.com, into a website or posting a link on LinkedIn to a video resume). However, companies can also develop their own UGC sections on a webpage and encourage users to post content directly onto the page. This is, of course, not without its risks. People may post problematic comments or videos that hurt the reputation of a company. Thus, asking for stakeholder participation requires a moderator who will ensure that offensive language is deleted, that there are no violations of copyright law, and that messages are relevant and audience appropriate. An example use of both administrator and UGC content are commercial websites like **www.amazon.com** and Yahoo! News (**www.news.yahoo.com**). On Amazon, products and prices are generally set by Amazon or its third-party sellers; however, customers are encouraged to write product reviews. Yahoo! News will publish the stories, but users comment upon and recommend stories to others. Sites that merge social networking and new media capabilities (like UGC) with traditional website functions, like **http://tumblr.com** does, are among the fastest growing sites on the internet (Nielson, 2011).

In the future, the traditional website may be replaced completely by social networking. It is important, therefore, to stay on top of trends. Also, consider the benefits and costs of social networking and UGCs. Question-and-answer forums are a great way to outsource technical support; however, if users are encouraging "fixes" to a product that damages the product or voids the warranty, then this will create more business issues than the UGC site resolves. Also, fashions in the social media world seem to come and go at a rapid pace. Thus, managing a variety of platforms can be difficult and labor intensive. Before starting a new project or promotional avenue, consider the long-term costs of maintaining them. Consultants can charge several thousand dollars to manage social networking and integrated marketing communication campaigns. This is great if you are on the consulting side, but is a business buzzkill. Nielson (**http://nielsen.com**) provides a variety of social media reports that are useful for continuing education. It publishes data that are useful for consultants and professionals who need to make marketing and promotion decisions. Among several other social networking and Internet tends, they monitor the demographics of online users, such as who watched videos longest, browsing and search patterns, and types of sites visited. To meet the needs of the ever-shifting fashions of social networkers, learn to collect and analyze these data. (Chapter 9 covers social networking in greater detail.)

Presentation Aids

Professional speaker Scott Berkun (2010) writes, "some people resist outlines because in our modern age they seem rigid, low-tech, and old-school, restricting ideas to the tyranny of two-dimensional hierarchy" (p. 66). In place of strong outlines, people choose to use less constrained forms of organization or they rely on their PowerPoint slides to guide them. "But," says Burkun, "there must be an outline of points supporting whatever you put into your talk for this reason: all presentations are narratives, and all narratives are a sequence of points. Even if your points are made by images, stories, or puppet shows, they must be linked together in a narrative to provide value to the audience" (p. 66). The most important presentation aid has been and always will be the organization pattern and outline. Along with practice, this point has been emphasized throughout this book.

It does not mean, however, that one should not utilize other types of presentation aids, such as props and graphics, to improve a presentation. However, these should not be used in lieu of the canon of memory (practice) and, therefore, as a crutch during delivery. Presentation aids should complement a rhetor's message and assist audiences with understanding. Berkun, who makes a comfortable salary as a professional speaker, likes using slides *in* a presentation, but he does not use them *as* the presentation:

> I usually present with slides. I love using images and movies to make points, but I never worry that these things won't work. . . . [By] working hard on a clear, strong, well-reasoned outline, I've already built three versions of the talk: an elevator pitch (the title), a five-minute version (saying each point and a brief summary), and the full version (with slides, movies, and whatever else *strengthens each point*). (p. 67; emphasis added)

Berkun is suggesting that presentation aids should strengthen points (an argument); he does not suggest that they should be used to entertain. Often rhetors will insert visuals into a presentation aid that does very little for the purpose of the argument—it just looks neat. All visuals should do something specific, such as summarize information or make complex ideas simpler to understand. A simple black-and-white line graph or Excel spreadsheets may not look pretty, but, when used appropriately, can present data well, whereas some of the flashiest charts, which may grab the audience's attention for a moment, can be useless if the data does not convey ideas or strengthen arguments. Of course, having a flashy presentation aid that achieves the goal of strengthening points is ideal.

Technically, presentation aids can be as simple as a name tag. As such, even these require forethought about design and use. For example, in the United States and most Western contexts, nametags should be worn on the right side of the chest. This assures that the nametag is visible in the direct line of the handshake. However, in some instances, such as in hotels or at trade shows, where people pass in rows, hallways, or aisles, the nametag could be placed on the left-hand side of the chest so it is visible to a passersby. On either side, however, the nametag should be above the breastbone and should optimally be readable from 10 feet away. This is why most nametags usually are designed so the first name is printed in larger fonts and in all uppercase letters. Because most tradeshows and conferences print generic and often unappealing nametags, paying money for a professional and reusable name tag, which can be worn by attendees, may be a wise choice for companies hoping to project a consistent and professional image in any context.

Using Presentation Aids

The right visuals, delivered through the proper medium, can improve the quality of any oral, written, or electronic communication. Information is very powerful. For the most part, however, presentation of information is very bland and unimaginative. This section first discusses the various technologies available for delivery and then the specific type of visual aids you might choose to use with(in) these technologies. Although specific details about how to design these visuals are presented here, the list of references in the continuing education section will be much more useful for those who want to exploit the full potential of visual aids and presentation technologies.

Technologies for displaying visuals. Before designing a visual, consider what technology will be available for presentation. Some visuals, such as film clips, require a significant amount of technology and have large file sizes, whereas a list or a table on a one-page handout can easily be prepared and presented. The file size is likely to be small, so it can easily be shared through email or IM. If technology is not a factor, design the visual for optimal effect and then choose the appropriate technology for display and distribution. In today's computer-mediated environments, it is likely that presentation aids will be embedded into artifacts and delivered across a variety of media. If something is widely distributed, attention to design is more critical (e.g., one should choose a more neutral color scheme); however, the nuances of design are far beyond the scope of this book. Courses in graphical design or self-guided teaching and practice with the books listed in the continuing education section will help you improve your skills. The following list of visual technologies is organized primarily from least to most complex. Handouts have been excluded because these would include a variety of the written concise and extensive artifacts discussed in Chapter 5.

Whiteboards (or chalkboards).   If available in a room, consider using the whiteboard to make specific notes or points before or during a presentation. Be sure to consider your use of the whiteboard as part of planning and practice. Keep writing on the whiteboard to a minimum during the presentation. If your handwriting is not of the highest quality, consider another option. Make sure to use dark colors so that the writing is easy to see. Consider the location of your audience and possible visual obstructions in the room.

When developing content for whiteboards, remember that long passages will be difficult to write and that each time you write something you must turn away from the audience. Use lists and keywords as much as possible. Write your notes for the board on a separate outline or embed them in your presentation outline in a way that they are easy to see when transferring to the board. Make notes in your outline that indicate when you should move toward the board.

Flip charts.   These are quick to develop and relatively inexpensive. Flip chart pages can be prefilled or they can be used during a presentation to generate a list of ideas from the audience or to transcribe a speaker's points (in place of a whiteboard). Given the overuse of projectors today, flip charts, especially those with professional-looking illustrations and pictures, can be refreshing. Some drawbacks to flip charts are that they are somewhat awkward to transport (they can be heavy), they may require use of someone with artistic talent, and they are not suitable to large audiences or venues.

When developing flip charts, consider the following: Each sheet should contain one idea, sketch, or theme; graphics, charts, illustrations, and other visuals must be large so the all audience members can see; use block lettering and capitalize all letters; use and vary colors for organizational purposes and to draw attention to key ideas and points.

Overhead transparencies.   Overhead transparencies are useful for audiences of 20 to 50 people and can be produced quickly, easily, and inexpensively. Most standard office copiers can make transparencies using acetate sheets that run through the machine like regular paper. This means any image, figure, picture, photo, or text can be made into a transparency. Adding specific notations during a presentation to preprinted outlines can add a unique and active element to a stale presentation. When transcribing notes onto premade images, the presenter does not need to concentrate on the difficult details, but he or she is doing something active with the audience and therefore is drawing them into the presentation. If creative and prepared, presenters can overlay transparencies for a cumulative presentation effect.

In many venues, transparency projectors have been replaced by document projector cameras (see next subsection). This means that if you want to use transparencies, you'll probably be lugging a clunky machine around with you (glare is the biggest problem with transparencies used on document projectors). However, the benefits of "going retro" could pay off, especially if you're creative. Keep in mind, however, that projected images can be hard to see from the back of a large room, often the images are distorted or tilted, it can be difficult to write on a transparency when it is on the projector, and the projector can obstruct the view of the audience. It is also difficult for the speaker to move around because he or she must change transparencies by hand.

When developing overhead transparencies, consider the following: Add color by cutting out colored pieces of acetate gel, which are available at art stores, and gluing or taping them to the original transparency; use water-soluble ink in a variety of colors; to actively participate with the audience, write content during the presentation; keep transparencies simple; use bold fonts; write words in uppercase letters.

Document cameras. Many classrooms and conference rooms have document cameras, which are attached to computer systems or projectors. This equipment is expensive and not likely to be widely available, though. The document camera works like an overhead transparency projector, with many of the same limitations; however, it comes with many additional benefits. The largest difference, and biggest benefit of the document camera, is that it does not require transparencies. Any document, including basic white paper (for writing on like a transparency), photographs, maps, magazines, and books, just to name a few, can be projected. The camera can also project three-dimensional shapes (3D), giving presenters the option to use props in new ways. For example, a speaker can demonstrate something with a prop on a stage that is located in a large venue. The prop is projected on a large screen so the audience can see. The cameras allow the user to zoom in and out, so small text can be easily projected. Finally, the document camera can save money on copies and handouts.

When developing presentation material for document cameras, understand their limitations. Many of the things to consider when using overhead projectors are similar to transparencies. However, note that there are size and weight limitations for these machines, so treat with care. Documents and other artifacts can be projected and then, using the "capture image feature," which is standard on many cameras, the presentation can be converted into an image that can then be incorporated into other presentational programs (e.g., PowerPoint or Apple Keynote), into post-presentation handouts, and into handouts that can then be distributed electronically (e.g., emailed to attendees or uploaded to a website).

Posters. Posters are prepared graphic devices that can be made of a variety of materials and media, such as text, photographs, diagrams, graphs, or any combination of these. Posters often work best in smaller-sized audience, such as trade shows, sales presentations, or academic conferences. Posters are useful because they are permanent and portable, can be simple or elaborate, can stand alone or be incorporated into a presentation, and are a recognizable media that can be easily displayed in a variety of locations. However, posters can easily become convoluted with too much detail, transporting them can be difficult if they are large or fragile, they can require extensive preparation, and often require the assistance of a design professional with expertise using technical software (e.g., Adobe InDesign). Today, many posters use sophisticated infographics, which require artistic interpretation of data, time, and expensive software.

When developing posters, consider the following: Each poster should contain one message or theme; words, charts, diagrams, and other symbols must be penned in a large size to be seen by everyone in the room; use all uppercase letters, and do not italicize; use color and vary it as appropriate; before printing, check color schemes from a distance to make sure the color works well and is not distracting. Remember that posters are somewhat permanent. They cannot be reprinted for minor typos or other graphical mistakes, so double check your work before sending to the printer.

Video, DVD, and Audio-Slide. Videos, especially those that are saved as digital files (e.g., .wmv, .mpeg4, .flv, and .avi), and those uploaded to video sites like YouTube.com or Vimeo.com, can easily be embedded into other presentation media (e.g., Microsoft PowerPoint). However, video itself can be treated as a stand-alone presentation tool. Similarly, presentation aids can be produced in the format of DVD or audio-slide and synchronized with a presentation. Audio-to-slide coordination can be developed within PowerPoint or video programs, such as Sony Vegas Movie Studio, in which voice-over or music is synchronized to slide transition. Photographers or presenters seeking a more old-fashioned feel may want to produce presentations with older audio-slide software. This technology synchronizes a 35-mm slide projector with music or sounds by way of electronic pulse.

Regardless of the medium used to achieve audio-visual coordination, or "slidecasting" as it is now called when distributed via web, consider the limitations of this presentation style. First, it requires a significant amount of technology both for production and for delivery. For production, you will need a computer capable of editing video and audio and burning DVDs. The older technology approach requires using a company that can create 35-mm slides. These are becoming harder to locate. For delivery, a room needs to be equipped with a projector and speakers. For smaller venues, a basic TV and DVD player could be used to present the video (one reason this is still a useful consideration). For the older audio-slide approach, you'll be bringing your own equipment. Additionally, it takes a lot of time to develop a script and to produce and edit the visuals. If you lack skills to do this on your own, it will require the expertise of a professional.

When developing audio-visual media, consider the following: Create a tentative production schedule; prepare a script or a storyboard and carry this script with you to the presentation; photograph or borrow slides of scenes that emphasize your points; keep images to one message per frame; test-run the show with enough time to re-edit if necessary; secure permission to use commercial or otherwise copyrighted music or material; provide credit to borrowed media; and use simple design for clarity. Refer back to Table 3.3 (Chapter 3) for a list of various audio and video programs, as well as useful tools and sites, for developing audio and videos. In addition to those programs, use services like FriendlyMusic (**http:// friendlymusic.com**) or AudioSwap (**http://youtube.com/audioswap_main**) to add music for free to non-commercial YouTube videos and presentations. To download others' online videos, perhaps for use in a PowerPoint presentation, you can use **http://saveyoutube.com** or similar site; however, note that YouTube and other video sites (and users) have use permission rules, so read the site's terms and agreements. Finally, if you want to record a screen shot and sound so that you can describe what you are doing for an online tutorial, then purchase or use screen capture software, such as Microsoft Encoder Screen Capture, Debut Video Capture Software by NCH Software, or the standard software for screen recorder that comes with Apple operating systems.

Digital Presentation Software (Slide Decks).   Most professionals (and just about everyone else) use presentation software, such as OpenOffice Impress, Microsoft PowerPoint, Google Documents, and Apple Keynote, to organize and present visual aids during a presentation. These programs allow users to design slides with basic text and a variety of other media, such as images, graphics, data, videos, and music. With a variety of templates and built-in professional-looking graphic design elements that make it easy to animate content, create slide transition effects, charts, graphs, and so on, it is easy to understand why they are so overused. A significant amount of skill is not required to develop professional-looking presentation aids. These presentations are easy to edit, update, and transport. They can easily be imported into online meetings, webcasts, and webinars and distributed in a variety of other ways (e.g., handouts, email attachments, or online via **wwwslideshare.net** or **www.scribd.com**).

Due to its widespread and often poor use, the slide deck is becoming tired and somewhat ineffective. The expression, "death by PowerPoint," summarizes both how an audience feels after a mind-numbing presentation as well as "*the end of a presentation* for the speaker" (note the double-entendre). Used well, however, slide deck presentations and other uses of digital presentation software can enrich an oral presentation by motivating and inspiring an audience in ways unachievable by words alone. The key is to keep presentations purpose-driven and simple and maintain continuity of design.

When setting up your slide deck, consider the following, which are summarized in Table A.6 (Appendix) and visually represented in Figure 6.4: how you will set up your slide deck, what type of content you will use, how you will navigate content, and how you will deliver your presentation. It takes some time to get comfortable with slides, so when you choose to use presentations aids, you're inevitably adding time to the production process and practice phase. Some key points in Table A.6 to note are to create a PDF version of your presentation as backup, to cite the sources of borrowed audio and videos, and to minimize slide content (and length). First, the PDF can often be imported into whatever slide deck presenter available at a venue. Second, many presentations cite research but not videos and audio. As with reports and written materials, be sure to cite sources and give credit to borrowed material. Third, note that Figure 6.4 is a presentation developed to deliver some of the points in Table A.6. Since Table A.6 works better as a handout, this could be delivered to the audience during or after a presentation. As far as presentations go, Figure 6.4 would be a hearty 10- to15-minute presentation and, because of the visuals, it would be more interesting to hear than a bullet point list of materials in Table A.6. Key ideas are reinforced, adding emphasis to the points in Table A.6. If everything was represented, the important points would be lost.

Presentation Software Alternatives: Prezi and Sliderocket.com.   Presentation software like PowerPoint and OpenOffice Impress are linear. In other words, slides transition in a step-by-step progression and data appears mostly as lists, which progress from top to bottom of each slide. In recent years, alternatives to the linear format have emerged. Two of the most popular are Prezi and SlideRocket. SlideRocket (**http://sliderocket.com**) is a cloud-based presentation program that functions like traditional presentation software, as well as offering the ability to link Internet resources to slides. With built-in social networking tools, for example, it allows presenters to quickly share presentation materials and to interact with audiences. It also features powerful analytical tools that can help businesses and organizations evaluate the performance of their presentations, down to audience reaction to specific points.

Prezi (**http://prezi.com**) is a cloud-based presentation program and storytelling tool. Ideas are presented on a virtual canvas in clusters and frames. The relative size and proximity of information distinguishes importance, relevance, and the relationship among information and ideas. The Zooming User Interface (ZUI) enables users to zoom in and out of content in

Figure 6.4. An example slide deck illustrating design practices.

such a way that frames can be embedded within each other. These features allow data, information, visuals, and multimedia to be explored both linearly and nonlinearly. The effect is that presentation of information is much more dynamic and stories can be delivered as a narrative. The movement is designated by a "path" rather than placement of material. This is great for spatially organized material. For example, if discussing three different countries, a Google Map can be embedded into the presentation and points about each country can be clustered on top of the specific country. When moving from one cluster to another, the Prezi will visually jump from one country (cluster) to the next.

Prezi provides a variety of useful tutorials and examples that can be used to help new users (see **http://prezi.com/learn**). Like any rhetorical artifact, though, one should consider audience, content, approach, design elements, and so on *before* beginning the construction process. Prezi, although new and unique, is not always the best option. For more routine presentations, for example, Prezi requires more time to design a presentation than with traditional presentation software. This may be unwarranted if the software need is to project simple ideas. Also, a benefit of traditional presentation software is that hyperlinks can be added that allow users to quickly navigate among slides (e.g., one can click a hyperlink that moves them from slide 8 to slide 22, or vice versa). With Prezi, the user is restricted to the designated path, which means that to move back to a cluster, a presenter must click the forward or back buttons until he or

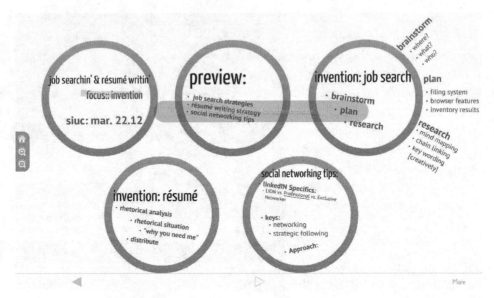

A screenshot of a Prezi canvas.

she lands on the correct visual. This can be annoying during Q&A sessions when you want to revisit a previous visual. However, Prezi does allow you to easily zoom in on content, such as specific words in a PDF. This is something that traditional presentation software does not allow. Again, the decision should be based on needs rather than a desire to use something flashy.

When working with Prezi, consider these specific points, which are not all that different from any other rhetorical process:

- *Create structure first; fill in details later*. If you begin with a blank canvas and begin developing your presentation on it, you'll waste a lot of time. Use your outline and sketch out a plan on paper, then transfer this to the canvas.

- *Choose a color and frame approach early and stick to it*. Part of the process of structuring your presentation requires you to be consistent. The frames and text are the structure of Prezi. Prezi actually does not offer many choices for designating frames or color schemes. Thus, if you use circles to bound larger concepts together, solid-box frames for larger points, and non-solid boxes for sub-points, repeat this throughout the presentation. This will help the audience understand the structure of content.

- *Think in frames*. Don't jump all over the place. Although you don't have to move linearly, it does not mean you should move all over the place, as many people tend to do in Prezi. Too much screen movement, although "fun," adds little to a presentation and disorients an audience. Some people even complain that it makes them nauseous (**http://etechlib.wordpress.com/2011/02/04/pondering-prezi**). Think like a movie director. Give an "establishing shot" and then zoom or pan into the details. Move frame to frame in a slow and coherent manner. Optimally, a frame should cover about 10 minutes of content. Thus, if you have 60-muinute presentation, begin with six large frames and build content within these frames accordingly. As with any other presentation software, don't overuse words.

- *Make sections bigger than you think you need to.* One feature of Prezi is the zoom function. If you are going to embed a bunch of ideas within a frame, make the initial frame larger than you think you'll need. You can then reduce the overall frame. Prezi will adjust everything within a frame proportionately.

- *Rein in ambition.* Remember, simplicity is usually more effective. One or two design decisions, used well, will be much more impressive than 10 executed poorly.

- *Use PDFs, not JPEGs or GIFs.* Prezi utilizes PDFs well. You can upload any PDF and zoom in on it without pixilation. This means that you can convert a traditional PowerPoint into PDF and upload the slides into Prezi. Use websites like **http://web2pdfconvert.com** to convert webpages into PDFs. When imported into Prezi, you can then zoom in on the appropriate sections. This is a great feature for professionals wanting to demonstrate web content.

- *Learn Prezi technical operations.* It is recommended that you create assets (e.g., pictures) in the resolution in which they will be presented. Optimally, work with 1024 x 768 screen resolution, which is the standard projector resolution. This means that if you are taking a screenshot, you want to do so when the screen resolution is set to 1024 x 768. Hold down shift key while creating frames. This creates a frame that will fill a 4:3 (or 1024 x 768) screen when projected. Also, learn the keyboard shortcuts, which dramatically increase the speed at which you can create Prezi content. All of this information is available in the Prezi manual (**http://prezi.com/learn/manual**). The problem, of course, is most people don't invest the time to learn software and web program features. Don't be this person. A little bit of time invested up front will pay awesome dividends later. You'll save a lot of time and avoid creating awful Prezis that do little for your oral presentation.

Although Prezis can be fun to use, they can be frustrating to create. If you don't understand some of the tips above, it may be necessary to work with someone who is trained in design and understands how to use the technical features of the program. If you are smart with design and understand certain technical features and how to implement them, you should add Prezi design to your list of communication consultation services.

Infographics and Specific Visual Aids

All of the above media often make use of specific visual aids, which present data like time frames, statistics, descriptions, statements, and references in creative and aesthetic ways. No presentation aid incorporates these elements with such a heavy emphasis toward design than informational graphics, or infographics. Infographics are often designed in software programs like Adobe InDesign and Microsoft Expression Design and presented visually in a variety of media, from print (e.g., brochures, cards, and posters) to digital (e.g., online videos, presentation software, and websites). Thus, learning to create information graphics may require investment in art and design classes or a lot of self-guided learning.

Infographics have been around for ages (e.g., maps). Today, however, they are important to the distribution of all types of information. Web users, with their diminishing attention spans, are inexorably drawn to these shiny, brightly colored messages with small, relevant, clearly displayed nuggets of information. Infographics, when designed well, are straight to the point, factually interesting, and rhetorically powerful. Infographics channel information in a visually pleasing, instantly understandable manner, making them not only useful, but extremely beautiful. (Some even look like art.) Figure 6.5 demonstrates a collection of different infographics elements.

Should you decide to design your own information graphics, or delegate the task to a design department, note

Figure 6.5. An example infographic with a collection of visual aids. *(Image © David Arts, 2012. Used under license from Shutterstock, Inc.)*

the following rhetorical components, which attend to the visual (how elements will appear), content (what data will be included), and knowledge (how facts will be deduced) components of such graphics:

- Keep it simple! Don't try to do too much in one picture. Remember form follows function. Infographics should present data in a compact way, communicate a message that is easy to understand, and analyze data to make a point, such as cause-and-effect relationships.

- Decide on a color and typography scheme early and use it consistently.

- Understand your purpose. Define the goal of the infographic. (Remember, an infographic is rhetorical, its primary and secondary goals are to inform, persuade, or entertain.) Without a clear goal, your data collection will be messy and your final product confusing.

- Think of it as a visual essay: Ensure your arguments hold and are relevant. Find the most effective visual metaphors.

- Remember that it's all about quickly conveying the meaning behind complex data.

- Draw conclusions for your audience; don't expect them to understand what pictures represent.

- Reference your facts in the infographic. Factual elements enhance credibility and effectiveness.

There are a variety of infographic types, but the most common are as follows:

- *Directional and instructional infographics.* The original infographics were directional (maps). These types of infographics assist readers with a variety of directions using symbols, pictures, maps, arrows, numerals, and so on. Diagrams can demonstrate product assembly or a recommended pattern of physical movement.
- *Quantitative infographics.* Pie charts, bar graphics, tables, and spreadsheets are typically used to assist in summarizing complex data.
- *Cause-and-effect infographics.* Information is presented to illustrate relationships between conceptual or physical entities. For example, an infographic may show the relationship between water shortages and commodity prices.
- *Comparison infographics.* Information and data are presented to draw comparisons between objects, events, places, and so on. Showing familiar objects of similar size or value to showcase differences in products and showing residential housing prices by neighborhood are common examples of information graphics using comparison.
- *Chronological infographics.* Typically based on timelines, chronological infographics present events or processes as they occur(ed) in time. Line graphs charting the monetary value of something over time is an example of a chronological infographic.

To learn more about infographics, check out the books listed in continuing education and check out a variety of blogs and websites on the topic. For inspiration, specifically check out the blog **www.coolinfographics.com** or search "infographics" in Google Images (**http://images.google.com**)

Table 6.1 summarizes a variety of visual aids that are used in infographics, as well as some programs that are useful for designing basic graphics, charts, images, and maps. Use visual aids to convey information clearly and concisely. Deciding how to present data is an important part of the invention process. To learn how to create effective slides and visuals aids, check out *slide:ology: The Art and Science of Creating Great Presentations* and the support websites for your data and word processing software, such as **http://office.microsoft .com/en-us/support** for Microsoft Excel and Word or **http://adobe.com/learning** for Adobe Illustrator.

Visual graphic editors come standard with Microsoft and Apple operating systems. However, if you plan to create complex graphics, upgrading to a professional design program can be worth the money. Adobe Photoshop and Illustrator are two of the best programs on the market, but they are also the most expensive programs. A relatively inexpensive program that offers a lot of power is Microsoft Expression Design. If you need to focus on process (e.g., a project schematic) or a sketch up of graphical user interfaces or 3D graphics, you may need to choose from among a variety of programs designed specifically for these types of projects: Google Sketchup; Microsoft Blend, Sketchflow, and Visio; Adobe InDesign; or Caretta GUI Design Studio.

Table 6.1   Common Visual Aids

Visual Aids	*Example*

Timeline
Use to show a series of events that occur in a chronological order. Can be much more effective than a simple bullet list.

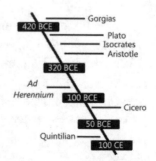

Flow chart
Use to show a process of steps or decisions. (Also makes a great brainstorming tool.) Use software designed specifically for flowcharting (e.g., MS Visio) or sketch freehand for a contemporary look.

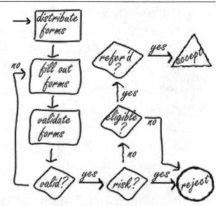

Venn diagrams
Use to demonstrate overlapping thoughts and ideas. Can contain several circles.

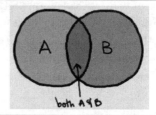

Pictograph (pictogram)
Use relevant graphics and images to represent an idea graphically. Pictographs are a type of chart/graph visually more interesting than raw numbers, lines, and bars.

Others
Here is a list of commonly used graphics: horizontal and vertical graphs, such as line graph, bar graph, and pie graph; diagrams; maps; and annotated maps. Augmented reality applications are an emerging graphical interface (see **www.augmentedreality.org**).

Conclusion

In addition to presentation aids, this chapter explored how to craft electronic communications. As online and mobile technologies continue to advance, there will be many new exciting ways to interact with and to represent the world. For example, *mashups*, a type of web application that integrates and combines data with multiple platforms (image or picture overlays in Google Maps), will change the way people will be able to visualize data. For example, WikipediaVision (**http://lkozma.net/wpv**) uses Google Maps to show semi-realtime updates of edits to Wikipedia. Another version of a mashup is augmented reality programs that allow users to use smart phones to project 3D visualizations of a street, for example. By holding up a smart phone and using the camera input, a person can aim the phone down a street and address and business information automatically populates the display, allowing a more dynamic representation of a map (Ricker, 2010).

Interaction among colleagues and workers is also changing. Electronic communications are becoming more advanced. The chat room/bulletin board was one of the earliest collaborative communication media, and it is still widely used. Chat rooms and bulletin boards are still useful today, especially for technology companies that encourage users to collaborate on solutions to problems with programs and devices. (This is an interesting form of outsourcing that simultaneously increases customer identification.) Chat programs now allow users to type and talk, share files, and, among other things, simulcast desktop applications.

Advancements in technology and improved Internet connection speed and availability have now made it possible for companies to invest in platforms that allow end-users to simultaneously work on shared documents. Google Docs is one of the most popular, although Microsoft and Apple both sell licenses to programs that allow documents to be written remotely and automatically updated when an Internet connection is available. Second Life applications, which allow users to collaborate in creative and dynamic ways using avatars, will continue to improve and grow in popularity, especially as the cost of basic goods and services continues to rise. Meeting in Second Life may be the next best option to actual face-to-face meetings. Although it may take people some time to get comfortable interacting virtually, the virtual presence of avatars allows from more focused interactions (Villano, 2008). These collaborative programs provide a variety of new possibilities for businesses to structure interactions internally and externally with stakeholders. However, these also come with many risks. Chapters 8 and 9 specifically address issues related to risk mitigation and social interactions within electronic spaces.

When creating electronic communications, think about how they will be shared. Will they be embedded in other communications? Will they be uploaded online, shared across an intranet, or burned to DVD? While these may seem like minor issues, there is always an issue of file size. You may want to create a dynamic infographic with embedded video, but distributing this could become an issue. It is difficult to transfer large files by email, so working within the cloud may resolve some design problems. In some cases, files can be transferred for free, or securely for a fee, through services like Adobe SendNow (**http://adobe.com/SendNow**), **www.sharefile.com**, **http://fileshare.com**, **www.yousendit.com**, **http://box.net**, and **www.huddle.com**. Time and money may also not be on your side. Being inventive at the beginning of the construction process will help resolve problems at delivery. Regarding delivery, several programs and services were provided in this chapter, and others will be discussed in Chapter 9. Presentation aids, documents, and multimedia artifacts can be uploaded online to **http://scribd.com, http://slideshare.com, http://issuu.com, http://mygazine.com, www.vimeo.com, http://youtube.com, www.picassa .com, www.flickr.com, http://foliolink.com, http://carbonmade.com, www.deviantart.com, http://illypads.com, http://peercast.org, www.shoutcast.com,** LinkedIn, and Facebook. Of course, the list could go on, and it is not always possible or desirable to share content on every site. Finding a distribution method that accomplishes your rhetorical objectives should be of primary consideration.

Be mindful of ethical considerations when working in collaborative platforms online. Although people may be working at a distance, rules regarding fair and equitable treatment still matter. Businesses should consider, for example, issues of accessibility for people living with disabilities. Technology can both be enabling and constraining. Focus on developing a caring work environment is discussed in Chapter 7. Regarding copyright, cite materials, especially photographs, videos, and so on. People often give credit to print materials in presentations, probably because it has been a focus in school. However, when borrowing an image from the Internet for a presentation, the image source is often not specified. When using others' images, figures, or other material, give credit. What is more, borrowed graphics should be used and cited in step with the permitted usage and rules (permissions) specified by the creator or distributor. For those creating and sharing materials, specify how materials should be used and monitor how they are used to ensure fair use.

Continuing Education: Recommended Texts and Resources

- *Resonate: Present visual stories that transform audiences* by Nancy Duarte. ISBN: 978-0470632017.

    Resonate helps presenters make strong connections with their audiences and lead them to purposeful action. The author's approach is simple: Building a presentation today is a bit like writing a documentary. Using this approach, you'll convey your content with passion, persuasion, and impact.

- *The exceptional presenter goes virtual: Take command of your message, create an ''in-person'' experience, and captivate any remote audience* by Timothy J. Koegel. ISBN: 978-1608320462.

    There is plenty of advice available on public speaking and in-person presentation skills. This book explains how to go about preparing and executing a high-quality virtual presentation. It is a short, easy-to-read book filled with guidance for overcoming the particular barriers that exist in virtual communication scenarios.

- *Creative workshop: 80 challenges to sharpen your design skills* by David Sherwin. ISBN: 978-1600617973

Creative Workshop provides 80 creative challenges that help readers achieve a breadth of stronger design solutions, in various media, within any set time period. Exercises include creating a typeface in an hour, designing a paper robot in an afternoon, and designing web pages and other interactive experiences. Each exercise includes compelling visual solutions from other designers and background stories.

- *Presentation zen: Simple ideas on presentation design and delivery* by Garr Reynolds. ISBN: 978-0321525659. (see also: presentationzen.com)

    Presentation Zen challenges the conventional wisdom of making "slide presentations" in today's world and encourages you to think differently and more creatively about the preparation, design, and delivery of your presentations.

- *slide:ology: The art and science of creating great presentations* by Nancy Duarte. ISBN: 978-0596522346.

    slide:ology is a visually stunning book that offers a lot of inspiration for slide design. It also provides a step-by-step guide to the development and design process. With shortcut tips, this is a must-have book for any rhetor serious about making awesome presentations without spending hours on actual slide development (overall design and invention always takes a lot of time).

- **Websites worth following:**

    - **Technology Entertainment Design ((http://ted.com):** This website distributes outtakes from TED Conferences, a global set of conferences owned by the private non-profit Sapling Foundation, formed to disseminate "ideas worth spreading." Observing these presenters will not only make you a better speaker, but they often have amazing presentation aids.

    - **Economist debates (www.economist.com/debate):** This website has a variety of debates on interesting and relevant topics. Over two weeks, two writers provide a series of editorials that argue for and against a motion. Readers can interact by voting for or against a motion.

    - **Neilson ratings (www.nielsen.com):** This site provides a variety of free and fee-based white papers and reports on social media. It is an excellent resource for business owners and consultants looking to stay at the forefront of trends.

References

Athavaley, A. (2007, June 27). A job interview you don't have to show up for: Microsoft, Verizon, others use virtual worlds to recruit; dressing avatars for success. *Wall Street Journal*. Retrieved from **http://online.wsj.com/article/SB118229876637841321.html**

Allen, M. W., Coopman, S. J., Hart, J. L., & Walker, K. L. (2007). Workplace surveillance and managing privacy boundaries, *Management Communication Quarterly, 21,* 172–200.

Arrington, M. (2010, August 4). Wave goodbye to Google Wave. Retrieved from **http://techcrunch.com/2010/08/04/wave-goodbye-to-google-wave/**

Berghel, H. (1997). Email — The good, the bad, and the ugly. *Communications of the ACM, 40,* 11–15

Berkun, S. (2010). *Confessions of a public speaker.* Sebastopol, CA: O'Reilly Media.

Brown, C. M. (2011, March 16). 8 Tips for using social blogging to grow your business. *Inc Magazine.* Retrieved from **www.inc.com/guides/201105/8-tips-for-using-social-blog-ging-to-grow-your-business.html**

Correia, A-P. (2008). Team conflict in ICT-rich environments: Roles of technologies in conflict management. *British Journal of Educational Technology, 39,* 18–35

Ducheneaut, N., & Bellotti, V. (2003). Ceci n'est pas un objet? Talking about objects in email. *Human–Computer Interaction, 18,* 85–110.

Enbysk, M. (n.d.) 10 tips for using instant messaging for business. Retrieved from **www.microsoft.com/business/en-us/resources/technology/communications/10-tips-for-using-instant-messaging-for-business.aspx?fbid=J7FuOt1vOkM**

Fox, J. (2009, April 19). Dominos uses YouTube to respond to PR crisis. *OneMarket Media.* Retrieved from **http://onemarketmedia.com/blog/2009/04/dominos-uses-youtube-to-respond-to-pr-crisis**

Fried, I. (2005, July 21). Driven to distraction by technology. *CNET | News.* Retrieved from **http://news.cnet.com/driven%20to%20distraction%20by%20technology/2100-1022_3-5797028.html**

Gregory, S. (2009, April 18). Domino's YouTube crisis: 5 ways to fight back. *Time.* Retrieved from **www.time.com/time/nation/article/0,8599,1892389,00.html**

Huberman, B., Romero, D. M., & Wu, F. (2009). Crowdsourcing, attention, and productivity. *Journal of Information Sciences, 35,* 758–765.

Jackson, T., Dawson, R., & Wilson, D. (2003). Reducing the effect of email interruptions on employees. *International Journal of Information Management, 23,* 55–65.

Mackay, W. (1988). Diversity in the use of electronic mail: A preliminary inquiry. *ACM Transactions on Information Systems, 6,* 380–397.

Moulds, J. (2007, November 19). SMS and IM replacing emails. *The Telegraph.* Retrieved from **www.telegraph.co.uk/finance/markets/2819755/SMS-and-IM-replacing-emails.html.**

Nielson. (2011). *Social media report:* Q3 2011. Retrieved from **http://blog.nielsen.com/nielsenwire/social/**

Panteli, N. (2002). Richness, power cues and email text. *Information & Management, 40,* 75–86.

Ricker, T. (2010, February 22). Nokia hints at augmented reality Maps and 3D smartphones in its future. *Engadget.* Retrieved from **www.engadget.com/2010/02/22/nokia-hints-at-augmented-reality-maps-and-3d-smartphones-in-its**

Robinson, J. (2010, February 12). Tame the e-mail beast. *Entrepreneur.* Retrieved from **www.entrepreneur.com/article/204980**

Sacco, A. (2007, July 13). Seven quick tips for videoconferencing beginners. *CIO*. Retrieved from **www.cio.com/article/123801/Seven_Quick_Tips_for_Videoconferencing_Beginners**

Santra, T., Giri, V. N. (2009). Analyzing computer-mediated communication and organizational effectiveness. *Review of Communication, 9,* 100–109

Smith, W. P., & Tabak, F. (2009). Monitoring employee emails: Is there any room for privacy? *Academy of Management Perspectives, 23,* 33–46.

Sumecki, D., Chipulu, M., & Ojiako, U. (2011). Email overload: Exploring the moderating role of the perception of email as a 'business critical' tool. *International Journal of Information Management, 31,* 407–414.

Turnage, A. K. (2007). Email flaming behaviors and organizational conflict. *Journal of Computer-Mediated Communication, 13,* 43–59.

Villano, M. (2008, February 10). The job interview, starring your avatar. *The New York Times*. Retrieved from **www.nytimes.com/2008/02/10/jobs/10pre.html**

Wang, J. (2010, October 20). New desktop app helps you 'CYA': ToneCheck is the e-mail nudge that will save you from yourself. Retrieved from **www.entrepreneur.com/article/217434**

Warkentin, M., Sayeed, L., & Hightower, R. (1997). Virtual teams versus face-to-face meetings: An exploratory study of a web-based conference system. In K. E. Kendall (Ed.), *Emerging information technologies: Improving decisions, cooperation, & infrastructure* (pp. 241-262). Thousand Oaks, CA: Sage.

Unit 3

Developing Skills for the Workplace and Communication Consulting

Image © Yuri Arcurs, 2012. Used under license from Shutterstock, Inc.

Chapter 7: Facilitating Safe and Collaborative Work Environments

Chapter 8: Gathering, Sharing, and Protecting Internal/External Communications

Chapter 9: Social Networking and Optimizing Online Presence

This unit applies rhetorical concepts to practical situations, such as employment in and management of organizations. Specific strategies for using rhetorical criticism in consulting scenarios are also provided. At the conclusion of this unit, students will have developed skills for facilitating collaborative and safe environments, which include working through conflict and improving employee relationships; will have improved understanding of how to gather and protect information; and will be able to use social media and the Internet to achieve personal and business-related goals.

Chapter 7

Facilitating Safe and Collaborative Work Environments

Image © Dmitriy Shironosov, 2012. Used under license from Shutterstock, Inc.

Starting Point

On September 8, 2009, a Yale doctoral student in the Department of Pharmacology, Annie Le, 24, was strangled in a university research lab. A lab technician, Raymond Clark, 24, responsible primarily for caring for animals and cleaning the lab, has since pled guilty for the crime (Reeves & Roupenian, 2011). Several authorities and experts describe the incident as an episode of workplace violence—"This was not about New Haven crime, or University crime, or domestic crime . . . [this] was workplace violence" (New Haven Police Chief James Lewis, as cited in Arnsdorf, Korn, Miller, & Needham, 2009). Supposedly, Clark sent Le a text message, complaining about the condition in which she left her workstations, and suggested they meet. It is not believed that Clark premeditated the murder, indicating that this was a random act of violence. However, other graduate research assistants said that Clark had bullied them about not following rules (Ferran, 2009).

According to the Occupational Safety and Health Administration (OSHA),

> Workplace violence is any act or threat of physical violence, harassment, intimidation, or other threatening disruptive behavior that occurs at the work site. It ranges from threats and verbal abuse to physical assaults and even homicide. It can affect and involve employees, clients, customers and visitors. Homicide is currently the fourth-leading cause of fatal occupational injuries in the United States. According to the Bureau of Labor Statistics Census of Fatal Occupational Injuries (CFOI), of the 4,547 fatal workplace injuries that occurred in the United States in 2010, 506 were workplace homicides. Homicide is the leading cause of death for women in the workplace. (Workplace violence, n.d.).

Workplace violence and workplace bullying, the latter of which is defined as "the repeated and prolonged hostile mistreatment of one or more people at work" (Keashly, 2010, p. 10), are not new phenomena. Recently, however, they have become a topic of both scholarly and public interest. Although the public often hears only about the most egregious cases, such as a workplace shooting (e.g., Star-Ledger Staff, 2011), workplace intimidation and bullying is widespread. OSHA, for example, receives nearly two million reports of workplace violence per year, and it is reasonable to assume that many incidents go unreported.

Given the above facts, it is highly probable that you will experience some degree of workplace bullying during your career, and you may already know someone who is a victim of it. Workplace bullying is fundamentally a systemic phenomenon grounded in an organization's culture (Keashly, 2010), so it is likely that you may also become an unwitting propagator of it. If you experience, observe, or instigate workplace intimidation, it is your responsibility to report it to management and curb it. As protected by the Occupational Safety and Health Act (OSH Act), one can report workplace intimidation and other occupational hazards without fear of employer retaliation or discrimination. Should an employer retaliate, employees have grounding for a civil lawsuit and the employer faces additional expensive civil penalties from OSHA.

The cost of workplace bullying to the employer and employee are significant. Estimates vary depending upon how data is collected and analyzed, but workplace bullying and violence is costly by any measure. The Workplace Bullying Institute (**www.workplacebullying.org**) estimates that, as a result of turnover and lost productivity, a bully could cost a Fortune 500 company an astounding $24 million per year. A more comprehensive study, although a bit dated, calculated the cost of lost work and legal expenses of workplace bullying to be approximately $4.2 billion (Anfuso, 1994). (Adjusted for inflation, that would be about $6.1 billion in 2011.) Financial matters aside, minor workplace bullying has a tremendous potential to escalate, drawing in others, including external stakeholders (e.g., customers), beyond the initial actor-target relationship. Its effects can be devastating and widespread.

Due to increased depression, trauma, and illness, victims and sometimes perpetrators of bullying are impacted financially. The financial impact is a result of missed work days (lost wages), lower commissions, fewer bonuses, increased medical expenses, and so on. Beyond financial issues, though, it is the psychological suffering that is most problematic: "Targets of bullying at work anticipate the workday with dread and a sense of impending doom. They steal through the workplace on a state of high alert, in anticipation of the next attack. Privately, they are profoundly ashamed of being victimized and are confused at their apparent inability to fight back and protect themselves" (Lutgen-Sandvik, Tracy, & Alberts, 2007, p.837). In short, bullying results in perceived power imbalances and creates a hostile work environment for employees who may not be direct targets (Salin, 2003).

In addition to workplace violence and bullying, professionals, entrepreneurs, managers, and consultants should be concerned about other "dark-side" issues of work, such as burnout, stress, sexual harassment, illegal activity, and customer and employee injury. These issues are often outcomes of poor leadership. Unsafe and unhappy workplaces are the result of managers' own improper behaviors or their unwillingness to address or resolve problematic issues. Failure of leadership can be a result of many factors, such as unawareness of a problem, a manager's own fears, and too much focus on short-term profit over long-term well-being.

But allowing behaviors that create hostility or dangerous workplaces should never be tolerated, and people who help to create these types of environments should be removed or rehabilitated. Stanford professor Robert Sutton (2007) calls people who create or allow hostile work environments "assholes": "The damage that assholes do to their organizations is seen in the costs of increased turnover, absenteeism, decreased commitment to work, and the distraction and impaired individual performance . . ." (p. 36). While thinking of problem-creators as "assholes" may be too aggressive, the point is clear: You must take proactive measures to curb inappropriate behavior in the workplace. Also, if you want to demonstrate strong leadership, you must work to create environments that engage employees, encourage positive communication, and are designed with ergonomic tools and with the workplace activity in mind—that is, objects and space are specifically designed for natural human body movements and cognitive and communicative activities.

Forethought in the design process can go a long way toward improving the health and happiness of employees. In the continuing education section of this chapter, several resources are provided that address ergonomic design for interactivity, safety, and employee management. These things matter: An office can be designed to promote more communication, silence, movement, efficiency, and so on. In this chapter, as with Chapters 8 and 9, focus is on the specific application of the concepts learned in the first two units. You will gain knowledge of techniques that demonstrate the applicability of rhetorical and communication principles in order to effectively mitigate issues related to workplace safety, work processes, team collaboration, networking (workplace promotions), and so on. This chapter specifically focuses on developing knowledge to address workplace issues through effective facilitation. The goal of learning to be a better team member and leader is to make the workplace a caring space, to improve team functions, to make meetings productive, and to work through conflict in the workplace.

Setting a Productive Rhetorical Tone

Within business and organizations development, the word "facilitation" refers to the process of designing and running a successful project, meeting, consulting relationship, group, or team. The word "facilitate," borrowed from French (*faciliter*), means "to render easy." The goal and task of facilitators and consultants is to make work processes more effective. Facilitators help others meet objectives. Thus, facilitating a safe environment for collaboration requires significant effort from managers and other decision-makers within the organizations, that is, those who "set the ground rules" by which interaction occurs. If the proper support and communication mechanisms are in place, employees and customers are able to effectively work together. What is more, the relationship between humans and equipment will also be safer. Focus on effectiveness in interaction leads to more efficient, safe, and caring organizations.

Facilitation requires a narrative that sets the right rhetorical tone through which practices are guided. Usually, these types of stories are closely associated with the "founder's narrative"—that is, those stories that point to what the founder would do in order to ensure safe collaboration. When safety and collaboration are institutionalized (formalized) within the organization, the stories of safety are written into policies and handbooks and embedded in training programs.

Three companies that seem to have been effective at establishing the proper rhetorical tone are Bob's Red Mill Natural Foods (BRM), Southwest Airlines, and Zappos.com. Bob's Red Mill was founded in 1978 by Bob Moore and his wife Charlee in Milwaukie, Oregon. The company is an outcome of Bob's love of healthy eating and old-world technologies. The company uses old milling techniques to produce a variety of whole-grain flours, cereals, and bread mixes. BRM has amassed an international following.

In 2010, Bob announced that he was giving his 200+ employees ownership of the company through an employee stock option plan (ESOP), a type of retirement plan in which the company contributes its stock to the plan to be held in trust for the benefit of its employees. This is consistent with the narrative that Bob is a compassionate businessperson.

An article announcing the plan (Tims, 2010) describes how employees think of Bob, but also tells a story that reinforces how employees should interact with each other: "'It just shows how much faith and trust Bob has in us,' said Bo Thomas, the company's maintenance superintendent. . . . 'For all of us, it's more than just a job. Obviously, it's the same way for Bob, too. . . .'" The article also helps sustain a narrative of Bob as an easy-going person: 'I may have given them the company' [Bob] said, chuckling, 'but the boss part is still mine.'" The story helps to sustain an image of a democratic, employee-, and customer-oriented company. When Bob eventually retires, one would expect that a leader that projects the same kind of light-hearted tone would be selected, likely from among the employees.

Southwest Airlines (NYSE: LUV) is a company that has received extensive attention. An Amazon search for hardcover books on "Southwest Airlines" produces no fewer than 230 results. Two of the books, *Lessons in Loyalty* and *The Southwest Airlines Way*, are recommended as continuing education. There are several biographies on its founder and former CEO

Herb Kelleher. Southwest is constantly named one of the top five Most Admired Corporations in American in *Fortune* magazine's annual poll. In the preface to *Flying for Peanuts*, Marty Thompson (2004) writes

> Southwest runs a very unique business! No airline customer service concept is as solidly founded on the premise that flying can be fun for both passenger and the airline and the airline employees, except Southwest. As a matter of fact, in today's business climate, Southwest is probably the only carrier in the airline industry that is, indeed, having any fun at all! (p. 1)

Such emphatic writing is typical to those loyal to Southwest and is an outcome of focused and careful image building.

Southwest is notorious for legendary stories, many of which are acceptably embellished. For example, legend has it that Herb Kelleher and Rolling King created the concept on a bar napkin. Just to get started, the company had to overcome several legal challenges, which involved appeals all the way up to the Supreme Court. The company overcame significant financial troubles, holding on by running three aircraft as if it had four (leading to the fastest ground turnaround times in the industry—dubbed "the 10-minute turn"). By flying shorter flights to smaller airports, fares could remain lower and there were fewer delays.

Probably one of the more unique Southwest stories involves a trademark dispute between Stevens Aviation and Southwest over the slogan "Just Plane Smart." This dispute culminated in an arm-wrestling match between the two companies' CEOs, Kelleher and Kurt Herwald, in lieu of a lawsuit. (The event became known as "Malice in Dallas.") Southwest ran a successful PR campaign to draw attention to the event, and employees were bussed to a large arena to cheer on their company founders. Although Kelleher lost the three-round bout, Stevens Aviation granted rights to the use of the slogan. Also, the proceeds from the event were generated to charity. The list of fun and quirky Southwest stories that suggest a friendly, fun, and creative organization could go on, but the most notable behaviors are the company's singing and dancing flight attendants, comedic pilots, and lovable gate agents that supposedly pull out personal credit cards to assist customers.

The culture of Southwest is partly due to the narrative and partly due to policy (Freiberg & Frieberg, 1998; Gittell, 2005). For example, the company has a rigorous probation period that retains its new employees more on this basis of their attitude than skills (Grubbs-West, 2005). Southwest understands that employees are "brand ambassadors" as well as skillful employees. The right attitude also pays off. Happier employees are less likely to cause accidents (Donald & Young, 1996).

Zappos.com was founded by Tony Hsieh, a serial entrepreneur who is "widely regarded as one of the most innovative Internet marketers of all time" (Chafkin, 2009). It has since been sold to Amazon.com. The Internet shoe store is wildly successful and offers impeccable customer service, including free return shipping. Hsieh is interested in the science of happiness and helped create a company culture with a focus on it. As Chafkin writes,

> That single-minded focus on happiness has led to plenty of accolades for the company, which routinely scores high on lists of the best places to work. But Zappos's approach to workplace bliss differs significantly from that of other employee-friendly businesses. For one thing, Zappos pays salaries that are often below market rates—the average hourly worker makes just over $23,000 a year. Though the company covers 100 percent of health care costs, employees are not offered perks found at many companies, such as on-site child care, tuition reimbursement, and a 401(k) match. Zappos does offer free food to its employees, but the pile of cold cuts in the small cafeteria loses its allure faster than you can say . Instead of buying his employees' loyalty, Hsieh has managed to design a corporate culture that challenges our conception of that tired phrase. (para. 10)

The culture of Zappos is maintained through a well-designed training program. For example, "all new Zappos employees receive two weeks of classroom training. Then they spend two weeks learning how to answer customer calls. At the conclusion of the program, trainees arc famously offered $2,000, plus time worked, to quit" (Chafkin, 2009)

The above examples demonstrate that setting the proper rhetorical tone for an organization, especially one that is going to be safe and fun to work in and will inspire employee collaboration, requires rhetorical effort—especially at the invention stage. Stories that illustrate the company's values are important to develop, tell, and distribute. Some of these stories may be deliberately created, others may emerge. They must be perpetuated both formally and informally within the organization. Webpages, for example, often have a link to "our history." Wikipedia pages and books, published about the company, help tell the preferred story of the company, which inspire the right kind of people to apply. These stories also shape current employees' perceptions about the company.

Use the power of interpretive rhetoric and tell a consistent story. As this will ultimate influence how employees and managers deliberate and facilitate within the workplace. Stakeholders can be both deliberately and subtly influenced by the tone of language in oral and written artifacts, so write and speak with a consistent and coherent authorial voice. The rhetoric of and about organizations will then cast its magic spell; it will motivate employees to work hard while maintaining a safe and collaborative environment. Stories, however, must be supported by proper policies and procedures, which include effective feedback systems. Many of the strategies and tactics listed in the following sections focus upon building and maintaining (i.e., facilitating) safe and collaborative work environments.

Facilitating Safe and Caring Work Environments

Creating safe and caring work environments requires attention to occupational health, which is a manifestation of healthy physical activities, emotional labor, and human relations. The World Health Organization (WHO) was one of the first organizations to address occupational health. WHO, in partnership with the International Labour Organization, outlined the following definition of occupational health in 1950:

> Occupational health should aim at the promotion and maintenance of the highest degree of physical, mental and social well-being of workers in all occupations; the prevention amongst workers of departures from health caused by their working conditions; the protection of workers in their employment from risks resulting from factors adverse to health; the placing and maintenance of the worker in an occupational environment adapted to his physiological and psychological equipment and, to summarize: the adaptation of work to man and of each man to his job. (Occupational Health, n.d.)

In the United States, occupational health is regulated primarily by the Occupational Safety and Health Administration (OSHA), an agency of the U.S. Department of Labor, which sets and enforces workplace safety standards and the Occupational Safety and Health Review Commission (OSHRC), which reviews enforcement priorities, actions, and cases (Occupational Health and Safety Act of 1970; U.S. Code, title 29, chap. 15). Within the United States, ensuing workplace safety is both an ethical and legal obligation of management. The following subsections list common types of physical and emotional concerns, as well as some ideas for managing these issues in the workplace.

Physical Concerns

Physical concerns at the workplace can range from minor injuries to death. According to OSHA, "an injury or illness is considered . . . to be work-related if an event or exposure in the work environment either caused or contributed to the resulting condition or significantly aggravated a pre-existing condition" (Occupational Safety and Health Definitions, n.d.).

Repetitive strain injuries—classified as musculoskeletal disorders (MSDs) and nervous system injuries—are common in contemporary organizations. These injuries are related to prolonged or repetitive tasks that cause strain on the body due to repetitive motion (e.g., typing), forceful exertions (e.g., lifting large loads), vibrations (e.g., drilling), mechanical compression (e.g., pressing against hard surfaces), or sustained or awkward positions (e.g., sitting in chair, bending, or looking down). Assembly line workers or construction workers may obtain these injuries by continuous repetitive motions that require force (e.g., hammering or drilling). Office workers may sustain injuries from typing, looking down (to read), and holding a phone to the ear. Common MSD injuries include sprains, strains, tears, back pain, nerve degeneration, carpal tunnel syndrome, and hernias. In many cases, these injuries require surgery or discontinuation of work tasks.

In addition to thwarting repetitive strain injuries, organizations should actively pursue measures to reduce workers' risk of skin disease, respiratory conditions, poisoning, hearing loss, and other bodily injuries, such as cuts and disfigurement. Many of these issues can be thwarted by creating a culture in which safety and happiness is a priority, by focusing on environment design (ergonomics), by maintaining and upgrading equipment, by implementing safety protocols and procedures, by training employees to properly use equipment, by making crisis management procedures and training a priority, and by focusing equally upon emotional and physical concerns.

Emotional Concerns

Within the scholarly field of organizational communication, researchers have studied the *emotions created and facilitated by the context of work* (e.g., Lutgen-Sandvik, 2003), as well as *the role of emotion required of work itself*, especially the emotional communication required of working with clients and customers (Sandelands & Boudens, 2000). According to Miller and Koesten (2008), there are two tracks of research that focus on the emotive rather than rational dimensions of work. The first track focuses on *emotional labor*, or the work required to project emotion and communicate in a way prescribed by management in the service of profits (e.g., Kruml & Geddes, 2000; Tracy, 2000). The second track focuses on *emotional work*, or the natural positive and problematic emotions that are part of interactions with clients and patients in human and social service occupations (e.g., Meyerson, 1998; Miller, Stiff, & Ellis, 1988). Emotional work can lead to authentic emotions that develop in client-provider relationships that are both intense and long-term. For example, in hospitals workers may form relationships with patients over time and have to deal with the grief that follows patients' deaths.

The effects of emotional work and emotional labor have significant impact on workplace climate and can affect workers mental and physical health (Miller & Koesten, 2008). For example, stress may be a psychological state, but it can reduce immune system responses, increasing illnesses (Dohrenwend & Dohrenwend, 1978). Depression, a psychological state, can lead to increased risk of cardiovascular disease (Kivimaki et al., 2003). Unlike physical labor, emotional labor and emotional work often extend beyond the boundaries of the workplace. Employees discuss emotional issues with their relatives and friends, increasing stress in non-work relation-

Stress in the workplace can lead to serious emotional and physical problems. (Image © Piotr Marcinski, 2012. Used under license from Shutterstock, Inc.)

ships (Montgomery, Panagopolou, de Wildt, & Meenks, 1986). These stressed employees talk incessantly about work issues, often to the annoyance of others, fret over minor issues, and give less emotionally to more important relationships (Montgomery et al., 1986).

Probably the greatest risk associated with emotional work and emotional labor is burnout. Burnout adversely affects both the employer and employee due to decreased morale and increased mistakes (Miller & Koesten, 2008). *Burnout is a state of emotional, mental, and physical exhaustion caused by excessive and prolonged stress.* It typically occurs when workers feel overwhelmed by workplace demands.

There are many causes of burnout; however, burnout experienced in the workplace stems from workers feeling or experiencing the following: little or

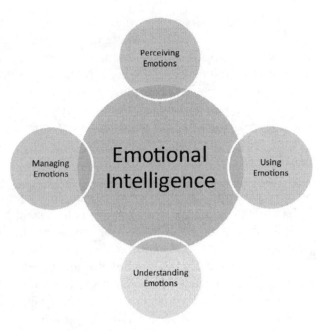

Figure 7.1. Emotional intelligence requires thoughtful use of emotions. (*Image © Kheng Guan Toh, 2012. Used under license from Shutterstock, Inc.*)

no control over their work, a lack of recognition or rewards for good work, unclear or demanding job expectations, work that's monotonous or unchallenging, or a chaotic or high-pressure environment. Some of the signs of burnout include fatigue; irritability; anxiety attacks; weight gain; teeth grinding; increased drug, alcohol, or tobacco use; nightmares; forgetfulness; low productivity at work; and an inability to concentrate (Rossi, Perrewe, & Sauter, 2006). Burnout also increases employees' risks of depression, anxiety, physical illness (i.e., stroke or heart attack), and suicide (Miller & Smith, 2007). Employees can, of course, take vacations, refuse over time work, and quit their job. From an employer's point of view, however, these are not amicable solutions. Employee turnover and the loss of qualified and quality employees come at a significant financial and social cost to the organization, often intensifying stress and burnout among remaining employees (Cox, Kuk, & Leiter, 1993). Thwarting or stopping this vicious cycle, which is often aggravated by physical issues listed above, as a manager or consultant, is important to crafting productive workplaces. This work requires what consultants describe as *emotional intelligence*, which is the ability to perceive, use, understand, and manage emotions productively (see Figure 7.1). Developing emotional intelligence requires attention to ethics, laws, and workplace designs. These issues, among others, are addressed in the next section.

Addressing Physical and Emotional Concerns

The following are suggestions for reducing workplace stress that leads to physical and emotional concerns within organizations.

Think ethically.   Actively pursuing the goal of being a good boss will significantly improve workplace relations. Managers and entrepreneurs have a propensity to micromanage, which can lead to stress and burnout among employees and decrease overall productivity and profitability (Wright, 1999). By actively striving to be a positive role model, by investing in the communicative process of giving employees positive feedback, and by addressing issues in a non-hostile manner, managers can have a significant impact on the overall tone of the workplace. If the overall work climate is positive, then workers will feel more comfortable coming to work and speaking up about problematic behaviors from coworkers and customers or equipment-related problems.

Unfortunately, many entrepreneurs, managers, and employees create the conditions for physical and emotional danger. For example, by purchasing inexpensive equipment, such as desks and chairs, workers are more likely to sustain physical injuries. Also, if they are uncomfortable they are more likely to be unhappy or hostile. By mistreating employees, managers create resentment and lower productivity. For example, workers often complain about meager bonuses. If a company talks up bonuses and benefits and then gives an unsatisfactory amount, this may cause more problems than offering no bonus (recall that Zappos has a happy workplace despite its lack of employee benefits). Thus, consider the rhetoric of the organization and match words with practices. *Inc. Magazine* and *Entrepreneur* regularly publish stories that describe creative management practices entrepreneurs use to facilitate happy work environments free of physical and emotional dangers.

Know the laws.   In the United States, two important laws that help promote and sustain a safe work environment are the Fair Labor Standards Act (FLSA) and the Occupational Safety and Health (OSH) Act.

The FLSA, passed in 1938, prescribes standards for wages and overtime pay that affect most private and public employment. The act requires employers to pay employees who are not otherwise exempt (e.g., salaried professionals) at least the federal minimum wage and overtime pay of one-and-one-half times the regular rate of pay. Some states and municipalities have higher minimum wage standards, so check state and local laws. The FLSA restricts the hours that children under age 16 can work and forbids the employment of children under age 18 in certain jobs deemed too dangerous. For agricultural operations, there are different labor standards. Information regarding the laws and mandatory reporting guidelines can be found online: **www.dol.gov/whd** and **www.dol.gov/whd/flsa**.

Adhering to FLSA guidelines not only protects businesses from potential civil or criminal investigations, it also ensures that children and laborers are not exploited in a way consistent with the examples in Upton Sinclair's *The Jungle* (1906/2010), a book that describes the atrocities of working in the Chicago stockyards (although the described experiences were common in many early-twentieth-century factories). The book's most disturbing illustration of life in the stockyards is that of people falling into meat grinders. Interestingly, many readers focused on food safety at first, not on the working conditions described in the book. The first legislation inspired by the book was the Meat Inspection Act, which eventually led to the creation of the Food and Drug Administration (established 1930). Contrasting labor practices today with those of a century ago, it is easy to see why governments need to regulate work practices. At the very least, the government can enforce safer work places and ensure against most worker exploitation. Contrasting contemporary workplaces with those of the past should also motivate you to avoid becoming complacent. It is necessary to advocate for a safe workplace and fair pay.

The OSH Act, passed in 1970, seeks "To assure safe and healthful working conditions for working men and women; by authorizing enforcement of the standards developed under the Act; by assisting and encouraging the States in their efforts to assure safe and healthful working conditions; by providing for research, information, education, and training in the field of occupational safety and health; and for other purposes" (Public Law 91-596, U.S. Code Title 29, chap. 15). The main goal of the law and its enforcement (via the Occupational Safety and Health Administration [OSHA]) is to ensure that private employers provide employees with an environment free from recognized hazards, such as exposure to toxic chemicals, excessive noise levels, mechanical dangers, heat or cold stress, or unsanitary conditions. Employers must follow strict protocols and file compliance reports. They must also be ready to undergo routine inspections of the workplace. Employees can report problems to OSHA without fear of employer retaliation. More information can be found online: **www.osha.gov** and **www.dol .gov/compliance/laws/comp-osha.htm**.

Other laws that ensure physical and emotional safe spaces are those that deal with worker's compensation and other forms of insurance (e.g., COBRA; see **www.dol.gov/ dol/topic/health-plans/cobra.htm**), payment of social security (**www.ssa.gov**) and other taxes (**www.irs.gov**), employee benefit security (Employee Retirement Income Security Act [ERISA]), birth and adoption of children (The Family and Medical Leave Act [FMLA]), Veterans Preference (see **wwwdol.gov/vets.**) and union rights and responsibilities (e.g., Labor-Management Reporting and Disclosure Act [LMRDA]). A list of applicable laws is available online at each state's Department of Labor website, as well as the as the federal Department of Labor website (**www.dol.gov**). For a discussion of general and specific questions regarding management practices, such as termination notices, computer monitoring, privacy and free speech, and language rules, visit **www.canmybossdothat.com**.

Be cognizant of environmental design. Surprisingly, in a society obsessed with efficiency, scant attention is given to office design. Design requires significant forethought and planning, long-term investments, and aesthetic approaches. Often, these are skirted in favor of inexpensive equipment and a preoccupation with output rather than process. However, attention to environment design and detail can lead to improved efficiency over time (Turner & Myerson, 1998). The study of efficiency in working environments, as it relates to technological and environment design and use, is called "ergonomics."

The International Ergonomics Association describes ergonomics as follows:

> Ergonomics (or human factors) is the scientific discipline concerned with the understanding of the interactions among humans and other elements of a system, and the profession that applies theoretical principles, data and methods to design in order to optimize human wellbeing and overall system performance. Practitioners of ergonomics, ergonomists, contribute to the planning, design

and evaluation of tasks, jobs, products, organizations, environments and systems in order to make them compatible with the needs, abilities and limitations of people. (Definition of Ergonomics, n.d.)

Commonly, people think of ergonomics as the use of specialized computer peripherals (e.g., mouse or keyboard) and chairs with specific design features. However, decisions regarding whether employees will have open work spaces or will work in cubicles are ergonomic decisions often with profound effects on communicative and collaborative processes.

Office design establishes boundaries, alters noise levels, and effects walking patterns. For example, an office with designated cubicles may reduce overall noise levels and distractions among workers; however, cubicles demarcate personal boundaries, establish "ownership" of a space, and provide privacy at a lower cost than walled offices. Cubicles, however, may reduce interpersonal communication among employees. Designating a space specifically for conversations (e.g., a break room) and giving employees time to interact can create a balanced environment with both privacy and interactivity. Designing the communication systems so that employees can fax or copy materials without leaving their desk or placing employees who use a copier frequently closer to the machine will reduce movement. Each decision is not necessarily better than another, so it is best to think in terms of tradeoffs that either satisfy or work against goals. Designing workspaces so employees must walk more may have social and health

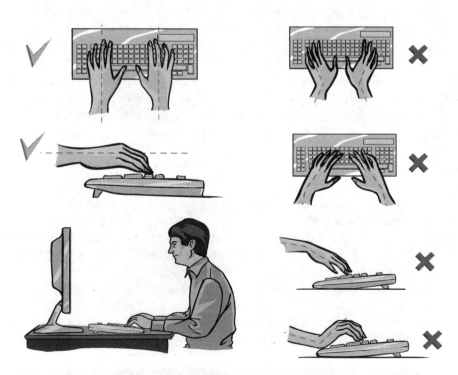

Repetitive strain injuries can be avoided by ergonomic design and practices.
(Image © hkannn, 2012. Used under license from Shutterstock, Inc.)

benefits; however, this decreases the amount of time they may be at their desk doing work-relat-ed tasks. To learn more about design, consider reading books on the subject (some listed in con-tinuing education), or visit the following websites: **http://iea.cc** and **http://osha.gov/SLTC/ ergonomics**.

Establish and utilize "quality circles."   Dr. William Edwards Deming, a professor and consultant, has been honored worldwide for his work on quality control. He is considered by many to be the founder of modern quality control systems and responsible for various con-sulting programs, such as Six Sigma (a business management strategy developed by Motorola). Deming conducted a significant amount of his research in Japan, a country that embraced his work earlier and with greater effect than the United States (Aguayo, 1990).

One of Deming's most significant contributions, and one that can be utilized by managers and consultants in the workplace, is the quality circle. A *quality circle* is a volunteer group com-posed of workers, under the leadership of a supervisor or team leader, who are trained to iden-tify, analyze, and solve work-related problems on their own. The goal of quality circles is to draw upon the collective wisdom of workers directly involved in manufacturing or service-related processes. Based on recommendations of the quality circle, the employees enact changes that improve processes. Over time, the quality circle will gain the confidence of management and be able to implement changes without management approval.

Quality circles can only be effective if they follow a step-by-step process known as the PDSA cycle (Scherkenback, 1986), which stands for Plan, Do, Study, Act. Today, it is frequent-ly referred to as the PDCA cycle (see Figure 7.2). The first task of a quality circle is to estab-lish objectives and processes (Plan). This requires significant "invention" on the part of deliberators. In other words, the objectives should be realistic and accomplishable and the processes, rules, and procedures of the group need to be thor-oughly considered and estab-lished before quality work can begin. During the second phase, the team implements the plan while adhering to the estab-lished process (Do). During this phase, workers collect data in order to chart and analyze out-comes against the initial objec-tives. In the third phase, workers study the results in order to determine needed corrections (Check). Over time, modifica-tions can be charted to deter-mine whether improvements are being made so that the targeted outcomes will be achieved.

Figure 7.2. Deming's Plan, Do, Check, Act (PDCA) Lifecycle. *(Image © S.john, 2012. Used under license from Shutterstock, Inc.)*

Information obtained during the check phase determines how future processes and work procedures should be modified (Act). Corrective actions will improve the processes over time.

Although quality circles are likely to improve communication processes, and they can be used to improve overall workplace quality (e.g., a quality circle dedicated to improving ergonomics or cross-cultural communication), it is challenging to establish effective quality circles in the United States, which is predominantly an individualistic culture (**http://geerthofstede.com/united-states.html**). The key to effective quality circles is to give employees the tools necessary to act outside the guidance of management. Employees must therefore be trained to deliberate, to collect data, and to calculate and interpret results. Providing the required training can be a hefty financial investment for organizations. Team building is also a top priority. All of this work can be for nothing without employee and management commitment to the idea of autonomous teamwork. If employees do not have the skills to work in a team or calculate and understand feedback systems, if employees do not catalog and log data correctly, and if management does not take the efforts of quality circles seriously, improvements to work process will be unlikely.

Utilize concepts in this book. To improve physical and emotional workplace safety, a variety of concepts from this book can be used. Consider, for example, using microblogs to send reminders about procedures in a "workplace tip of the day." Encourage employees to log issues and to describe how they resolved them in a wiki, thus encouraging employees to create a manual over time. Establish groups based on identity markers (e.g., gender or ethnicity) to discuss problems they are facing and to make recommendation to management for positive changes (these needn't be as formal as quality circles).

Creating internal and external communication systems can positively affect workplace relations and mitigate threats. For example, there are a variety of private crisis intervention hotlines that partner with businesses to provider 24-hour, professional support to company employees. These services offer a hotline for employees to call to file complaints confidentially or to help deal with a crisis. Such hotlines ensure that professionals, who are trained in handling crisis, help workers cope with stress and other work-related issues in a confidential setting. These hotlines can be effective not only in reducing workplace stress, but also in encouraging employees to express problems. Problems are filed confidentially, but reported to the company. In addition to a safer workplace, these services can help lower an organization's insurance and culpability should a claim be filed with federal or state regulators. It is important, however, for management to follow up with employees and work to resolve issues. Failure to do so can actually increase culpability. Providing health insurance that includes counseling services is also effective.

These programs are ineffective if employees are not encouraged to use them. Thus, crafting documents that advertise the availability of these programs and services, as well as crafting extensive artifacts that outline policies and procedures, is important. In addition, proper forms, assessments, and research that review employee behavior, assess hazards and security, poll employees about issues, establish control and prevention procedures, provide training and education, and maintain accurate record keeping can make a significant difference in the climate of an organization. The canons of rhetoric, as applied to the invention and crafting of these artifacts, will make a difference in how effective they are.

A Special Note about Regulations

Although this section focused primarily on acting ethically and legally, one could easily criticize the adherence to regulatory bodies and governmental agencies. Although discussing the proper role of government in civil society is beyond the scope of this book, it is necessary to note that we have an ethical and moral obligation, as rhetors, to treat our contemporaries with respect. Although many businesses do provide safe workplaces, one needn't ask too many people before hearing a story about awful workplace conditions or horrible bosses, ones that create a hostile work environment. Organizations need to create and enforce their own regulations of inappropriate behavior.

Some entrepreneurs, even those on the political right (who arguably seek less government oversight), look at regulations as a challenge to make business operations more effective. For example, Fred Keller, CEO of Cascade Engineering, a West Michigan plastics manufacturer, as reported by *Inc. Magazine* (Bluestein, 2011), works to adhere to OSHA, the Department of Labor, and the Environmental Protection Agency. Working against the grain, he has aggressively pursued cutting greenhouse gas emissions by 20% between 2005 and 2010, well above EPA regulations. He has taken a contrarian position to the National Manufacturers' Association, his industry's lobbying powerhouse, which bemoans about EPA regulations. Keller not only exceeds government regulations, but he also adheres to voluntary regulations in order to obtain certifications from the International Standards Organization, which certifies quality management processes and the LEED and B Corporation guidelines for social and environmental responsibility.

Keller's business employs over 1000 employees and is valued at more than $250 million. Despite the difficult economic times, his business is thriving. As Keller explains, instead of seeing regulations from OSHA as a nuisance, he sees them as a blueprint for improvement. Keller suggests that the business school mantra of profit maximization is a head-based approach. A heart-based approach requires doing something good. A practicing Methodist, Keller follows the guiding principles of John Wesley instead of capitalist economists like Milton Friedman:

> *Do all the good you can*
> *By all the means you can*
> *In all the ways you can*
> *In all the places you can*
> *At all the times you can*
> *To all the people you can*
> *As long as ever you can.*

Keller is known to pull this list from his pocket in the middle of meetings and read it to remind people of what's important to him and the company (an excellent use of a rhetorical artifact). This advice is useful to keep in mind when facilitating groups and meetings.

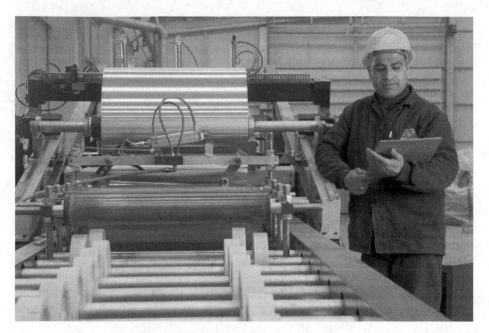

Formalized procedures, checklists, and practices can reduce workplace injury. (Image © Levent Konuk, 2012. Used under license from Shutterstock, Inc.)

Facilitating Teams and Groups

Creating a caring environment within an organization requires leadership. There are a variety of perspectives on leadership, such as the early trait approaches that look at what personality traits are required to be a "Great Man" (Cheney, Christensen, Zorn, & Ganesh, 2011) and the stylistic or behavior approaches that focus on styles of leadership, such as autocratic (authoritarian), democratic (participatory), and *laissez-faire* (hands off approach) (Lewin, Lippitt, & White, 1939). In recent years, there has been a focus on transaction or transformational approaches to leadership (Burns, 1978). The latter approach fits somewhat into the more interpretive and critical approaches to leadership discussed by leadership scholar Keith Grint (1997, 2000), who describes a more constitutive approach to leadership, which places rhetoric at the forefront of the process of creating social perception. According to Grint, the management of meaning is strongly linked to the use and abuse of language. Consistent with the constitutive approach to rhetoric outlined in Chapter 2, constitutive leadership assumes we use rhetoric to artistically shape our world, but also account for the fact that rhetoric also shapes us.

Grint (2000) argues that the earlier approaches to leadership are flawed in assuming that we can objectively categorize persons and situations. Such perspectives also assume that leaders are far more influential and transformational then they probably are. Followership, situational variables, and other important factors, such as who is on the team, for example, largely influence outcomes. While entrepreneurs are important to creating successful ventures, assuming that their success is somehow determined by innate psychology dispositions takes for granted too many other factors. The constitutive approach suggests that leaders and entrepreneurs must attend to the socially constructed nature of things and must, therefore, consciously attempt to influence others' interpretations, including how others see situations and problems. Thus, while leadership styles matter, for example, it is how these leadership styles are used in situations that ultimately determines whether a project will fail or succeed. At times, authoritarianism may be necessary, and at other times a team-based approach, which places a higher concern on people than production, may be the better approach (Blake & Mouton, 1964).

Keeping in mind, however, the important role of ethos, pathos, and logos, it is more likely that leaders who adopt a more proactive and caring approach to working with people, and who are conscientious of active listening practices, will be more effective. Leaders who can make others feel like they've been genuinely heard, even if their ideas are not adopted, are likely to be better facilitators. This book cannot go into all of the details of leadership, although there are some recommended books in the continuing education section. It is largely assumed that many readers will take courses in leadership and communication and organizational communication, which cover these topics in greater depth. In thinking about business and professional communication within the workplace as an employee, manager, or consultant, there are two areas worth focusing upon: facilitating meetings and working through conflict. These two concepts are discussed below, although primarily from a pragmatic perspective.

Facilitating Meetings

In order to have effective and productive meetings that encourage participation, the burden cannot be on a single individual. Instead, everyone must work together to ensure that a meeting has a clearly stated purpose and agenda. Participants should be chosen carefully, invited in professional manner, and given sufficient information (e.g., agenda and handouts) before the meeting. As part of the rhetorical process, it is also important to determine what type of meeting it is (e.g., informational or deliberative), the cultural environment at the time (e.g., hostile or productive), and so on. While the ideas presented below are generally helpful for any type of meeting, the meeting will need to be set up differently if it is dealing with crises rather than routine matters. If it is likely that participants may become passionate about a topic, scheduling time for one-on-one discussions between parties with different opinions can facilitate better outcomes. The facilitator will also have to prepare opening and closing comments differently. More time may be necessary when dealing with difficult problems. Sticking to a single topic per meeting and spreading meetings over several days (if possible) may help reduce concerns that someone's ideas are not adequately addressed. When time is short, preparation may require polling participants to get a sense of what agenda items ought to be included. Facilitators should, in most cases, make this process transparent so people feel included.

Pragmatically, preparation means attention to little details, such as room bookings, catering, audio-visual equipment, and invitations and reminders. To schedule a meeting and to distribute materials, consider the use of cloud-based collaborative software. Google Docs and Google Calendar, for example, can be used to share documents and to plan a meeting time. Other resources provide scheduling platforms, such as **wwwdoodle.com.** or Meeting Wizard **http://meetingwizard.com**. A planner can propose times and have people select those that work for them. After everyone supplies their available times, the organizers choose the time that most participants can meet. To prepare an agenda, give as much detail as possible, but be brief. Distribute the agenda by the most effective means. When extensive information may be necessary, consider attaching it in a separate file and refer to it in the agenda. Stylistically, there are a variety of agenda templates available online (see, especially, **http://office.microsoft.com/en-us/templates**).

Facilitation requires a single person or designated group to be responsible for guiding the meeting and keeping things on time and on track. An important role of the facilitator is to focus on process and enforce established rules. This reduces claims by participants that others received favorable treatment. By setting ground rules, and enforcing them, people will feel that the process was fair, even if the outcomes are unfavorable to their positions. Consider some of the following tactics to improve overall meeting processes:

- Review the agenda at the beginning of the meeting and invite questions, comments or additions about its content.
- Arrange (before the meeting if possible) to have someone different present each item on the agenda.
- Encourage the expression of various viewpoints and expect differences of opinion. If handled well, they can contribute to creative solutions.
- Be suspicious of agreements reached too easily—test ideas to make sure there really is agreement on essential points.
- Don't let a discussion continue between two people; seek comments from others.
- Don't allow comments to become repetitive.
- As much as possible, hold people accountable to their comments. Don't allow them, in other words, to use general statements. Instead, encourage statements that refer to specific people and opinions ("I believe that . . ."; "Jim said that . . .").
- Look for common (even if only minor) points of agreement and point them out.
- Try to help others understand that conflict can be good and encourage collaboration as much as possible. (See next section.)
- Try using tactics that reduce frustration: humor, affirmation, small buzz groups, change of locations, information chats, and so on.
- If drawn into the discussion in support of one particular position, suggest that someone else take over the facilitation until that item is decided.
- Remember that any meeting will benefit from breaks in proceedings.

Remember, however, that often one needs to be flexible and invent creative ways to handle the unpredictable course of meetings.

It is not the facilitator's sole responsibility or burden to ensure meetings run smoothly. Facilitate the process, but invite others to help. Co-facilitators and neutral-party observers can help ensure fair meetings. (This is why many large groups have "parliamentarians.") It is the facilitator's responsibility to set the tone and to ensure that the whole group is included, not just specific and vocal individuals. Sometimes facilitating can be daunting, especially in environments with intense politics. Ideally, however, facilitation is easy if you try to inspire the group and remain committed to the principles of collaboration.

Inspiration is probably the most overlooked aspect of everyday meetings. All the attention to detail and process can push the opportunity for spontaneity and enthusiasm aside. Build in activities that engage participants, use strategies to generate discussion, or visual aids to grab attention. At the conclusion of meetings, inspire future work by recapping the reason for the gathering and create a bond by singing a song, taking a moment of silence, standing in a circle, or shaking hands.

Meeting should always be results-oriented, which means that every meeting should be directed toward one or more outcomes. Participants must feel that something has been accomplished, and they must see meetings as part of the bigger strategy to involve them in the future of the organization. Achievements at one meeting should be recapped in the next, and so on. Getting people to participate in meetings with enthusiasm can be difficult, but with some rhetorical effort—a positive and happy tone, projection of one's own enthusiasm, and explanation of important issues that the audience can identify with—will get others more involved. People also respect effective processes, so thinking about how to create the conditions for a more democratic forum can lead to much better results. Breaking meetings into segments and reducing face-to-face time by utilizing technology (e.g., brainstorming can happen within a virtual space rather than taking up 20 minutes of time at the physical meeting).

During a meeting, be an active listener and provide feedback. Active listening is hard work. When we practice active listening, we become part of the transaction and take responsibility for understanding others. We set up situations in which others have an opportunity to be heard, such as setting and enforcing time for discussion and trying different techniques to involve people (e.g., group breakout sessions). Active listeners try to reduce barriers to active listening. They show interest, remain respectful, do not ambush others, or pay attention only to facts, and they do not fake sincerity. Instead, active listeners prepare for the meeting, paraphrase the content of others, express understanding, and ask questions (Golen, 1990). Active listeners are much better facilitators and leaders because people who feel heard are much more inclined to share ideas, believe in the mission, and follow leaders' directives.

In addition to listening, effective meeting processes require feedback systems, a critical element of constitutive-oriented leaders. How are people supposed to understand how to interpret and change if never given feedback? Below are some guidelines that work toward effective feedback for both givers and receivers.

Be descriptive. For those who must give feedback, be descriptive rather than evaluative. Don't mention that a person's behavior is wrong. Focus more on describing the behavior and how it can be improved. Also, focus on process, the group's needs, and delivering comments at a time that is appropriate. Be as honest as possible, but mitigate when it will help soften the blow (e.g., provide a positive comment that buffers the bad news).

Listen. For those receiving feedback, be aware that being nervous is normal. Don't compensate nervousness by creating barriers to listening. Try to understand that observers are trying to help. Don't become defensive. Concentrate on how feedback can help improve behaviors. Notice if several independent observers make similar recommendations for improvement. Focus on these areas to improve. Consider everything observers say. Some of the comments may not be useful, but attempt to understand the point of view of the observer. If it doesn't apply, let it fly. Ask questions to clarify the feedback. The feedback is an opportunity for change.

Follow-up. After meetings, don't assume that ideas discussed during a meeting or feedback session will be put into action or even remembered. To ensure follow-through and accountability, a meeting should be followed up with minutes. Ensure that minutes are produced and promptly distributed to all attendees, including guests (if applicable). Meeting minutes don't need to include everything everyone said. However, nowadays podcasts can be distributed. If the meeting notes need to be transcribed, often software (e.g., Dragon Naturally Speaking) or a transcription kit (foot pedal and software) helps create full-detail written accounts in a timely manner. In most cases, however, the following data are sufficient: date, time, location, attendees present, key points raised, decisions made, motions and voting results (if votes were taken), parties responsible for follow-up action and details, and name of recorder. Minutes are also often distributed with notes, or as one document. In some cases, minutes are required by law (e.g., corporate board meetings). Minutes and notes can be distributed by email or interoffice mail and archived online or in office files.

Facilitators or leaders often need to provide a gentle nudge to remind people about completing action items. Leaders should check to ensure that action is taking place as agreed. Check-ins can be conducted by email, phone, or microblog. With important issues, a special follow-up meeting dedicated to progress reports can improve outcomes (this is part of the "check" phase in quality circles). Failure to check in or follow up after a meeting, a very common occurrence in many organizations, sends a message that not much action is really expected. Every goal and action item needs to be addressed. Often designating a "point person," who is responsible for specific action item, can ensure that progress is being made. The point person also reports on results, reducing information overload for a specific facilitator. What is more, having a variety of people checking on progress reduces the perception that a leader is micromanaging, and it helps give greater control over item implementation.

Conflict and Collaboration

Creating an environment that encourages participation will inevitably create conflict. Although people tend to view conflict negatively, communication scholars tend to see conflict as a natural part of human communication, and generally as a good thing. As with leadership, there are a variety of classes and books on the subject of conflict. This section will introduce concepts of collaboration and explain how to use metaphors to work through conflict.

In communication studies, conflict is defined "as an *expressed struggle* between at least two *interdependent parties* who *perceive* incompatible goals, scarce resources, and interference from others in achieving their goals" (Wilmot & Hocker, 2001, p. 41; emphasis added). The importance of this definition for communication is that conflict is expressed and involves perception (and by extension judgment). As an expressed struggle, conflict interactants use rhetoric to advocate for their positions. Thus, conflict is observable and open to systematic study by a rhetorical critic. As a perceptual activity, interactants in an expressed dispute must also interpret other parties' claims (along with other external stimuli) using cognitive schemata, "which function to shape and define what the interaction is about, the valence of the interaction, and attributions about others' motives and intentions" (Rogan, 2006, p. 158). Also important to this definition is interaction. If one party discontinues interaction (e.g., a coworker leaves the organization), then there is no conflict, although both parties may still have strong negative feelings about the other. Because conflict is expressed, it cannot be solely an intrapersonal struggle. In other words, if a person is upset but gives no verbal or nonverbal cues about being upset, then there is no conflict.

A common depiction of conflict styles is the Thomas-Kilmann Conflict Instrument, which is presented in Figure 7.3 (see also Wilmot & Hocker [2001, p. 131]). As this figure demonstrates, and research consistently shows, people often approach conflict with a variable degree of concern for self (assertiveness) and a variable degree of concern for other parties (cooperativeness). If, for example, someone has a high concern for his or her goals and a low concern for others' goals, then he or she is likely to use more aggressive tactics and offer few concessions (low cooperativeness). This type of style is competitive. Of course, people tend to use tactics variably depending on the situations, although they often demonstrate a stylistic preference.

Constitutive leaders work to create cultures in which people use collaborative approaches to conflict. A collaborative environment is characterized by a high concern for self and a higher concern for the other. What this often means is that people embrace conflict and use it as a means to creative unique outcomes. For example, if we use the sharing of a pie as an analogy, avoiders and accommodators would likely give up most of the pie, even if they are unsatisfied that they received a small piece. Competitors would try to get bigger pieces. Compromisers would make arguments in favor of splitting the pie equally. Collaborators, however, would find a way to make a bigger pie so that everyone got a bigger piece. Collaboration is not always ideal or possible, but constitutive leaders will work hard to create the environmental conditions where creative solutions are frequently sought. They would, in essence, embrace the metaphor of conflict as cultivating a garden.

One approach to understanding conflict and working through it is to try to use different metaphors to discuss conflict. Wilmot and Hocker (2001) suggest that "conflict brings up such strong feelings that metaphoric analysis, of both the process of conflict and specific conflicts, aids in analysis, intervention and lasting change" (p. 17). Metaphors can be divided into three categories, according to their impacts on conflict dynamic: 1) negative ones that undermine the capacity for conflict resolution, 2) neutral ones that do no harm or good, and 3) positive ones that expand the potential for strategic transformation.

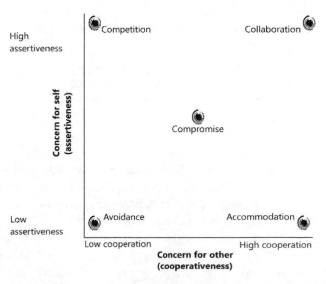

Figure 7.3. Conflict styles based on Thomas-Kilmann Conflict Instrument *(Adopted from Wilmot & Hocker [2001, p. 131].)*

Negative metaphors frame conflict as a battle, struggle, or animalistic behavior. Wilmot and Hocker (2001) observe that "war and violence is the central metaphor of conflict in the United States and Western Europe" (p. 17). People describe conflict with these metaphors: "she just blew up at me," "we hurled accusations back and forth," "your comments are right on target," "let's cross that bridge when we come to it," "my boss has a short fuse," and "we are in a battle to the death." Negative metaphors greatly restrict the emergence of original ideas for conflict resolution, since a perception of warring groups fighting against each other on a battlefield usually moves parties into antagonistic positions, each pushing hard for a , instead of a mutually acceptable resolution.

Neutral metaphors tend to describe conflict as a game, heroic adventure, or balancing act. Although the outcome is still win-lose, it is not a loss of significant proportion and the process of playing is considered more important than the outcome. Common metaphors involve the following types of sayings: "I guess the ball is in my court," "we are going back and forth," and "I struck out." By recognizing all parties as equal game players, neutral metaphors allude to a certain degree of mutual respect. Nevertheless, since this metaphor is based on the assumption of existing rules, its effectiveness is limited. Only when parties involved follow the same set of rules—that is, "play fair"—can desirable goals be achieved.

Positive metaphors, which often lead to more collaborative outcomes, position conflict as a bargaining table, as a tide, as a dance, or as a garden. Common positive metaphoric expressions include the following: "this presents us with a fun challenge," "you have a good point; what can we do together to resolve it?", "we're cultivating some real ideas here," "things ebb and flow," "we've got everything on the table," "looks like the tide is turning," and "that's a great seed of an idea." As Wilmot and Hocker (2001) note, "The whole idea of dancing with partners is to create something beautiful, graceful, and inspiring that depends on each person's skill, training, and individual expression" (p. 24) Such a collaborative image can help parties develop the proper rhetorical and interpretive frame for collaboration. Each party searches for a favorable outcome from which each party can benefit. For more discussion of metaphors, see also McCorkle & & Mills (1992).

As this process illustrates, simply adopting a new way of talking about conflict is likely going to affect how it is approached. If the general language of the culture is to think of conflict positively, and to believe language is constitutive of reality, then it is easy to see how saying "let's incubate that idea," rather than saying "if that's all we've got, we're on a road to destruction," will affect conflict outcomes. Since conflict is everywhere—even in deciding routine and mundane matters that don't look like conflict (because we are so used to thinking of conflict as negative)—choosing a collaborative frame and speaking with positive metaphors, will begin to facilitate a safer and more caring environment. A constitutive and transformational leader will not only believe in the principles of collaborative negotiation—a bigger pie is possible!—but will work to create an environment in which people seek collaboration too. Training activities, formal documents, Tweets with positive messages, and asking behavioral questions at the interview stage that solicit references to metaphors (and hiring candidates who use positive ones) is a proactive way to develop a collaborative workplace that draws on rhetorical approaches and artifacts discussed in this book. (For another way to think about negotiations, read the book *Getting to Yes*, which offers ideas for principled rather than positional bargaining.)

Conclusion

This chapter provided evidence to suggest that workplace violence and injuries are a serious concern for today's businesses and organizations. However, several mini case studies were provided to show that for-profit business can be caring. Setting aside the mantra of profit-maximization—a head-based logic—in favor of safety and care maximization—a heart-based logic—and by facilitating the enactment of a caring environment, managers and employees can create a fun and safe workplace. Safe and caring environments improve efficiency and effectiveness while reducing the threat of burnout.

Creating such an environment requires managers and consultants to create and maintain a positive rhetorical tone by adopting a positive and caring attitude and by seeking a collaborative approach to conflict. Sustaining this narrative is easy: Just apply communication principles and craft communications in the ways suggested in this book. If one must be motived by the logic of the dollar, research provided in the chapter shows that caring and safe environments, that is, those that consider the effects of the rhetorical and physical environment (open space increases communication), are more profitable.

Should you find yourself in a hostile work environment, the OSH Act protects you from retaliation. It is important as a manager, consultant, or employee to point out problems and use emotional intelligence to design and cultivate a beautiful workplace.

Continuing Education:
Recommended Texts and Resources

Unlike other chapters, the following list of books do not include a description of the applicability of each book's content to improved business and professional communications. Instead, they have been categorized under general themes: addressing workplace bullies, building collaborative workspaces, and designing safe office environments. Each book is consistent in theme with the others in its list yet offers a unique perspective as well.

The following books provide strategies for creating safe workplaces and addressing workplace bullies:

- *The no asshole rule: Building a civilized workplace and surviving one that isn't* by Robert I. Sutton. ISBN: 978-0446526562.
- *The bully at work: What you can do to stop the hurt and reclaim your dignity on the job* by Gary Namie and Ruth Namie. ISBN: 978-1402224263.

The following books provide strategies for facilitating meetings, building collaborative workplaces, and resolving conflict in the workplace:

- *Successful meetings: How to plan, prepare, and execute top-notch business meetings* by Shri Henkel. ISBN: 978-0910627917.
- *Second edition of the Deming route to quality and productivity* by William Scherkenbach and W. Edwards Deming. ASIN: B005E8F5R6 [Kindle]
- *Resolving conflicts at work: eight strategies for everyone on the job* by Ken Cloke and Joan Goldsmith. ISBN: 978-0787980245.

- *Working through conflict: Strategies for relationships, groups, and organizations* by Joseph P. Folger, Marshall Scott Poole, and Randall K. Stutman. ISBN: 978-0205569892.
- *Getting to yes: Negotiating agreement without giving in by* and . ISBN: 978-0143118757.
- *Lessons in loyalty: How Southwest Airlines does it—An insider's view* by Lorraine Grubbs-West. ISBN: 978-0976252856.
- *Leadership: Theory and practice* by Peter G. Norhouse. ISBN: 978-1412974887.
- *The Southwest Airlines way: Using the power of relationships to achieve high perform-ance* by . ISBN: *978-0071396837*
- *The leadership challenge (4th ed.)* by James M. Kouzes. ISBN: 978-0787984922.

The following books provide strategies for designing office environments that increase collaboration and reduce musculoskeletal disorders and repetitive strain:

- *Workplace by design: Mapping the high-performance workscape* by Franklin Becker and Fritz Steele. ISBN: 978-0787900472.
- *'Extra-ordinary' ergonomics: How to accommodate small and big persons, the disabled and elderly, expectant mothers, and children* by Karl H.E. Kroemer. 978-0849336683.
- *Workplace safety: A guide for small and midsized companies* by Dan Hopwood and Steve Thompson. ISBN: 978-0782136044.

References

Aguayo, R. (1990). *Dr. Deming: The American who taught the Japanese about quality.* New York: Fireside.

Anfuso, D. (1994). Deflecting workplace violence. *Personnel Journal, 73*(10), 66–77.

Arnsdorf, I., Korn, H., Miller, Z., & Needham, P. (2009). *Yale Daily News.* Retrieved from www.inc.com/magazine/20110501/social-entrepreneurs-the-case-for-more-not-less-regulation.html

Blake, R., & Mouton, J. (1964). *The managerial grid: The key to leadership excellence.* Houston: Gulf Publishing Co.

Bluestein, A. (2011, May). The case for more (not less) regulation. Retrieved from www.inc.com/magazine/20090501/the-zappos-way-of-managing.html (1978). *Leadership.* New York: Harper and Row Publishers.

Burns, J. M. (1978). *Leadership.* New York: Harper and Row Publishers.

Chafkin, M. (2009). The Zappos way of managing. *Inc. Magazine.* Retrieved from

Cheney, G., Christensen, L. T., Zorn, T. E., & Ganesh, S. (2011). *Organizational communica-tion in an age of globalization* (2nd ed.). Long Grove, IL: Waveland Press.

Cox, T., Kuk, G., & Leiter, M. P. (1993). Burnout, health, work stress, and organizational healthiness. Professional burnout: Recent developments in theory and research. In W. B. Schaufeli, C. Maslach, & T. Marek (Eds.), *Professional burnout: Recent developments in theory and research* (pp. 177–193). Philadelphia: Taylor & Francis.

Definition of Ergonomics. (n.d.). Retrieved from www.iea.cc/01_what/What%20is%20Ergonomics.html

Dohrenwend, B. S., & Dohrenwend, B. P. (1978). Some issues in research on stressful life events. *Journal of Nervous and Mental Disease, 166,* 7–15.

Donald, I., & Young, S. (1996). Managing safety: An attitudinal-based approach to improving safety in organizations. *Leadership & Organization Development Journal, 17,* 13–20.

Ferran, L. (2009, September 17). Raymond Clark sent to max security prison for Annie Le murder. *ABCNews.* Retrieved from http://abcnews.go.com/US/annie-le-case-police-arrest-ray-clark-murder/story?id=8598755#.TsgpRGOzFEp

Freiberg, K., & Frieberg, J. (1998). *Nuts! Southwest Airlines' crazy recipe for business and personal success.* New York: Broadway Books

Gittell, J. H. (2005). *The Southwest Airlines way.* New York: McGraw-Hill.

Golen, S. (1990). A factor analysis of barriers to effective listening. *Journal of Business Communication, 27,* 25–36

Grubbs-West, L. (2005). *Lessons in loyalty: How Southwest does it—an insider's view.* Dallas: Cornerstone Leadership Center.

Grint, K. (Ed.). (1997). *Leadership: Classical, contemporary, and critical approaches.* Oxford,UK: Oxford University Press.

Grint, K. (2000). *The art of leadership.* Oxford, UK: Oxford University Press.

Keashly, L. (2010). Some things you need to know but may have been afraid to ask: A researcher speaks to ombudsmen about workplace bullying. *Journal of the International Ombudsman Association, 3*(2), 10–23.

Kivimaki, M., Virtanen., M, Vartia, M., Elovainio, M., Vahtera, J., & Keltikangas-Jarvinen, L. (2003). Workplace bullying and the risk of cardiovascular disease and depression. *Occupational and Environmental Medicine, 60,* 779–783.

Kruml, S. M., & Geddes, D. (2000). Exploring the dimensions of emotional labor: The heart of Hochschild's work. *Management Communication Quarterly, 14,* 8–49.

Lewin, K., Lippitt, R., & White, R. (1939). Patterns of aggressive behavior in experimentally created social climates. *Journal of Social Psychology,* 271–301.

Lutgen-Sandvik, P. (2003). The cycle of employee emotional abuse: Generation and regeneration of workplace mistreatment. *Management Communication Quarterly, 16,* 471–501.

Lutgen-Sandvik, P., Tracy, S. J., & Alberts, J. K. (2007). Burned by bullying in the American workplace: Prevalence, perception, degree and impact. *Journal of Management Studies, 44,* 737–862.

McCorkle, S., & Mills, J. L. (1992). Rowboat in a hurricane: Metaphors of interpersonal conflict management. *Communication Reports, 5*(2), 57–66

Meyerson, D. E. (1998). Feeling stressed and burned out: A feminist reading and re-visioning of stress-based emotions within medicine and organizational science. *Organizational Science, 8,* 103–118.

Miller, K., & Koesten, J. (2008). Financial feeling: An investigation of emotion and communication in the workplace. *Journal of Applied Communication Research, 36,* 8–32.

Miller, K., Stiff, J. B., & Ellis, B. H. (1988). Communication and empathy as precursors to burnout among human service workers. *Communication Monographs, 55,* 250–265.

Miller, L. H., & Smith, A. D. (2007). Anxiety at work—The road to burnout. *HealthyPlace.* Retrieved from www.healthyplace.com/anxiety-panic/main/anxiety-at-work-the-road-to-burnout/menu-id-69

Montgomery, A. J., Panagopolou, E., de Wildt, M., & Meenks, E. (1986). Work-family interference, emotional labor and burnout. *Journal of Managerial Psychology, 22,* 36–51.

Occupational health [definition]. (n.d.) World Health Organization. Retrieved from www .who.int/occupational_health/en

Occupational safety and health definitions. (n.d.) *Bureau of Labor Statistics.* Retrieved from www.bls.gov/iif/oshdef.htm

Reeves, M., & Roupenian, E. (2011). Raymond Clark pleads guilty to murder of Yale grad student Annie Le. *ABCNews.* Retrieved from http://abcnews.go.com/US/raymond-clark-pleads-guilty-murder-yale-grad-student/story?id=13158057#.Tsgja2OzFEo

Rogan, R. G. (2006). Conflict framing categories revisited. *Communication Quarterly*, 54, 157–173.

Rossi, A. M., Perrewe, P. L., & Sauter, S. L. (2006). *Stress and quality of working life: Current perspectives in occupational health.* Charlotte, NC: IAP Information Age Publishing.

Salin, D. (2003). Ways of explaining workplace bullying: A review of enabling, motivating and participating structures and processes in the work environment. Human Relations, *56,* 1213–1232.

Sandelands, L. E., & Boudens, C. J. (2000). Feeling at work. In S. Fineman (Ed.), *Emotion in organizations* (2nd ed., pp. 46-63). London: Sage.

Scherkenback, W. W. (1986). *The Deming route to quality and productivity: Road maps and roadblocks.* Washington, D.C.: George Washington University Continuing Engineering Education Press

Sinclair, U. (1906/2010). *The jungle.* New York: Oxford University Press USA.

Star-Ledger Staff. (2011, November 11). Details emerge about gunman and day of slaying in Mountain Lakes. *Star-Ledger* (NJ.com). Retrieved from www.nj.com/news/index.ssf/2011/11/co-worker_mountain_lakes_shoot.html

Sutton, R. (2007). *The no asshole rule: Building a civilized workplace.* New York: Warner Business Books.

Thompson, M. (2004). *Flying for peanuts: The ABCs of flying Southwest Airlines.* Chandler, AZ: Five Star Publications.

Tims, D. (2010, February 16). Founder of Bob's Red Mill Natural Foods transfers business to employees. *The Oregonian.* Retrieved from www.oregonlive.com/clackamascounty/index.ssf/2010/02/bobs_red_mill_natural_foods_ro.html

Tracy, S. J. (2000). Becoming a character for commerce: Emotion labor, self-subordination, and discursive construction of identity in a total institution. *Management Communication Quarterly, 14,* 90–128

Turner, G., & Myerson, J. (1998). *New workspace, new culture: Office design as a catalyst for change.* London: Gower.

Wilmot, W. W., & Hocker, J. L. (2001). *Interpersonal conflict.* New York: McGraw-Hill.

Workplace violence. (n.d.). Occupational Safety & Health Administration, United States Department of Labor. Retrieved from

Wright, R. R. (1999). Effect of micro management on job satisfaction & productivity: A case study. *Vision: The Journal of Business Perspective, 3,* 51–61.

Image © nasirkhan, 2012. Used under license from Shutterstock, Inc.

Chapter 8

Gathering, Sharing, and Protecting Internal/External Communications

Starting Point

In 1996, a Pennsylvania district court ruled that an at-will employee of the Pillsbury Company, Michael A. Smyth, had no reasonable expectation of privacy when sending emails. This was true even though the company promised, as noted in the complaint, that "it would neither read employee e-mail, nor terminate or reprimand an employee based on the content of such e-mail" (*Michael Smyth v. The Pillsbury Company,* 1996). Smyth was discharged after Pillsbury management intercepted his emails with content that they felt was inappropriate and unprofessional. Smyth sent an email that negatively referred to the firm's sales management team and noted that he was going to "kill the backstabbing bastards." He also referred to a company's social event as "the Jim Jones Kool-Aid social affair." As the court concluded: "[W]e do not find a reasonable expectation of privacy in e-mail communications voluntarily made by an employee to his supervisor over the company e-mail system notwithstanding any assurances that such communications would not be intercepted by management" (*Michael Smyth . . .* , 1996).

In tort and common law, employers are held responsible for employee conduct under the doctrine of *respondeat superior*—a common-law doctrine that makes an employer liable for the actions of an employee when the actions take place within the scope of employment. As Smith and Tabak (2009) note, "Someone who has sustained damage through the misconduct of an employee may hold the employer accountable if the employer knew about the misconduct but failed to prevent it, or even if the employer was unaware of the misconduct but should have known. . . . Sexual harassment provides a good example of this doctrine" (p. 34; see also Areneo, 1996; Fazekas, 2004).

It is not surprising that organizations take measures to mitigate potential problems, especially regarding electronic communications. Here are some interesting statistics regarding this point, as reported by The American Management Association's (2007) review of workplace monitoring and surveillance (see also Smith & Tabak [2009]:

- 84% of employers have email-use policies in place.
- 43% engage in some active form of email monitoring.
- 28% have terminated employees for inappropriate email use.
- 24% of organizations had email records subpoenaed in the year prior of the report.
- 43% have policies aimed at IM use.
- 12% address employees' work-related blogs.
- The growth of email monitoring software is growing at approximately 30% per year.

The U.S. legal system does not currently address rights and responsibilities associated with email in the workplace, and the U.S. Constitution is largely unhelpful in application to non-public workplaces. The most important piece of legislation in the United States that defines the extent to which an employer can monitor email and other electronic communication is the Electronic Communications Privacy Act (ECPA) of 1986. Given that it is somewhat dated and allows for a variety of workplace exemptions, the law is decidedly pro-employer in the age of GPS, social networking, and mobile smart phones (Hornung, 2005). When courts interpret the laws that exist, a difficult task given that legislation lags far behind advances in technology, they too tend rule in favor of the employer. As Smith and Tabak (2009) note: "In spite of this legal vacuum, courts have consistently supported the rights of employers to monitor employee e-mails" (p. 34; see also Muhl, 2003). Given the dearth of specific laws, it is not surprising that most issues are resolved through case law. Consistent with tort law, however, the basis of culpability of a claim based on intrusion of privacy is whether a claimant (e.g., employee) had a reasonable expectation of privacy and whether a "reasonable person" would find the actions of an employer egregious. When students are polled in various classes, they tend to side with the employer or are rather indifferent toward privacy, a suggestion that the reasonable person standard is also pro-employer (personal non-scientific experiment). The courts have largely interpreted the law that the reasonable person has little expectation of privacy in the workplace and an employer (and organization) can monitor any message that is passed through its network. People generally have little expectation of privacy. (It has not yet been challenged, but messages sent via a university's or coffee shop's wifi may be legally intercepted by the organization. Does a reasonable person have an expectation of privacy when communicating on a borrowed wifi connection?)

Business and professional communication is now a global affair. Email and other types of electronic communication link people together. However, email content and the right to monitor such content shifts as it traverses geographical boundaries. Thus, organizations face different legal and cultural conditions with respect to monitoring, particularly in the European Union. According to Smith and Tabak (2009):

> Privacy in the United States is operationalized in a different manner than in countries such as Canada or members of the European Union. In the United States, privacy can be viewed as a commodity, meaning that it can be bartered away when individuals feel it is in their interests to do so. In Europe, however, privacy is viewed as more fundamental, something that persons cannot be induced to forfeit. (p. 41).

Compare, for example two similar cases *Onof v. Nikon* (France) and *McLaren v. Microsoft* (United States). Both deal with the retrieval of an employee's communications in a folder marked "personal," although stored on a company computer. Both employees were dismissed for violating company policies. France's Supreme Court ruled in favor of Onof, claiming that the employer is not permitted to read employee email and that doing so is a "violation of the fundamental right of secrecy in one's private correspondence even if that correspondence is conducted on the employer's e-mail system and in violation of company policy" (Lasprogata, King, & Pillay, 2004, p. 54). A Texas court of appeals ruled in favor of Microsoft, claiming that "interest in preventing inappropriate and unprofessional comments, or even illegal activity, over its e-mail system would outweigh McLaren's claimed privacy interest in those communications" (Case No. 05-97-00824, 1999 Tex. App. Lexis 4103). The interpretation of the Microsoft case, as it applies to all business communication and work, is that the ownership of the computers and the network and the transmission of email message to others on a network preempt any reasonable expectation of privacy (Rustad & Paulsson, 2005).

Although this chapter deals with the collection, distribution, and protection of internal and external communications more broadly, this introduction suggests that in each of these three parts of the process, one must consider ethical obligations and legal ramifications of decisions. Although the focus and interest is primarily on electronic communications, it is also important to consider the treatment of print artifacts. In this chapter, we will consider the implications of choosing to use overt and covert methods and the type of tone this sets in the workplace. These are key concerns that are important to address, especially if the goal is to create and facilitate a safe and collaborative work environment, as discussed in Chapter 7. Following the brief section on setting the right rhetorical tone, concepts and practices related to gathering, sharing, and protecting data are discussed. Finally, the chapter, as with others, concludes with recommendations for texts for continued education.

Setting the Right Rhetorical Tone

Within the United States, the legal precedence for conducting surveillance on employees is on the side of employers. Technology has especially made it easy to keep tabs on employees. For example, GPS tracking devices can be installed on company vehicles, telephone conversations can be recorded, Facebook accounts can be monitored and their contents used against coworkers, and text messages sent to and from company phones, even if private, can be logged. With the breakdown of work-life boundaries, there can be some confusion regarding which communication and practices are within the scope of employment and which are private. For example, if you have been given a company phone and encouraged by your employer to use it for personal and private communications, and you send a text message from home to a colleague about non-business issues, do you have a reasonable expectation of privacy? How about if the message is sent to a relative who is not employed by the company? Addressed below, these issues also pertain to corporate and organizational espionage, which involves the collection of information and data (or "intelligence") on another organization for purposes of strategic decision-making (sometimes intercepting their communications in nefarious, although legal, ways). These issues are also not mutually exclusive. Given the risk of corporate espionage and the potential that employers are liable for workplace hazards created by employees own maleficence, there are many legitimate reasons that employers and managers may want to monitor their workplaces covertly. Nevertheless, this can lead to a feeling of resentment among employees. Thus, using overt methods, when possible, is more likely to set a positive rhetorical tone over covert methods, but monitoring of any kind may make employees feel that they are not trusted by their employers.

Issues related to workplace safety and organizational decision-making can be addressed through rhetorical processes. For example, employees can be invited to participate in dialogue with management regarding the need to establish a safe and productive workplace. Explanations that are reasonable and sound can be offered to employees as the rationale for monitoring. Although employees may not ultimately like the idea of being watched, employees will better understand the need to do so if management involves them in the decision-making process. Employees should be encouraged to provide comments and feedback regarding alternatives to the more oppressive approaches to surveillance and monitoring. Inducing favorable behavior vis-à-vis rewards may be better than threats of punishments.

Gathering Information and Communication

Gathering information and communications (hereafter data) is important to the rhetorical process. Data help rhetors understand audiences and plan effective persuasive strategies. Gathering data is also important if stakeholders want to justify decisions, and in most cases this means that the decisions appear rational. Thus, the primary reason for data gathering within organization is planning—businesses and organizations do not operate in a vacuum and must understand what is going on in the external environment and respond to changes. In other words, organizations are open systems—that is, they take in resources from the external environment (e.g., labor and raw materials) and transform them into outputs (e.g., services and products). Understanding the external environment and adapting to it requires effective feedback systems and processes for dealing with minor and major issues. Figure 8.1 shows a basic open-systems model.

James D. Thompson (2003), an organization and management theorist, suggested that the primary goal of organizing processes is to protect the technology of the organization, which he defines as all the people, equipment, and processes that make the production of goods and services possible. According to Thompson, there are three primary types of technology: long-linked, mediating, and intensive.

Long-linked technology involves a series of sequential steps in the transformation process, such as those found in a factory (A must occur before B and B before C, and so on). Long-linked technology is characterized by a medium level of communication for decision-making across units. In place of extensive communication, organizations coordinate action through the use of plans, schedules, and feedback processes. For example, a car manufacturer will have a purchasing department and supply warehouses that will ensure that workers and equipment on the factory floor (the technology) keep operating. The purchasing department is, therefore, classified as a boundary-spanning unit (BSU) because it protects the technical core by buffering it from the external environment. Workers in the purchasing department head out into the external environment to communicate with suppliers, and the warehouse stockpiles raw materials to ensure that they are ready at hand. Although the location of the warehouse is likely to be close to the factory, the purchasing department can essentially be located anywhere, most likely where there is a concentration of suppliers.

Mediating technology is defined as the organizational process of mediating a relationship between suppliers and customers. For example, a clothing store mediates the relationship between clothes manufacturers and customers who want to buy clothes, and banks link depositors with borrowers. Independent outlets (stores) and bank branches will not have to communicate much in order for decisions to be made. Data and resources, as well as communication, are pooled together via a headquarters. Coordination of activities is accomplished by

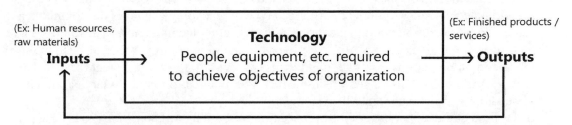

Figure 8.1. A basic open-systems model.

standardization, rules, and procedures. As with bank branches and stores, BSUs, headquarters, and other branches are not likely to be located close together.

Intensive technologies are characterized by a high level of communication, tightly coupled units, that is, located close together, and a variety of ad hoc meetings. Coordination is achieved through the mutual adjusting of behaviors. Although there are some standard operating procedures, these are likely only guidelines. The expectation is that interactants will adopt protocols and procedures to the contingencies of a situation. Hospitals, especially surgical teams and emergency rooms, are examples of organizations that use intensive technology. Counseling centers, in which an individual counselor is paired with a specific client, is another example. Counselor and patient adapt to each other over time and the therapist makes different recommendations based on individual information provided by patients. University settings, especially labs in research universities, are another good example of the use of an intensive technology within an organization. Ideally, advisors, mentors, researchers, and teachers adapt to the knowledge of each student and the demands of specific research projects.

Given that many organizations have become conglomerates, it is often likely that they will have several different businesses using a variety of technologies. For example, a clothing store may manufacture its own clothing. This form of vertical integration gives some control over the quality of the inputs (i.e., clothing), although it also increases the managerial demands of the organization and environment uncertainties (there is more to be concerned about). For example, the organization becomes responsible for maintaining relationships with suppliers of raw materials rather than just one partnership with an outlet. Thus, the organization becomes more susceptible to the increases in the prices of raw materials.

Many organizations try to move away from intensive technologies because of the expense of maintaining individual relationships with each client. Mediating technology and long-linked technology are more predictable and less expensive. For example, catering to the individual needs of students in a university can become difficult. While ideally each student would have a tailored experience based on his or her career goals and previous experience, today's universities have become somewhat long-linked in fashion. Students are "tracked" into specific programs and given a standardized set of classes to take, and in a specific order. Doctor-patient relationships should also be intensive; however, nowadays doctors try to diagnose a problem and get patients onto a regimented prescription drug plan. In a way, doctors are outsourcing care to pharmaceutical companies, reducing the uncertainties that come from intensive relationships with patients (thus decreasing risks of malpractice).

Figure 8.2 summarizes the three types of technology and the types of interdependence and coordination mechanisms required of each. Each type of technology changes the communication demands. For example, in organizations with mediating technologies, one would find a stronger need to create extensive artifacts, such as standard operating procedures and manuals. Since communication is low, one might expect a newsletter to be sufficient for distributing updates. In more intensive setups, immediate communication is necessary, so updates would need to be immediate rather than sporadic.

BSUs protect the technology of the organization. According to Thompson (2003), the primary functions of BSUs are *buffering* and *smoothing*. Buffering involves protecting the input

Type of technology	Form of interdependence	Degree of communication	Priority for locating units close together	Type of coordination
Long-linked Ex: Factories	**Sequential** Inputs ↓ → A → B → C ↓ Client	Medium	Medium	Plans, schedules, feedback, meetings
Mediating Ex: Banks, schools	**Pooled** Inputs ↓ ↓ ↓ Client Client Client A B C	Low	Low	Standardization, rules, procedures
Intensive Ex: Research labs	**Reciprocal** Inputs ↓ ↓ A ←┬→ B ↓ Client	High	High	Mutual adjustment, frequent meetings, ad-hoc decisions

Figure 8.2.   Summary of Thompson's Classification of Technology (Thompson, 2003).

side of the organization. For example, when a company stockpiles equipment, it ensures that materials will still be available if a supply shortage occurs. Smoothing occurs on the output side and can include running promotions and discounts to get rid of excess inventory. When there are not enough inputs or too many outputs, this is not an ideal state for an organization.

When either buffering or smoothing fail to protect the operations of the company, an organization resorts to *rationing*. In normal circumstances, for example, a hospital will have enough supplies and doctors to ensure that all patients are attended to in a timely manner. In other words, the ideal organizational state of a hospital is no prioritization of care at any time. However, shortages occur during times of crisis, and there are times when patients must wait hours for emergency room care (unanticipated need). In these situations, hospitals must prioritize care at the technical core. As Thompson notes, it is a failure of the BSUs. Scheduling departments, warehouses, educational campaigns, and so on, should decrease shortages or a large number of patients suddenly arriving at the emergency room. Thus, a brochure that explains what people can do at home during a time of crisis will help keep some people away.

Nevertheless, budgets have limits and in some extreme circumstances (e.g., war, contagious disease, or natural disasters), it is impossible to have stockpiled enough supplies.

As another example of the importance of BSUs, consider the university. Within a university, faculty members do not need to worry about recruiting students or ensure that they have paid tuition or obtained the necessary financial aid. These roles fall to the BSUs recruiting, billing, and financial aid. This ensures that when engaged in technical core function (i.e., learning), teachers and students do not need to be concerned about the external environment. Generally speaking, faculty members do not worry where the next group of students will come from or whether graduates find jobs. These are functions performed by the registrar's office and career services. By protecting the processes of learning, BSUs serve a vital function. They shield students and teachers from changes in the external environment. Of course, when these BSUs fail to protect the technical core, often due to serious financial exigencies, universities resort to rationing. Permanent faculty members are replaced by adjuncts, programs are eliminated, classes are cut, class sizes swell, and so on. The activities of protecting an organizational technical core require communication among units and with external stakeholders. Thus, all of the communication artifacts are deployed for very specific reasons—to protect the organization from external environment changes. Of course, effective communication should have the desired effect. Advertising will recruit more customers. Executives will receive reports with analytical information for proper decision-making. Marketing departments will collect data with surveys and report these to other branches. Budgets will be emailed. Memos will explain protocols. The list, of course, could go on. However, the point should be clear: Rhetorical artifacts sent and received in an organization serve an important coordinating function, and part of the failure of businesses could be the failure to utilize rhetorical artifacts effectively. (Figure 8.3, for example, shows a person using a checklist, a mundane form of significant importance.)

Because of the important role that BSUs play in protecting the organization and coordinating activities, they often have a significant amount of power. In many cases, they may even have more power than those working at the technical core. For example, marketing and advertising departments may be the last to be cut during times of financial uncertainty. This fact explains why, in many cases, the people working at the technical core (e.g., faculty or factory workers) are often paid less than many of the people working in BSUs. Faculty salaries may be frozen before funding for "institutional development" is cut (the goal of these folks is to increase third-party revenue). When looking for a job, determine the importance and relevance of the unit that you will work in. Is it an important BSU to technical core activities? If so, it may be an excellent place to work. Also, consider developing skills that will make you more effective in handling BSU functions (e.g., statistics, marketing, sales, advertising, and logic).

Given that sole proprietors and small businesses do not have BSUs, ample consulting opportunities exist for professionals with strong written and verbal communication skills, research skills, and sales skills. Public relations specialists, technical writers, and social media and search engine optimization consultants often are hired on a temporary basis to fulfill the important boundary-spanning unit functions, such as marketing, promotions, technical document production, fundraising, procurement, and so on.

Figure 8.3. Warehouses serve in important organizational function. Consider using your communication and analytics skills as a procurement specialist, wholesale buyer, or logistics specialist. *(Image © Marcin Balcerzak, 2012. Used under license from Shutterstock, Inc.)*

Effective Information Gathering

Effective information gathering requires an understanding of data needs. What issues need to be identified or resolved? How will they be identified (i.e., what method is best for the data needed)? How will data be analyzed and managed (i.e., what software and filing systems will be used)? How will information overload be avoided? In order to identify organizational needs, rhetors must spend some time deliberating about what data are relevant and useful. Answering these questions is part of the invention phase of rhetoric and requires concerted rhetorical effort (deliberation) on the part of stakeholders, such as customers, employees, managers, and consultants. What good is any data collection effort if the data collected are not useful?

Finding the appropriate measurement is often difficult. Proxy measures, therefore, are frequently used. One of the default proxy measures for many organizations is increases in users or profits. For example, universities have become fixated on increasing enrollment numbers, and organizations, even non-for-profit organizations, have become fixated on cash measurements (profits, donation values, and so on). While financial information can provide important information on the year-to-year health of an organization, it often cannot tell the whole story. While profits may be soaring, it may be at the expense of necessary maintenance.

Thus, year-to-year profits should only be one measurement—hence the use of the executive "dashboard" as described in Chapter 5. Other measurements may be new employee hires, new customer accounts, and improvement in supplier relations. These may lower profitability in the short term, but establish the conditions necessary for higher profitability in the long run.

Consider, however, the desire to measure "improved relations with suppliers." While more suppliers could be healthy, measuring improved relations can be difficult. Likely this would require some form of qualitative feedback, which is difficult to quantify (like profitability). Here is a more familiar example: A university is in the business of "knowledge transfer" and "skill development." However, how can one effectively measure these items? Of course, pre-tests, mid-tests, and post-tests could be administered, but this is costly and also can have adverse effects (increased cheating, especially if merit pay is linked to students' exam scores). Thus, universities often measure success by post-graduation job placement. This is hardly an effective measure for measuring "knowledge transfer," but one that is used nevertheless. Some universities also measure the quality of faculty members by their publication record in top-tier journals, which now have "impact factor" ratings (a complex algorithm that scores a journal based on citations, supposed readership, and so on—one can download an article and cite it without reading it). As these examples illustrate, it is often hard to account for what really counts.

A second issue related to the collection of data is information overload. The best way to thwart information overload is to have a plan of action before engaging in the research process. This increases the chance that only relevant data will be collected—hence the need to think through the process and identify what data are really needed. Malcolm Gladwell has an excellent article in *The New Yorker* that describes the challenges of information overload experienced by intelligence agencies (e.g., CIA). As he notes, "the central challenge of intelligence gathering has always been the problem of 'noise': the fact that useless information is vastly more plentiful than useful information" (Gladwell, 2003). Deciding what data should be obtained and explored will certainly reduce information overload. This also means that some data will be missed because you are not looking for it.

When making decisions, a rational approach to decision-making is often preferred (see Figure 8.4). Often,

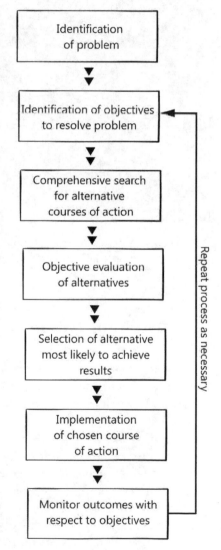

Figure 8.4. Rational decision-making model.

because of time constraints and other factors (e.g., capacity or cost), it is not possible for people to be absolutely rational. Exploring a comprehensive list of possible alternatives is not possible or always desirable. Thus, organizational decision-makers often engage in what Herbert Simon calls "satisficing" (a combination of the words satisfy and suffice), a type of decision-making strategy that attempts to meet criteria for adequacy rather than optimality. Decision-makers maximize their decision process by choosing the most satisfactory solution with the information they have available. When hunting for an apartment, for example, renters often base their impressions on a loose set of criteria and their impressions of previously viewed apartments. This is the essence of satisficing, and it represents a more realistic picture of actual decision-making practices. Ideally, one would want to make the best decision based upon all information available. However, we are bound by limits of time, information, and foresight, so we must make a reasonably good decision and rationalize it *ex post facto*.

Some methods that are commonly used in businesses and organizations, and worth learning more about, are the Performance Evaluation and Review Technique (PERT), Nominal Group Technic, and the Delphi method. In addition, the use of brainstorming, buzz sessions, idea writing, and focus groups, as well as decision-making aids, such as fishbone diagrams and flowcharts, can help improve decision making (see Chapter 2). The use of these processes and tools can improve overall decision-making, but they are only effective if people are committed to the process and their use. Due to the cost of implementation and the time required to implement these devices, many businesses, organizations, groups, and teams fail to use them. To learn more about creative decision-making techniques and enhance your skills, review the book *Creative Problem Solving for Managers* by Tony Proctor. This book provides an accessible and imaginative approach to problem solving skills; for example, how to improve computer-assisted problem solving.

Using Common Communication Research Methods

A variety of communication research methods are used to collect data. In the continuing education section, there is a list of books that are excellent introductions to communication research. Regardless of whether your specific program of study requires the courses, take courses in qualitative and quantitative research methods, as well as statistics. These courses, at some time in your career, will be very useful. To be a consultant, graduate-level research courses will be very useful. For example, marketing communication specialists need to understand how to design and analyze research. The purpose of this section is to introduce a variety of methods.

Rhetorical criticism (rhetorical analysis).   Rhetorical criticism, or the examination of how symbols act on people, is probably one of the most useful research methods for entrepreneurs, professionals, and consultants interested in the rhetorical approach to communication. Rhetorical critics analyze how symbolic artifacts (words, phrases, images, gestures, performances, texts, films, and discourse in general) construct rhetorical situations or influence people within rhetorical situations. Rhetorical analysis is important because, as Lloyd Bitzer (1968), the first to define the rhetorical situation in contemporary terms, notes:

> . . . a work of rhetoric is pragmatic; it comes into existence for the sake of something
> beyond itself; it functions ultimately to produce action or change in the world; it per-
> forms some task. In short, rhetoric is a mode of altering reality, not by the direct
> application of energy to objects, but by the creation of discourse which changes real-
> ity through the mediation of thought and action. The rhetor alters reality by bringing
> into existence a discourse of such a character that the audience, in thought and action,
> is so engaged that it becomes mediator of change. (p. 68)

The goal of the rhetorical critic, whether he or she is an academic or a professional seeking to understand a company's interviewing process (for example), is to discover how rhetoric will best instruct, inform, entertain, move, arouse, perform, convince, or persuade the target
audience, including whether and how the company might improve its audience.

The process of rhetorical criticism, outlined in Chapter 2, involves a process of selecting
an artifact, analyzing an artifact, formulating a question, and expressing findings. On the sur-
face, this process seems simple. However, selecting the proper artifacts can be difficult. For
example, learning about the internal workings of a company may not be possible through
analysis of publicly available materials. Access to the most useful artifacts, in other words,
may be limited. When analyzing artifacts, there is no guarantee that the findings will be of
explicit utility. As an interpretive method, there are often many plausible ways to understand
an artifact. As Kuypers (2009) notes, "criticism is an art, not a science. It is not a scientific
method; it uses subjective methods of argument . . . " (p. 14).

Critics analyze an artifact that reflects a target audience's attitudes. Interpretations, although
subjective, are based on the historical and situational context of the rhetorical artifact. Many people think research should be objective. In most personal and professional situations, however,
often rhetorical criticism is the only methodical approach that is useful, and it is better to be systematic in analysis even if, methodological gods forbid, it is subjectivist. By analyzing position
announcements to craft a résumé, as suggested in Chapter 4, you will be able to address the needs
of the target audience and generate a list of more thorough and thoughtful questions during the
interview phase. Too often, however, people see the title of a position announcement and send a
template résumé. Conducting a thorough analysis of the position announcement, although subjective, ensures that candidates address audience-specific concerns (i.e., employer interests).

There are a variety of rhetorical criticism methods, such as metaphor analysis, narrative
analysis, ideological analysis, and feminist analysis. While most of these methods are aimed
at social critique, that is, they are more useful for academics, they can be applied in practical
terms within the workplace. A feminist analysis of promotional materials, internal corporate
communications, office design, and so on, may uncover symbolic representations that create
a hostile or less caring business environment. Individuals trained in rhetorical criticism and other
communication research methods are now providing important services to the U.S. Department
of Defense (see **http://comops.org**), showing the growing utility of interpretive approaches to
strategic communication in understanding organizations.

Survey-based research.   Surveys are one of the most frequently used research tools,
so the public is generally used to them. However, this also means that getting the public to

complete a survey can be an arduous task. Often, therefore, companies and researchers must provide incentives. For example, it is common to offer a random drawing for a significant amount of money. This raises some issues regarding whether the data obtained are useful. People may choose to complete the survey solely for the prize. People who are not motivated by the incentive—who likely have different opinions—will not complete the survey. Also, people may complete the survey quickly just to register for the drawing. (Many surveys, therefore, often have quality control questions.)

Technically, the survey can be divided into two categories: the questionnaire and the interview. Most people think of the questionnaire when they think of surveys. Interviews are addressed separately in the next sub-section. Questionnaires are usually paper-and-pencil or online instruments that the respondent completes. Interviews are completed by an interviewer who writes down interviewee responses. If the survey is semi-structured, the interviewer will ask follow-up questions based on respondent's answers (it is necessary to train interviewees to ensure reliability). Often it's hard to tell the difference between a questionnaire and an interview. For instance, some people think that questionnaires always ask short, closed-ended questions while interviews always ask broad open-ended ones. Questionnaires can be designed with open-ended questions (although they do tend to be shorter than interview questions), and there will often be a series of closed-ended questions asked in an interview. The choice to use one over another depends on concerns regarding bias and time.

As a method for studying business-related issues, questionnaires possess several important strengths. First, their nature makes it possible to study a relatively large group (sample) of people with greater ease than other methods. For example, a link to an online survey can be distributed by email or online, as a QR-code on a poster, or printed and mailed. In some cases, questionnaire-style interviews can be conducted by telephone. Second, because survey responses are often quantifiable, surveys can facilitate a comparison of respondents' answers. Third, surveys are considered to produce unbiased results and rank high in the measure of reliability, or the confidence that one would consistently achieve the same results. Surveys arguably have less influence over the process because there is less researcher-subject interaction. Responses that are forced (such as those on 1-to-7 Likert scale) produce more consistent responses and are less open to researcher interpretation (assuming respondent interpret questions largely in the same way). Finally, questionnaires, especially forced-answer questionnaires, allow for faster analysis. Data can be easily fed into analysis software, such as Excel or SPSS, as numerical quantities. This allows organizations to more quickly make decisions based on "predictive analytics" (data analysis used to uncover patterns in customer or employee behavior). Among other things, analyzing patterns or trends allows managers to prevent high-value customers from leaving, sell additional services to current customers, develop successful products more efficiently, or identify and minimize fraud and risk.

Surveys are also limited by several factors. First, responses are often limited in depth. They can only record perceptions held by stakeholders, leaving the explanations of choices unobserved. To understand *why* a person holds a belief or opinion and what a response *means* to him or her requires follow-up questions. Second, surveys tend to be acontextual. Thus, the nuances and rich details of answers, often context dependent, are left unaccounted for in the process. Third, surveys are not as "natural" as conversations (interviews). People do not tend to think about things on a scale, thus a survey may force a respondent to think about something in an uncommon way. Fourth, people often may think about an issue in nuanced ways; however, surveys often force respondents to choose a single response. What is more, without additional clarification, each respondent may interpret questions differently and thus provide inconsistent responses. Finally, respondents may not have much thought about something until the receive the survey. Thus, the survey forces feigned interest in a topic.

To conduct a survey, receive training in questionnaire design and analysis. Generally, to design a survey, you need to determine the question content, scope and purpose of the survey, the response format for collecting information from respondents (e.g., forced-choice or open-ended questions), and question wording (the goal is to reduce inconsistent interpretations and get at the issue of interest without leading respondents). Surveys tend to be generic and boring. Even edgy organizations tend to replicate stuffy survey and questionnaire design. As with all business communication, consider the audience and create artifacts consistent with image. A questionnaire provides an opportunity to project an image and create identification. Figure 8.5 provides an example section from a survey used to solicit feedback from students' use of technology. Notice that some of the questions are edgier. This does not guarantee that the survey will be completed; however, at least it is not boring to read.

Courses in quantitative methods and statistics may be required to analyze data in a way that produces validity, a concept that describes whether data are believable representations of a population's beliefs, attitudes, opinions, and so on. In general, consider issues related to pop-

SURVEY

Do you use or contribute content to any of the following media or social networking tools?
(Check all that apply.)

	WTF is this?	Avoid it	I fiddle	Hell yeah	Addict
1. Tumblr	☐	☐	☐	☐	☐
2. Blogs (Blogger / WordPress)	☐	☐	☐	☐	☐
3. Twitter	☐	☐	☐	☐	☐
4. Facebook	☐	☐	☐	☐	☐
5. +You (Google)	☐	☐	☐	☐	☐
6. LinkedIN	☐	☐	☐	☐	☐

Assignments/Exams

Did assignments help you improve your overall writing? --------------- Yup! | 50/50 | I right da same

Did assignments help you improve your understanding
of the rhetorical process? --- Watch out Aristotle! | 50/50 | No

Figure 8.5. There is no reason survey content should be boring. Make surveys that are fun to read and fit your audience. This one is used to survey student in a Biz and Prof Comm course.

ulation, sample (actual group from population that is contacted), question design, respondent bias, and administration costs. Table 8.1 lists some of the strengths and weaknesses of survey research.

Interviews and focus groups.   As noted, interviews can be used for survey-based research. When people refer to the interview, however, they are typically referring to the unstructured or semi-structured qualitative interview, which seeks to understand the meanings of central themes in the life world of the subjects. The main objective in conducting qualitative interviews is to understand the meaning of what the interviewees say.

Table 8.1   Strengths and Weaknesses of Survey Research

Strengths:
- Surveys are relatively inexpensive (especially self-administered surveys).
- Surveys are useful in describing the characteristics of a large population. No other method of observation can provide this general capability.
- Surveys can be administered from remote locations using mail, email, or telephone.
- Consequently, very large samples are feasible, making the results statistically significant even when analyzing multiple variables.
- Many questions can be asked about a given topic, giving considerable flexibility to the analysis.
- There is flexibility at the creation phase in deciding how the questions will be administered: as face-to-face interviews, by telephone, as group administered written or oral survey, or by electronic means.
- Standardized questions make measurement more precise by enforcing uniform definitions upon the participants.
- Standardization ensures that similar data can be collected from groups then interpreted comparatively (between-group study).
- Usually, high reliability is easy to obtain—by presenting all subjects with a standardized stimulus, observer subjectivity is greatly eliminated.

Weaknesses:
- A methodology relying on standardization forces the researcher to develop questions general enough to be minimally appropriate for all respondents, possibly missing what is most appropriate to many respondents.
- Surveys are inflexible in that they require the initial study design (the tool and administration of the tool) to remain unchanged throughout the data collection.
- The researcher must ensure that a large number of the selected sample will reply.
- It may be hard for participants to recall information or to tell the truth about a controversial question.
- As opposed to direct observation, survey research (excluding some interview approaches) can seldom deal with "context."

Steinar Kvale (2008) suggests that interviewing, in its truest sense, is the sharing of multiple views, or "inter-views," on a topic so that consensus can be achieved through dialogue. As a research approach, therefore, interpretive interviewing is probably one of the most natural. According to Kvale, interviews are particularly useful for getting the story behind a participant's experiences. The interviewer can pursue in-depth information around the topic. Interviews may be useful as follow-up to certain respondents to questionnaires, e.g., to further investigate their responses.

In informal, conversational interviews, there are no predetermined questions. A theme may be suggested but interviewees largely lead the direction of the conversation. The researcher "goes with the flow." In more structured approaches, the interviewer follows a stricter protocol of questions and often does not ask unstructured questions. If, however, the interviewer is supposed to ask follow-up questions, he or she is often trained to ask specific types of follow-up questions. This ensures that the same general areas of information are collected from each interviewee; this provides more focus than the conversational approach, but allows a degree of freedom and adaptability in getting the information from the interviewee. The strictest protocol is the closed, or fixed-response interview. All interviewees are asked the same questions and asked to choose answers from among the same set of alternatives. This format is useful for those not practiced in interviewing. The more structured approaches to interviewing are optimal when there are multiple interviewers or time is short. The open, unstructured interviews can last several hours.

Focus groups tend to take a more structured approach at the beginning as researchers query respondents for specific answers. However, the idea of a focus group is to allow an organic conversation to emerge and for participants to take over the conversation. Although many focus groups are placed in rooms where they can experience products or services (e.g., taste food or play with a new gadget), some focus groups seek to uncover trends through talk. In these situations, it is critical for people to feel comfortable. Conducting focus group research in an office that looks more like a living room, providing food and beverages, and encouraging more informal "coffee shop talk" can help participants feel more relaxed, thus encouraging more natural conversation.

Interviews are frequently recorded with digital audio devices and then transcribed. Transcribing can be an expensive and time-consuming process. However, there are few tricks of the trade. For example, transcribing only the sections that are relevant can save a lot of time. Once data are transcribed, they can be more easily analyzed. Interpretive approaches to interviewing do not often seek to "code" data in the sense that responses to questions and conversations are placed into pre-established categories. Often data are "thematized" as concepts emerge from among various respondent answers. Should researchers desire a more quantified approach, they can categorize responses after the interview is transcribed. Researchers seeking to code interview data will need to create categories and then identify content in the interview transcripts that fits these categories. If multiple researchers are coding transcripts, seek inter-rater reliability—a statistical score that demonstrates consensus among reviewers. If the results fail to have inter-rater reliability, then it could mean raters or data are inconsistent.

Interviews are useful when respondents lack reading skills, when researchers need to address complex topics or obtain a nuanced opinion, and when researchers want to more deeply understand answers provided by respondents. Because of the personal nature of interviews, they often produce higher response rates than surveys, although the overall number of respondents is likely to be lower. Some of the drawbacks of interviews include the following: Interviewers can affect the data if they are not consistent; it is a time-consuming method (this is a general concern of most qualitative research); and the interviewer can bias interviewee responses.

Observation (ethnography).   Ethnography is the writing of culture. It is often the product of field observations that are obtained by a researcher, who either watches cultural or organizational practices without influence or participates in cultural practices in order to understand them better. The goal of observation research is to watch activities as they unfold naturally.

Observational research is largely unstructured. Researchers often "enter the field" and begin collecting observations of mundane organizational or professional life. Observations can focus on both people and objects. The observer's role is to record group interactions and behaviors using various qualitative inquiry tools (e.g., field notes, interviews, and narratives). Although observers can try to observe objectively, without interference, most researchers prefer the participant-observer approach, through which researchers attempt to become part of community and to adopt roles as participants.

Through observation and participation, researchers build accounts of cultural practices by taking notes. The ethnographer focuses on specific practices that seem important to the people or objects they are observing. The practice of observational research involves taking detailed field notes and often interviewing cultural participants to check the validity of these notes. Field notes are meant to be read by the researcher to generate an understanding of the culture, social situation, or phenomenon being studied.

Popular forms of observational research in business include the mystery shopper or mystery customer technique to test the quality of consumer experiences and customer service. Others include the disposable camera technique, where respondents are asked to take snapshots of their life or of others using specific products or services. (Pictures are then analyzed using a narrative technique to understand how products and services are consumed.) Today, shadowing—a technique that involves following specific person or object for some time—has become a popular method for virtual and non-virtual work (Engstrom, 2012).

Observational research is useful when one wants to account for the complexity of group behaviors, when a researcher wants to uncover the interrelationships among multifaceted dimensions of group interactions, or when it is necessary to understand the context of practices. Immersion and prolonged involvement in a setting can lead to the development of rapport and foster free and open speaking with research subjects. Observation fosters an in depth and rich understanding of a phenomenon, situation, or setting and the behavior of the participants in that setting. Observation is an essential part of gaining an understanding of naturalistic settings and members' ways of seeing. Observation can provide the foundation for theory and hypothesis development.

Doing quality observational research, however, requires a significant investment of time. It involves prolonged engagement in a setting or social situation and requires a collection of a significant amount of data, much of it useless. Sorting through data can be difficult, frustrating, and just as time consuming as the data collection process. Observational research for academic studies can take several years to complete. Within business settings, however, this is particularly problematic because by the time data are understood, trends in the environment could be shifting. Thus, ethnographic research within business settings requires accelerating the pace of observation and data analysis, often reducing the quality of the research. In any case, ethnographic research requires a well-trained researcher, which often is achieved through several years of graduate-level study. Other issues to consider include too little data leading to false assumptions about behavior patterns. Conversely, a large quantity of data may not be effectively processed. Data collectors' first impressions can bias what details they pay attention to during the course of a study. Today, many researchers prefer to record practices by video or audio. In public setting, for example, cameras can record interactions without audio. Thus, mall security cameras (for example) can be analyzed to better understand shopping practices.

Other qualitative approaches. In addition to the above methods, communication researchers and consultants use a variety of other methodological and theoretical approaches to the collection and analysis of data. These include the following:

- Narrative inquiry
- Discourse analysis
- Hermeneutics
- Case study
- Short-term observation
- Ethnomethodology
- Grounded theory
- Phenomenology
- Kinesics
- Introspective analysis (autoethnography)
- Content analysis
- Online/virtual research
- Critical social research

These methods can be researched on your own. For a comprehensive introduction read Lindlof and Taylor's *Qualitative Communication Research Methods.*

To learn more about the above methods and develop the skills necessary to use them in practice, you will need to take graduate-level research courses. However, knowing about them is helpful should you ever need, in a management position, to collect data. Companies can hire the services of firms who specialize in the collection of qualitative research, such as those offering services through the Qualitative Research Consultants Association (**https://qrca.org**). Table 8.2 summarizes some of the benefits and drawbacks of most qualitative research.

Table 8.2   Strengths and Weaknesses of Qualitative Research

Strengths:
- Data are usually collected in naturalistic settings in qualitative research.
- Data are based on the participants' own categories of meaning.
- It is useful for studying a limited number of cases in depth.
- It is useful for describing complex phenomena.
- It provides individual case information.
- It provides understanding and description of people's personal experiences.
- It describes in rich detail practices as they are situated and embedded in local contexts.
- It can determine how participants interpret ideas, objects, and practices.
- It is responsive to local situations, conditions, and stakeholders' needs.
- It can include observations of changes that occur during the study (a major life event may shift consumer behavior).
- Qualitative data in the words and categories of participants lend themselves to exploring how and why phenomena occur.

Weaknesses:
- Knowledge produced is not generalizable.
- It is difficult to make quantitative predictions.
- It might have lower credibility with some constituents.
- It involves a significant amount of time to collect and analyze data compared to quantitative research. (It takes time to build trust with participants that facilitates full and honest self-disclosure).
- Time and costs can render the research impractical, especially in businesses that require decision-making in a dynamic environment.
- Short-term observation studies, a way around issues of time, may lead to hasty generalizations.
- The results are influenced by the researchers' idiosyncrasies.
- Researcher bias can influence the design, implementation, and analysis of the study.
- Some subjects may be previously influenced and affect the outcome of the study.
- Study groups may not be representative of the larger population.
- Any group that is studied is altered to some degree by the very presence of the researcher.

Covert Data Gathering Methods

Organizations use a variety of covert methods to conduct research on employees, customers, and competitors. Covert methods are generally detection and prevention oriented. In the United States, people generally assume that many of their practices in the workplace are likely to be monitored. Employees assume, for example, that their emails and telephone calls can be monitored at any time. (In some states it is required that all parties be informed that their conversations are being monitored.)

Some data gathering may seem benign. For example, a web cookie, a type of computer code that allows origin websites and browsers to communication, can be used to authenticate a user, session, user preferences, shopping cart contents, or any browser stored text. Cookies are not software, so they are generally safe. However, they can be used by spyware to track users' browsing activities or stolen by hackers to gain access to users' accounts. Data collected from cookies during a user session provide companies with detailed information about users' browsing habits. From these data a website can be modified to better suit search patterns. Algorithms also often adapt to user habits, allowing content-driven sites to recommend specific content based on preferences, previous purchases, browsing patterns, and so on. Website analytics programs provide companies with information regarding which links are generating leads. This helps a company determine if its paid advertising is working. Today, companies may encourage users to use a mobile applications or social networking tool, such as FourSquare or Groupon. These sites allow merchants to track user activity. Stores and shopping centers are also deploying mobile phone tracking technology that allows them to track customer movement based on the identification number of cell phones, although often businesses warn customers of this practice (see Censky, 2011).

Some data collection efforts can seem questionable. For example, organizations monitoring individuals' private social networking accounts or conducting credit checks on their employees may seem a little more questionable. Stealing another company's trash in order to identify key suppliers or possible strategic plans, paying competitor employees to work as spies, or monitoring hotel bookings near a corporate headquarters in order to determine if a company is about to launch a new product (companies tend to bring investors, employees, and key customers together before a major announcement or launch), are all strategies described by Eamon Javers (2010a) in his book *Broker, Trader, Lawyer, Spy: The Secret World of Corporate Espionage*. Despite the questionable nature of these practices, corporate espionage is a growing business: "In the midst of two wars and the fight against Al Qaeda, the CIA is offering operatives a chance to peddle their expertise to private companies on the side—a policy that gives financial firms and hedge funds access to the nation's top-level intelligence talent" (Javers, 2010b).

Generally speaking, the most common types of covert data collection involve undercover investigations, surveillance, electronic monitoring, background investigations, and skip tracing. *Undercover operations* are essentially intelligence or "spy" operations within any given unit of an organization. An obvious advantage of this type of operation is that it gives management an accurate picture of what is happening in detail. If surveillance is expected, workers may have a way to be dishonest "under the radar." Once a person gains rapport with the "inner circle," the undercover operative can participate in the behavior in order to gain additional intelligence or document the policy violation or crime first hand. Undercover operations may occur at random or be undertaken due to suspicious activities of investigative targets. A variation of undercover operations, frequently used to check and monitor quality assurance, is "secret shopper" programs. A person hired as a mystery shopper will act like a regular customer and report on his or her experience. Often it is the threat that a mystery shopper could visit a store at any time that motivates employees and managers to comply with company protocols.

Surveillance is the visual monitoring of a location or individual to uncover misconduct. The visual monitoring is logged by video, photograph, and text. These are often then described in a report, which is given to management or the client. Learning to take detailed and effective field notes, record or photograph activities, install hidden cameras, and covertly follow people is important for consultants wanting to work with private investigation companies or as internal security managers. Often organizations place employees under covert surveillance when they are suspected of stealing products or customers, or are suspected of helping competitors (this is a type of countersurveillance). For example, a delivery service may steal products during transportation, or a valet company may have employees who steal from cars. Sometimes companies don't want to prosecute offenders, because this could lead to bad press. They simply want to isolate the incident and dismiss problematic employees.

Electronic monitoring is a variation of surveillance. As briefly noted above, it involves tracking a person's online activities or offline activities by means of an electronic device. Common forms of electronic monitoring involves recording phone calls, observing vehicles with GPS trackers, monitoring computer activity, and using website analytics. Businesses can utilize information obtained by covertly monitoring customer practices. This reduces the bias often associated with traditional observational research. Businesses can reduce legal and civil liability by monitoring practices of employees' online search activities. For example, an employee visiting websites with illegal content (e.g., gambling or child pornography) can be caught, terminated, and arrested before the company is caught off guard by an undercover police operation. Also, restricting and monitoring employee online search practices can reduce the threat of malicious software or hackers and can increase productivity. A company can reprimand or fire the employee in order to reduce culpability and encourage only work-related searches from its other employees. As noted in the introduction, monitoring employees' electronic communication is generally acceptable in the United States, although knowing the applicable laws in each state is important (read *Navigating the Legal Minefield* by Ron Hankin [2008]).

Background investigations and *skip tracing* are frequently used types of covert surveillance, although some tactics are overt (e.g., calling applicant references). Although covert, they are not deliberately so. Background investigations involve searching a person's history, social relationships, online activities, routines, and financial history. Organizations can use background investigations as part of the pre-employment screening process (in addition to interviews). This information can be valuable because prior behavior is predictive of future behaviors. An employee with a poor employment history, history of theft, or questionable online social comments is likely to continue these behaviors once hired. This is not to say that we should not believe in reform. A person can change. A thorough background investigation, however, can lead to better decision-making practices, such as hiring a person on specific conditions. A longer probationary period, for example, gives managers time to screen and monitor the employee. Credit checks are part of the due diligence process. They are important to conduct, for example, before one enters into long-term contracts and partnerships. A background investigation could reveal liens or other financial issues that could be connected to important company assets.

Skip tracing, which means tracing the activities of someone who "skipped town" in order to find him or her, is often used to track down people who owe money or are trying to avoid civil litigation. Hiring a company to find someone who does not want to be found can be a worthwhile investment, even if at a financial loss. Such practices help maintain and enforce important social and financial obligations. In short, they reproduce social order.

With many city and states cutting funding to public police departments, many companies are on their own to protect their assets or conduct investigations of stolen property. This is one reason the U.S. Bureau of Labor Statistics anticipates a 22% growth in the private detective and investigator profession over the next decade. Although there are many benefits to covert data collection, it is not without its drawbacks. When employees, potential business partners, suppliers, and other organizations learn of cover surveillance practices, it often creates an atmosphere of distrust or undermines otherwise healthy relationships. Consider options for overt data collection and weigh the costs and benefits of covert methods.

Ethical Considerations of Data Collection

When conducting any type of primary research, consider the ethical implications of the activities. Table 8.3 lists ethical considerations specific to common communication research methods (see also Chapter 2). Generally speaking, regardless of when or where data are collected, one must obtain or provide *voluntary participation, informed consent, privacy (confidentiality, anonymity, and security),* and *rights to service.*

Corporate espionage, a growing field, involves covertly observing the activities of competitors, investors, and customers. (Image © rj lerich, 2012. Used under license from Shutterstock, Inc.)

Table 8.3   Ethical Considerations of Research

Keep in mind the following concerns:

- Obtain the permission of the people you will study.
- Not all types of research require permission. For example, when analyzing data that is publicly available (such as in the case of commercials or public message boards), you do not need author permission.
- Don't do anything that would cause physical or emotional harm to subjects. Be careful, for example, with how you word sensitive or difficult questions during interviews.
- Be sure your own personal biases and opinions do not get in the way of research; give all sides a fair consideration.
- Many types of research, such as surveys or observations, are conducted under the assumption that respondents will remain anonymous. Many interviews, however, are not done under the condition of anonymity (e.g., focus groups). Let research subjects know whether your research results will be anonymous.
- When doing research, do not take advantage of easy-to-access groups of people simply because they are easy to access (e.g., undergraduate college students). Choose subjects based on what would most benefit the research topic.
- Some types of research done in a university setting or for third parties (e.g., grant funding agencies) require Institutional Research Board approval.
- When reporting results, accurately represent observations and interviewee responses. Do not take interview responses out of context and do not discuss partial observations without putting them into the appropriate context.

Voluntary participation requires that people not be coerced into participating in research. This is especially relevant when researchers rely on "captive audiences," or those with potential conflicts of interest (e.g., prisoners and students).

Closely related to the notion of voluntary participation is the requirement of *informed consent*—the idea that prospective research participants must be fully informed about the procedures and risks involved in research. Research subjects must give their consent to participate. This is especially important if there may be risk of physical or psychological harm. Often research participants sign a consent form that describes the study and their rights and responsibilities. Privacy must be guaranteed by the researcher.

There are three standards that are applied in order to protect participants' *privacy*. Researchers should attempt to provide reasonable guarantee of *confidentiality*—a guarantee that identifying information will not be made available to anyone who is not directly involved in the study. A stricter standard is the principle of *anonymity,* which essentially means that the participant will remain anonymous throughout the study—even to the researcher(s). *Security* guarantees that participants' information will be protected by security measures. For example, subjects may be assigned a number, which is used to label data. These may be secured in separate locations, often protected by surveillance and electronic monitoring. Increasingly, researchers have had to deal with the ethical issue of a *person's right to service*. Good research practice often requires the use of a control group. The control group is often denied the services of the non-control groups. When a service, product, treatment, or program may have beneficial effects, persons assigned to the "no-treatment" control group may feel their rights to equal access to services are being curtailed. As with all ethical issues, the choice to use or not use these practices are never easy, and the benefits and risks should be weighed thoroughly.

In regard to covert data collection methods, some people feel that any covert methods are unacceptable. While this is not the position advocated in this book, rhetors must consider the legal, political, and ethical challenges of using covert methods. It is highly recommended to always hire a qualified expert to conduct undercover or covert research (e.g., a licensed private investigator). Laws and acceptable professional "best practices" frequently change. Professional investigators and information gatherers have a better grasp of these changes because they are required in most states to take continuing education courses.

Hiring a professional to conduct undercover research can reduce personal and corporate liability. Undercover operations can be legally high-risk activities, so a professional investigator, trained in the laws of surveillance, assumes the risk of the investigation. Nevertheless, simply outsourcing security and monitoring does not absolve executives, managers, or other stakeholders from the crimes that may be committed by professional investigators. Avoid establishing a condition where investigative agents feel they must provide outcomes and do anything to please the client. The Hewlett-Packard (HP) spy scandal is a good case study (read the following articles listed in this chapter's reference list: Hewlett Packard (2006, September 12), Kaplan, (2006a, September 12), Kaplan (2006b, September 12), and Robertson (2009, August 12). Appendix C provides a short case study of the incident. The HP case involved a California private investigator illegally monitoring the phone calls of HP board members and journalists. Although HP chairperson, Patricia Dunn, who hired the investigator, denied involvement in the investigator's illegal activities, she was forced from the board. This case explains why it is important to be familiar with laws that affect business practices. It also suggests that it is important to hire ethical surveillance specialists.

Sharing Information and Communications

Once various business and professional rhetorical artifacts have been created, analyzed, and distributed, you must save your work products. Thanks to cloud computing, as well as the various methods described in other chapters, making data widely available has never been easier. However, there are some things to consider when saving documents that will make them easier to protect, share, and download.

Saving and organizing documents is a taken-for-granted practice that often is not given conscious thought among business owners and professionals until there is a problem locating files. Establishing a system to organize electronic and, especially, hard files should be part of the invention process. Archiving is itself an established profession with its own associations (e.g., SAA [**www2.archivists.org**]) and scientific journals (e.g., *American Archivist*). Like all rhetorical processes, sharing data and documents requires consideration of the audience, situation, rhetor and interpreter abilities, and availability of technology.

Saving "Hard" Files

Saving files requires discipline and an investment in the proper tools. But nothing is more important than planning. The keys to good filing practices are 1) filing only what needs to be filed, 2) filing it in a way that facilitates easy access, and 3) following protocol for removal. To execute these practices, spend time thinking about the record management system.

A file plan is more than a simply list of the file folders currently in file cabinets. A file plan is really only one component of a records management system, which is a set of policies and procedures for organizing and identifying files or documents to speed their retrieval, use, and destruction.

When establishing a records management system, establish procedures for filing documents and maintaining the file as well as a list of subjects. Keep your system up to date. Make the filing designations broad enough that to avoid creating a new file for every document. For example, when filing documents by customer, it may be necessary to create a new file for each customer. This is fine if the business has a significant number of repeat clients and work with these clients generates a significant amount of paperwork. However, with few repeat customers, filing paperwork by date may reduce the number of individual file folders needed.

Once a file folder system has been created, create a coding system that allows users to recall data quickly. Files are generally filed with chronological, numeric, alphabetical, or alphanumeric systems. Chronological systems arrange files by date. This is useful for small

Establish procedures for filing documents and maintaining files. (Image © Heinz Koenig, 2012. Used under license from Shutterstock, Inc.)

files and for records that have a very short life span; data can be purged in a systematic order (by date). Numeric files are arranged by number. In its simplest form, a serial arrangement begins with the lowest number and proceeds, but more complex systems can be used for large series. Alphabetical files are arranges from A-Z. This is the basic arrangement for most subject files. There are books written on both how to assign the titles that are put in alphabetical order and how to alphabetize the folder. Be consistent when filing by subject. For example, it would not make sense to file "University of Colorado" in "Cs" and "University of Illinois" in "Us." Creating a filing protocol and following it will save you a lot of time and frustration.

Nowadays, many documents can be archived as electronic documents. This is particularly helpful in reducing storage costs. However, developing an electronic system is also very important.

Saving Electronic Files

Saving printed documents requires significant planning; however, because these have a material dimension, they are not likely to "disappear" in the same way that electronic files can. One of the greatest risks for electronic storage of files is that an older version may be overwritten by a newer version. Another concern is incorrect filing, which could lead to productivity losses or accidental deletion of files. These concerns are mitigated through the use of well-planned saving procedures. The larger the organization, the more training this will require. Surprisingly, few small businesses spend time discussing the procedures necessary for end users to save documents effectively. The following procedure is one approach, although others have been developed by professional organizers and archivists. This section focuses primarily on basic saving procedures for personal computing (e.g., a student saving classwork files). These practices, however, can be used as the seed for developing a larger filing system.

Step 1: Plan strategy.   The first step in an effective strategy for saving electronic documents is to plan the saving process. This should be determined by how the document will be accessed or shared and how it is likely to be intuitively remembered. For example, whether on an internal drive, external drive, or shared network, files should be placed into folders that make sense. Remember, the desktop is not a folder. It is useful to place permanent shortcuts to frequently used programs or accessed files on the desktop, or to temporarily store files that are being used for a specific session. However, a cluttered desktop is likely to be lead to increased stress (like email overload), confusion, and slower computing speeds. The best place for folders on a computer is in "My Documents" or some other properly named folder (e.g., "My Work Documents" or "Consulting Documents"). Categorizing folders and compartmentalizing files into specific types of work, and then into specific subjects, will make saving and retrieving documents easier. As a general rule, keep folders to fewer than seven levels.

When saving files on the computer, plan a strategy like the one that follows (each » represents a level):

```
My Documents »SchoolWork   » 2011     » Fall      » COM113
                                                  » COM221
                          » 2012     » Spr      » COM315
                                                  » COM317  » Assignments  »File1.docx
                                                                           »File2.pptx
                                                             » Lectures     »File1.docx

                                       » Fall      » COM320
               »Personal   » Photos   » Trip 1    » Photo1
               »Research   » Articles  » Article1.pdf
```

Notice that in the above example, SchoolWork is separate from research. This is because research, in general, may extend beyond the classroom. It makes sense to save files obtained from research in a separate folder so that they can be accessed for another class or after graduation. Dumping these files into their own folder means that you don't have to recall what class you were in when you obtained a useful article. However, by creating specific folders for each class, and then for each semester, the risk of overwriting one class paper with another is reduced. (Obviously, "File1" or "Photo1" are names used in the example. In practice, the files would be saved with a more useful name, such as "FinalPaper.docx" [see Step 3].)

Step 2: Find appropriate software.   A variety of software programs are available that help users organize and keep track of files. These are useful when managing a large number of documents. For example, one can purchase a software or cloud-based application specifically designed for storing and organization files for internal and external use. Popular versions of these programs are Firmex (**www.firmex.com**), policytech (**http://info.policytech.com**), docAssist (**www.docassist.com**), and CentralDesktop (**www.centraldesktop.com**). Microsoft Office 365 allows users to manage files more easily with common Microsoft tools and programs.

If on a limited budget, utilize programs that you already have. For example, Microsoft OneNote now comes standard with most versions of Microsoft Office. Using it with SkyDrive or SharePoint, files and notes can easily be organized and shared through the cloud or on the hard drive. OneNote helps maintain and track active links and changes in those links. Researchers and writers may already have EndNote, a bibliography management program that makes citing materials, sharing references, and searching databases easier. The program links to specific files and documents, so the program can help manage research articles. You can also create another library and use it to build links to other files. Because the program allows users to choose keywords, use it to code and organize files. This makes organizing and searching for files easier. The program, in short, can be used as an ad-hoc database.

Step 3: Save documents with thoughtful names.   When saving files, create a logical system and stick with it. When in a rush, it is easy to forget to update or maintain files. One may quickly save a file, planning to organize it later. As time passes, more files accumulate with the same expectations, only to develop a mess of files, which take time to sort through. A well-designed system is only as good as it is used.

Unfortunately, many students and entrepreneurs, based on observation, tend to save documents without much of a system at all. For example, it is not uncommon for students to start a paper and continue to edit the same version, day after day, without creating backups. For smaller papers, this approach may be fine. However, for larger reports, it is useful to always begin a new writing session with a new file, typically identified by date. This ensures that if content is accidently deleted, if a file becomes corrupt, or if an initial thought or section is determined to be unnecessary only to later be determined to be important, there are previous versions to return to. Beginning with a new file each day will reduce potential problems due to computer or user error. This practice is particularly important when sharing documents for editing. A final paper for the Business and Professional Communication course, for example, could be saved as follows: AhmedS_COM319-Finalpaper_12.1. Then, the next day the student would save the document as AhmedS_COM319-Finalpaper_12.2. Should the student delete something in the new version, then later decide that she or he wanted to use that section, she or he could return the "12.1" version. When sharing this document with a colleague, in hope of obtaining some feedback, the student could send the file as AhmedS_Com319-Finalpaper-v1, then Finalpaper-v2, and so on, until the document is finally labeled AhmedS_COM319-Finalpaper_final and uploaded into BlackBoard or Moodle, sent by email, or printed.

In the above examples, notice the lack of spaces and quotations in the file name, and the use of the underscore (_) and hyphen (-). Although one can save files and documents with spaces, it is not recommended. When files are shared, uploaded into a website and set as a downloadable hyperlink, or managed with software (e.g., EndNote), spaces create errors in the code. This means that before sharing the file the sender would have to delete the spaces and insert the recommended characters, often a frustrating and time-wasting task. Many programs deal with this problem by inserting the ISO-Latin international standard for spaces (%20). So, if the file is saved as "Jones J – COM 319," and it shared online, the file name will be converted to Jones20%J20%-20%-COM20%319. This is hardly an easy to read file name.

File names with hyphens are easier to use when optimizing websites and are important for search engine indexing. For example, to index a picture so that Google Images finds it, one must either give it a metadata name—a special line of HTML code that tells "crawlers" a little about the picture (see Chapter 9)—or save it as suggested. The latter is easier because it does not require knowledge of coding or special software and can be indexed on third-party sites (e.g., **www.google.picassa.com**). Thus, an online photos saved as Jane-Jones.jpg, will be picked up by Google Image search when a user searches "Jane Jones." A file named Image1, without metadata, would not be found by the search engines. When creating files that will be saved as a URL (e.g., **http://someurl.com**), it is better to use the hyphen. The underscore may not be easily identifiable when the URL is underlined in print. Note the difference between **http://someurl.com/Jane-Jones.jpg** and **http://someurl.com/Jane_Jones.jpg**. (There is an underscore between Jane and Jone (Jane_Jones) in the second URL.)

Finally, thoughtful file names assist in the organization of files and, when they include enough information, can assist users in quickly identifying documents. Where the file is stored is obviously an important part of this process. For example, a document stored in a folder named "research articles" will be obviously different than articles stored in a folder named "news articles." Because research articles are often referenced by name, it makes sense to save the file beginning with the last name of the first author. For example, the following article could be saved in the folder "ResearchArticles" with the following name: SimsR_2010_A-study-of-deviance-as-a-retaliatory-response-to-power:

Sims, R. (2010). A study of deviance as a retaliatory response to organizational power. *Journal of Business Ethics, 92*, 553–563.

To organize the most frequently accessed files or folder, use numbers. For example, if someone accesses a folder named "ResearchArticles," it will be located below the folder "Pictures" or "Programs." Dialing down the window can become frustrating if you access the file frequently to send documents. By saving the file as 1-ResearchArtices, this will always be located at the top of the window when the "list view" option is selected in the file menu.

Step 4: Backing up and transporting documents.   The final step in organizing data is the backup and transportation (or distribution) of documents. People now frequently move among a variety of devices, from computer to laptop to tablets to smart phones, all of them capable of editing documents. In some cases, users transport documents across a variety of platforms with external flashdrives. Moving all of these documents can get complicated, and there is an increased risk of losing, corrupting, and overwriting files. Thus, it is recommended to use the portable device as the primary device, with frequent or automatic backups. Getting into the habit of backing up the drive, with a specified folder, properly labeled (PDBackup_1-23-12; PDBackup_1-25-12) will reduce the risk of losing files. As mentioned several times, however, using the cloud to save or backup files eliminates a lot of these complications. Popular cloud providers and programs include Microsoft 365, ZumoDrive, Amazon, Google, and Qvidian.

Cloud services, however, are not without risks. Files can also be lost or at risk of hacking. These companies do take special care to back up their servers and to reduce security risks, but there is never full certainty in any situation. So far, no major problems have been reported with these services. However, the watchdog group Privacy Rights Clearinghouse (PRC) provides the following reminder: "When users store their data with programs hosted on someone else's hardware, they lose a degree of control over their sensitive information. The responsibility for protecting that information from hackers, internal breaches, and subpoenas then falls into the hands of the hosting company rather than the individual user. This can have many possible adverse consequences for users" (What are the risks of cloud computing?, n.d.). PRC's list of reminders and suggestions to consider before saving on the cloud include the following:

- Read the host company's privacy policy and terms of service.
- Gain knowledge of the location of the servers, because this might change the applicable laws that govern the access to information.

- Remember that government investigators or civil litigants may try to subpoena information, and they could approach the hosting company without notifying the data owners.
- Hosting companies do not have the same motivations as their clients to not disclose information to government sources.
- Understand that some companies may willingly share sensitive information with marketing companies (hence, the first bullet).
- There is risk that a company may shut down its operations, file bankruptcy, or sell to another company, resulting in changes to terms of service and access.
- Currently, technology is light years ahead of laws, so there are still many questions and uncertainties regarding regulations, rights, and responsibilities of all parties.

Although this list may seem scary, cloud computing, with the right company, can be the right choice for many small businesses trying to save money. Such businesses can avoid expensive equipment purchases, IT maintenance, and security against viruses and other threats.

Saving and storing documents is only one part of the important process of protecting sensitive information. It is also important to take measures to protect data, information, and communications when sharing and storing it.

Storing files on the cloud can be a safer and cost-effective solution for many small businesses. (Image © .shock, 2012. Used under license from Shutterstock, Inc.)

Protecting Information and Communications

The revelation of sensitive government and corporate information from WikiLeaks, beginning in 2006, demonstrates that even the most protected organizations are not protected from data theft. Protecting important business documents from theft is an essential security function.

Protecting internal and external communication requires limiting access to data and ensuring that only the appropriate and approved information is delivered to the appropriate and approved audience. This essentially entails restricting access to content and distribution channels. Keeping important documents in a locked room or cabinet, password protecting electronic files, creating firewalls, maintaining up-to-date virus and malware protections, and monitoring access (by video, key code, and so on) are all important security measures. Blocking or protecting wireless connections and having strict company protocols regarding maintaining and distributing information are also essential. For the most sensitive information, access may require several levels of approval to retrieve.

Since most business owners and professionals are only concerned with protecting data on a smaller scale, the following list of important reminders is primarily restricted to simple protective measures. For more detailed information, see the Privacy Rights Clearinghouse (PRC; **www.privacyrights.org/fs/fs18-cyb.htm**), which is a great resource on laws regulating data privacy, protection standards and protocols, and industry and technology trends. PRC, as well as the books *Information Storage and Management* and *Securing Intellectual Property* provide far more detail and helpful tools than those covered here.

Know the laws. Professionals and entrepreneurs who are familiar with laws are likely to make better decisions regarding the protection of their documents and avoid errors that could lead to certain types of data from being exposed (e.g., a violation of a law could lead to a subpoena, opening data for the public's view). Some laws, such as Sarbanes-Oxley, which regulates accounting and documentation practices for publicly traded companies, can easily create data exposure for businesses. Adhering to legal requirements about data collection and monitoring, and assuring clients and suppliers do as well, can actually benefit businesses.

Use the law. Trade secret law and contract law can be helpful to businesses with a need to protect processes, products, and services secrets. The complexity of laws regulating technology and intellectual property is complicated and will require the assistant of experts. However, small business owners and managers must direct their legal counsel. An attorney can give advice, but knowing what to ask for is also crucial. For example, an entrepreneur may need to ask that an attorney craft a nondisclosure agreement that employees will sign as a pre-condition for employment. Instructing the attorney to craft nondisclosure agreements, no-compete agreements, third-party contracts, and other end-user agreements, and what these agreements should specifically address, will make the attorney's work easier. An attorney can only do the work that he or she is instructed to do. Knowing some practices of the law, therefore, is important. Consultants must explain to businesses what information they need to collect, how they will protect it, and their clients' potential risks. These issues are often spelled out in the agreement for services.

Utilize technology. Basic technology, such as cameras and email attachment blocking programs, can keep people from accidently or maliciously sending documents. Also, badges, key codes, scanners, and so on can be used in organizations with more sensitive information.

Purge and shred files. It is easy to let documents build over time. However, these documents can contain sensitive data. Unnecessary paperwork not only clutters, it is also a potential liability. Having a system in place to get rid of excess and unnecessary documents will reduce the risk of potential theft. Delete computer files and, if the data are really important, be sure to destroy the files with programs like File Shredder.

Practice due diligence. Pre-employment screening and exit interviews can help ensure that the right employees are hired and that those leaving the organization have an opportunity to share their reflections on data security. The exit interview is also an opportunity for reminding the employee of his or her rights and responsibilities. Should an employee have access to sensitive information, it is necessary to verify that he or she has properly destroyed or returned company property. If he or she signs an affidavit verifying this is true, then he or she could be arrested for perjury should information be disclosed. A legal verification that the exiting employee will adhere to the original conditions of employment will make it easier to get an injunction, if necessary. Also, random audits of work practices and testing technology for security holes are two quality control measures that are useful for protecting data storage and retrieval systems.

The above list is not, of course, complete. However, it, like all of the topics discussed in the previous section, will lead to more productive research, storage, and protection of business and professional data, information, and communications.

Conclusion

This chapter discussed processes related to the gathering, protection, and distribution of data and documents. Companies use a variety of research methods to collect data, from surveys to observation. They use both quantitative and qualitative procedures to analyze data. There are a variety of tools on the market to assist in analysis, from SPSS (quantitative) to ATLAS.ti (Qualitative).

As data travels through an organization during the various steps of collection, analysis, write up, and distribution, it is important to have a filing system in place that is intuitive and easy to maintain. Creating and implementing effective filing systems require rhetors to use forethought (invention) and discipline. For example, determining how to arrange files is an important step to reducing information overload. Files that are not properly organized and maintained not only increase wasted time and stress, they are often a security risk.

Data and communications must also be protected. A variety of tips and important websites and books on the topic were provided for improving data and communication security. A well-organized filing system is only one important part of an effective data security system. For companies with a limited budget, cloud computing offers a low-cost alternative for data distribution and improved security. However, cloud computing is not without its risks and therefore requires a well-thought-out system of file organization as well.

Continuing Education: Recommended Texts and Resources

The following books, organized by category, are worth reading. The descriptions are excluded because the list is longer than in previous chapters, and many of the books will be specific to professional interests. They are organized by personal preference.

Communication Research

- *Creative problem solving for managers: Developing skills for decision making and innovation* by Tony Proctor. ISBN: 978-0415551083
- *Media and communication research methods: An introduction to qualitative and quantitative approaches* by Arthur Asa Berger. ISBN: 978-1412987776
- *Qualitative communication research methods* (3rd ed.) by Thomas R. Lindlof and Bryan C. Taylor. ISBN: 978-1412974738
- *Qualitative inquiry and research design: Choosing among five approaches* by John W. Creswell. ISBN: 978-1412916073
- *InterViews: Learning the craft of qualitative research interviewing* (2nd ed.) by Steinar Kvale and Svend Brinkmann. ISBN: 978-0761925422
- *The coding manual for qualitative researchers* by Johnny Saldana. ISBN: 978-1847875495

File Organizing and Data Management

- *Records management* by Judith Read and Mary Lea Ginn. ISBN: 978-0538731416
- *The office: Procedures and technology* by Mary Ellen Oliverio, William R. Pasewark, and Bonnie R. White. ISBN: 978-0538443548

Security

- *Broker, trader, lawyer, spy: The secret world of corporate espionage* by Eamon Javers. ISBN: 978-0061697203
- *Process of investigation: Concepts and strategies for investigators in the private sector* (3rd ed.) by Charles A. Sennewald, CPP, and John Tsukayama, CPP, CFE, PCI. ISBN: 978-0750679503
- *Navigating the legal minefield of private investigations* by Ron Hankin. ISBN: 978-1932777734
- *A practical guide to security assessments* by Sudhanshu Kairab. ISBN: 978-0849317064

• *Securing intellectual property: Protecting trade secrets and other information Assets* [Corporate Author]. ISBN: 978-0750679954

References

American Management Association. (2007). *AMA/ePolicy 2007 survey of electronic monitoring & surveillance survey*. Retrieved from http://press.amanet.org/pressreleases/177/2007-electronic-monitoring-surveillance-survey

Areneo, J. (1996). Pandora's (e-mail) box: E-mail monitoring in the workplace. *Hofstra Law Review, 14*, 339–365.

Bitzer, L. (1968). The rhetorical situation. *Philosophy and Rhetoric, 1,* 1–14.

Censky, A. (2011). Malls track shoppers' cell phones on Black Friday. *CNNMoney*. Retrieved from http://money.cnn.com/2011/11/22/technology/malls_track_cell_phones_black_friday

Engstrom, C. (2012). Shadowing virtual work practices: Describing subjects and objects as action nets. In S. Long (Ed.), *Virtual work and human interaction research*. Hershey, PA: IGI Global.

Fazekas, C. P. (2004). 1984 is still fiction: Electronic monitoring in the workplace and U.S. privacy law. *Duke Law and Technology Review, 15.*

Gladwell, M. (2003). Connecting the dots. *The New Yorker*. Retrieved from www.gladwell.com/2003/2003_03_10_a_dots.html

Hewlett Packard. (2006, September 12). *George Keyworth resigns as HP director* [Press Release]. Retrieved from www.hp.com/hpinfo/newsroom/press/2006/060912b.html

Hornung, M. S. (2005). Think before you type: A look at e-mail privacy in the workplace. *Fordham Journal of Corporate & Financial Law, 11*, 115–160.

Javers, E. (2010a). *Broker, trader, lawyer, spy: The secret world of corporate espionage*. New York: HarperBusiness.

Javers, E. (2010b). CIA moonlights in corporate world. *Politico*. Retrieved from www.politico.com/news/stories/0110/32290.html

Kaplan, D. A. (2006a, September 12). Hewlett-Packard sets emergency board meeting. *Newsweek.com*. Retrieved from www.newsweek.com/2006/09/07/hewlett-packard-sets-emergency-board-meeting.html

Kaplan, D. A. (2006b, September 12). Suspicions and spies in Silicon Valley. *Newsweek.com*. Retrieved from www.newsweek.com/2006/09/17/suspicions-and-spies-in-silicon-valley.html

Kuypers, J. A. (2009). *Rhetorical criticism: Perspectives in action*. Lanham, MD: Lexington Books.

Kvale, S. (2008). *InterViews: Learning the craft of qualitative research interviewing*. Thousand Oaks, CA: Sage.

Lasprogata, G., King, N. J., & Pillay, S. (2004). Regulation of electronic employee monitoring: Identifying fundamental principles of employee privacy through a comparative study of data privacy legislation in the European Union, United States and Canada. *Stanford Technology Law Review, 4.*

Michael Smyth v. The Pillsbury Company. (1996). 914 F. Supp. 97 (E.D. Pa., 1996). *Lawdex.* Retrieved from http://lawdex.com/docs/Smyth_v_Pillsbury.pdf

Muhl, C. J. (2003). Workplace e-mail and internet use: Employees and employers beware. *Monthly Labor Review, 126(2),* 36–45.

Robertson, J. (2009, August 12). Sentencing looms in HP phone-record scandal. *The Christian Science Monitor.* Retrieved from www.csmonitor.com/Innovation/Responsible-Tech/2009/0812/sentencing-looms-in-hp-phone-record-scandal.

Rustad, M. L., & Paulsson, S. R. (2005). Monitoring employee e-mail & internet usage: Avoiding the omniscient electronic sweatshop: Insights from Europe. *University of Pennsylvania Journal of Labor & Employment Law, 7,* 829–904.

Smith, W. P., & Tabak, F. (2009). Monitoring employee e-mails: Is there any room for privacy? *Academy of Management Perspectives, 23*(4), 33-48.

Thompson, J. D. (2003). *Organizations in action.* Edison, NJ: Transaction Publishers.

What are the risks of cloud computing? (n.d.). Privacy Rights Clearinghouse. Retrieved from www.privacyrights.org/fs/fs18-cyb.htm#riskscloudcomputing

Chapter 9

Social Networking and Optimizing Online Presence

Image © Mihai Simonia, 2012. Used under license from Shutterstock, Inc.

Starting Point

Lately, many aspiring entrepreneurs are turning to **www.kickstarter.com** to help them raise capital to launch their small businesses. The concept of crowdfunding and crowdsourcing sites is clever in its simplicity. Following the traditional model of borrowing money from friends and family to raise capital to launch small businesses, entrepreneurs now turn to the web and tap more people who want to support fledgling businesses or to help "kick start" novel projects. For example, Caroline Mak and Antonio Ramos used Kickstarter.com to raise capital to upscale their Brooklyn Soda Works (BSW) operation. BSW is a new company that creates handmade, artisanal carbonated beverages made with sustainable produce sourced from local farms whenever possible (see **http://brooklynsodaworks.com**). Through Kickstarter, Mak and Ramos planned to raise a modest $1,500 to buy necessary equipment. As they noted on their Kickstarter profile page:

> We need equipment to scale up to bring our soda to the public, starting with the Brooklyn Flea Market this summer.

> We've proven we can make soda at home in small batches, but
> we need to purchase an industrial juicer, kegs, CO_2 tanks, reg-
> ulators and a freezer in order to carbonate on a large scale. We
> will minimize the waste produced by using compostable cups,
> and encourage the public to bring their own reusable contain-
> ers. (Brooklyn Soda Works, n.d.)

By incentivizing donations—e.g., offering a coupon for two free sodas for those who
donated $10 or a "deluxe package" of goodies for those donating $50 or more—Mak and
Ramos raised $2,849, almost double their goal.

Kickstarter.com, started by Perry Chen, is designed as an online community that helps
artists, musicians, athletes, inventors, and filmmakers raise small sums of money. It has been
used to produce small-scale "fun" projects and larger projects—for example, leaving a disposable camera in the park (raised over $3,000 of the requested $500) and recording a studio album
(Allison Weiss, raised over $20,000 of the requested $12,000).[1] The site functions in an eBay-
like fashion. Pitchers set deadlines, ranging from a day to a few months, and they must raise the
entire amount of money they request. If they miss their goal, they don't get the money (McCarthy,
2008). As Chen notes, the benefits of Kickstarter is that funding is determinate: "The thing about
the projects is that they are finite. You are telling people *if you support me with these funds, you
are going to get this thing. . . .*" (as cited in Logorio, 2010). In other words, people are not investing in shares of the company. Thus, there is no long-term return on investment for supporters, and
they don't even get to write off donations for tax purposes. This fact, however, hasn't stopped close
to 100,000 people from pledging money to Kickstarter projects (Logorio, 2010). Diaspora, an
open-source social network with extra privacy features, recently raised more than $200,000 from
nearly 6,500 donors on Kickstarter (6 Cool Crowdsourcing Business Tools, n.d.).

Kickstarter.com is just one of many new startups in the area of crowdsourcing, a type of
social networking platform that leverages the talents and work of many distributed individuals who have a loose and ad-hoc relationship with a company or professional who needs help.
For example, individuals may request help with writing a book. Each chapter could be completed by an independent contractor with expertise in the chapter content. Large projects can
be completed in a significantly shorter periods of time and often at lower costs. Short-term
projects can be completed without long-term employment or complicated contractual com-
mitments. Crowdsourcing, which taps the collective wisdom of individuals working across
space and time, leads to increased productivity and more accurate results, as crowds tend to be
far superior to individual expertise on a topic (Surowiecki, 2004).

Although a young industry, it is a becoming an institutionalized business model. Companies,
like Crowdflower and Spigit, develop technology and services specifically designed for crowdsourcing, and professional associations—e.g., **www.crowdsourcing.org**—have emerged (6
Cool Crowdsourcing Business Tools, n.d.).

The main competitive advantage to crowdsourcing is that projects are funded or completed at an accelerated pace. Facebook, for example, has engaged thousands of its members to
translate the site into more than 65 languages. Pizza Hut uses virtual order-takers through the

---

[1]Profile pages: www.kickstarter.com/projects/238859335/leaving-a-disposable-camera-in-the-park?ref=spotlight;
www.kickstarter.com/projects/allisonweiss/allison-weiss-does-it-again-with-your-help?ref=spotlight

cloud to reduce call volume at specific stores. A small technology company can start a **http://getsatistfaction.com** page, which provides a platform for customer service. Product and service users answer each other's questions. This reduces support costs and provides insight into new ways that customers might be using a product. Companies seeking new logo designs can now tap into a collection of designers through 99Designs (**www.99designs.com**). Individuals or companies needing human translators can use application program interface (API) services (e.g., **http://mygengo.com** or Amazon Mechanical Turk [**www.mturk .com**]) to upload articles, blog posts, or any other content, and they can have it worked on in small bits by people scattered throughout the world. CastingWords, an Internet-based transcription service, for example, posts its clients' files on Amazon Mechanical Turk and pays people small amounts of money to transcribe long or short segments of audio as chunks. This allows long audio files to be transcribed in 24 hours or less. Nonprofits and micro-lending companies, like **www.kiva.org** and **http://samasource.org**, help connect small-donor philanthropists with people in underdeveloped countries seeking access to small loans (often $100 or less) to develop small businesses.

In this chapter, you will be introduced to a variety of concepts that will help improve your online presence. Understanding how to utilize social networking through websites, such as crowdsourcing sites, and learning how to optimize online presence through search engine optimization (SEO) will help improve your own marketability. It could also lead to new career and consulting opportunities. For example, a basic knowledge of HTML, CSS, and Graphical User Interfaces will set you on a path to becoming a more effective small business and communication consultant.

As with all the concepts presented in this book, some of the information and ideas may seem basic. However, things are not always as easy as they first appear. For example, projects listed on Kickstarter.com must be approved. As Logorio (2010) notes, "Although Kickstarter is potentially open to everyone, each project must be approved by the site before it is given the go-ahead to post photos, videos, and a plea for pledges. Highly inventive projects are usually shoe-ins; a business venture with apparently adequate existing funding is not." Learning how to describe a project in a creative and suave way (i.e., rhetorically) will go a long way. In other words, some businesses need rhetorical assistance to help them articulate their visions through creative writing. For example, a project that is described as "a plan to travel while creating location-inspired couture or mailing hand-designed postcards back home to donors could be approved; just saying 'I want to backpack ' might not" (Logorio, 2010). What is more, Kickstarter is optimized when those making a pitch already have a strong social network, so kairos becomes important. First develop a strong social following, and then pitch on Kickstarter. As a consultant, instructing and helping clients to build a business image before going to Kickstarter can make a significant difference in outcomes. As is often the case with most things, people are more likely to support a project that is already well supported. The faster a project's funding requirements are met, and the faster it is exceeded, the more likely others will be called into the contagion. Describing the incentives and offering the right ones, all rhetorical choices, can also increase chances for positive outcomes.

While this chapter can only be an introduction to concepts, thinking about how to apply rhetoric to social networking can make a difference between online success and failure. Getting to the top of a Google search is no easy task, but it is also not impossible. SEO practices are almost 100% rhetorical efforts. The right keywords, clustered together (density), and descriptions that are aesthetically appealing and fun to read (reducing "bounce rates") are some of the most important parts of building an online identity and profile that will appease the Google (and other search engine) Gods.

Applying the Five Canons

Social networking is a learnable skill. Of course, some people do make it seem like an art and have a knack for getting others to like them. However, with concerted effort, you can improve your ability to engage in online conversations and develop long-term relationships and followers. For example, reading news articles will increase your knowledge of the world, improving the chance to identify something of common interest with another person during conversation. Also, practicing and engaging in conversation will help you learn to be more relaxed when speaking with others. Little efforts, like dressing appropriately for the context will influence others' perception of you. Studies show a correlation between attractiveness and persuasiveness and relatability. One study, conducted by Marc-Andr, Messner, & Ludwig Sporer (2006), found that attractive male and female salespersons were more likely to induce more positive attitudes and stronger intentions to purchase a product than unattractive salespersons. Attractiveness, however, can be enhanced with positive and caring rhetoric. Effective use of the canons of rhetoric can make a significant difference in how others perceive you. A physically appealing person who speaks poorly or aggressively will quickly lose the tenuous advantage that physical attractiveness provides.

Application of the canons of rhetoric, as noted throughout this book, increase communicative competence. All things being equal, people who are more competent are likely to be better liked (Aronson, 1998). One way to build competence is continuing education, hence the list of recommended readings at the end of each chapter. Another way to build competence is to engage collaboratively with others, to learn, and to practice. However, be thoughtful about how competence is projected. Just because you know something does not mean that you should always reveal this fact. Research on problem-solving groups has demonstrated that those who are considered to be more competent and have the best ideas tend not to be the best liked (Bales, 1958). In other words: Don't make others feel incompetent!

Whether social networking occurs online or offline, balancing a narrative of competence with a narrative of care is a rhetorical endeavor, as is all other activities in the social networking process. Specific strategies will be provided in the following section. To illustrate this process, consider the activity of introducing yourself at a party to an important person whose time is being monopolized by one core group of people, all of them relatively important. You may feel you are not worthy of being part of the group and, therefore, hover nearby, waiting for an opportunity to move in. Not only is this likely to make the group uncomfortable, it will lead to a poor use of time. Understanding the context—it is a gathering for meeting—should help you feel more comfortable approaching the group. It is expected. Others, as long as they are also good rhetoricians, will understand the rules of engagement. Walking up to the group and introducing yourself may make you appear confident—generally considered a good thing in the United States. Of course, you don't want to be rude. Asking permission to join a group, and participating in the conversational topic already in play with intelligent and thoughtful comments, will increase your ethos. Similarly, identifying an appropriate time to exit, and practicing good rhetoric—for example, saying "I can see you two want to catch up with each other" when two people seem to want some time to speak privately—will generally lead to a more favorable impressions of you as a considerate person.

The goal of social networking is to promote and sustain a chosen narrative. For example, you may perceive yourself as a caring and compassionate person. Speaking and living in a way that is coherent with this image will sustain a narrative that others reinforce when they speak about you. By social networking in a thoughtful way, rhetors can develop an image as being caring and courteous. When your narrative about yourself is consistent with others' image of you, then you achieve narrative fidelity (see Fisher, 1985; see also Chapter 1). Whether the goal is to be recognized as a caring professional, an expert, or both, you'll need to be consistent in words and deed.

Traditional Social Networking: Tips and Strategies

To be an effective social networker, be mindful of oral communication—don't mumble, make and keep eye contact, listen actively, and focus on audience needs. Whether you are an excellent communicator or highly knowledgeable, perhaps even an "expert," keep in mind the two cardinal rules of networking:

- *Rule 1:* The ultimate goal is to help others.
- *Rule 2:* It's far more important to understand others' needs before telling them about your needs.

These two rules are consistent with the idea that networking is a two-way street, as briefly noted in Chapter 4. In addition to assisting in job searches, networking is important to salespeople, who network to build and maintain potential clients. Professionals network to obtain referrals and additional knowledge. Recruiters network to obtain job leads. Managers and executives network in order to gain referent power—a type of power based upon connections and loyalty (French & Raven, 1968).

When networking, remember that you're trying to develop a relationship with someone, which means you should be thinking about that person. It's your job to understand the people in your network, where they are coming from, and what's important to them. In addition to the cardinal rules, be sure to set expectations, reach out, and put in some work to maintain the relationships. For example, send cards for birthdays and holidays, suggest relevant and useful connections to contacts in your network, and share information of interest. Your contacts will appreciate your efforts and it reinforces your commitment to the relationship.

In setting realistic expectations, begin the process from the point of view that professionals don't need to know most people; they just need to know the right people. Building a small group of strong connections rather than an insignificant number of weak links should be your primary goal (this applies to online connections, too). This point, unfortunately, seems to escape many people who seem to accept every request they receive.

Having a large network means that you will not be able to offer genuine help to others. It is easy to overpromise and underdeliver. In practice, maintain an expectation of not receiving anything in return. The fact that a networker has reached out and made contact with you does not put them in your debt. No one is required to "pay you back." Instead of approaching networking with the goal of gaining favors, try reaching out with curiosity. Take some time to define what you are looking for and build a network strategically, in a way that builds a profile and identity. In so doing, you will not waste time building social and professional relationships that actually distract from professional goals. When networkers know what they are looking for, they go beyond the immediately obvious connections and forge relationships in other industries. Furthermore, don't expect that you'll be able to immediately identify who may be a quality connection. Dismissing people leads to lost referrals. Thoughtful connections can make you an important mediator of relationships. You will help others connect in useful ways. This generates, as noted, referent power.

In reaching out to people, be considerate of their needs and time. For example, quantifying the relationship can be an excellent way to provide professional courtesy. People are busy. Often the first thing that comes to mind when someone begins talking is, "How long is this person going to talk with me?" or "How much time is this going to take?" Address those concerns from the start by saying something like, "Hi. I have one item that I'd like to briefly discuss with you. It should only take two minutes. Do you have time now, or would you have time later?" Saying this shows respect for others' time. However, don't start a relationship with requests or favors, even if the favor is for a moment of someone's time or a lunch meeting. Sure, everyone enjoys a free lunch; however, this is an overused tool that is suspicious. It is better to begin the relations with a compliment. If using email or technology, keep communication short. Gather intelligence on the people with whom you hope to connect and consider creative ways to obtain face-to-face meetings. For example, attend the same club or a conference they attend.

Finally, it is necessary to put some effort into the process. Building a social network takes effort and can be a frustrating process. In some respects, it can be analogous to cold calling. The kind of work that effective networkers put forth includes trying to provide as much value to others as they possibly can. Creating value requires thoughtfulness and effort, but it is a time-consuming endeavor. In addition to obtaining referrals, it is necessary to introduce others. By connecting like-minded people, who may enjoy nothing more than the same book, you can expand your network. While the relationship may blossom outside of your purview, people who are connected will remember the common contact—that is, you stay in their minds. However, don't assume people want to be connected. Ask them, in advance, if they'd be interested in meeting the mutual acquaintance. Even if they don't, they will appreciate the offer.

You must also nurture your network. Don't forget about relationships you already have. Program an electronic calendar to remind you of important dates, such as birthdays and anniversaries, and be sure to send them something (just a note is fine). These are the best opportunities for you to check in to see if there is any new knowledge or referrals you can obtain. Keep at it, even when you receive a lot of rejections. Set reasonable goals. For example, try to reach out to one new person per day. Set aside 30 minutes a day to do some intelligence gathering on someone and send him or her thoughtful compliments. Obviously, networkers receive many rejections or never hear from a person again. But don't take "no" personally.

Don't pester anyone; give a potential new contact a few weeks to respond. If you don't receive a response, be persistent. For example, drop in to talk face to face. This often produces better results than generic emails do. Sometimes switching the method is all you need to do. Over time, you will learn what your contacts prefer as the method of relationship maintenance. For some, they will want to meet up for beers; others will appreciate a card during the holidays.

If you're not a great networker and seem to fail to obtain and maintain connections, keep developing your skills. You will hone this skill over time. Sometimes the issue is with your approach; like most things, you will refine this through practice. Spend time reflecting on the rhetorical process. Perhaps something you're doing or saying is being interpreted by an audience in a way other than intended. If you fail in obtaining a response through one medium, try another. Networking requires more than just electronic communications, as these are easy to ignore. (Just because you are in someone's LinkedIn network does not mean that person added you with any forethought about the relationship.) Online social networks, discussed next, are often designed by users with the intention of having as many links as possible. Another strategy is to develop only useful links. The links people develop are often weak ones. Networking involves attentive effort. Box 9.1 provides some tips and strategies specific to networking at a social gathering. To improve your game, try some of the approaches listed. Even people who are skilled at networking, such as diplomats and executives, find social gatherings unnerving. So, relax.

Online Social Networking: Tips and Strategies

In many regards, social networking online is similar to networking in nonvirtual spaces. It requires adherence to the etiquette of the space, it requires attention to the others' needs, and it requires sustained effort. Given the proliferation of multiple sites to maintain, keeping on top of various networks can be a time-consuming affair. At the very least, time should be set aside each day to engage with and update online profiles. As a topic of research, social networking research has primarily focused on consumer rather than professional behavior. Surprisingly, research shows that it does not lead to a significant increase in social pressure to purchase products or services (see Iyengar, Han, & Gupta, 2009; Raice, 2011). One conclusion is that personal contacts and offline relationships are still more important to social influence. In short, engage in online social networking but do not do so in a way that gets in the way of developing meaningful offline relationships.

Many people and businesses approach online social networking as a game in popularity, trying to develop as many "friends" or "followers" as possible. In some situations, especially for companies trying to get others involved in the promotion of sales, games, and activities, in order to increase identification with products and services, having a large network is important. However, who "friends" and "de-friends" the company webpage may be of little concern. When developing an online profile as a professional, however, more consideration about who is in your network and how many people you can reasonably connect with is warranted.

Box 9.1: Networking at the Social Gathering

Social networking at a gathering is similar to giving informal speeches. The truth is that most of our social life is conversational, so you already have years of experience networking. Keep in mind that social gatherings, like parties, are spaces where people expect to engage. So, don't stress about striking up a conversation. In these situations, it is easier rather than harder to talk with others. Consider using some of the following strategies:

- Look for a person standing alone or a couple that is not engaged in a conversation.
- Begin a conversation in the food line, at the hors d'oeuvres table, or with the person seated next to you.
- Have a "wing person," who is familiar with the group, introduce you to a few people.
- Begin with, "Hi my name is. . ." and a "here and now" (literally what is in front of you). Example: "Hi, my name is. . . . Have you tried this dish?"
- Lead the conversation with some creativity. Don't be dull by asking "What do you do?" Instead, mention the event: "The organizer really did a fantastic job. What is your relationship with the organizer?"
- Focus on the other person. Follow up responses with more specific questions. For example, if the person mentions that she or he was sent by his or her company to the event, ask, "Are you enjoying yourself? Sure is nice to get away from work, no?" However, don't engage in a game of 20 questions. The goal is to find common ground and then have a conversation about that topic.
- Establish common ground by making connections, even if broad. "Oh, you're a college teacher at the University of Wyoming. I have a friend who lived in Laramie for some time, she loved it."
- Be pleasant and courteous. Ask questions but try not to pry or interrogate. Try complimenting the other person on something he or she is wearing and ask a question about it. Example: "That is a lovely tie. Where did you get it?"
- Don't be negative. Unless you know the person well, don't complain. Even then, don't be cynical. Negative comments, especially at social events, are usually unwelcomed.
- Keep in mind that the goal is networking, so don't spend too much time with a single person. Have a short conversation and leave on a high point, just after you've said something funny or you receive a positive reaction from the other.
- Bring business cards and other materials. Follow up after the social event through LinkedIn, email, or post.
- If the other is disinterested, move on and don't take it personally. Some people just aren't that social.
- At conferences, people sometimes meet up with others they haven't seen for a while. When speaking with someone and another person approaches him or her, use it as an opportunity to exit. Get introduced to the other, give and receive a business card, thank the person with whom you've been speaking for his or her time, and say, "Seems like you all want to catch up; I'll see you around."

The most important thing about online social networking is to send the correct message. Online social networks, like Facebook and LinkedIn, when used by businesses and professionals, are not sales platforms. They are better conceptualized as public relations platforms. Virtual social networking helps build relationships with current and potential clients, but only if one is sending a consistent message that reflects a narrative identity. The goal is to influence image, or external perceptions. This is accomplished with rhetoric that has narrative rationality—that is, rhetoric that has narrative coherence (the story of your professional life makes sense) and narrative fidelity (the story of your professional life is true) (Fisher, 1985).

Sales pitches are highly discouraged in online social networking. A blatant sales pitch in a tweet or a Facebook message can seem presumptuous. Most people use Facebook, Twitter, Google+, and other networks to communicate, engage, and share with like-minded individuals, friends, family, and social contemporaries. Thus, it is more important to engage with others in a friendly and fun way. Build identification by communicating more than sales.

In most situations, the key to a successful online presence is a strong offline one. For most businesses and professionals, their followers are the ones who already identify strongly with a product or person's expertise. Generally, clients who follow a company or profile online do so in order to stay up to date on trends and relevant information. Although companies like **www.groupon.com** and **www.livingsocial.com** have turned social networking into a way to get great deals-of-the-day, most followers of business and professionals could care less about "red hot sales" on products or an upcoming seminar. Instead, they want to be engaged. If you have built a solid and strong relationship with an online audience, they will be more likely to respond to your sales message. Building this type of business relationship requires effort, and many people are just unwilling to invest the time to do this (hence opportunities for communication consultants to help small business develop strong social networks). Because of the effort required to maintain quality relationships, it is necessary to invest in followers and customers who are loyal rather than the fickle customers only searching for deals. Many of the customers who look only for deals do not translate into long-term customers, the ones that will matter in the long run. This has been a complaint of businesses who have partnered with Groupon.com (Mitaru, 2011). There is a growing movement within business to divorce bad customers and focus only on the best ones. The rationale is that the "bad customers"—those that offer a low return on investment because of their time demands or desire only to shop deals—distract from more loyal customers willing to pay a premium (see Joyner, 2009).

Accept the rhetorical burden of invention and spend time developing an online strategy. Plan the overall message and goals and consider the type of audience that should follow you. Then, modify the strategy so it fits the culture of each site. Facebook is different than LinkedIn; both are different than Twitter. Each social networking platform has audiences that expect different approaches. The message should be consistent; however; how it is presented, in terms of arrangement, style, and delivery, will be unique. In any case, take it easy on the marketing lingo from the start. Use social media for its intended purpose. Engage with as many fans and followers as possible by starting conversations, asking questions, responding to customer service issues in public, sharing meaningful information, showing personality, using humor and creative writing, creating dynamic content (audio, video, or infographics), and talking about an unrelated subject from time to time. In the following sections, there are variety of additional tips and strategies for networking online, as well as building a strong online presence.

An Important Note about Social Networking

Whether online or offline, social networking is an important part of business and professional development. While online social networking is important, be mindful of offline activities and cultivate long-term friendships. A recent Cornell study revealed that while we have been able to remain connected with high school friends, associations, and so on, we now have fewer close friends (Brashears, 2011). As the economy becomes more volatile, job security decreases, and prices of food increases, having strong social connections will matter. As Potter (2011) explains, the implications of fewer personal friendships has significant impact: "We may 'friend' more people on Facebook, but we have fewer real friends—the kind who would help us out in tough times, listen sympathetically no matter what, lend us money or give us a place to stay if we needed it, keep a secret if we shared one." Use the tips about protecting your communications discussed in Chapter 8. Be wary of people who may be phishing or trolling—a way to acquire information such as usernames, passwords, and credit card details by masquerading as a trustworthy entity. Change your online passwords frequently. Offline, get to know people well before investing in their enterprises.

Actively promoting who you are, and building a comprehensive narrative offline and online, can be enhanced by utilizing concepts in this book. A well-articulated pitch, a well-crafted email sent after conversation (or handwritten note, depending on context), and a personal web-

Social networking is important for building and maintaining strong relationships.
(Image © Monkey Business Images, 2012. Used under license from Shutterstock, Inc.)

site that captures the essence of your professional identity—whether you're fun, witty, or sentimental—will lead to an enhanced professional image and narrative (i.e., identity). In the remainder of this chapter, we will look at some strategies that you can use to build a professional image. We will also explore specific technical practices that rhetors can use to increase their chances of landing at the top of search engine results when people search specific terms.

Establishing Online Presence

A presence on the web is accomplished primarily in two ways. The first is through a website and the second is through social media and user-generated sites. Companies that are solely web-bases, such as online retailers, require sophisticated websites. A cadre of high-tech equipment and software and professional designers and programmers is required to build and maintain these types of websites. For many small businesses and professionals, who use their websites for promotional and informational purposes only, a simple website is sufficient. Learning some of the techniques and tools used to build, maintain, and promote a basic website can be useful. Learning a little more about the most important social networking tools can improve web presence, with or without the addition of professional-looking website.

Websites

Whether using a template or coding a site using development software, spend time thinking about structure, design, and overall theme. This may be easy if you already have a particular narrative or image; however, a web presence can be influential in shaping and changing an image. When working with clients or on your own ventures, choose a tone, style, and design that is going to be consistent and coherent with your image. Recall from Chapter 3 that writing down specific design directives *before* beginning a project can lead to consistent development and fewer mistakes. For example, create a document that explains font choices, color choices, and so on. Using the same colors, styles, and fonts across media lead to stronger audience identification. It is also important to choose a user name (handle) and use it consistently. Now, more than ever, one must consider user names and check their availability across multiple sites before naming a business. One can easily do this by using profile search services like **http://namechk.com** or **http://knowme.com** to see whether a username is available on dozens of popular social networks. If it's not, these sites can help identify a username that will be available across a variety of social networks. A webpage URL name (e.g., www .proCommunication.me) consistent with your username on a variety of popular sites and that is easy to remember will help people identify your content across multiple Internet platforms. (A single username for multiple sites also makes managing them easier.)

As part of the invention process, research others' websites to get ideas for content and style. If developing a business website, analyze competitors' sites to gain intelligence on the kinds of keywords that will be used for searches. Remember that people are inundated with information, so using more images and infographics, short paragraphs, and creative writing can be much more compelling than long blocks of text. In most cases, a website is just a vehicle for inspiring people to call your business or connect with you in other ways. The first page of a website, therefore, is the most critical. What you include and exclude has significance effects on visitors. People do not spend much time on webpages. If they are not inspired within a few seconds, they will go elsewhere. At most, average users read about 28% of the words on a site during a visit (Weinreich, Obendorf, Herder, & Mayer, 2008). Thus, think of a slogan that captures the essence of your company or your client's company, and your own professional image. A slogan should create an emotional response and provide a clear message about what you, your company, or your client's company does. For a discussion on the rules of slogan writing, check out Donnelly (2011). Remember to keep writing interesting. According to Carol Tice (2011), people expect websites to "cop an attitude" (see also Fried, 2010).

After determining what you want to include or exclude from a website, sketch an outline of the structure of the site (see Figure 9.1). This will help to determine how many pages are needed and the topic of each page. It is critical to think through the content before coding a site. Some pages may end up with too much information or too little. With most website plans, rhetors can have as many pages as they want. However, always aim for fewer pages with less content. People don't want to read or go deep into websites. A general sense among web designers is that if it isn't on the first page, it is likely to be missed. Consider using download-

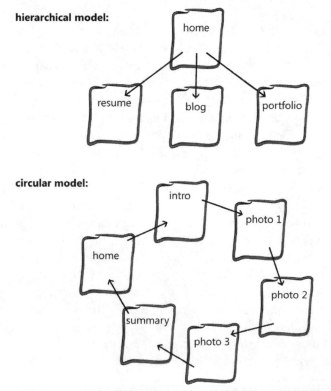

Figure 9.1. Examples of website outlines (hierarchical or circular models).

able content rather than linking to separate pages. For example, when designing a website to function as a portfolio or résumé, consider using a single-page site and embed items, such as a video résumé, directly on the first page or create a link with a downloadable PDF version of a functional or chronological résumé (refer to Chapter 4).

When placing content into pages, consider how people read websites. Research suggests that users begin at the upper-left corner of a website and scan horizontally downward toward the right. If a company relies primarily on getting people to call, for example, then placing a phone number at the right-hand side of the screen, just below content, as demonstrated in Figure 9.2, is an excellent way to make sure visitors see what's important. Other research, using heat map sensors that track eye movements, shows that for content-heavy sites, such as Google search listings or Wikipedia pages, people have a tendency to read in an F-shaped pattern (Nielson & Pernice, 2010). Such research also reveals these interesting nuggets of information that are helpful to consider when placing content onto a webpages:

- Headlines draw eyes before pictures.
- People scan the first couple words of a headline.
- People scan the left side of a list of headlines.
- The headline must grab attention in less than 1 second.
- Smaller type promotes closer reading.
- Navigation at the top of the page works best.
- Short paragraphs encourage reading.
- Introductory paragraphs enjoy high readership.
- Ad placement in the top and left positions is optimal.
- People notice ads placed close to popular content.
- People read text ads more than graphic ads.
- Multimedia works better than text for unfamiliar or conceptual information.

Figure 9.2. Example webpage home. *(Courtesy of United International Investigations.)*

People are likely to read content that is surrounded by white space, small type, and will gravitate toward bulleted items, an occasional bold font, short sentences and fragments, explanatory subheadings, and lists (Agger, 2008). Of course, creative writing helps. This has already been mentioned throughout this book, but repetition reinforces important ideas. For more design tips see Folino (2010) and Logorio and Markowitz (2010).

Once design decisions have been made and content determined, rhetors can use either a graphical user interface (GUI) design program, which allows them to sketch or design program prototypes that are then sent to coders, or they can use development software or an online program to design the site. GUI programs consist of Microsoft Blend, Caretta Softwarem Axure, and DesignerVista.

For simple websites, the kind that you are likely to code, choose among a variety of HTML development software programs, such as Adobe Dreamweaver (the industry-leading web authoring and editing software). Dreamweaver provides both visual and code-level capabilities for creating standards-based websites. Dreamweaver also allows users to code desktop, smartphone, and tablet applications. While Dreamweaver is a great program, it is more difficult to use and is significantly more expensive than Microsoft Expression Web, which also creates standards-based websites.

A variety of companies offer templates that can save coding time. For templates, see **www.templatemonster.com, www.templatesspot.com,** and **www.websitetemplates.org.** Basically, download the templates, open them with a program like Expression Web, and make changes to text and design. It is necessary, however, to know the basics of HTML and CSS (see section "generating content" below). Downloading templates and editing them with a software program is better for consulting because small businesses often already have a hosting company. Also, these often look more professional than the templates provided by hosting companies.

If unfamiliar with website design, use a web-based template platform provided directly through hosting packages—e.g., **www.godaddy.com, www.fatcow.com, http://bravenet.com, www.ipage.com, www.bluehost.com,** Yahoo Small Business webhosting (**http://smallbusiness .yahoo.com**) and **www.networksolutions.com**. Again, these do not look as professional but they are functional. The benefit of using templates offered by these sites is that are loaded automatically into the webpage, so you don't have to worry about uploading or "FTPing" them to the host server. Often one just clicks and drags content. Each hosting company offers a variety of benefits and risks. Understand your or your clients' needs and select a service that offers the highest level of service for the best price.

For a free and easy-to-use service (creating websites is as simple as clicking, dragging, uploading, and copy + pasting content), try Google Sites (**https://sites.google.com**). Functionality is limited, but this saves one from the pain of having to learn any programming languages. Another easy-to-use program, which allows users to easily update content and is often included as an installed application through hosting companies, is Joomla! (**www.joomla.org**). Joomla! is a free and open-source content management system (CMS) for publishing content on the Internet. A CMS is based on a platform that keeps track of every piece of content on a website; much like a local public library keeps track of books and stores them.

Content can be simple text, photos, music, video, documents, or just about anything one can think of adding. A major advantage of using a CMS is that it requires almost no technical skill or knowledge to manage. Since the CMS manages content, rhetors don't have to worry about formatting extensions. Many universities and large nonprofit organizations use Joomla! because it is easy for end-users to update. As described by company designers:

> Joomla is designed to be easy to install and set up even if you're not an advanced user. Many Web hosting services offer a single-click install, getting your new site up and running in just a few minutes. / Since Joomla is so easy to use, as a Web designer or developer, you can quickly build sites for your clients. Then, with a minimal amount of instruction, you can empower your clients to easily manage their own sites themselves. (**http://joomla.org/ about-joomla.html**)

As this brief note indicates, it is important to select a webhosting company that has a single-click Joomla! install. Without this feature, things can easily get complicated. Many hosting companies offer Joomla!-based themes and templates. Like WordPress (**http://wordpress.org**), one can easily change themes without changing content. A site that allows a hybrid of website functionability and social networking, blogging, and microblogging features is Tumblr (**www.tumblr.com**).

Regardless of webhosting and design choices, knowing a little about generating content with actual code, or at least understanding what is going on "under the hood," helps rhetors to better develop and manage online presence.

Generating Content

When generating webpages, there is a choice to use a variety of codes (e.g., HTML, HTML4, CSS, XHTML, and XML). Unless you are a professional programmer, understanding how to code in these languages is not a major concern. However, there are a few basic things one should know about generating content for the web. Understanding some of the basics of (X)HTML and CSS will help you to get a site up and running. For those using templates or user-generated content sites, knowing a little HTML can help resolve minor technical issues. Learning how to read HTML code allows communication consultants to also offer legitimate advice regarding search engine optimization. To get a handle on HTML code and webpage design, read Elizabeth Castro's (2007) best-selling book *HTML, XHTML, & CSS*. It is easy to read and offers clear explanations of basic concepts. It also includes a nice guide on syndication and podcasting.

CSS.   The old version of HTML combined content, structure, and formatting instructions in a single document, which was simple but not very powerful. It also required repetitive coding. If a designer wanted fonts to be the same on each page a website, for example, then he or she would code this on each page. The World Wide Web Consortium (W3C), the standard-setting organization for web content (**www.w3.org**), has created formatting instructions called *Cascading Style Sheets* (CSS) to separate content from format. The benefit of this format is that a single "style.css" file is created that tells all other pages on a site how to format something.

For example, in the following line of code the reference in bold "<h2>" is linked to the "style.css" file on the server.

Web page code:

```
<h2><strong><em>Dallas Private Investigator</em></strong></h2>
```

Any text on any webpage on the site with the tag <h2> will appear the same. In other words, each webpage reads the CSS file, which has the following line of code:

Style.css file:

```
.header_text h2 { font: normal 18px Arial, Helvetica,
sans-serif; color:#808080; padding:5px 0; margin:0;
text-align:center;}
```

This code indicates that any page on the website with the code <h2> will appear as a light gray, 18-pixel font, as demonstrated in Figure 9.3 (just below the company name). Any other

Figure 9.3. Example webpage home. *(From www.covert-pi.com by COVERT INVESTIGATIVE SERVICES. Copyright © 2010 by COVERT INVESTIGATIVE SERVICES. Reprinted by permission.)*

text within the site marked "h2" would look exactly the same, with the caveat that the additional code in the line indicates that the text should be bold (coded as <strong>) and italicized (coded as <em>). (Note: The forward slash and repeat of a code indicates the end of a particular feature.)

So let's say that a company wanted to make all text with "h2" tag orange, in the spirit of Halloween or because the company is changing its identity and thinks its colors need to also change. Instead of going through each page in the site, which would take a lot of time, the company webmaster or consultant would simply change the color code in the "style.css" file (in bold above) to an orange color (e.g., #F1A629). With one change to the .css file, all text marked with the "h2" code, regardless of where it is located in the site, would automatically update to the coded color. Of course, the color code may seem somewhat confusing. However, one does not need memorize all of these codes. Most of the programs listed earlier do the coding for designers (including setting up the CSS files), and there are a variety of websites online that list tags. Begin learning code by visiting this useful website **http://w3schools.com/tags/ref_byfunc.asp** or reading the appendix in Castro's *HTML, XHTML, & CSS* (which includes a color palette with all the necessary codes like #FFFFFF [white]).

(X)IITML.   HTML has two essential features—hypertext and universality (Castro, 2007). Hypertext means that links can be created so that users can jump around the Internet; so long as a link and destination are provided. Here is the common reference code for a link:

<a href="thepagename.html"</a>

Universality means that HTML documents are saved as text only files, so virtually any computer can read a web page. It doesn't matter which device or program is interpreting the data. This does not mean, however, that everyone experiences the text and its corresponding reference (e.g., embedded content) in the same way. Not all browsers or screen sizes are the same. So while HTML is universal, it is not very strict. As noted above, W3C has tried to create standards, which led to CSS. It also led to XML (*Extensible Markup Language*), a type of language that can be used to create other languages. This code is too strict for it to be useful to most web designers. The code is picky, for example, about upper- and lowercase letters in its code. As an illustrative example, HTML would read #FFFFFF (white color) the same as #Ffffff. XML, however, would not be able to read the code if the code needed to be in all uppercase letters. There are already billions of pages on the Internet, and most of them are not up to W3C standards. Even Google homepage, according to the W3C validator **http://validator.w3.org** (a site that identifies errors in webpages), has 37 errors, and 2 warnings (as of December 2011).

Because XML is not very lenient and not everyone has the ability to code in XML and HTML is relatively easy to use, the solution was to rewrite HTML using XML. The result was XHTML, which is now labeled X/HTML5. Again, this may sound very complicated to beginners. This solution, however, was genius because it means that you can make mistakes in code (refer to the example regarding white font in the previous paragraph). In short, it kept the process of coding simple for people like you. HTML is easier to learn than a foreign language and, with only a few different syntax rules for (X)HTML, programmers are still able to write in basic HTML language. To optimize website rankings in search results for your own website or for clients' websites, you only needs to learn to read HTML and understand a few basics of the code.

Look back at Figure 9.3; notice that below the name of the company and "Dallas Private Investigator" that "Home" in the menu bar (Home | Service | FAQ. . .) is in a lighter gray color than the others in the list. In the code below, notice the following tags: <li> </li> (list item), <a href> </a> (URL link), class="active" (item in list that is active). It is the "active" tag (in bold for demonstration purposes only) that makes the box a lighter color. The color of the active code is, of course, written into the style.css file. To change the color of the active tag, say to orange, you would just edit the code in the CSS file. Each page on the website would automatically update.

```
<li><a href="index.html" class="active">Home</a></li>
```

Look again at Figure 9.3. Notice that there is an option for "Blog" in the list of links. Note that the blog link is inactive. By reading the following code, we can ascertain that when users click on the area labeled blog a new browser or tab window will open. We know this fact because of the code in bold (target="_blank"). If you want the file to open in the same window and tab, you would just delete the phrase target="blank".

```
<li><a target="_blank" href="http://covert-pi.com/blog">
Blog</a></li>
```

If a programmer does not want to code using CSS for a specific page, perhaps because the page is unique to the overall site, this is also easy to do. Just delete the following code, which is the line of code that tells the browser to read the CSS file for a specific page.

```
<link href="style.css" rel="stylesheet" type="text/css" />
```

In the absence of these files, all text sizes, colors, and other features (e.g., tables) must be coded specifically for the individual page. In the absence of these codes, text becomes the standard default text of a browser (e.g., Arial 12 point).

Now, look at the following code and see if you can read it:

```
<h2><strong><a href="http://youtube.com">YouTube</strong>
</a></h2>
```

Visually, it would look something like the following on a webpage:

YouTube

(Note that it would be a hyperlink. Clicking on the text above would take browsers to **http://youtube.com**.)

If we remove the <h2> and <strong> tags, the code would read as follows:

```
<a href="http://youtube.com">YouTube</a>
```

And, the text on the webpage would look like this:

YouTube

The above mini-tutorial may seem difficult, but it really is not. With a little motivation, you can quickly pick up HTML code and various tricks. In many cases, UGC websites provide the necessary code. For example, to embed a YouTube video, click the "share" link and copy and paste the code into a website. Also, if you like a feature on a website and want to replicate it, simply search for the feature online. There are a variety of wikis and forums that explain how to code websites. (Alternatively, copy and paste the code from the website of interest.) For more complicated websites, one needs to take courses in computer programming. However, for basic informational sites—the kind small businesses and professionals often need—self-guided learning is optimal. Basic (X)HTML is easy to do with the assistance of programs (e.g., Microsoft Web Expression), web providers (e.g., **http://ipage.com**), resources (see continuing education), and templates (e.g., **http://templatemonster.com**). Learning the basics of web programming enables communication consultants to offer website search engine optimization (discussed later in chapter).

Social Networking and UGC Sites

In addition to developing a website, you must maintain a presence within social networking and user-generate content sites. In this section, specific strategies and resources are provided to help improve and enhance online professional profiles. The techniques described will teach you how to build a better presence for businesses, whether as a manager planning strategies and directing others to implement ideas, as a public relations specialist for your employer, or as a small business owner or consultant.

LinkedIn. LinkedIn is easy to use. However, there are a few things that professionals can do to use it more effectively as a social networking and business lead generator.

Keep your profile audience focused. It is easy to make a LinkedIn profile read like a curriculum vitae or résumé. Resist this temptation. Instead, tell a story. Provide an informal description of why you are unique to a profession and how you can or have helped others.

Maintain a cohesive professional narrative. Your expertise and the skills and knowledge you possess should be clear. Your narrative should be consistent with other social networking sites where you have a public presence. Link to your personal website, company website, Facebook, and Twitter, and consider the LinkedIn account as a launching point to other accounts. Project a positive tone that that will interest an audience. LinkedIn is for professional networking, but it needn't be stuffy. One can be conservative without being dry, so have fun.

Be creative. One way to make a profile stand out is to be creative with words. Given that so many people suck at writing a creative profile, this is yet another consulting opportunity. Charge by the hour to write and manage others' online presence (assuming you're a good writer). LinkedIn has a variety of apps that allow users to share in creative ways. For example, use the Amazon app to list books in your library, add polls to engage others, use the Twitter app to make the page a bit more dynamic, and among other things provide infographics through the SlideShare app.

Get connected, but have a strategy. The most powerful tool of LinkedIn is its search function. Use it to find new clients and business partners. Outlook, Yahoo, Gmail, or other contacts can be imported directly into LinkedIn. More direct connections lead to more opportunities. Nevertheless, choose a connection strategy. There are two types of LinkedIn users: LIONs (LinkedIn Open Networkers) and "Trusted Partner" networkers. LIONs connect with as many people as possible and treat their account as a phone and email bank. A benefit is a lot of potential contacts to choose from when searching for a referral, but it is likely to be populated by weak links. A networker taking the trusted partner approach develops deeper relationships and therefore is likely to received stronger referrals. For job seekers, professionals, and consultants looking to have a big list of trusted folks, a hybrid strategy that involves finding new people, developing a strong relationship, and only then expanding is a great way to build both a large and deep database of contacts.

Use "LinkedIn search" to find potential clients and partners. LinkedIn is the ultimate in specificity search. Users can search by company, by geography, by name, by job title, or other parameters. Members can search across their entire networks at once or can look at the contact list of an individual to see if there's anyone with whom they'd like to be connected. If you identify people that you'd like to be introduced or referred to, give a mutual connection a call or send an email to ask him or her for a referral. This approach is more polite than going directly to a connection, and it's much more likely to be successful. Premium members can send an "InMail" message to a person with whom they are not connected. Premium account holders can appear more serious about networking and are likely to receive positive responses.

Give testimonials. LinkedIn allows users to write testimonials and recommendations. These are excellent ways for users to gain more credibility. However, remember to give in order to receive. Like all rhetorical efforts, consider how a testimonial will reflect upon your identity. Be selective in your referrals and write testimonials with a professional tone. When asking for a testimonial, give directives. What specifically would you like the person to write in his or her brief message?

Have a helpful headline. When people find you in searches on LinkedIn, or when you contribute to group discussions, questions and answer forums, polls, and other LinkedIn activities, the initial thing others see is a "profile box" with a name, photo, and "headline." The default headline is current job title (e.g., "Owner at Some Company" or "Manager at Some Company." Yawn! Change this manually with the "edit profile" feature. A basic job title is not only "yawn-o-rific," it doesn't communicate what you can do for others. Treat the headline like an introductory line in face-to-face meetings: "I'm pretty damn good at creating websites."

Join groups to connect and interact. Be an expert. Participate in the LinkedIn Q&A section. Posing thoughtful questions and responding intellectually to questions will help you develop a reputation as a person who knows what he or she is talking about. Follow groups, such as alumni associations, professional associations, interest groups, and various companies. Participate in their discussions. If you're an active blogger, these discussions can be great places to find new topics to write about. They are also great places to promote your articles and blog posts.

Update. Don't forget to keep active. If you don't stay on top of your account, you'll miss opportunities to connect with others. Update information at least once a month to keep you on top of others' minds. When contacts log in, they receive status updates. This is a non-intrusive way to maintain relevance. If you don't update, then you'll likely never appear on the front page of a contact's profile. For really high-profile contacts, step outside of LinkedIn and surprise them with a phone call or invitation to a face-to-face meeting.

Watch others' status updates. Keep an eye on status updates from others. As with networking in general, you need opportunities to initiate contacts at times other than when you need something. Sending notes at random can be awkward or annoying. However, when a contact updates something, use this as an opening to get back in touch. Even small status changes can start a conversation—the sort of small talk needed to help relationships grow.

Proactively link others together. Don't wait for others to initiate a request to be linked up to other contacts. Review your contact list regularly and look for ways to link together clients, former colleagues, and other people. LinkedIn doesn't offer a functional way to do this, so just send each contact a separate email and recommend the connection. (This email also helps you stay connected with others.)

Facebook.   Facebook offers exceptional, low-cost marketing opportunities for small businesses and professionals. It is a powerful platform on which to build an online presence, promote new products and services or sales, solicit feedback, and gain new customers through referrals. When a Facebook user likes or follows a business, those who are associated with the particular user will see this and may be inclined to visit a particular Facebook page, which could lead to a sales conversations and new professional contacts.

When consulting, it is imperative to get clients signed up for and to show them how to utilize its most important features. Box 9.2 provides a list of best practices for Facebooking for

Box 9.2: Best Practices for Businesses on Facebook

In one of its ebooks, *How to Use Facebook for Business* (2011, pp. 30–32), HubSpot provides the following list of best practices (direct citation of list):

1. Be interactive, fun and helpful.
2. Embed videos on Facebook pages.
3. Create a connection between Facebook and the outside world.
4. Create contests on Facebook.
5. Integrate traditional advertising with Facebook.
6. Use Facebook to grow email lists, and vice versa.
7. Introduce new products on Facebook first.
8. Welcome new page visitors.
9. Integrate social content on the Facebook Page.
10. 'Like' other businesses' Facebook Pages.

The above list is suggestive of the following key points. First, Facebook users generally expect pages to be interaction, so include relevant advertising, discounts, contests, surveys, and so on. Second, businesses need to keep people on their Facebook page as long as possible. Therefore, companies should embed content into the Facebook page. Don't send users to YouTube or Vimeo to watch clips. Third, Facebook should enhance outside relationships and generate leads, so make Facebook fans feel valuable (e.g., by introducing new products or exclusive deals to them) and use their data to interact outside of Facebook (hence the recommendation to generate email lists). Finally, remember that Facebook is a platform for social *networking,* which means that it is important to visit and engage with others' pages, especially those with whom there is a strategic partnership (e.g., suppliers).

business. Once you've signed up for a personal Facebook account, secure your company's username. Navigating Facebook as both a personal and business user is unnecessarily complicated. If you reserve a company name for a personal account, you won't be able to use it for your Business Fan Page, so create a personal account before registering a company account. Fan Pages have special rules regarding usernames, so read up on this issue in Facebook's Help Center (**www.facebook.com/help**).

A business can set up a basic account or create a Fan Page, the latter of which requires a personal account. A Business Fan Page offers more functionality, such as fan interaction. Although Facebook can offer an inexpensive way to interact with customers and provides a contemporary form of word-of-mouth advertising, it is recommended that businesses pay for hyper-local ads to target Facebook users in a geographical area or, if a business is not geographically limited, to advertise to clusters of people that meet specific customer demographics. Skimping on paid advertising is likely to reduce possible conversions. So include online paid advertising into marketing budgets.

Once registered, search for competitors and evaluate their Facebook presence. What types of pages have they built? How many fans or "friends" do they have? Spend some time looking at their posts and analyzing their photos and videos to understand how they're using Facebook. If, for example, a competitor is using an edgy narrative, consider using a more tempered approach (or be edgier). One can also target specific customers, poaching them from competitors by offering a one-time deep discount to try the business.

Twitter.   Twitter can be used in many ways. For example, Business Week published a list of the 20 ways businesses use Twitter (see Israel, n.d.), and there are some very creative ideas worth noting: *IBM uses it as a big company newsletter, Zappos uses it to develop its service-focused culture (and maintain a near-zero marketing budget)*, and *Stocktwits is specific to Twitter, allowing analysts to share stock picks in a rolling fashion.*

Although Twitter is limited to 140 characters and is a great tool for sharing links to news and other web content or advertising promotions and sales, it can be used by organizations in a variety of other ways, both internally and externally. For example, a small company can use Twitter, so long as the content is not sensitive, as a messaging board. As noted in Chapter 6, a company can send daily outtakes from the employee handbook or code of ethics to encourage adherence to policy. Alternatively, workers can Tweet what they are doing and, over time, help collect details about day-to-day functions. Tweets can be protected, and thus limited to only those who are "approved followers." In this sense, information is internal. However, the information sent through Twitter is stored on Twitter's servers, and rigorously analyzed (see Sipping from the fire hose, 2011). If information is sensitive, having it stored or sold by Twitter to Gnip or DataSift may not be ideal, so an internal system can be installed on the company's servers (e.g., Status Net [**http://status.net/product**]).

To leverage Twitter, learn and use some of its advanced tools. These include desktop and mobile Twitter clients likeTweetDeck, Seesmic, and Tweetie. Desktop clients give users more flexibility and more control over Twitter strategies than the Twitter website. Among other things, the products allow users to predefine searches (e.g., to monitor certain keywords, including a business name) and group people in way that minimizes "noise." In short, these desktop applications keep Tweeters focused on relevant content. Also consider using a web tool like Twitterfall, which allows users to define (and color-code) various custom searches, which can then be reviewed when desired. Twitterfall is also useful for following trending topics.

Monitor and analyze web presence, including Twitter feeds. By collecting data on followers, such as what they like to (Re)tweet and who they follow, one can obtain information that can be used to offer custom products or services. There are a variety of programs and apps available to generate useful analytics on Twitter users, such as Twittercounter (**http://twittercounter.com**), Tweetstats (**http://tweetstats.com**), and xefer (**http://xefer.com**).

Others sites and ideas.   In addition to the above, consider using blogs, wikis, multimedia content (e.g., YouTube videos), and social networking platforms (e.g., Foursquare), as part of your arsenal of business and professional communications. By integrating many of these tools together—for example, embedding videos into Facebook fan pages and blogs—sites become more dynamic and gain greater exposure on the Internet. Of course, the more sites one belongs to and must generate content for, the more complicated managing these sites becomes. Monitor various platforms using software and services specifically designed for this purpose. For example, Hootsuite (**http://hootsuite.com**) allows users to manage multiple social profiles, schedule messages and tweets, track brand mentions, and analyze social media traffic. Companies should hire someone, permanently or as a consultant, to focus specifically on social media management. Of course, as a communications student, this person could be you.

Social networking, just like regular networking, requires giving and receiving. Spend time participating in discussions on other people's blogs. It takes time to build a reputation and establish credibility, and you can't always expect everyone to come to you. Sometimes, you have to go out and build credibility and a reputation. Identify three or four blogs, Twitter profiles, Facebook pages, and LinkedIn profiles in an industry, or those that focus on small business, and get into the habit of regularly reading the content and participating in discussions. Whenever you can, add value by sharing a personal story or relevant information in the comments section. Get to know the writers. They'll be valuable contacts. Analyze the rhetorical strategy and keep a journal by writing down ideas that are interesting, or create a toolbar folder that maintains a list of interesting ideas, strategies, and so on. To participate in blogs focusing on small business and consulting issues, start at Technorati's list of blogs (**http://technorati.com/blogs/directory**).

Managing an Online Presence

Once an online profile has been created, monitor and care for your reputation. To be found by search engines, use search engine optimization (SEO) practices.

Social media relations requires participation in some of these important activities. (Image © maigi, 2012. Used under license from Shutterstock, Inc.)

Monitoring Online Reputations

With review sites, such as Yelp.com, Angie's List, Yahoo! Local, Citysearch, MerchantCircle, and Google Places, proliferating and increasing in use, businesses now have many outlets for additional online advertising. As part of an SEO strategy, discussed below, businesses should claim their listings. However, it is also important to use these services to build a reputation by encouraging customers to leave feedback. Unfortunately, these sites invite negative feedback as much as they do positive ones. Often people who have a negative experience are highly motivated to leave a negative review. Both positive and negative reviews create rhetorical opportunities for dialogue. When possible, responding to both positive and negative reviews by sending coupons, addressing the issue, and trying to rectify problems can help build an even better reputation. Although negative reviews are not ideal, don't worry about a few. People understand that one can't please everybody. As long as you or your client receives largely positive reviews, a reputation will remain intact.

Actively generate buzz about work and monitor reputations. Get positive testimonials on a LinkedIn page. Address positive and negative comments about your work, presentations, writing, and so on by monitoring the blogosphere, Facebook, Twitter, and others. Engaging in these practices assists in developing and maintaining a reputation that will generate job offers, invitations to events as a speaker or guest, and marketing opportunities.

There are a variety of websites that are in the business of online reputation monitoring. For example, **www.reputation.com, www.yext.com, www.naymz.com, www.rapleaf.com, www.trackur.com,** and **http://myreputationmanager.com** offer premium monitoring services and will fix problems with rankings in major search services, such as Yahoo! Local and YellowBot. However, you can do a lot of this work yourself, for free, by doing some very basic things. When building a reputation, never fake reviews or testimonials. Ask happy customers and individuals in your professional circle to write positive reviews about your work. This will ensure that you always have more positive reviews than negative ones. Don't freak out about negative reviews. If there are any negative reviews, follow up with that person by contacting him or her. Try to make the follow-up experience a positive one.

To ensure that you do not miss comments about your work and services, set up (**http://google.com/alerts**). Google Alerts are free email updates from Google search results about any topic. For example, track your name, the name of high-status professions in your field, names of competitors, and certain other terms that are relevant to your profession or business. Anytime Google indexes something with the specified keyword, you'll receive an email notification with a link to the item. Alerts can be set up for web, blog, news, video, or group searches.

Second, review the results as web analytics data (see SEO section below). Google Analytics is a free tool from Google that provides detailed and very useful information about website traffic and the effectiveness of website marketing efforts. When building a website, add tracking tags to properly monitor them in Google Analytics. Monitor analytics because, without such data, it is impossible to evaluate the success of social media marketing efforts. Analytics show which sites feed traffic to the monitored site.

Third, search Facebook using its real-time search engine. Search to see whose talking about you or a company and collect these statements. Bing (**http://bing.com**), Microsoft's search engine, now includes friends' opinions and "likes" for particular products and servic-es directly in its search results. You'll get an impression of what others are saying about you, about your business, or about your client's business just by running a Bing search.

Fourth, search Twitter. Currently, one can search Twitter for real-time results. One easy way to monitor conversations is to search for concepts of interest (e.g., your name). Use Bing and Google's Social Search to find what Buzz you or your company is generating within the Twitterverse. As mentioned, Twitter clients like TweetDeck or Seesmic can be used to search, monitor, and save results in real time. These results are indexed in an easy-to-read format directly on the desktop.

Finally, take advantage of services that will push relevant data to you. BackType, a Twitter company, is a real-time search engine that indexes online conversations in thousands of blogs and social networks. Use this service to keep up on conversations across the web. Set it up so that every day you receive emails from BackType with links to comments that include the key-words you're monitoring. Without these alerts, it is almost impossible to monitor blogs, thus your ability to respond to posts would be very limited.

Monitoring online reputations can take a lot of time. However, set aside at least a few hours every week to check in. Develop a disciplined strategy for responding to both positive and neg-ative buzz. Working as a communication consultant, you'll be surprised how little people know about online reputation monitoring. Being able to get people up and running with some of these services, and helping them monitor and maintain their reputation, is a highly valuable service.

It is very difficult to engage in all online conversations, so spend time learning the various networks and decide where to focus efforts. Looking at website analytics data—if you own an online business—will greatly benefit your (or a client's) business. If most traffic originates from Twitter and Facebook, for example, then spend more time cultivating relationships on these services. Part of getting high-ranking in search results is to push unique and repeat users to a website. Analytics used to monitor and maintain a reputation can also be used to improve mar-keting on the web. The efforts to get websites and other social profiles ranked high by search engines is called search engine optimization (SEO), and it is a decidedly rhetorical effort. In a way, SEO is the practice of persuading search engines to choose a website when people search key words.

Search Engine Optimization (SEO)

This section will introduce simple SEO practices that can make a big difference to your or your clients' online status. To offer SEO consulting to others, gain more knowledge by engag-ing in continuing education efforts. Specifically, read HubSpot.com's white papers on SEO and social networking topics, as well as Google's extensive collection of information on the topic, which is available in Google's Webmaster Tools Help (**http://google.com/support/web-masters**). Stay abreast of important changes relevant to helping others maintain their online presence.

Before beginning search engine optimization for a person, business, topic, or other param-eter, run a Google, Yahoo, and Bing search of relevant keywords. For example, a private inves-tigator in Dallas would search "Dallas Private Investigator" and note the companies with the highest ranking (top 10). Look not only at how sites are designed, but note specific keywords that are used in the home page descriptions, how many pages are typically included in a site, other relevant pages and information, and the various links from the site. As explained below, content is king. Google, for example, likes descriptive and concise text that is relevant to a page. High-quality writing that is written for target audiences will not only make the web crawlers (spiders) happier, such writing will reduce "bounce rates" (when a visitor does not spend sufficient time on a page). A high bounce rate can reduce rankings.

When analyzing sites, look "under the hood" by viewing page source information. All web browsers allow users to look at the page source code. If using a Windows-based system, just right-click on the page in any browser and select "view page source." Or, get to this by clicking on the toolbar menu and selecting the "view page source option." A window will open that reveals the HTML code, as demonstrated in Figure 9.4. Of particular interest is the <title> or <h1> tag and the "meta elements," specifically the tags. Meta elements are the HTML or XHTML <meta . . .> code that provide structured metadata about a webpage. It is content that does not appear on the page viewed by visitors to a site, but content that is read by search engines.

Meta elements are often used to specify page description, keywords, and any other meta-data not provided through other head elements and attributes (e.g., title). Of particular importance is the keyword meta tag (Figure 9.4). These are the keywords that search engine crawlers search for when indexing sites. Using the same keywords as competitors is important to competitive ranking. Of course, some sites do not use optimal keywords, and sometimes people search using keywords that may not seem intuitive. To help generate keywords, try Google's

```
<!DOCTYPE html PUBLIC "-//W3C//DTD XHTML 1.0 Transitional//EN"
"http://www.w3.org/TR/xhtml1/DTD/xhtml1-transitional.dtd">
<html xmlns="http://www.w3.org/1999/xhtml">

<head>
<title>Dallas Private Investigator + Process Server</title>

<meta name="Description" content="We are Dallas Private Investigators specializing in surveillance
and have more than 30 years of experience investigating
domestic civil and criminal cases" />

<meta name="keywords" content="Dallas Private Investigator, Process Service, PI, Surveillance,
Cheating Spouse, Infidelity, Small Business Investigations,
Background Checks, Insurance Investigations, Child Custody, Civil Litigation" />

<meta http-equiv="Content-Type" content="text/html;charset=ISO-8859-1" />
<meta name="Classification" content="private investigator" />
<meta name="robots" content="all" />
<meta name="revisit-after" content="5 days" />
<meta name="msvalidate.01" content="0823CD1CE42B5CB0688891335DC9DCBA" />
```

Figure 9.4. Under the hood. View page source code to see what meta tags others use to promote their websites to search engines.

AdWords Keyword Generator (**http://google.com/AdWords**), which is especially helpful when running paid advertising through Google. Other keyword generator tools include Alexa (**www.alexa.com**), KeyRow (**www.keyrow.com**), and KPMRS (**www.kpmrs.com**).

Once you've completed your research on relevant words and content, begin the process of developing material that will help in search ranking. According to Google (Search engine optimization starter guide, n.d.), at a minimum, you should do the following:

- Create unique, accurate page titles
- Make use of the "description" meta tag
- Improve the structure of site URLs
- Make sites easier to navigate
- Offer quality content and services
- Write better anchor text
- Use heading tags appropriately
- Make effective use of robots.txt
- Notify Google of mobile sites
- Guide mobile users accurately
- Promote websites in the right ways (e.g., don't spam links)
- Make use of free webmaster tools

The specifics of each of these are outlined in Google's *Search Engine Optimization Starter Guide*. However, Google is not the only search engine. Two other important search engines, Bing and Yahoo, have different algorithms (the program code that ranks websites). There are differing opinions, but several search engine optimization specialists believe that writing to W3C standards (HTML5 / CSS) matters more for Bing and Yahoo rankings than it does for Google rankings (Mazur, 2010). Either way, it never hurts to create a website free of coding errors. Create interesting website content that is interesting and well-written, cluster relevant keywords together, update content frequently (keep it fresh), and use meta tags. By following these rules, sites should receive preferential treatment by search engines.

Relevant content is critical.   Anyone can set up a website in a matter of minutes and fill it with other people's content by using aggregators, bots, links, and so on. What matters most, especially for developing a brand or identity, is to write informative, helpful, and descriptive content that captures a consistent, coherent, and unique voice. Search engines respect high-quality text with some links pointing to this content. Google considers websites that constantly add content much more useful than websites that add content infrequently. For this reason, set a realistic target for the production of new content and stick to it. If you don't plan to change content on a home page frequently, consider embedding a blog on the site that can be updated at least once a month. A 250-word entry is easy to write, and linking to articles relevant to a profession or customers is a cinch. A blog can also help build a loyal following of readers, which will increase visitors to a site and decrease bounce rates. The ideal word count for each page is between 500 and 1,500 words. The critical element, however, is to keep content fresh.

Write for your audience, not search engines. Obsession with search engine optimization has led to a tendency for people to write content to "game the system." Search engines have caught on. Clustering keywords on a page, especially when absent other content, can actually hurt rankings. Sure, a private investigator wants keyword like "cheating spouse" and "private investigator" in the content of his or her homepage; however, just listing these absent content and repetitively throughout a webpage not only makes the page unappealing to readers, but search engines will consider the site to be spam. What is more, the website will have higher bounce rate and, as a result, lower search rankings. It is more useful to write a compelling narrative that integrates relevant keywords.

Write a specific title. The title is the single most important part of a webpage and should not be neglected. It tells audiences and search engines what a website is about. Use and make them as unique as possible, but relevant. The title shows up in search engines as the hyperlink and in the web browser's tab. Notice in Figure 9.5, line 4. The title is "Dallas Private Investigator + Process Server." When someone searches for any of these keywords, this is more likely to be grabbed by the search engine. Also, in the search results, it is clear what the page is promoting (see Figure 9.6). If you create a webpage for a professional résumé, write your name and what you do. For example: Emma Robertson Life Coach.

Use the h1 and keyword tags. The h1 tag is a title tag that is useful for SEO. The h1 tag tells search engines what the main title of the page is, that is, the primary heading. It is like the <title> tag, but does not show up in the web browser or search engine, rather it shows up

Figure 9.5. Line 4 is the meta tag title, which shows up in web browsers (see Figure 9.6).

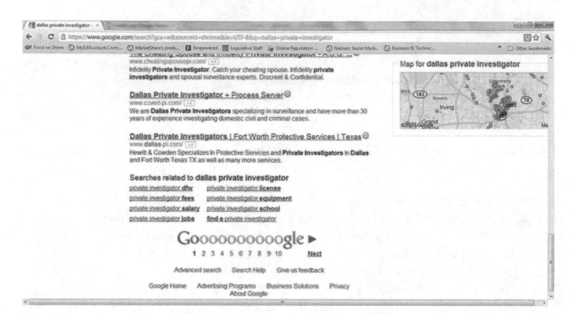

Figure 9.6. What appears in a Google search engine based on meta data information (see Figure 9.5).

at the top of the page in the browser tab. The <h1> tag in Figure 9.3 is Covert Investigative Services. Although this is the company name, it could be something more descriptive: Dallas Private Investigator. This company, however, has a company name with keywords "Investigative Services," so it is okay to use. The h1 tag is an incredibly powerful tool and Google takes it seriously, providing it is substantiated by the page's content. In other words, the words in the h1 title tag should also appear in the main text. Using the h1 tag is an excellent way to optimize a page for specific keywords.

Placing keywords in a variety of other places in a site is also important. For example, keywords should appear in the h2 and h3 tags consistently. These are the subheadings, making the content of a page hierarchical. The subheading h2 tag for Figure 9.3 is "Dallas Private Investigator," the most popular search people conduct when searching for private investigators in the Dallas-Fort Worth area. This placement of keywords in the title, the h1 and the h2 tag, tells search engines what the page is about. Also, it is useful for visitors as well. Naming a business so it is search engine friendly is important. At one time, back in the days when printed Yellow Pages were the go-to guide for business, it was useful to choose a name optimized for these books. Hence, a proliferation of "A1 whatevers"—e.g., A1 Bail Bonds or A1 Storage. Today, naming a business with a high-frequency search keyword is critical.

Other locations to embed keywords "under the hood" is in the description tag (see Figure 9.5, line 5), which is the text that goes below the link in search engines. Figure 9.6 shows how the search "Dallas Private Investigator" appears in the search result list. (Notice that the company is listed on the front page of this search, although not ideally at the top.) The description text below the URL is exactly what is in Figure 9.5, line 5. The image "Alt tag" is also useful. Not only can it be used to place keywords in metadata, but it is helpful for indexing in image search sites. For example, the following HTML, which is also shown in Figure 9.4, line 6, indicates to the web browser what the image is about.

```
<li><a href="http://covert-pi.com/contact.html"><img
src="images/civil-process-service-investigations.JPG"
width="700" height="380" alt="civil process service crimi-
nal investigations" /></a></li>
```

Note that the file name and the alt tag use keywords relevant to the profession of private investigating. To conduct an image-only search for the phrase "civil process service criminal investigations," this picture would appear in the search results. Of course, nobody is likely to search for something this way. However, a search for civil process service in regular search could lead a potential customer to this webpage because it will be ranked higher—the keywords are identified in the search.

Use keywords frequently in webpages and articles and provide relevant URL links (anchor text). The density of keywords should be about 10 for each 1,000 words. Consider underlining, bolding, or changing keyword color to assist visitors. To analyze the keyword density of a website, try this free tool: **www.tools.seobook.com/general/keyword-density.** If you blog with Word Press, try **http://keywordwinner.com**.

Use links and backlinks.   Linking to other sources is not only a great way to show appreciation of others' content, but it is a SEO strategy. Getting others to link to your site or blog indicates to search engines that your work is relevant. Quality, rather than quantity, is important to gaining relevant backlinks for SEO. Validating posts, videos, podcasts, and so on can generate quality links. External links (inbound) will have more importance if they are coming with or from high-authority domain sites (trusted and popular).

Other strategies.   Engage with social media audiences. Building relationships and interacting with connections helps build a brand, exposure, and most importantly, increased website visits. Embedding videos, picture, infographics, and other relevant data (using meta tags and keyword to describe this content), and sending out PR announcements can also generate site traffic. To assist people with sharing, use AddThis (**www.addthis.com**) to allow users to share content with the click of a button. The AddThis button HTML, demonstrated below, is automatically generated by AddThis, so just copy and paste it into websites, blogs, and so on. In Figure 9.3 the AddThis button is located in the upper right-hand corner.

```
<!—AddThis Button BEGIN —>
<script type="text/javascript">var addthis_config =
{"data_track_clickback":true};</script>
<script type="text/javascript"
src="http://s7.addthis.com/js/250/addthis widget.js#user-
name=craigstrom"></script>
<!—AddThis Button END—>
```

Add a XML site map to a site and validate it with search engines. Once a site is built, go to **www.xml-sitemaps.com**. This free tool generates a XML site map that can be easily uploaded into the website servers. This will help search engines understand the structure of a site and Google recommends it. All of the major search engines (Yahoo, Bing, and Google) validate sites as well. Each gives a site-specific code or file, which can be embedded into websites or home pages. These validators indicate to the search engine that the site is authentic. Figure 9.5, lines 11 and 12 demonstrate this code for Bing and Yahoo.

Because Facebook is becoming one of the most popular search tools on the web, it is important to do Facebook-specific SEO strategies, some of which are described in Box 9.3.

Box 9.3: SEO Strategies for Facebook

Facebook pages are increasingly becoming a "second home page" for businesses online. Facebook has created ways for businesses to get more exposure and traffic through search engine optimization (SEO) practices. Facebook's "viral channels"—the News Feed, invitations, and messages—play a central role in the spread of content through Facebook to connections. However, employing SEO tactics within a Facebook page can help generate more Facebook exposure across the entire Facebook userbase. Below is a list of tactics worth trying:

- Choose the best name for a Facebook page—and don't change it.
- Select the best URL (Facebook username) for a Facebook page.
- Use the "About" textbox to place keyword-dense prose near the top of a page.
- Use the "Info" tab to include more important keywords, text, and high priority links on a page.
- Create "Static FBML" boxes and tabs to place lengthy content and more static links on a page.
- Post direct links to your website (or other relevant sites) in a page's stream.

There are a variety of other ways to boost Facebook profiles, such as getting more fans, linking to and from Facebook on other sites, adding photos, descriptions, discussion forums, and participating in others' forums. As with regular SEO strategies, building and expanding a Facebook page presence requires creative planning and consistent execution.

Analyzing Results

Use Google Analytics (Figure 9.7 and 9.8), a free tool (although they offer a premium service), AddThis analytics, mini URL tracking services (e.g., **https://bit.ly**), Facebook analytic tools ("interactions"), and website analytics provided by sites like **www.yourbuzz.com** and **http://hootsuite.com** to track patterns of website visitors. These data are useful for making decisions regarding website content and services. For example, with the data in Figures 9.7 and 9.8, it is easy to see that the company is getting hits from people in the Dallas area, the targeted region. It also shows day-to-day traffic patterns and the relatively high bounce rate. Working to reduce the bounce rate, perhaps with special offers, an automatic text messaging request service, or targeting deals on the high-volume days can help keep traffic on the site longer, which would perhaps increase search engine ranking. Of course, if most of the traffic is coming from Dallas, making special offers only to these visitors or writing content that would be relevant to this demographic could help increase business sales.

Conclusion

This chapter described how to put all of the rhetorical strategies and efforts described in this book toward the development of a strong social presence online and offline. A variety of strategies were offered for developing a stronger social network. In addition, a variety of strategies for building, maintaining, optimizing, and monitoring online social networks and websites were provided, as well as an introduction to some of the basics of website design.

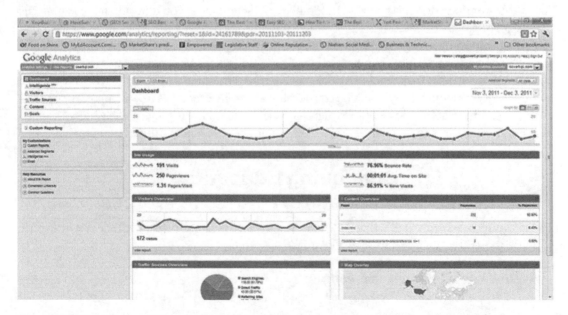

Figure 9.7. Google Analytic's Dashboard.

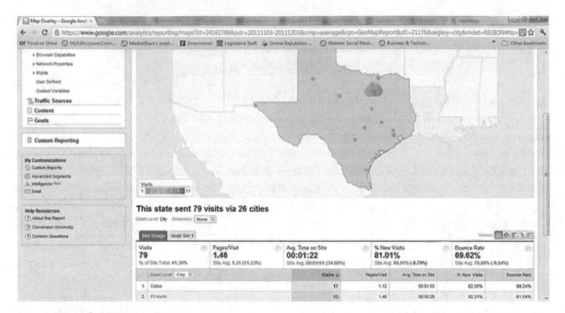

Figure 9.8. Google Analytic's traffic location infographic.

Obviously, a textbook can only offer so much. Continue to develop and hone your rhetorical and technical skills beyond this class. It took several centuries to develop the technology necessary for us to communicate and interact in the ways that we do today. However, business and professional communication has changed little since Socrates' day. If you draw upon the canons, use the classical appeals of rhetoric, and create a compelling story, and observe all of the available means of persuasion in any social-professional situation, you'll be more successful as a professional and consultant. Identifying the available means of persuasion requires expertise of rhetorical and technical skills that cannot be developed in a single course. However, as you master these skills through continuing education, you can develop a lucrative career as a contemporary sophist— a type of communication consultant-teacher—and help other professionals and businesses achieve their rhetorical desires in a variety of rhetorical situations, especially online situations.

Continuing Education:
Recommended Texts and Resources

The following texts and sites will help you develop your SEO skills. As with the previous three chapters, these are clustered by specific areas.

Website development and coding:
- *HTML, XHTML, & CSS (6th ed.)* by Elizabeth Castro. ISBN: 978-0321430847 (see also: www.elizabethcastro.com/html6ed/)

- *Dreamweaver CS5 for Windows and Macintosh: Visual quickstart guide* by and . ISBN: 978-0321703576
- *Sams teach yourself Microsoft Expression Web 4 in 24 hours* by Morten Rand-Hendriksen. ISBN: 978-0672333460
- W3C Consortium: www.w3.org/
  - Tutorial: www.w3schools.com/html/

Search Engine Optimization (SEO):

- HubSpot.com white papers and camp: http://camp.hubspot.com/
- Google webmaster central: www.google.com/webmasters/
- *Search engine optimization (SEO) secrets* by Danny Dover and Erik Dafforn. ISBN: 978-0470554180
- *Ranking number one: 50 essential SEO tips to boost your search engine results* by James Beswick. ISBN: 978-1452849904
- Read articles in Inc. Magazine (inc.com) and Entrepreneur (entrepreneur.com) to discover what other businesses are doing.

References

6 Cool Crowdsourcing Business Tools. (n.d.) *Inc Magizine.* Retrieved from www.inc.com/ss/how-use-crowdsourcing-business.

Agger, M. (2008, June 13). Lazy eyes: How we read online.*Slate.com.* Retrieved from www.slate.com/articles/technology/the_browser/2008/06/lazy_eyes.single.html.

Aronson, E. (1998). *The social animal* (8th ed.). New York: Worth Publishers.

Bales, R. (1958). Task roles and social roles in problem solving groups. In E. E. Maccoby, T. M. Newcomb, & E. L. Hartley (Eds.), *Readings in social psychology* (3rd ed., pp. 437–447). New York: Holt.

Brashears, M. E. (2011). Small networks and high isolation?: A reexamination of American discussion networks. *Social Networks, 33,* 331–334.

Brooklyn Soda Works. (n.d.) *Kickstarter.* Retrieved from www.kickstarter.com/projects/1427166211/brooklyn-soda-works-artisanal-handmade-sodas-ma.

Castro, E. (2007). *HTML, XHTML, & CSS* (6th ed.). Berkeley, CA: Peachpit Press.

Donnelly, T. (2011, January 31). The new rules of writing a memorable slogan. *Inc. Magazine.* Retrieved from www.inc.com/guides/201101/new-rules-of-writing-a-memorable-slogan.html.

Fisher, W. R. (1985). The narrative paradigm: In the beginning. *Journal of Communication, 35*(4), 74–89.

French, J. R. P., & Raven, B. (1968). The bases of social power. In D. Cartwright & A. Zander (Eds.). *Group dynamics: Research and theory* (pp. 259–269). New York: Harper & Row.

Fried, J. (2010, May 1). Why is business writing so awful? *Inc. Magazine.* Retrieved from www.inc.com/magazine/20100501/why-is-business-writing-so-awful.html.

Folino, L. (2010, February 5). How to design the best website for your business. *Inc. Magazine.* Retrieved from www.inc.com/guides/how-to-design-best-website-for-small-business.html

How to use Facebook for business: An introductory guide. *HubSpot.* Retrieved from www.hubspot.com/marketing-ebook/how-to-use-facebook-to-grow-your-business/.

Israel, S. (n.d.). 20 ways businesses use Twitter. *Business Week.* Retrieved from http://images.businessweek.com/ss/09/10/1006_twitterville/index.htm.

Iyengar, R., Han, S., & Gupta, S. (2009). Do friends influence purchases in a social network? *Harvard Business School Working Paper, 09-123.* Retrieved from www.hbs.edu/research/pdf/09-123.pdf.

Joyner, A. (2009, October 1). You're fired: Getting rid of bad customers. *Inc. Magazine.* Retrieved from www.inc.com/magazine/20091001/youre-fired-getting-rid-of-bad-customers.html.

Logorio, C. (2010, May 19). How to use Kickstarter to launch a business. *Inc. Magazine.* Retrieved from www.inc.com/guides/2010/04/using-kickstarter-for-business.html.

Logorio, C., & Markowitz, E. (2010, October 29). 7 deadly web design sins. *Inc. Magazine.* Retrieved from www.inc.com/guides/2010/10/7-deadly-web-design-mistakes.html.

Marc-Andr, R., Messner, M., & Ludwig Sporer, S. (2006). [RTF bookmark start: }Result_7Explicit persuasive intent and its impact on success at persuasion—The determining roles of attractiveness and likeableness[RTF bookmark end: }Result_7. *Journal of Consumer Psychology, 16,* 249–259.

Mazur, C. (2010, May 4). Does W3C validation really matter? *Top Ranking Solutions.* Retrieved from www.topranksolutions.com/does-w3c-validation-really-matter.

McCarthy, R. (2008, July 8). The get ahead guide: Perry Chen thinks his website could be as big as YouTube. *Inc. Magazine.* Retrieved from www.inc.com/magazine/20080701/the-get-ahead-guide-perry-chen-website-could-be-youtube.html.

Mitaru, I. (2011, June 7). Why Groupon sucks for small businesses. *Bizfeed.* Retrieved from www.pcworld.com/businesscenter/article/229644/why_groupon_sucks_for_small_businesses.html.

Nielson, J., & Pernice, K. (2010). *Eyetracking web usability.* Berkley, CA: New Riders.

Potter, N. (2011, November 8). More Facebook friends, fewer real ones. *ABC* News. Retrieved from www.abcnews.go.com/Technology/facebook-friends-fewer-close-friends-cornell-sociologist/story?id=14896994#.T1pCLjEgfdk.

Raice, S. (2011). Facebook targets huge IPO. *The Wall Street Journal.* Retrieved from http://online.wsj.com/article/SB10001424052970203935604577066773790883672.html.

Search engine optimization starter guide. (n.d.). Google [corporate document]. Retrieved from www.google.com/support/webmasters/bin/answer.py?answer=35291.

Sipping from the fire hose: Making sense of a torrent of tweets. (2011, October 1). *The Economist.* Retrieved from www.economist.com/node/21531025.

Surowiecki, J. (2004). *The wisdom of crowds.* New York: Doubleday.

Tice, C. (2011, April 18). Why your website should cop an attitude. *Entrepreneur.* Retrieved from www.entrepreneur.com/blog/219502.

Weinreich, H., Obendorf, H., Herder, E., & Mayer, M. (2008). . *ACM Transactions on the Web, 2.*

Appendix A

Useful Tables and Figures

Table A.1 Useful research resources

Sources	Location
Bureau of Labor Statistics	bls.gov/home.htm
• *Occupational Outlook Handbook*	
• Consumer data (CPI, inflation, pay & benefits)	
Central Intelligence Agency Library	cia.gov/library
• *The World Factbook*	
• *World Leaders*	
• *CIA Maps & Publications*	
Etymology Dictionary	etymonline.com
FedStats	fedstats.gov
• Provides access to information from 100+ U.S. Federal Government agencies.	
Infomime (scholarly collections)	infomine.ucr.edu
International Monetary Fund	imf.org
• World Economic Outlook Database	
IPL2 (Internet Public Library)	ipl.org
Library of Congress	loc.gov
National Center for Research Resources	ncrr.nih.gov
Newszines (recommended)	
• *Economist*	economist.com
• *Huffington Post*	huffingtonpost.com
• *Spot.us*	spot.us
• *Washington Post Top-Secret-America*	projects.washingtonpost.com/
Online Databases (see librarian):	top-secret-america
• *EBSCOhost Academic Search Premier*	search.ebscohost.com
• *InfoTrac*	infotrac.thomsonlearning.com
• *ProQuest*	proquest.com
• *FirstSearch*	oclc.org
• *Lexis/Nexis*	lexisnexis.com

Table A.1   Useful research resources (*continued*)

Sources	Location
SCORE	**.score.org**
• Business advice, business templates, etc.	
Secretary of State Website (check your state)	.Ex: **cyberdriveillinois.com**
• Information on business filings and state economic data	
The Free Dictionary by Farlex	**.thefreedictionary.com**
Thesaurus.com	**.thesaurus.com**
Uniform Commercial Code	**.law.cornell.edu/ucc**
U.N. Bibliographic Information System	**.unbisnet.un.org**
U.S.A.gov	**.usa.gov**
• Federal laws and public records	
U.S. Bureau of Justice Statistics	**.bjs.ojp.usdoj.gov**
• Data on crime, law enforcement, and prisons	
U.S. Census Bureau	**.census.gov**
• American Fact Finder	
• *Statistical Abstract of the U.S.* (1879—)	
• Various publications on jobs, business, foreign trade, etc.	
U.S. Geological Survey	**.usgs.gov**
U.S. Small Business Administration	**.sba.gov**
• General business and regional marketing data	
• Legal information and support	
Wikipedia	**.wikipedia.org**

Table A.2 Communication media advantages and disadvantages

Media	Advantages	Disadvantages
Face-to-face (Oral)	• ***Rich medium.*** All verbal and nonverbal modalities available • Rich and simultaneous verbal and nonverbal feedback and cues • Immediate opportunities for clarifying points • Typically fewer distractions • Ease of interaction and emotional expressivity	• Such a rich medium that micro-expressions and contextual factors cannot be replicated or properly understood at a later time • Ephemeral. Unless recorded, there is no verifiable record of interaction. • Restricted to only those who are present • Pressure to respond quickly, reducing opportunities to interpret information and prepare rebuttals • Reduced control over rhetorical process

Synchronous	Conversations, interviews, team meetings, luncheons, town-hall meetings
Asynchronous	Public addresses, situations interrupted by other factors (e.g., time or disruptions by another party), and situations involving interpretation/translation among languages

Media	Advantages	Disadvantages
Written	• ***Lean medium***. Nonverbals limited; At most, communicators can create text-based nonverbal expression (emoticons) • Able to plan and edit message, providing greater control over content • Message can be distributed widely and in a variety of formats and languages • Can read message several times and spend more time interpreting meaning of message • Can take time to draft a response or avoid immediate interaction • Provides a permanent record • Minimized distortion and deemphasized emotional components	• Limited opportunities for quick feedback • Takes more time and resources to distribute • Requires additional technical kills (e.g., grammar, punctuation, and design), especially if document is elaborate • Fewer opportunities to clarify unclear information and emotional position

Synchronous	Instance messaging, text messaging, interactive computer chat
Asynchronous	Reports, memos, letters, blogs, bulletin boards, email

Table A.2 Communication media advantages and disadvantages (*continued*)

Media	Advantages	Disadvantages
Audio or Visual only (e.g., graphs/ charts, audio recording, or video recording)	• **Semi-rich medium.** Only graphical, vocal, or nonverbal cues available • Can convey complex ideas and relationships quickly and dynamically • Graphics are visually attractive and oral or video messages require less investment of time and effort than written text • Reduce opportunities for misunderstanding and language-related issues	• Requires technical and artistic skills to design and create • Requires more time and technology to develop and distribute • More difficult to transmit, store, share, etc. than basic text (file size, for example, is significantly larger) • Can require special equipment or programs to view or listen

Synchronous	Working within cloud environment to allow others to interact and change visuals (e.g., Crowdsourcing projects, Google Charts)
Asynchronous	Presentations (e.g., Prezi), voice mail, video recording (viewed later), Audio distributed on CD

Media	Advantages	Disadvantages
Computer-mediated communication (CMC)/Electronic	• **Semi-rich medium.** Verbal and nonverbal cues available (though potentially obscured). • Can more thoroughly, creatively, and instantaneously integrate oral, audio and visual components • Deliver message quickly across a controllable and broad distribution radius • Increased interest and persuasiveness due to use of multimedia formats • Increased accessibility and openness	• Requires technical skills and proficiency in new and emerging technologies to thoroughly utilize (cost of training can be high) • Can be too easy to use, creating information overload • Mistakes are not easily rectified and require significant investment in time • Requires large capital investments • Creates security and privacy risks • Can increase distractions and lower productivity (if not used appropriately)

Synchronous	Videoconferencing, telephone conferencing, second life, webinar
Asynchronous	Email, online videos, podcasts

*Note: These are not mutually exclusive. For example, you could have face-to-face communication electronically (e.g., video conference), while using visual communication (projected charts and graphs). This illustration simply seeks to isolate the advantages and disadvantages of each.

Table A.3 Logical and argumentative fallacies

Appeal against a person (*argumentum ad hominem*): Attack against another person instead of the argument itself; suggests that a claim is false *solely* because of person making it. "Politicians are slick, so until we have additional evidence we can't believe what she said."

Appeal to consequences (*argumentum ad consequentiam*): An argument that concludes a premise (usually a belief) as either true or false based on whether the premise leads to desirable or undesirable consequences. "Starting a restaurant is a smart choice: People like to eat out!"

Appeal to (inappropriate) authority (*argumentum ad verecundiam*): An argument in which an authority is used to make a point. Often people draw on an inappropriate authority, i.e., someone outside of his or her field of expertise or experience. "My speech teacher said that the labor law is unjust and likely unconstitutional."

Appeal to fear (*argumentum ad metum*): An attempt to create support for an idea by increasing fear and prejudice. "If you don't do X, Y (something awful) will happen." The opposite is *appeal to hope*: "If you do X, Y will happen; therefore, if you want Y to happen, do X."

Appeal to ignorance (*argumentum ad silentio*): Appealing to ignorance as evidence of something. "We have no evidence that aliens don't exist, therefore they must exist."

Appeal to novelty (*argumentum ad novitam*): Prematurely arguing that something (idea or physical entity) is better or superior, *exclusively* because it is novel or contemporary. "The latest tablet computers will increase productivity."

Appeal to pity (*argumentum ad misericordiam*): Instead of giving carefully documented reasons, evidence, and facts, a person appeals to another's sense of pity and compassion. "For just a few dollars a month you can help resolve world hunger."

Appeal to pride or loyalty (*argumentum ad superbiam*): A glaring oversimplification appealing to one's (previous) commitment. "If you love your country, you should vote to give more money to the military."

Appeal to repetition (*argumentum ad nauseum*): Restating a point, often in a slightly different way. An argument that assumes the more something is said, the truer it becomes. This is a favored tactic of propagandists. "We've been warned a thousand times. . ."

Appeal to the number (*argumentum ad numerum*): A variation of an *ad populam* argument that asserts that truth or correctness equates with mass (numerical) support. "Eight out of 10 people prefer this gadget, so it must be the best on the market."

Appeal to the people (*argumentum ad populam*): Concludes a proposition to be true because many people (supposedly) believe it to be true. "Capitalism is the best economic approach for democratic governance."

Bandwagon: An argument in favor of doing what others, particular popular individuals, are doing. "Do X because that's what persons (of status/other cluster) are doing."

Begging the question: Assumes the answer, usually through circular reasoning. "Kids in school are having sex at a younger age. If we teach safe sex in schools, then more children will be having sex."

Table A.3   Logical and argumentative fallacies (*continued*)

Equivocation: Occurs when the same word is used, but has two or more different meanings, leading to easy confusion. A word is used one way to make a point, but is later used differently to make another point. "Rhubarb pie is better than *nothing. Nothing* is better than pie." (This confuses the rhetor's meaning of "nothing."

False cause (*cum hoc ergo propter hoc*): Without real proof that a causal relationship actually exists, claiming A causes B. This is often the result of two unrelated events occurring at the same time. "If you want to motivate employees, give them a sales commission. As soon as our company implemented a sales commission policy, profits soared." (Other factors may have caused the increase in profits. Also, there may be no cause-effect relationship between motivation and profits.) See also *post hoc ergo propter hoc*.

False dichotomy (either/or fallacy): The audience is offered a choice A or B. Rejecting one item acts as a selection of the other. C is never an option. "You're either with us or against us."

Gambler's fallacy: An argument that implies that chance is affected by more than random events. An argument that something will happen because it is "overdue." "I've lost three nights in a row, so I am sure to win big tonight. I always have a hot streak after three losses."

Half truths: Only offering evidence consistent with argument; excluding information that could undermine argument. "His (or her) fingerprints were at the scene of the crime" . . . but so were a few others.

Hasty generalization: Quickly make an inference from one example to a population of examples. "X is true of A, B and C. Therefore, X is true of everything."

Loaded questions: Ask a question with an embedded assumption that, if answered, indicted implied agreement. "Have you stopped cheating yet?"

Many questions (*plurium interrogationum*): Ask many different questions to confuse. Also a demand to know a simple answer to a complex question. "Tell me, where do you want me to be and how often do you expect that I am there and what do you want me to do while there?" "Who is to blame for the poor stock performance?"

Name-calling: Misusing labels to pejoratively reject or glitteringly support a person, group, or thing. "X candidate is a true patriot."

Non sequitur ("It does not follow."): An inference or conclusion that does not follow from established premises or evidence; also, moving from one statement to the next in a manner that does not make sense. "There are many corporations. I want to make money. Therefore I should start a corporation."

Poisoning the well: Discrediting someone before she or he speaks, or discrediting topic or argument before debate. "Sharron does not have a degree, but I suppose she has a few interesting things to offer to this discussion." "Talking about salary increases is a waste of time in this economic climate, but go ahead and ask."

(continued)

Table A.3 Logical and argumentative fallacies (*continued*)

Post hoc ergo propter hoc: Latin for "It happened after, so it was caused by." Similar to a non-sequitur, but time dependent. "She got sick after she visited China, so be aware that travelling to China is not good for your health." (Perhaps her sickness derived from something entirely independent from China.) See also *cum hoc ergo propter hoc*, which is less dependent on the chronological ordering of the correlation.

Propaganda tactics: Bandwagon (see above), repetition (see Appeal to repetition), stereotyping, confidence without warrant, glittering generalities, slogans, scapegoating, testimonials, appeal to plain folks, statistics without context, and manufactured problems.

Red herring: When the arguer diverts the attention by changing the subject. X is the topic. Y is mentioned. The conversation changes to Y. "*Person A:* This is expensive, I don't think I should buy it from you. *Person B:* Did you hear we are getting a raise soon?'"

Reification fallacy: Treating an abstract belief or hypothetical construct as if it represented a concrete event or physical entity. "Freedom is a gift given by god."

Sacred cows: Argument in favor of something held in such respect that it cannot be criticized (symbolic belief). "When you criticize the president, you criticize all that s/he stands for: democracy, the American way of life."

Shifting the burden of proof: The burden of proving an argument is always on the person asserting it. Shifting the burden to the person who denies the assertion avoids providing evidence for one's own case and assumes that the other's failure to support a position proves the initial claim true. "Since you cannot offer any valid reason why we should not downsize, as I propose, downsizing must be the best option."

Slippery slope (Absurd extrapolation): A series of statements that have a superficial connection with one another, and which lead into a rather far-fetched conclusion. "If we allow doctor-assisted suicide, then eventually the government will control how we die."

Statistics of small numbers: Similar to observational selection and hasty generalization. "My parents smoked all their lives and they never got cancer." "I don't care what others say about Yugos, my Yugo has never had a problem."

Straw man: Rather than argue against an opponent's stronger argument, selecting the weaker point (also misrepresenting the other's argument as weaker than it actually is). Typically, the rhetor creating the "straw man" then presents own position more forcefully. "You're in favor of taxing profits, which means that you must prefer to be against job growth."

Two wrongs make a right: The rhetor justifies what she or he did by accusing someone else of doing the same. "You cheated first."

Weak (false) analogies: A comparison of two like things or events for which a comparison cannot be made. "Guns are like hammers."

Table A.4   Editing and proofreading marks for instruction: A useful tool for educators and consultants

Notation	*Explanation*
apv	avoid passive voice; write in the first person
	example: Use "I propose that. . ." rather than "It will be argued that. . . ."
aq	avoid quotation; use your own words to explain
ar	avoid repetition
awk	awkward sentence; rework for clarity
c?	connection among parts of sentence, or successive sentences, is unclear
cap	capitalization problem
frag	sentence fragment
run-on	run-on sentence
m?	meaning is unclear; I don't understand what you are trying to say.
para	issue with parallelism
punc	punctuation problem
qp	quotation problem
ra	read aloud: Is this what you want to say? If you read this aloud, you'll hear how awkward it sounds.
sg/pl	singular and plural forms are mixed
sp	spelling problem
syntax	syntax tangle
vague	sentence is vague and unclear
wcp	word choice problem

This is a modified version of a document used by Dr. Lenore Langsdorf (Professor Emerita, Southern Illinois University Carbondale) in her graduate-level seminars.

Table A.5 Common email mistakes and remedies

1. *Sending before you mean to.* Press the wrong keys in some email systems and your message will send when you're typing.

 ◇ Enter recipients' addresses only when the email is ready to be sent.

2. *Forgetting the attachment or uploading the wrong attachment.* Forgetting the attachment requires the embarrassing "oops" email and creates email overload. Sending the wrong attachment can be problematic if it contains sensitive information.

 ◇ Upload files *before* composing message. Refer to attachments in message and double-check references to attachments to ensure that all belong and all are included.

3. *Expecting an instance response.* Email is designed as an asynchronous communication system. Allow at least two business days for a response.

 ◇ Use IM or phone if an immediate response is needed.

4. *Waiting too long to respond.* Waiting more than two business days to acknowledge receipt is bad email etiquette.

 ◇ If you need more time to respond, send a quick email indicating what day you will respond. If you are going on vacation, set the email to send automatic "vacation responses." Be specific with the date you will be able to respond to emails. Give yourself a few days.

5. *Forwarding useless emails.* Don't send forwards or spam to others. This is unprofessional and increases email overload.

 ◇ Don't do it. If you want to forward a joke or some kind of charity email, send it to your friends from your personal email. Even then, do you really want to be "that friend?"

6. *Hitting "reply all" without consideration.* Don't include or exclude people in your reply without considering the possible interpretations of your actions.

 ◇ The "reply all" feature is handy only when everyone needs to be included in a response. Omit people who do not necessarily need to see the reply. Include all people in the initial response to avoid creating animosity.

7. *Including email signature when it is not necessary.* Many email systems allow you to include an email signature and additional information (e.g., "Information in this email is private . . ."), which is automatically populated into messages. This can save you time from retyping your name and contact information, but it can also create unnecessary clutter.

 ◇ When sending emails to colleagues or people who know you well, delete your email signature. If an email is part of a thread, only include your email signature once.

8. *Failing to include basic greetings.*

 ◇ Don't forget to use proper salutations and greetings. Write emails as you would a professional letter.

Table A.5 Common email mistakes and remedies (*continued*)

9. ***Emailing when you are angry.*** Sending emails that contain abusive, obscene, or derogatory language, referred to as "flaming" is never appropriate.

    ◇ If you are upset, take some time to cool down. Run your email by someone else to have them comment on your tone. Use ToneCheck (**http://tonecheck.com**). Keep in mind that your employer may have a monitoring system in place to monitor questionable language.

10. ***Not paying attention to the subject line.*** The subject line is very important. It is your headline. The appropriate subject line allows people to better manage their mailboxes and helps them prioritize responses.

    ◇ Make your subject line specific and interesting. Make your heading (and message) context specific. (Remind them why you are sending the email.) If the conversation is changing direction, start a new thread with a new subject line.

11. ***Misusing "cc:" (copy) and "bcc:" (blind copy).*** You want to make sure the proper people are included in a message; however, simply including a manager or executive is often unnecessary and can upset subordinates. Consider the power dynamics of your organization.

    ◇ Copy people only when they need to receive the message. Follow company policy and protocol. Follow the same guidelines as you would for memos. Just because you can easily send a message to anyone in the organization does not mean you should. Follow the proper chain of command, including who needs to receive evidence of a message.

12. ***Relying too much on email.*** Consider context and the rhetorical situation. If a message is urgent, don't simply indicate this with a "flag." This will not receive the same attention that a voice message will.

    ◇ Think about your delivery method during the invention stage. This applies to all messages, but people tend to use email without forethought.

13. ***Other considerations.*** The following list will help keep messages professional and reduce information overload.

    • Don't overuse emoticons or abbreviations.

    • Don't request an auto-confirmation of email delivery or receipt (sent when message is opened). "Return receipt requested" is only appropriate for the most critical messages.

    • Keep on top of your messages. If your inbox piles up, you'll miss important messages and could communicate aloofness. Also, seeing many emails in your inbox will increase your stress. Open, respond, file, and delete messages.

    • Read all messages that are part of thread before responding.

    • Keep your message focused on your audience. Like a good rhetorician, adapt the formality of your message and the content to keep your audience interested.

    • Don't send long or complex messages by email. Use another method.

    • Use auto response when you'll be away for a while (e.g., vacation).

Table A.6:   How to avoid "death by PowerPoint"

Setup	*Explanation*
Software:	Use software you are comfortable with; this will allow you to work fast and utilize design features (e.g., transitions, animations, and shapes). The standards are Apple Keynote, Microsoft PowerPoint, and OpenOffice Impress.
File format:	Verify what equipment will be available and which file format is preferred. Although you will lose transition and animations features, always have a PDF version of the presentation available—at least you'll have something to project.
Size:	1024×768 at 96 dpi (dots per inch) is a safe bet because it is the standard output for most projectors. Also, the file size will be lowers. Set your computer screen resolution to 1024×768 in Start Menu: Control Panel: Appearance and Personalization (Windows) or Apple Menu: Monitors and Sound.
Transitions:	Although transitions can add a nice touch, they are not usually necessary. A simple advance to the next slide is usually sufficient. Use a transition when it reveals information in an interesting way.
Templates:	Slide design should be uniform and coherent, which means it should have a consistent style throughout the presentation. This can help with organization of thoughts. Design should also speak to your subject matter, so templates are rarely helpful. Nevertheless, a template can inspire ideas. In companies, or to enhance identification, create a standard template and use it consistently throughout a company.
Structure:	Slides should follow a pattern of arrangement consistent with the overall rhetorical approach. In other words, slides should correspond to the outline and should be ordered topically, chronologically, narratively, spatially, and so on.

Content	*Explanation*
Text:	Use standard serif or sans serif typefaces, especially if transporting files (or convert image to graphic). If you use non-standard typefaces, the operating system of the computer at a venue may not recognize them. Take it easy on fonts. Overusing bold or underline, colors, sizes, or other features can distract viewers. Try to keep the presentation within four levels. Use font changes instead of bullets (e.g., use black for section and red for subsection). Don't write in all caps, and aim for at least 28-pt fonts. Use high-contrast colors. If possible, don't use bullet points. Instead, use photographs or illustrations. Aim for fewer than 15 words per slide.

Table A.6:   How to avoid "death by PowerPoint" (*continued*)

Content	*Explanation*
Images:	Keep images to one per slide. Vary images as much as possible. Use a mix of photographs, illustrations, maps, and so on. Place image centrally within the slide. (Text should usually go higher to ensure everyone in the room can read it.) Remember that bigger and simpler is better—use vector images to avoid pixilation and don't make visuals difficult to read or understand. If you have to explain them, they are not likely effective visuals. (In some cases, however, complex data may need to be explained and the visual will help. Try to use a two-level design—a foreground (the image) and the background (the image). Don't use, for example, three colors in the background.
Video & audio:	Insert audio and video when it will enhance your presentation, not in place of it. In other words, keep video and audio brief. Be sure to load the audio and video directly into the presentation for transportation—don't rely that an internet connection will be availed. Use **http://keepvid.com** to download YouTube videos to files.
Copyright & permissions:	Whenever borrowing content, read the terms of use and permissions. Some sites, for example, require that the image indicate that the image or graphic was obtained from its site, with special reference to the contributor. For more information on borrowing content for a variety of situations (e.g., academic, professional, and corporate), visit **http://creativecommons.org**.

Navigation	*Explanation*
Navigating slides:	Utilize a title slides to give capture the essence of presentation and develop ethos. Show audience what is coming in during presentation by projecting navigation slide—slide that preview what is coming. Main points on navigation slides should correspond to the topics covered. Maintain parallelism by dedicating the same amount of speaking time to each point.
Hyperlinks:	Use hyperlinks to job to external content or to other slides in the presentation. These are especially effective during Q&A. When embedding files and hyperlinks (e.g., audio), make sure to have a standard folder to maintain integrity. Should you move a file to a separate folder, make sure to update the link. To minimize frustration, make one folder and dump all linked content into it. Number the files to correspond to their location within the presentation (slide1.mp3). Of course, this requires prior practice.

(continued)

Table A.6: How to avoid "death by PowerPoint" (*continued*)

Delivery	*Explanation*
Outline:	Even if you are using a presentation aid, don't forget to use an effective outline, with an introduction, a preview, a body, and a conclusion.
Practice:	Run through your presentation with and without slides several times to get comfortable with the material.
Surprise yourself:	Although you need to practice a lot, allow yourself to deviate from the script from time to time. Surprise yourself. If you surprise yourself, you'll surprise others too.
Follow up:	Part of delivery is thanking your audience and, if possible, sharing your slides. Post slides on **http://slideshare.com** and allow your audience download them for future reference or use. If you include your contact information, this is a great way to keep others thinking about you.

Symbol	Meaning	Symbol used in context	Corrected copy
PUNCTUATION MARKS	**Insert...**		
	apostrophe	You've got to use an apostrophe.	You've got to use an apostrophe.
	colon (or semicolon)	We need the following:	We need the following:
	comma	Use a comma, dude.	Use a comma, dude.
	ellipses	She said, "Let's go there!"	She said, "Let's go...!"
-/n	en dash (hyphen)	Show self confidence!	Show self-confidence!
-/m	em dash	My goal confidence!	My goal--confidence!
( )	parantheses	(add parantheses)	(add parantheses)
	period (or other stop)	The end of a sentence	The end of a sentence.
	slash	Circle: yes/no	Circle: yes / no
	quotation marks	She said, "Let's go there!"	She said, "Let's go there!"
OPERATIONAL & TYPOGRAPHICAL SIGNS			
	align horizontally	this is funky	this is funky
||	align vertically	1. alligned 2. needs alligned	1. alligned 2. needs alligned
	begin new paragraph	...when needed. Start a new paragraph	...when needed. Start a new paragraph
	bold face	a bold-faced line	**a bold-faced line**
	capitalize	captitalize cheyenne	captitalize Cheyenne
] [	center	]Center this text.[	Center this text.
	close up space	too much space	too much space
	delete	deleete; and delete all	delete
(ds)	double space	double space these lines	double space these lines
missing	insert missing material	ins missing material	insert missing material
#	insert space	insert space	insert space
(ital)	italicize	Communication Quarterly	*Communication Quarterly*
(stet.)	let stand (error)	stet! I shouldn't have marked this.	I shouldn't have marked this.
/	lower case	Don't Over Use Caps	Don't over use caps
	move down	move down	move down
[	move left	[lefty	lefty
]	move right	righty]	righty
	move up	this is too low	this is too low
	run lines together	run these lines together	run these lines together
(ss)	single space	single space these line	single space these lines
(sp) or	spell out	B2B Kendall Hunt Pub.	Business to Business Kendall Hunt Publishing
	start new line	from here start another line	from here start on another line
~	transpose	transpose words these	transpose these words

Figure A.1

Appendix B

Résumé Writing: A Look at the Consulting Process

Overview

In this brief appendix, a thorough discussion of relevant and contested items will be provided. This will be followed with two consulting examples that demonstrate the writing and feedback process from beginning to end of a consulting relationship. This should sufficiently show you the résumé consulting process so that you can provide your own consulting services, should you desire. The average income from each client is approximately $125, which is an average wage of $75 per hour.

What Matters?
Relevant and Contested Résumé Items

The following items are the résumé items that are often included in a résumé. However, the relevance and usefulness of these items are debatable. It is important to consider these thoroughly before developing a résumé or providing feedback to others.

Name and Contact Information

Employers need to identify the applicant and how to contact him or her. For aesthetic reasons, this information is often presented in large, bold fonts. A permanent and temporary physical address is optional, especially for students. If an applicant does not currently live in the location of the business, or he or she wants to save space, it is now possible to exclude mailing addresses (employers infrequently contact candidates by post). Instead, provide a URL to a personal website, e-portfolio, or social media résumé or pages. These places may or may not include a physical mailing address. Use a tinyurl format for lengthier URLs.

Always include an email address and phone number(s) that are checked regularly. These are the most used contact methods. Choose an email address that looks professional and not likely to change. For example, do not use an email address to which you could lose access (e.g., a school account) or one that looks questionable (e.g., "carlyhotboots88@..."). Free email accounts are fine (e.g., ymail.com, gmail, and hotmail). Consider including a Skype username.

Personal Statements and Objectives

It was once popular to include objectives, but not so much today. The objective is assumed—to obtain a job within a specific profession. Most people want to advance in their careers, so it is not necessary to state the obvious. Describing short- or long-term career objectives may actually be a turn off to an employer, especially if it sounds like the current position is merely a stepping stone to another career.

Some résumés, especially electronic ones expected to be optically scanned, now include keyword summaries, qualification summaries, or career summaries. These are useful to employers because they summarize the information presented in the résumé. Title these sections generically, such as "Summary of Qualifications." Make the information aesthetically pleasing by using bullets, hyphens, or commas to separate information. Place any summary toward the top of the résumé, just under your name and contact information. The résumé in Figure 4.2 (chapter 4) provides an example keyword summary.

Education

For current college students, for those who have recently graduated, or for those who have extensive training and certifications, education is one of the strongest selling points (place it at the top). If, however, one has been out of school for some time or has amassed extensive experience, then education will be less important (move it toward the bottom of the document). Unless they are relevant, exclude high school or military training.

It is assumed you graduated from high school if you are in college. Although some employers may be impressed by military services, your résumé should focus on relevant skills. As a single-line bullet point under employment history, list your military service. Then, use only relevant transferrable skills obtained in the military. Example 1 below provides an example of how military service can be used. Unfortunately, veterans may be discriminated against. Following the Vietnam War, discrimination against war veterans was so rampant that the U.S. Congress passed the *Vietnam Era Veterans' Readjustment Assistant Act of 1974* to force equal employment opportunity. Although discrimination is terrible, always consider how information could be interpreted. Remember to choose wisely revelatory information.

Students have a tendency to list majors and minors, when simply listing a degree may be enough (e.g., "B.S., Communication"). For special concentrations or minors, consider listing them together instead of distinguishing between majors and minors (e.g., "Concentrations in Communication, Public Relations, and Marketing"). This is particularly useful if you are just shy of a minor degree. Consider dedicating a section of the résumé to relevant courses. Alternatively, state in the cover letter specific areas of study and how this knowledge will be beneficial to an employer. It will likely not matter to an employer whether a student majored or minored in a subject. They want to know what knowledge an applicant possesses. To highlight a double major or the time required for degree completion (e.g., to show one is a hard worker by completing a degree in less than four years), state this in the application letter instead of placing this information awkwardly in the résumé. Stellar GPAs can be listed, but it is not necessary. Not so stellar GPAs can be excluded, unless a position announcement requires it. Provide only "Major GPA" if it is better than an overall GPA (this is often the case). To save space, don't list scholarships individually. Instead, consolidate the information into a single bullet—e.g., "Received eight competitive academic scholarships.")

Regardless of how information is presented, be ready to answer clarification questions during the interview. *Remember this important point:* applicants do not need to reveal all degrees or qualifications, especially if one may appear "overqualified."

Experiences, Skills, and Other Interesting Substance

In this section of the résumé, provide information that demonstrates how past experiences will contribute to an employer's future. Specifically, use prior accomplishments (not duties) from previous jobs or activities to demonstrate that you are a mover and shaker. Duties describe job functions, they do not demonstrate what one has learned or achieved as a result. Thus, instead of writing "Served customers," write "Provided excellent customer service, as demonstrated by an average customer tip rate of 18.5% and high performance reviews by store managers." Use action verbs, active voice, and specific details that are relevant to the position.

When listing jobs, use reverse chronological order (i.e., start with the most recent). Emphasize the job that has the most relevance by providing more details. Include service, internships, and part-time or temporary jobs only if they are *relevant*. If applying for a position as a junior public relations strategist, for example, would a two-year career as a nanny indicate much of relevance for the position? No. Exclude this information, except only as career history. For many traditional college students, who often only have worked a few jobs or in the retail or service sector (e.g., McDonald's), the functional (hybrid) résumé is best. It accounts for work history, but details relevant (functional) information. When someone has a significant career history worth noting, the chronological résumé is better (see Figure 4.2, chapter 4).

While it is notable that one worked full time while going to school, a service-oriented position is not going to generally going to stand out. However, skills obtained in leadership, management, customer service, knowledge about food safety, and so on, may be valuable for certain careers. For example, in our hypothetical public relations position, one could make them relevant if the position is for a food service company. For position in other sectors, however, applicants could note that they helped manage a small public service announcement campaign for the local McDonald's drive to raise money for the Ronald McDonald House Charities. This may have been completed as part of a basic position, but it can be noted, especially in a functional résumé, as something outside of the usual job function of a fry cook.

When listing activities and awards, provide only those that occurred outside of a working context (if possible). For example, volunteer work for Habitat for Humanity that is part of a work-related volunteer day, is not technically volunteering with Habitat. Keep in mind to only individually list services that will appeal to others and fit the position. Involvement in charity work and an extensive volunteer history will certainly be attractive to an organization focused on charity work, but may mean little to a corporate managers. Study abroad experiences and being bi- or multilingual may appeal to organizations that do business internationally. It may not appeal to managers hiring entry-level positions in production.

Generally, avoid listing membership or involvement in political or religious activities. Doing so may lead to prejudicial treatment. Of course, if this information is relevant to the position or is likely to weigh positively on an applicant's candidacy, it should be included. If applying to a Christian think tank, positions held in a church hierarchy are relevant. If applying to a company that provides financial advising, however, avoid disclosing specifics. Consider using general references such as "large nonprofit organization" or "community social group." If you do not have a lot of work experience or volunteer experience because of involvement in athletics or some other co-curricular activity, mention these as evidence of use of time. Co-curricular activities are likely to have developed certain transferrable skills, so focus on functions rather than positions. For example, don't just write: "President of XYZ Sorority," write "Strong communication and conflict management skills" (explain in an interview how you developed or demonstrated these skills).

Today, nearly every Fortune 500 company and many small employers use scanning software to quantify candidates. According to the National Résumé Writers' Association, 80% of employers now use software to scan résumés, especially those posted to job sites (e.g., **www.monster.com**). It is important, therefore, to sprinkle industry- and job-specific keywords throughout the résumé. Rhetorically analyze several job descriptions and position announcements within a profession to generate a list of words to populate application materials with. The words used within these documents will most likely be the words used to motivate the search software. Draw from the specific position announcement provided by the company when modifying your application package for a specific job.

Personal Data and References

Never include information, especially in the United States, which reveals certain demographical information: age, gender, disability, sexual orientation, religious or political affiliations, marital status, salary history, socioeconomic status, and identification numbers (e.g., driver's license or social security numbers). If such information is a *bona fide occupational qualification* (e.g., nationality because an international firm can only hire host-country nationals), applicants may be asked to provide some of this information. Of course, names and dates listed in the résumé can inadvertently reveal some of this information (video résumés reveal even more). Providing this information can create problems, especially if the résumé is read by prejudiced recruiters. Because of stringent employment laws within the United States, providing this information can create problems for companies. It is not wise to place recruiters in an awkward position at any point in the hiring process, but especially right away.

It is always assumed that one can provide references. So writing "References available upon request" wastes valuable résumé real estate. Unless asked to include references, expect that these will be requested later in the hiring process. Be sure that references have agreed to support your candidacy for a position. If you suspect they may be contacted, give them advanced warning. When asked to provide references in the résumé or application package, use the same layout and design as other materials to maintain aesthetic consistency.

The following examples demonstrate how some of these concepts are used to provide feedback to clients. Note that the end result is not perfect, but much better than the original. Also keep in mind that feedback is provided based on specific position announcements. Unfortunately, the position announcements cannot be included due to copyright issues. Use these examples in class to discuss not only the résumés, but whether the feedback is appropriate and useful. How might the process have been improved?

Example 1: Original Document

M. H.
0000 Street Place
City, St 12345
(555)555-5555

Profile
Texas State Board Certified - Social Studies 8-12, Life Science 8-12
Committed and compassionate teacher seeking to use my talent and abilities to serve the community.   Adaptable, patient, and persistent; nonjudgmental and very caring.
Additional strengths include:

Teaching experience	Ability to motivate and inspire	Leader
Positive and confident attitude	Organizational skills	Proficient in Spanish

Education
B.A. History and Military Science	2003
University of Texas at Arlington: Arlington, TX	
Education Certification, Ottawa University: Phoenix, AZ	2005

Present Experience
Student teacher/ Substitute teacher   01/2005-05/2005
Red Mountain, Mesa Unified School District (Arizona)
    Taught U. S. Government for 5 months
    Taught all grade levels while substituting   10/2004-12/2005
Substitute teacher for the Dallas Independent School District
    Teach all grade levels   02/2006-Present

Related Experience
U. S. Army
    Platoon Sergeant/ Trained and counseled Soldiers
    Taught classes for Soldier readiness
    Serverd in "Operation Desert Watch" (Saudi Arabi)   12/1996-12/2000
U. S. Army Reserves
    Taught class for Soldier readiness   01/2001-Present
    Company Commander of (59) personnel for (1) year.   01/2006-5/2007
    Captain/ Platoon Leader-Responsible for the technical and tactical training and
    professional development of twenty-one Soldiers   02/1994-12/1996
    Served in "Operation Iraqi Freedom". Awarded bronze star medal
                                                            04/2007-08/2008
Youth Group Minister
    Mentor and educator for students learning about their faith with the Church
                                                            08/2008-Present

Example 1: Round 1 Feedback

Examples are provided to client, as well as one-page of written feedback.

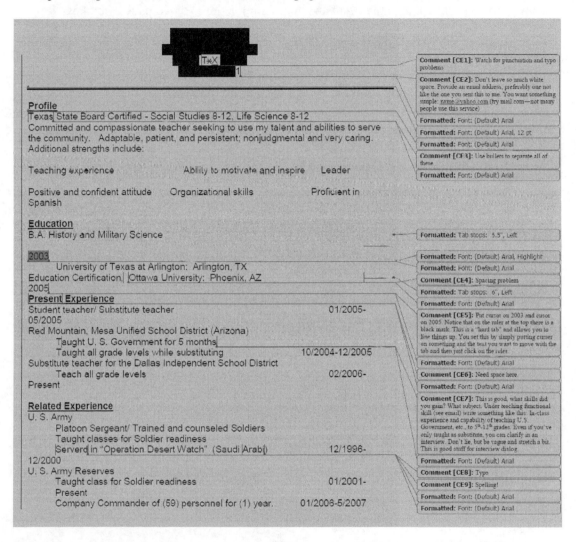

Profile

Texas State Board Certified - Social Studies 8-12, Life Science 8-12

Committed and compassionate teacher seeking to use my talent and abilities to serve the community.   Adaptable, patient, and persistent; nonjudgmental and very caring. Additional strengths include:

Teaching experience   Ability to motivate and inspire   Leader

Positive and confident attitude   Organizational skills   Proficient in Spanish

Education

B.A. History and Military Science

2003

    University of Texas at Arlington: Arlington, TX

Education Certification. Ottawa University: Phoenix, AZ

2005

Present Experience

Student teacher/ Substitute teacher   01/2005-05/2005

Red Mountain, Mesa Unified School District (Arizona)

    Taught U. S. Government for 5 months

    Taught all grade levels while substituting   10/2004-12/2005

Substitute teacher for the Dallas Independent School District

    Teach all grade levels   02/2006-Present

Related Experience

U. S. Army

    Platoon Sergeant/ Trained and counseled Soldiers

    Taught classes for Soldier readiness

    Serverd in "Operation Desert Watch" (Saudi Arabi)   12/1996-12/2000

U. S. Army Reserves

    Taught class for Soldier readiness   01/2001-Present

    Company Commander of (59) personnel for (1) year. 01/2006-5/2007

Comment [CE1]: Watch for punctuation and typo problems

Comment [CE2]: Don't leave so much white space. Provide an email address, preferably one not like the one you sent this to me. You want something simple: name.a.yahoo.com (try mail.com—not many people use this service)

Formatted: Font: (Default) Arial

Formatted: Font: (Default) Arial, 12 pt

Formatted: Font: (Default) Arial

Comment [CE3]: Use bullets to separate all of these

Formatted: Font: (Default) Arial

Formatted: Tab stops: 5.5", Left

Formatted: Font: (Default) Arial, Highlight

Formatted: Font: (Default) Arial

Comment [CE4]: Spacing problem

Formatted: Tab stops: 6", Left

Formatted: Font: (Default) Arial

Comment [CE5]: Put cursor on 2003 and cursor on 2005. Notice that on the ruler at the top there is a black mark. This is a "hard tab" and allows you to line things up. You set this by simply putting cursor on something and the text you want to move with the tab and then just click on the ruler.

Formatted: Font: (Default) Arial

Comment [CE6]: Need space here.

Formatted: Font: (Default) Arial

Comment [CE7]: This is good, what skills did you gain? What subject. Under teaching functional skill (see email) write something like this: In-class experience and capability of teaching U.S. Government, etc., to 5th-11th grades. Even if you've only taught as substitute, you can clarify in an interview. Don't lie, but be vague and stretch a bit. This is good stuff for interview dialog.

Formatted: Font: (Default) Arial

Comment [CE8]: Typo

Comment [CE9]: Spelling!

Formatted: Font: (Default) Arial

Formatted: Font: (Default) Arial

Example 1: Round 3 Feedback

This version, third in the process, focuses on content. The organization is looking better after two revisions. The client is applying to an education position, so two pages are okay.

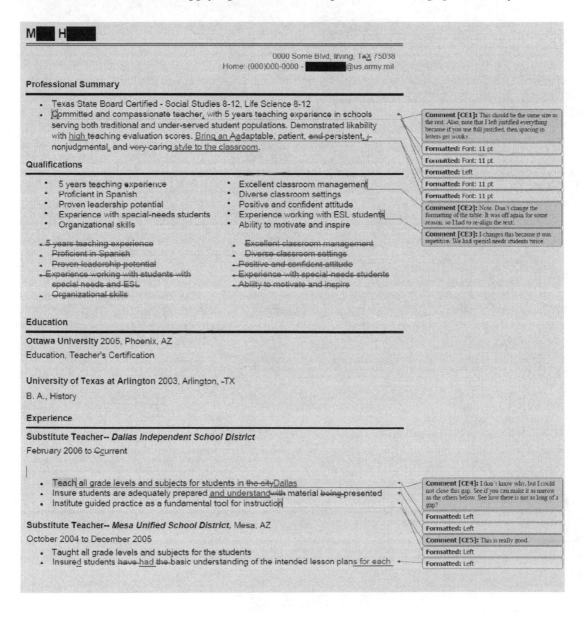

class meeting
- Delivered the proper guidance and correspondence during class that prepares students for examinations

Experience (cont'd)

Student Teacher—Red Mountain High School, Mesa, AZ
January 2005 to May 2005
- Taught U. S. Government for 5 months to seniors

Certifications

- Texas State Board Certified in Social Studies and Life Science grades 8-12

Leadership Expertise

Captain/ Platoon Leader

January 2001 to ~~Current~~current

U. S. Army Reserves – Grand Prairie, TX
- Responsible for the professional development of twenty-one Soldiers.
- Served in "Operation Iraqi Freedom" Worked with a diverse population of Iraqi citizens in order to maintain positive relations.
- Cared for troops through strategic planning and by facilitating effective communication among Soldiers and Department of Defense civilians

Platoon Sergeant

December 1996 to December 2000

U. S. Army – Ft. Bliss, TX
- Trained and counseled Soldiers to be tactical and technically proficient
- Taught 80 classes for "Soldier readiness" to insure ~~they~~ troops were knowledgeable about mitigating combat risk
- Demonstrated enhanced cross-cultural communication skills while serving in "Operation Desert Watch" (Saudi Arabia)

Community Involvement

As a Youth Group Minister and Mentor, I have been educator and guidance counselor for students interested in learning about their spirituality

Affiliations

- Golden Key Honor Society
- Member of the United States Army Reserves

Formatted: Left

Comment [CE6]: Never separate a section from itself. Unless it is a really long list.

Comment [CE7]: This is optional, but I think it looks sexier. Not that I want to make out with it sexy, but more like Helvetica sexy.

Comment [CE8]: The bullet to the left is larger than all others. You want this to be balanced. NEVER MIND. FIXED IT.

Comment [CE9]: Can you think of one more bullet to add? Did you get any kind of high recommendation or honor? Did you implement anything that the teacher liked and said she or he would continue to use?

Comment [CE10]: Technically, the lower case is grammatically correct, but it's your call. Some people like that Caps because it looks more balanced.

Formatted: Left, Tab stops: 0.46", List tab + Not at 1"

Formatted: Left, Tab stops: 0.46", List tab + Not at 1"

Formatted: Left, Tab stops: 0.46", List tab + Not at 1"

Formatted: Left, Tab stops: 0.46", List tab + Not at 1"

Formatted: Left, Tab stops: 0.46", List tab + Not at 1"

Formatted: Left, Tab stops: 0.46", List tab + Not at 1"

Example 1: Final Version

Name Redacted

0000 Redacted, CITY, TX 00000

Home: (000)000-0000 - aaaa.aaaaa@us.army.mil

Professional Summary

- Texas State Board Certified - Social Studies 8-12, Life Science 8-12
- Committed and compassionate teacher, with 5 years teaching experience in schools serving both traditional and under-served student populations. Demonstrated likability with high teaching evaluation scores. Bring an adaptable, patient, persistent, nonjudgmental, and caring style to the classroom.

Qualifications

- 5 years teaching experience
- Proficient in Spanish
- Proven leadership potential
- Experience with special-needs students
- Organizational skills
- Excellent classroom management
- Diverse classroom settings
- Positive and confident attitude
- Experience working with ESL students
- Ability to motivate and inspire

Education

Ottawa University 2005, Phoenix, AZ

Education, Teacher's Certification

University of Texas at Arlington 2003, Arlington, TX

B. A., History

Experience

Substitute Teacher-- *Dallas Independent School District*

February 2006 to current

- Teach all grade levels and subjects for students in Dallas
- Insure students are adequately prepared and understand material presented
- Institute guided practice as a fundamental tool for instruction

Substitute Teacher-- *Mesa Unified School District,* Mesa, AZ

October 2004 to December 2005

- Taught all grade levels and subjects for the students
- Insured students had basic understanding of the intended lesson plans for each class meeting
- Delivered the proper guidance and correspondence during class that prepares students for examinations

Experience (cont'd)

Student Teacher—Red Mountain High School, Mesa, AZ
January 2005 to May 2005
- Taught U. S. Government for 5 months to seniors

Certifications

- Texas State Board Certified in Social Studies and Life Science grades 8-12

Leadership Expertise

Captain/ Platoon Leader

January 2001 to current

U. S. Army Reserves – Grand Prairie, TX

- Responsible for the professional development of twenty-one Soldiers.
- Served in "Operation Iraqi Freedom" Worked with a diverse population of Iraqi citizens in order to maintain positive relations.
- Cared for troops through strategic planning and by facilitating effective communication among Soldiers and Department of Defense civilians

Platoon Sergeant

December 1996 to December 2000

U. S. Army – Ft. Bliss, TX

- Trained and counseled Soldiers to be tactical and technically proficient
- Taught 80 classes for "Soldier readiness" to insure troops were knowledgeable about mitigating combat risk
- Demonstrated enhanced cross-cultural communication skills while serving in "Operation Desert Watch" (Saudi Arabia)

Community Involvement

As a Youth Group Minister and Mentor, I have been educator and guidance counselor for students interested in learning about their spirituality

Affiliations

- Golden Key Honor Society
- Member of the United States Army Reserves

Example 2: Original Document

Use this example to do your own analysis.

J████████ R████████

Some Address, Elmhurst, IL 60126

(000) 000-0000, email@net.elmhurst.edu

OBJECTIVE

To obtain a position as a corporate recruiter for Groupon where I can apply my previous experience with my interpersonal and intercultural skills to recruit multiple sales representatives

EDUCATION

Elmhurst College, Elmhurst, Illinois

Bachelor of Science   Anticipated Dec. 2011

    Major: Intercultural Studies with a concentration in Human Resource Management and Diversity

    Minors: Business Administration and Communication Studies

    GPA: 3.83/4.00

Relevant coursework:

Diversity Recruitment	Human Resource Management
Business and Professional Communication	Intercultural Communication
Cultural Diversity in Organizations	Interpersonal Communication
Managerial Development for Women	Writing in Professional Fields

Capstone Project:

    Devised a strategic plan to attract diverse members, specifically in the lesbian, gay, bisexual, and transgendered community, to organizations and focused on how retention rates can be kept high and turnover rates low

Elmhurst College Study Away Experience, Cape Town, South Africa, Summer 2011

South Africa: Service and Interdisciplinary Study

- Volunteered at Mokone Primary School in the Langa township
- Led and instructed two fourth grade classrooms containing sixty students despite linguistic and cultural barriers
- Established rapport quickly with individuals in an unfamiliar environment
- Examined South Africa's political history, traditional and colonial cultures, religions, the "new South Africa" of the post-apartheid era, and social challenges related to education, poverty, and healthcare

Triton College, River Grove, Illinois, May 2009

General Education Studies

EMPLOYMENT

Recruiting and Development Intern, Northwestern Mutual, Oak Brook, Illinois, Oct. 2010-Present

- Aid the Director of Recruitment and Selection in sourcing possible full-time candidates
- Create and implement incentive plans for which existing employees are rewarded upon generation of full-time candidate referrals
- Participate in on-campus classroom presentations to recruit for the Financial Representative internship program and assist in the intern interview process
- Network with professors to discover qualified candidates for the internship program
- Coach and develop ten Financial Representative interns

Sales and Service Associate, JPMorgan Chase, Elmhurst, Illinois, Feb. 2008-Apr. 2009
- Investigated fraudulent account issues
- Resolved customer complaints in a professional and ethical manner
- Assisted in the preparation of loan documents
- Examined customers' financial situations and suggested appropriate services
- Worked alongside manager to complete daily banking tasks

Teller, JPMorgan Chase, Elmhurst, Illinois, Sept. 2006-Feb. 2008
- Processed financial transactions
- Executed the opening and closing procedures of the branch
- Evaluated customers' needs and referred them to the proper financial representative

VOLUNTEERISM
Feed My Starving Children, Schaumburg, Illinois, Apr. 2011-Present
- Hand-pack meals that are specifically formulated for malnourished children

Public Action to Deliver Shelter (P.A.D.S.), Elmhurst, Illinois, Oct. 2009
- Aided and facilitated in the preparation of comfortable surroundings for the homeless

HONORS

Transfer Excellence Scholarship	2009-Present
Phi Theta Kappa Scholarship	2009-Present
Elmhurst College Dean's List	2009-Present
Phi Theta Kappa Honors Society	2008-Present
Triton College Scholars Program	2008-2009
Triton College President's Honors List	2006-2009

ACTIVITIES

Global Poverty Club	2011-Present
Elmhurst College Mentoring Program	2011-Present
Triton Accounting Club	2007-2008

SKILLS
Fluent in English and Spanish
Strong interpersonal communication skills
Experienced in Microsoft Office Suite, Microsoft Publisher, and Microsoft Outlook
Independent and self-disciplined while being sensitive to the needs of others
Intercultural sensitivity
Excellent multitasking abilities

REFERENCES
Available upon request

Example 2: Final Document

After two revisions, this is the final document. How does this compare to your notes?

| J█████████ R█████ | ██████████ Willow Street (630) 202-████ |
| | ████████ IL   e-mail:██████████@net.elmhurst.edu |

Education

Elmhurst College – Elmhurst, IL   Feb. 2012
    Bachelor of Science   3.83 GPA
    Intercultural Studies I Human Resources Management and Diversity

    Relevant Coursework:

Diversity Recruitment	Human Resources Management
Business and Professional Communication	Intercultural Communication
Cultural Diversity in Organizations	Interpersonal Communication
Managerial Development for Women	Negotiations Theory and Practice

Relevant Employment History

2010-Present	Recruiting and Development Intern	Northwestern Mutual	Oak Brook, IL
2006-2009	Sales and Customer Service Associate	JPMorgan Chase	Elmhurst, IL

Areas of Experience and Transferable Skills

Human Resources
- Knowledge of the Americans with Disabilities Act
- Managed ten financial representative interns to assist them in attaining their weekly professional objectives
- Assisted the Director of Recruitment in screening and recruiting prospective full-time candidates
- Established and implemented an incentive plan for which existing employees were rewarded upon generation of full-time candidate referrals
- Created a job description and established guidelines for a marketing internship position for a large financial services company

Diversity and Training
- Devised a strategic plan to attract diverse members, specifically in the lesbian, gay, bisexual, and transgendered community, to organizations and focused on how retention rates can be kept high and turnover rates low
- Prepared and delivered a series of informational presentations on a variety of diversity-related issues

Communication
- Fluent in Spanish and English
- Delivered formal and informal presentations to audiences in both business and academic settings
- Communicated and provided cross-cultural instruction to sixty students in South Africa
- Completed numerous college-level communication courses, specifically in the areas of interpersonal and intercultural communication
- Intermediate level skill in Microsoft Office (Word, Excel, PowerPoint) and Microsoft Outlook

A Mini Case Study of the HP Spy Scandal

Overview

In the run-up to CEO Carly Fiorina's tumultuous and forced departure from Hewlett-Packard (HP) in early 2005, sensitive and damaging boardroom information was leaked to the press. A *Wall Street Journal* article, for example, provides a descriptive account of an off-site retreat in which board members discussed the company's pressing problems. Reportedly, the board was becoming increasingly frustrated with its CEO and wanted Fiorina to hand over some responsibilities to fellow executives. Although Fiorina's days were numbered, she made it clear that the leaks had to stop by phoning "each board member personally" and giving each one "a stern lecture on the importance of confidentiality" (Kaplan, 2006b).

Until early 2006, it had appeared that the drips of secretive information to the press had ceased. Then CNET, an online technology news site, published an article about HP's long-term strategy and provided clues from an anonymous source that only a person attending high-profile meetings would have known. While the CNET article has been generally interpreted as "upbeat and innocuous" (Kaplan, 2006b), HP's non-executive chairperson, Patricia Dunn, vowed to uncover the source of the leaks and finally put an end to them. Thus, the investigation that would eventually end with a public relations nightmare, criminal investigations, and civil lawsuits was launched.

At a board meeting on May 18, 2006, Dunn provided details of the surveillance and outed the leaker as George Keyworth, the longest serving member of the board. Keyworth admitted to being the CNET leak, apologized to the board, and noted, "I would have told you all about this. Why didn't you just ask?" (Kaplan, 2006a). Keyworth was asked to resign at this meeting, but refused. He resigned on September 2006, just after the first articles about the spying scandal were going to press, so that "every aspect of this unfortunate matter [can] be put in the past" (Hewlett Packard, 2006). In the press release regarding his resignation, he criticized the investigation, maintained that he had done nothing wrong, and suggested that he was not the source of earlier leaks:

> The invasion of my privacy and that of others was ill-conceived and inconsistent with HP's values. I acknowledge that I was a source for a CNET article that appeared in January 2006. I was frequently asked by HP corporate communications officials to speak with reporters—both on the record and on background—in an effort to provide the perspective of a longstanding board member with continuity over much of the company's history. My comments were always praised by senior company officials as helpful to the company—which has always been my intention. (Hewlett Packard, 2006)

If what Keyworth notes is accurate, the investigation and its aftermath demonstrates the limitations and potential problems of organizational intelligence gathering and begs to question whether it is reliable or an effective means of obtaining information. Also it raises concerns that its widespread use of covert operations led to a culture of paranoia and additional ethical and legal challenges for an organization.

Outsourcing the Investigation, or "Plausible Deniability"?

According to one of the earliest reports regarding the scandal, "Dunn referred the matter [regarding leaks] to HP's general counsel [Ann Baskins]. In turn, that office contracted out the investigation to security experts who then recruited private investigators who took the extraordinary step of spying on the phone records of all the directors (including Dunn), as well as journalists (including the CNET reporter)" (Kaplan, 2006b). The external private investigators obtained phone records by "pretexting," a common practice whereby security consultants use "false pretenses" and other deceptive tactics to obtain another's non-public information.[1] As part of their investigation into the leak, private investigators called phone company providers (e.g., AT&T and Verizon) and obtained phone records by providing no more than a home address, account number, and the last four digits of the account holder's Social Security Number. By cross referencing telephone numbers, the investigators were able to deduce which board member had been making calls to the CNET reporter.

As chairperson of the board, Dunn was obligated to protect the organization and its shareholders. Whether press leaks were a legitimate threat to the company is perhaps a matter of perspective. Nevertheless, Dunn felt that identifying and punishing the culprit(s) was in HP's best interest. There are various ways in which the issue could have been addressed. While CEO,

---

[1]Read this interesting *The New York Times* article by William Safire (2006), which includes a discussion of the "language of pretexting": www.nytimes.com/2006/09/24/magazine/24wwln_safire.html

Fiorina personally called all the board members and reminded them about the importance of confidentiality (Kaplan, 2006a). Having decided to open an investigation into the matter, however, it is reasonable that Dunn outsourced the matter so that she could attend to other matters while the investigation was ongoing.

Dunn maintains that she thought that the phone records could be obtained through legal methods. During the course of the investigation and congressional hearings, she noted that she didn't realize that pretexting involved identity misrepresentation. Nevertheless, concerns have been raised that Dunn could have intentionally avoided knowing details about the investigation and that the long list of people to whom the matter was outsourced was an attempt to create "plausible deniability"—the denial of knowledge of the activities of people lower in the chain of command and hierarchical order of an organization (Kaplan, 2006b). Because only the lowest-ranking member of all the actors involved faced jail time (Robertson, 2009), one could argue that people in higher positions of authority, and with greater amounts of power, can engage in ethically and legally questionable behavior with little chance of being held accountable.

Discussion Questions

1. Do you think that Patricia Dunn should be held ethically or legally accountable for the actions of the private investigator?

2. Do you think pretexting (faking a profile to obtain information) should be legal? Is it ethical?

3. Given the plethora and availability of technological devices that can easily record and store sensitive data, or accidentally or purposefully expose a company to threats, how should managers deal with these devices?

4. Should employees be offended if they are not allowed to bring electronic devices into their workplace?

5. Faced with leaks of sensitive information, what activities should a company engage in to protect itself?

6. What are the ethical problems that might arise through undercover policies or practices?

7. How would you have responded to the board leaks if you were in a position to do so?

8. How do your responses fit with the creation and maintenance of a collaborative work environment (draw upon material from Chapter 8)?

References

Hewlett Packard. (2006, September 12). *George Keyworth resigns as HP director* [Press Release]. Retrieved from www.hp.com/hpinfo/newsroom/press/2006/060912b.html

Kaplan, D. A. (2006a, September 12). Hewlett-Packard sets emergency board meeting. *Newsweek.com.* Retrieved from www.newsweek.com/2006/09/07/hewlett-packard-sets-emergency-board-meeting.html

Kaplan, D. A. (2006b, September 12). Suspicions and spies in Silicon Valley. *Newsweek.com.* Retrieved from www.newsweek.com/2006/09/17/suspicions-and-spies-in-silicon-valley.html

Robertson, J. (2009, August 12). Sentencing looms in HP phone-record scandal. *The Christian Science Monitor.* Retrieved from www.csmonitor.com/Innovation/Responsible-Tech/2009/0812/sentencing-looms-in-hp-phone-record-scandal.

Index

Ability in interpretive
    rhetoric, 25
*About Face: Reviving the
    Rules of Typography*
    (Jury), 100–101
Abstract in report, 200
Action in Monroe's
    Motivated Sequence,
    192
Action verbs, 152
Active voice, 71, 88
Ad hominem arguments,
    203
Adobe Acrobat Pro, 202
Adobe InDesign, 239
AdWords Keyword
    Generator, 340
Agenda templates, 268
Amazon Mcchanical Turk,
    315
Ambiguity, 28
American Institute of
    Certified Public
    Accountants, 130
American Management
    Association, 278
Analytical reports, 199
Analytic skills, 7
Annotated maps, 242
Apostrophes, 89
Appearance in employment
    search process, 167
Appendixes in reports, 202
Apple Final Cut Pro, 105
Apple iPad, 108
Application letter, 156–60,
    180, 182–83
    body, 157–58
    closing, 158
    example of, 159

salutation and opening,
    156–57
Application program
    interface (API)
    services, 315
Approach, 53–54, 55
Archiving, 300
Argumentative fallacies, 85
Aristotle
    canons of rhetoric and,
        33–37
    classes of rhetoric
        identified by, 32–33
    kairos and, 42–43
    persuasive appeals
        described by, 25,
        38–40
    rhetoric defined by, 25
Arrangement
    as cannon of rhetoric, 34,
        35
    in crafting concise and
        extensive artifacts,
        173, 175
    in résumés, 145–50
Articulation in oral delivery,
    113
ASCII documents, 155
*Associated Press Stylebook,
    The,* 80
Asterisks in email, 216
Asynchronous messaging,
    214
Attention in Monroe's
    Motivated Sequence,
    191
Audience
    characteristics, 51–53
    critical and conflicted, 55
    hostile, 55

résumés, 141–42
    in rhetorical situations, 41
    in search engine
        optimization, 341
    type, 55
Audio editors, 226
Audio slide, 235
Augmented reality
    applications, 242

Background investigations,
    131, 297
Backlinks, 343
Back matter in reports, 202
BackType, 338
Balanced design, 95
Baskins, Ann, 380
Behavioral interviews, 162
Benefits, negotiating, 167–68
Berkun, Scott, 231
Biased language in
    quotations, 81
Bibliography in reports, 202
Birth and adoption of
    children, 261
Blackboard, 227
Blackshaw, Pete, 230
Bloggers, 218
Blogging services, 218
Blog hosting sites, 14
Blogs, 218–20, 335
    corporate recruiting, 136
    invention and, 219
    style of, 219–20
Body
    of application letter,
        157–58
    of letters, 181–82
    of reports, 200–202
Boeing, 23

Boilerplating, 57–58

Boldface, 101, 102

Bona fide occupational qualifications (BFOQ), 166

Bookmarks, 133–34

Bottom marker, 98

Boundary-spanning unit (BSU), 281, 282–84

Brainstorming, 54, 56

BRIC countries, 5

Bridges in paragraphs, 79

Briefings, 192–93

Brochures, 189–90
  panels in, 190
  printing and distributing, 190
  templates for, 190
  writing and designing, 189–90

Broker, Trader, Lawyer, Spy: The Secret World of Corporate Espionage (Javers), 297

Brummett, Barry, 28

Bullying in workplace, 252

Burke, Kenneth, 28

Burnout, 259

Business periodicals and newspapers, 136

Business to business connections (B2B), 229

Buzz sessions, 58

Callicles, 24

Canons of rhetoric, 33–38
  in arrangement, 34, 35
  in concise communications, 172–76
  in delivery, 36, 37

in electronic communications, 211–13

in extensive communications, 172–76, 202

in invention, 34, 35

in memory, 36, 37

in pitches, 191

in questions and answers, 193

in résumés, 140–56

in social networking, 316–17

in style, 34, 36, 37

in writing and designing a brochure, 189

Capital letters
  in email, 216
  to emphasize important headings or words, 101

Career choices, 9–12

Cascade Engineering, 265

Cascading Style Sheets (CSS), 155, 327–29

CastingWords, 315

Categorical pattern, 64

Causal (cause-effect) pattern, 65

Cause-and-effect infographics, 241

Center tab stop, 98

Chen, Perry, 314

Chicago Manual of Style, The, 80, 81

Chronological infographics, 241

Chronological (temporal) pattern, 64

Chronological résumé, 146–47, 149

Cicero, 33

Citations, 81

Clark, Raymond, 251–52

CLEAR, 196

Closing, 158, 182

Cloud computing, 6
  collaborative software, 267
  files saved and backed up with, 305
  presentation programs, 236–37
  telephony services, 222

Clustering, 56–57

CNET, 379–81

Collaboration in teams and groups, 270–73

Collaboration skills, 7

Collapse of sensemaking, 7

Colloquium, 205

Color, 100

Columns, 100

Comments that excite and concern, 144–45

Communications
  concise, 171–95
  design, 94–104
  distribution, 104–16
  electronic, 209–45
  evaluation, 116–21
  extensive, 195–205
  format of written and verbal, 34
  four-step artifact construction process, 47–90
  gathering, sharing, and protecting, 277–310
  gathering information and, 280–300
  information and, 280–308
  media, advantages and disadvantages of, 352–53

résumés, 127–69
rhetorical approach to, 21–44
writing process, 47–90
Communication students. *See also* Text
approach to class by, 9–14
career choices, 9–12
continued learning, 16
interpretive frame of mind and, 2–5
majors, declaring, 14
questions asked by, anticipated, 5–8
skills, obtaining and improving, 13, 16
theoretical focus, integrated, 15–16
Community of Science, 198
Comparison infographics, 241
Complete (memory and delivery), 83–89
argumentative fallacies, 85
grammatical and mechanical errors, 85–89
revising, 83–85
writing tips, 84
Complex sentence, 76
Compound-complex sentence, 76–77
Compound sentence, 76
Computer monitoring, 261
Concise communications, 171–95
brochures, 189–90
cover letter (transmittal), 182–83
delivering information, canons applied to, 172–76

forms, 187–89
letters, 178–82
memorandum (memo), 183–85, 186
oral briefings, 192–93
pitches, 191–92
press releases, 185–87
questions and answers, 193–95
spoken types of, 190–95
strategies for crafting, 177–78
written types of, 178–90
Conclusion, 82–83, 202
Conflict in teams and groups, 270–73
Confrontational approach to communication, 54, 55
Consistent design, 95
Constraints in rhetorical situations, 41
Consumer Price Index, 167
Contact information on résumé, 365–66
Contingency plans, 196
Continuing education, 16, 136–37
Continuing pages in letters, 182
Conversations, 160
Corporate espionage, 296
Corson, Christopher, 23
Cosmology episode, 7
Cost of distribution, 106
Counseling, career or wellness, 138
Cover letter (transmittal), 180, 182–83. *See also* Application letter
Covert data gathering methods, 295–98

background investigations, 297
electronic monitoring, 297
ethics in, 300
skip tracing, 298
surveillance, 297
undercover operations, 297
Creative Problem Solving for Manager (Proctor), 287
Credit checks, 297
CREDO*Reference,* 136
Criminal record, 154–55
Critical and conflicted audience, 55
Criticism, rhetorical, 31, 287–88
Crowdsourcing, 313–15
Curriculum vitae, 128

Dashboard software manufacturers, 201
Death by PowerPoint, 236, 360–62
Decimal tab stop, 98
Declarative sentence, 77
Deletions and omissions, 80
Deliberative rhetoric, 32
Delivering information, canons applied to, 172–76
arrangement, 173, 175
delivery methods, 175–76
invention, 173, 174
memory, 175–76
style, 175
Delivery
as cannon of rhetoric, 36, 37

Delivery (*con't*)
   in crafting concise and extensive artifacts, 175–76
   in résumés, 155–56
Delphi method, 287
Deming, William Edwards, 263
Demographic trends, 5–8
Department of Labor, 257, 261, 265
Department of Professional Regulation, 132
Department of the Secretary of State, 132
Design, 94–104
   balanced, 95
   of brochures, 189–90
   consistent, 95
   document formatting, 95–102
   email, elements used in, 216–17
   embedded objects, 103–4
   restrained, 94–95
Diagrams, 242
Digital presentation software (slide decks), 236
Direct approach
   to communication, 54, 55
   to messages, 174–75
Directional infographics, 241
Directions, willingness to follow, 7
Directive memo, 185
Direct quotations, 80–81
Direct text marketing campaigns, 214
Distribution, 104–16
   availability, 106
   cost, 106
   oral delivery, 108–14

presentation aids, 115–16
rhetorical impact, 104, 105–6
security and privacy, 107
social media, issues specific to, 107–8
time, 106
Document cameras, 234
Document formatting, 95–102
   color, 100
   columns, 100
   footers, 99
   headers, 99
   headings, 98–99
   justification, 97–98
   lists, 99–100
   margins, 97, 98
   notes, 99
   page layout, 95–96
   shading, 100
   tabs, 97, 98
   typography, 100–102
   white space, 96–97
Documents
   backing up and transporting, 305–6
   saving with names, 303–5
Domains for personal sites, 13
Domino's, 230
Doodling, 57
Double-space between paragraphs in email, 217
Doyle, Patrick, 230
Dress in employment search process, 167
Due diligence in protecting information and communications, 308
Dunn, Patricia, 300, 379–81
DVD, 235

Eats, Shoots & Leaves (Truss), 48
Eat Tweet (Evans), 171–72
Editing marks for instruction, 357
Education, continuing, 16, 136–37
Educational management systems, 227
Education on résumé, 366–67
Elective courses, 14
Electronic communications, 209–45
   blogs, 218–20
   canons applied to, 211–13
   email, 215–18
   instant messaging, 214–15
   microblogs, 228–29
   podcasting, 225–26
   Second Life, 227
   social networking and, 228–31
   social networking sites, 229
   teleconferencing, 222–25
   text messages, 213–14
   user-generated content sites, 229–31
   voice messages, 220–22
   written, 213–20
Electronic Communications Privacy Act (ECPA), 278
Electronic files, saving, 302–6
   backing up and transporting documents, 305–6
   saving documents with names, 303–5

software, finding appropriate, 303
strategy for, planning, 302–3
Electronic folders, 133–34
Electronic monitoring, 297
Electronic résumé, 149–50
Email, 209–11, 215–18
design elements used in, 216–17
effect on business and organizational processes, 209
example of, 218
memos attached to, 183, 184
mistakes and remedies, 358–59
problems associated with, 210
protocols for writing, sending, and replying to, 210–11
security and privacy in, 217–18
sending as web page, 217
workplace monitoring and surveillance, 278–79
Email platforms, 216
Embedded objects, 103–4, 105
Em dash in email, 217
Emotional concerns in work environments, 258–65
Emotional intelligence, 259
Emotional labor, 258–59
Emotional work, 258–59
Employee benefit security, 261
Employment search process, 129–69

application letter, 156–60
continuing education, 136–37
conversations, 160
counseling, 138
dress and appearance, 167
institutional environments, 130, 131
institutional trends, 131
interviews, 160–66
occupations, 129, 132
opportunities, searching for, 133–36
professional associations, 130
professions, 130, 132
resignations, 168
résumés, writing, 139–56
salary and benefits, negotiating, 167–68
shadowing, 132–33
social networking, 137–38
End notations in letters, 182
Enthymemes, 39
Epideictic rhetoric, 33
E-portfolios, 149–50, 155
Equal Employment Opportunity Commission (EEOC), 165, 166
Ergonomics, 261–63
Ethics
in gathering information and communications, 298–300
professionalism and, 7
technological implications, 6–7
in work environments, 260

Ethnography, 293–94
Ethos, 39–40
in proposals, 198
in résumés, 151
Evaluation, 116–21
feedback, 117, 118–21
reading and listening, 117–18
Evans, Maureen, 171–72
Excel, 289
Excel spreadsheets, 232, 241
Exclamatory sentence, 77
Executive dashboard, 201, 286
Executive summary in reports, 200–201
Exigence in rhetorical situations, 41
Experience, skills, and interesting substance on résumé, 367–68
Extensive communications, 195–205
canons applied to, 172–76, 202
colloquium, 205
forums, 203–4
panels, 204–5
plans, 195–97
proposals, 197–99
reports, 199–202
symposium, 205
verbal types of, 202–5
written types of, 195–202
Eye contact in oral delivery, 113–14

Facebook, 229, 314, 333–35, 344
Facebook analytic tools, 345
Facial expression in oral delivery, 114

Facilitation, defined, 254
Fair Labor Standards Act
    (FLSA), 260
Fallacies
    argumentative, 85
    logical and
        argumentative, 354–56
    syllogisms leading to, 39
Federal Business
    Opportunities, 198
Feedback
    preparing, 117
    providing, 118–21
    receiving, 121
    résumé, 371–73
FindRFP, 198
Fiorina, Carly, 379, 380–81
Fishbone diagramming, 58
Fisher, Walter, 26
Five Ws and one H of
    journalism, 186
Flexibility and stress
    management, 7
Flip charts, 233
Flow charts, 58, 242
Flying for Peanuts, 255
Focus groups, 58, 292
Font, 101–2
Food and Drug
    Administration,
    260–61
Footers, 99
Forensic rhetoric, 32–33
Foreward in report, 200
Formal reports. *See* Reports
Format of written and verbal
    communications, 34
Form-design software,
    188–89
Forms, 187–89
Forums, 203–4
Foss, Sonja, 31

Foundation Center, 198
Four-step artifact
    construction process,
    47–90. *See also
    individual headings*
    complete (memory and
        delivery), 83–89
    organize and outline
        (arrangement), 63–68
    prepare and research
        (invention), 49–63
    summary of, 50
    write (style), 68–83
Free speech in work
    environments, 261
Friedman, Milton, 265
Front matter in reports, 200
Full-block style, 178, 179
Functional résumé, 148, 149

Gathering information and
    communications,
    280–300
    boundary-spanning units
        in, 281, 282–84
    covert data gathering
        methods, 295–98, 300
    effective, 285–87
    ethical considerations in,
        298–300
    information overload, 286
    informed consent, 299
    intensive technology in,
        282
    long-linked technology
        in, 281
    measurements, 285–86
    mediating technology in,
        281–82
    privacy, 299
    research methods in,
        287–95

    rights to service, 299–300
    voluntary participation,
        299
General purpose of business
    messages, 53
Gestures in oral delivery,
    114
Gladwell, Malcolm, 286
Glossary in reports, 202
Google, 216
Google Alerts, 337
Google Analytics, 337, 345
Google Calendar, 267
Google Docs, 267
Google Image, 304
Google+, 229
Google Voice, 222
Gorgias, 24, 43
GoToMeeting, 212
Government agency forms,
    189
Grammatical and mechani-
    cal errors, 85–89
    apostrophes, 89
    hedging sentences, 87
    parallelism, 88
    passive voice, 88
    phrases, 87
    repetition, 87–88
    singular-plural
        agreement, 88–89
Graphs, 242
Greetings in letters, 181
Grint, Keith, 266
Groups. *See* Teams and
    groups, facilitating
Gutters, 96

Hanging indent, 98
Hankin, Ron, 297
Hard files, saving, 301–2
Headers, 99

Headings, 98–99, 181
Hedging sentences, 87
Helvetica (film), 101
Hermeneutical rhetoric, 25–26
Hermeneutics, 25
Herwald, Kurt, 255
Hewlett-Packard (HP) spy scandal, 300, 379–81
H1 tags, 341–43
Hootsuite, 336
Hostile audience, 55
Hsieh, Tony, 255
HTML (hypertext markup language), 155, 216, 329–31

Iacocca, Lee, 33
Idea pitch, 192–93
Idea writing, 58
Identification, rhetoric and, 31
Illinois Private Detective, Private Alarm, Private Security, Fingerprint Vendor, and Locksmith Act of 2004, 130
Imperative sentence, 77
Impression management, 7–8
Impromptu oral delivery, 111–12
Index in reports, 202
Indirect approach
    to communication, 54, 55
    to messages, 174–75
Indirect quotations, 81
Inexperience, 154
Infographics, 239–41
Informational brochures, 189

Informational reports, 199
Information and communications
    gathering, 280–300
    protecting, 307–8
    sharing, 300–306
Information overload, 286
Information Storage and Management, 307
Information tracking sheet, 134
Informed consent, 299
Inside address in letters, 181
Instant messaging (IM), 214–15
    platforms, 214
    tips for using, 215
Institutional environments, employment search and, 130, 131
Institutional trends in employment, 131
Instructional infographics, 241
Integrated marketing communications (IMC), 28
Intensive technology, 282
Intention in sentence construction, 77
Interactive résumé, 150
Intercultural sensitivity, 7
Intermittent underlines in email, 217
International Ergonomics Association, 261
International Labour Organization, 256–57
International sensitivity, 7
International trade and governance, 5

Interpretive frame of mind, 2–5
Interpretive rhetoric, 25–29
    defining, 25–26
    means of persuasion in, 25
    particularity in, 25
    value of, 27–29
Interpretive skills, 7
Interrogative sentence, 77
Interview questions, 163–66
    behavioral, 164
    BFOQ, 166
    common, 163–64
    EEOC regulations, 165, 166
    illegal, 165–66
    by interviewee, 164–65
Interviews, 160–66
    behavioral, 162
    follow-up, 166
    informal, conversational, 292
    interpretive, 292
    negotiation stage, 161
    open-ended, 161–62
    panel and group, 162
    questions (*See* Interview questions)
    screening stage, 160, 161, 166
    Second Life, 163
    selection stage, 161, 166
    situational, 162
    stress, 162
    for survey-based research, 291, 292–93
    telephone, 162–63
    transcribing, 292
    types of, 161–62
    video, 163
    work, 162

Intrapersonal deliberation, 32
Introduction, 82, 201
Invention
    as cannon of rhetoric, 34, 35
    in crafting concise and extensive artifacts, 173, 174
Invention in résumés, 140–45
    audience, understanding, 141–42
    job description, analyzing, 142–45
    SWOT analysis, 140–41
Invitational approach to communication, 54, 55
Invitational rhetoric, 177
Invitation for bid (IFB), 197–98
Isocrates, 43
Italics, 101

Javers, Eamon, 297
Job changes, frequent, 153
Job description, analyzing, 142–45
    comments that excite and concern, 144–45
    word choice, patterns in, 142–44
Job sites, 134–35
Journalism, five Ws and one H of, 186
Journalistic approach, 57
Jungle, The (Sinclair), 260
Jury, David, 100–101
Justification, 97–98

Kairos, 42–43
Kelleher, Herb, 255
Keller, Fred, 265

Kemple, K. Richmond, 196
Keynote, 197
Keyword generator tools, 340
Keyword tags, 341–43
Keyworth, George, 379–80
Kickstarter.com, 313–14
Kvale, Steinar, 292

Language rules in work environments, 261
Laws
    to promote and sustain safe work environments, 260–61
    in protecting information and communications, 307
Le, Annie, 251–52
Left-justified (ragged-right) margins, 98
Left tab stop, 98
Lessons in Loyalty, 254
Letters, 178–82
    body, 181–82
    closing, 182
    continuing pages, 182
    cover, 180, 182–83
    end notations, 182
    heading, 181
    inside address, 181
    salutation, 181
    style, 178–80
    templates for, 178
    writer's signature block, 182
LinkedIn, 229, 331–33
Links, 343
Listening skills, 7, 117–18
Lists
    in document formatting, 99–100
    of figures in report, 200

Logos, 38–39
    in proposals, 199
    in résumés, 153–55
Long-linked technology, 281
Lorem ipsum text, 96

Majors, declaring, 14
Mak, Caroline, 313–14
Manuscript, oral delivery by, 109–10
Maps, 242
Margins, 97, 98
Marking quotations, 80
Mass customization printing websites, 190
Materials, inserting in quotations, 81
McLaren v. Microsoft, 279
Means of persuasion in interpretive rhetoric, 25
Meat Inspection Act, 260
Mechanical errors. *See* Grammatical and mechanical errors
Mediating technology, 281–82
Medium, 63, 134
Meetings in teams and groups, 267–70
Memorandum (memo), 183–85, 186
Memory
    as cannon of rhetoric, 36, 37
    in crafting concise and extensive artifacts, 175–76
    oral delivery by, 110–11
    in résumés, 155–56
MetaLab Whiteboard, 227
Metaphoric analysis, 271–72

Michael Smyth v. The Pillsbury Company, 277–78
Microblogs, 228–29
Micro-lending companies, 315
Microsoft Excel, 232, 241
Microsoft Expression Design, 239, 241
Microsoft Lync, 212
Microsoft Office Publisher, 189
Microsoft OneNote, 303
Microsoft templates
    agenda, 268
    for brochures, 190
    for letters, 178
Microsoft Word, 98, 241
Mikogo, 212
Mind mapping, 56–57
Mini résumé, 150
MLA Style Manual, The, 80, 81
Mnemonic devices, 175–76
Moderator, 203, 204, 205
Monotype Imaging Holdings Inc., 101
Monroe, Alan, 191
Monroe's Motivated Sequence, 191–92
Moodle, 227
MP3 (.mp3) file format, 226
Multimedia content, 335
Multimedia Messaging Service (MMS), 213
Multimedia object and document software programs, 105
Musculoskeletal disorders (MSDs), 257, 262
Myspace, 229
Mystery shoppers and customers, 293

Name on résumé, 365–66
Narrative rhetoric, 26–29
    defining, 26–27
    value of, 27–29
National Labor Relations Board, 23
Navigating the Legal Minefield (Hankin), 297
Need in Monroe's Motivated Sequence, 191
Negative metaphors, 272
Negotiation skills, 7
Negotiation stage, 161
Nervous system injuries, 257
News releases, 185–87
Nielson Online, 230, 231
Nominal Group Technic, 287
Nominal group technique, 56
Nonprofit companies, 315
Notes, 99

Objectives on résumé, 366
Observational research, 293–94
Occupational Outlook Handbook (BLS), 132, 167
Occupational Safety and Health Act (OSH Act), 252, 260, 261
Occupational Safety and Health Administration (OSHA), 252, 257, 261, 265
Occupational Safety and Health Review Commission (OSHRC), 257
Occupations, 129, 132

Omissions, 80
Online content, generating, 327–31
    Cascading Style Sheets, 327–29
    HTML, 329–31
Online portfolios, 213
Online presence. *See also* Social networking
    content, generating, 327–31
    establishing, 323–36
    managing, 336–45
    reputations, monitoring, 337–38
    search engine optimization, 336, 338–44
    UGC sites, 331–36
    websites, 323–27
Online résumé, 149–50, 155
Online social networking, tips and strategies, 319, 321–22
Onof v. Nikon, 279
Open call problem, 13
Open-ended interviews, 161–62
Opening of application letter, 156–57
OpenOffice Impress, 236
Operational plans, 196
Opportunities, searching for, 133–36
Oral briefings, 192–93
Oral delivery, 108–14
    articulation, 113
    eye contact, 113–14
    facial expression, 114
    gestures, 114
    impromptu, 111–12
    by manuscript, 109–10
    by memory, 110–11
    message, preparing, 109

Oral delivery (*con't*)
pitch, 112
by simple outline, 110
speaking rate, 112–13
staging, 114
volume of speaker's
voice, 112
Organizational devices,
175–76
Organizational pattern in
pitch, 191–92
Organizational pattern that
limits scope, 64–66
causal (cause-effect)
pattern, 65
chronological (temporal)
pattern, 64
problem solution, 65
pro-con arrangement,
65–66
spatial pattern, 64–65
topical arrangement, 64
Organizational skills, 7
Organize and outline
(arrangement), 63–68
organizational pattern
that limits scope,
64–66
purpose-focused outline,
66–68
Orphan, 100
Outline, purpose-focused,
66–68
Overhead transparencies,
233–34
Over-qualification, 154

Page layout, 95–96
Panel and group interviews,
162
Panels, 204–5
Paragraphs, 78–80
bridges in, 79

coherence of, 79–80
elements of, 78–79
length of, 79
mechanics of, 79–80
support sentences in, 79
topic sentences in, 78–79
unity of, 79–80
Parallelism, 88
Particularity in interpretive
rhetoric, 25
Passive voice, 71, 88
Pathos, 40
in proposals, 198–99
in résumés, 151, 153
PBXs (private branch
exchanges), 222
PDSA (Plan, Do, Study,
Act) cycle, 263
Performance Evaluation and
Review Technique
(PERT), 287
Personal data on résumé,
368–69
Personal statements on
résumé, 366
Persuasive appeals, 38–40
ethos, 39–40
logos, 38–39
pathos, 40
Phrases, unnecessary, 87
Physical concerns in work
environments, 257,
259–65
Pictograph (pictogram), 242
Pitches, 191–92
Pitch in oral delivery, 112
Pizza Hut, 314–15
Plagiarism, 81, 196–97
Plain-text (ASCII) résumés,
155
Plans, 195–97
Plato, 24, 43
Podcasting, 225–26

Point of view (POV), 69–70
Portable document format
(PDF), 14, 155
Portfolio-sharing sites, 14
Positive metaphors, 272
Posters, 234–35
PowerPoint, 197, 213, 235,
236
death by, 236, 360–62
Preface (synopsis) in report,
200
Prepare and research
(invention), 49–63
audience characteristics,
51–53
medium, 63
primary research, 58–59
purpose and approach,
53–54, 55
research checklist,
reminders, and tips, 62
rhetorical situations,
50–51
secondary research,
59–61
what you know and need
to say, 54, 56–58
Presentation aids, 115–16,
231–42
audio slide, 235
digital presentation
software (slide decks),
236
document cameras, 234
DVD, 235
flip charts, 233
infographics, 239–41
overhead transparencies,
233–34
posters, 234–35
presentation software
alternatives, 236–39
Prezi, 236, 237–39

SlideRocket, 236–37
technologies for
     displaying visuals,
     232–39
using, 232–39
video, 235
visual aids, 241–42
whiteboards, 233
Presentation software, 236
Presentation software
     alternatives, 236–39
Press releases, 185–87
Prezi, 236, 237–39
Primary research, 58–59
PrimoPDF, 155
Prison Entrepreneurship
     Program, 153
Privacy
     in distribution, 107
     in email, 217–18
     in gathering information
     and communications,
     299
     in work environments,
     261
Privacy Rights
     Clearinghouse (PRC),
     305–6, 307
PRLOG, 186
PR Newswire, 186
Problem solution, 65
Pro-con arrangement, 65–66
Proctor, Tony, 287
Production software, 213
Professional associations,
     130
Professional
     communications.
     See Communications
Professionalism, ethics and, 7
Professions
     defined, 130
     learning about, 132

Proofreading marks for
     instruction, 357
Proposals, 197–99
Protecting information and
     communications,
     307–8
     due diligence in, 308
     laws in, 307
     purging and shredding
     files, 308
     technology in, 308
*Publication Manual of the
     American
     Psychological
     Association,* 80, 81
Public Relations Quarterly,
     196
Punctuation in quotations,
     81
Purging files, 308
Purpose and approach,
     53–54, 55
Purpose-focused outline,
     66–68
Purpose of business
     messages, 53–54, 55

*Qualitative Communication
     Research Methods*
     (Lindlof and Taylor),
     294
Qualitative Research
     Consultants
     Association, 294
Quality circles, 263–64
Quantitative infographics,
     241
Question-answer chain,
     57
Questions and answers
     (Q&A), 193–95
Questions asked by students,
     anticipated, 5–8

Questions to ask when
     revising, 83
Quotations, 80–81
     deletions and omissions,
     80
     direct, 80–81
     indirect, 81
     inserting materials, 81
     marking, 80
     punctuation in, 81
     within quotations, 81
     typos or biased language
     in, 81
Quoting references in email,
     217

Ramos, Antonio, 313–14
Rationing, 283
Reading, improving, 117–18
Recruiting blogs and
     periodicals, 136
Reference list in reports, 202
References
     quoted in email, 217
     on résumé, 368–69
Regulations in work
     environments, 265
Repetition, 87–88
Repetitive strain injuries,
     257, 262
Reports, 199–202
     back matter, 202
     body, 200–202
     front matter, 200
     types of, 199–200
Repurposing, 57–58
Request for proposal (RFP),
     197–98
Research. *See* Prepare and
     research (invention)
Research methods, 287–95
     focus groups, 292
     interviews, 291, 292–93

Research methods (*con't*)
  observation, 293–94
  rhetorical criticism,
    287–88
  strengths and weaknesses
    in, 291
  survey-based research,
    288–91
Research resources, 350–51
Resignations, 168
Respondeat superior, 278
Response in email, 217
Response memo, 186
Restrained design, 94–95
Résumé, 127–29, 365–78
  action verbs, 152
  blunders, 154
  curriculum vitae, 128
  feedback, 371–73
  final version, examples
    of, 374–75, 378
  original, examples of,
    370, 376–77
  sharing online, 13–14
  speaking about, 160–66
    (*See also* Interviews)
Résumé, arrangement in,
    145–50
  elements, common and
    disputed, 145
  salutation and opening,
    156–57
Résumé, canons in, 140–56
  arrangement, 145–50
  delivery, 155–56
  invention, 140–45
  memory, 155–56
  style, 150–55
Résumé, writing, 139–56.
    See also Application
    letter
  canons, applying, 140–56
  rhetorical situations, 139

Résumé formats, 145–50
  chronological, 146–47,
    149
  electronic, 149–50, 155
  functional, 148, 149
  interactive, 150
  mini, 150
  video, 150, 155
Résumé items, 365–78
  education, 366–67
  experience, skills, and
    interesting substance,
    367–68
  name and contact
    information, 365–66
  personal data and
    references, 368–69
  personal statements and
    objectives, 366
Retweeting, 228
Review sites, 337
Revising, 83–85
RFP Database, The, 198
Rhetoric
  Aristotle and, 25, 32–37
  cannons of, 33–38
  classes of, 32–33
  concepts of, 29–30
  defining, 23–29
  deliberative, 32
  in distribution, 104,
    105–6
  epideictic, 33
  forensic, 32–33
  interpretive, 25–29
  invitational, 177
  kairos and, 42–43
  narrative, 26–29
  persuasive appeals and,
    38–40
  skills in, 7
Rhetorical criticism, 31,
    287–88

Rhetorical Criticism:
  Exploration and
  Practice (Foss), 31
Rhetorical situations
  audience in, 41
  constraints in, 41
  defined, 25–26, 41–42
  elements of, 41
  exigence in, 41
  kairos and, 42–43
  in prepare and research,
    50–51
  in résumés, 139
  in writing résumés, 139
Rhetorical tone
  in work environments,
    safe and collaborative,
    254–56
  in workplace monitoring
    and surveillance, 280
Right indent marker, 98
Right-justified (or ragged-
    left) margins, 98
Rights to service, 299–300
Right tab stop, 98
Robinson, Annabeth, 227
Role-playing, 58
Roman typeface, 101, 102
Ronick, David, 197
RSS (really simple
    syndication), 226
RSS/Atom validator, 226

Salary, negotiating, 167–68
Sales brochures, 189
Salutation, 156–57, 181
Satisfy in Monroe's
    Motivated Sequence,
    191
Screen capture software, 235
Screening, 100
Screening stage, 160, 161,
    166

Search engine optimization (SEO), 315, 336, 338–44
  audience, 341
  h1 and keyword tags, 341–43
  links and backlinks, 343
  other strategies, 343–44
  relevant words and content, 338–40
  results, analyzing, 345
  search ranking, 340
  title, 341
Search engines, 134–35
Search ranking, 340
Secondary research, 59–61
Second Life, 163, 227
Securing Intellectual Property, 307
Security
  in distribution, 107
  software for email, 217–18
Selection stage, 161, 166
Sensitivity, intercultural and international, 7
Sentences, 75–78
  complex sentence, 76
  compound-complex sentence, 76–77
  compound sentence, 76
  intention, 77
  structure, 76
  stylistic construction, 77–78
  support, 79
  topic, 78–79
Sequence of claim, 54
Shading, 100
Shadowing, 132–33
Sharing information and communications, 300–306

archiving, 300
electronic files, saving, 302–6
hard files, saving, 301–2
Short Message Service (SMS), 213, 214
Shouting, 213
ShowDocument, 212
Shredding files, 308
Simmons, Annette, 69
Simple outline, oral delivery by, 110
Simultaneous broadcast (simulcast), 222
Sinclair, Upton, 260
Single sourcing, 57–58
Singular-plural agreement, 88–89
Situational interviews, 162
Skills
  demonstrating and enhancing, 13
  important for success, 7
  impression management, 7–8
  improving, 16
  obtaining, 13
Skip tracing, 298
Skype, 158–59, 161, 214, 220, 222
Slidecasting, 235
Slide decks, 236
Slide:ology: The Art and Science of Creating Great Presentations, 241
SlideRocket, 236–37
Sloodle, 227
Small Business Administration, 195, 196
Smyth, Michael, 277–78

Social media distribution, 107–8
Social media résumés, 149–50, 155
Social networking, 313–47. *See also* Online presence
  canons applied to, 316–17
  in electronic communications, 228–31
  in employment search process, 137–38
  important note about, 322–23
  online, tips and strategies, 319, 321–22
  search engine optimization, 336
  traditional, tips and strategies, 317–19, 320
Social networking sites, 229
Social security payments, 261
Socrates, 24, 39
Software for saving electronic files, 303
Solicited proposals, 197
Sophism, 43
South Park (TV series), 229
Southwest Airlines, 254–55
Southwest Airlines Way, The, 254
Spatial pattern, 64–65
Speaking rate in oral delivery, 112–13
Specific purpose of business messages, 53
SpectorSoft, 218
Speech. *See also* Tone and voice
  articulation, 113
  speaking rate, 112–13
SPSS, 289
Staging in oral delivery, 114

Status reports, 192–93
Stevens Aviation, 255
Storyboarding, 57
Story Factor, The
    (Simmons), 69
Storyline, 68–69
Strategic plans, 196
Stress interviews, 162
Stress management,
    flexibility and, 7
Students. *See*
    Communication
    students
Style. *See also* Write (style)
    as cannon of rhetoric, 34,
        36, 37
    in crafting concise and
        extensive artifacts, 175
    of letters, 178–80
Style in résumés, 150–55
    ethos, 151
    logos, 153–55
    pathos, 151, 153
Style manuals, 80, 81
Stylistic construction of
    sentences, 77–78
Subject line in email, 217
Support sentences, 79
Support websites for data
    and word processing
    software, 241
Surveillance, 297
SWOT analysis, 140–41
Syllogism, 38–39
Symposium, 205
Synchronous messaging, 211

Table of contents in report,
    200
Tables and figures, 349–63
    communication media
        advantages and
        disadvantages, 352–53

death by PowerPoint,
    avoiding, 236, 360–62
editing and proofreading
    marks for instruction,
    357
in email, 217
email mistakes and
    remedies, 358–59
fallacies, logical and
    argumentative, 354–56
research resources,
    350–51
Tabs, 97, 98
Tactical plans, 196
Taxes, 261
Teams and groups,
    facilitating, 266
    collaboration, 270–73
    conflict, 270–73
    meetings, 267–70
Technical skills, 7
Technological challenges for
    global workforce, 6–7
Technology
    boundary-spanning units
        in, 281, 282–84
    intensive, 282
    long-linked, 281
    mediating, 281–82
    in protecting information
        and communications,
        308
Teleconferencing, 222–25
    considerations in
        purchasing or using,
        222–23
    etiquette guidelines,
        223–25
Telephone interviews,
    162–63
Termination notices, 261
Text
    approach to, 9–14

benefits of, 8–9
distinguishing features of,
    14–16
objective of, 8
in reports, 201–2
Text messages, 172, 213–14
Theoretical focus,
    integrated, 15–16
Thomas-Kilmann Conflict
    Instrument, 271
Thompson, James D., 281
Thompson, Marty, 255
3D graphics, 241
Timeline, 242
Title
    in report, 200
    in search engine
        optimization, 341
Tone and voice, 70–75
    active and passive, 71, 88
    appropriate, 70–75
    cultural insensitivity and
        biased language,
        71–74
    establish, 54
    expressive and concrete
        words, 74–75
    pitch in oral delivery, 112
    volume of speaker in oral
        delivery, 112
ToneCheck, 211
Topical arrangement, 64
Topic sentences, 78–79
Top marker, 98
Trade publications, 136
Traditional social
    networking, tips and
    strategies, 317–19, 320
Transcription services,
    Internet-based, 315
Transmittal (cover letter),
    180, 182–83
Truss, Lynne, 48

Twitter, 171–72, 228, 335
Twitter clients, 335, 338
Twitterspeak, 228–29
Typefaces, 101–2
Typography, 100–102
Typos in quotations, 81

Undercover operations, 297
Uniform Resource Locator
    (URL), 13
Union rights and
    responsibilities, 261
University of Montana, 153
Unsolicited proposals, 198
Uppercase letters. *See*
    Capital letters
User-generated content
    (UGC) sites, 229–31,
    331–36
  Facebook, 333–35
  LinkedIn, 331–33
  other sites and ideas,
    335–36
  Twitter, 335

Venn diagrams, 242
Video as presentation aid,
    235
Videoconferencing, 222–23
Video interviews, 163
Video résumé, 150, 155
Virtual meetings, platforms
    for, 212, 213
Visual aids, 241–42
Visual graphic editors, 241
Visualization in Monroe's
    Motivated Sequence,
    191
Visuals, technologies for
    displaying, 232–39.
    See also Presentation
    aids

VocationVactions, 132
Voice. *See* Tone and voice
Voice messages, 220–22
Voice over Internet Protocol
    (VoIP), 161, 214,
    220–21
Voluntary participation,
    299

Warrant, 66
WAV (.wav) file format,
    226
Web conferences, 213
Web cookie, 296
Web crawlers, 339
Webinars, 213
Web 2.0, 16
Wessel, David, 23
Whiteboards, 233
White space, 96–97
Widow, 100
Wikipedia, 230
Wikis, 335
Wired PR News, 186
Word choice, patterns in,
    142–44
Work environments, safe
    and collaborative,
    251–74. *See also*
    Teams and groups,
    facilitating
  emotional concerns,
    258–65
  facilitating, 256–66
  physical concerns, 257,
    259–65
  regulations, 265
  rhetorical tone in,
    254–56
Worker's compensation,
    261
Work history, gaps in, 154

Work interviews, 162
Workplace bullying, 252
Workplace monitoring and
    surveillance, 277–310.
    See also Information
    and communications
  of email, 278–79
  global, 279
  rhetorical tone in, 280
World Health Organization
    (WHO), 256–57
Write (style), 68–83
  citations, 81
  conclusion, 82–83
  introduction, 82
  paragraphs, 78–80
  point of view, 69–70
  quotations, 80–81
  sentences, 75–78
  storyline, 68–69
  tone and voice, 70–75
Writer's signature block in
    letters, 182
Writing process. *See*
    Four-step artifact
    construction process
Writing tips, 84
Written proposals, 197

(X)HTML, 329–31
XML (Extensible Markup
    Language), 329–31

Yahoo!, 216
Yelp community, 53–54
Yoga Alliance, 130
YouTube videos and
    presentations, 235

Zappos.com, 255–56
Zooming User Interface
    (ZUI), 237